4th Joint SIGHUM Workshop on Computational Linguistics for Cultural Heritage, Social Sciences, Humanities and Literature (LaTeCH-CLfL-2020)

Held online due to COVID-19

Barcelona, Spain
12 December 2020

ISBN: 978-1-7138-2821-1

COLING 2020

The 4th Joint SIGHUM Workshop
on Computational Linguistics for Cultural Heritage,
Social Sciences, Humanities and Literature

**Co-located with the 28th International Conference
on Computational Linguistics COLING'2020**

Proceedings

December 12, 2020
Barcelona, Spain (Online)

Copyright of each paper stays with the respective authors (or their employers).

Preface

These are very strange times. LaTeCH-CLfL has joined the swelling ranks of virtual scientific meetings. We all have next to no experience with such events – and yes, we hope that next year we will not need that experience any more. The format of the workshop is an experiment. You can access on-line, in advance, all talks and all posters. We will not bother you with detailed introductions, other than to say that the range of topics of the accepted papers has met a good deal of the expectations in the call for papers.

The actual workshop will consist of an invited talk (thank you, Elke Teich), brief Q&A sessions for the oral presentations (which you will have watched by then), and a poster session during which you will be able to chat with any author you like.

Here is a bit of statistics for those who care about such numbers. We have received unusully many submissions (thanks, everyone). We have accepted 20 papers for the 42.5% acceptance rate. Let us express our deep appreciation for the work of our wonderful program committee: you rock!

Keep well.

Stefania, Nils, Stan, Anna

`https://sighum.wordpress.com/events/latech-clfl-2020/`

Invited Talk

Linguistic variation and the dynamics of language use

It is widely acknowledged that linguistic variation is a core feature of language, affecting all linguistic levels from the phonetic to the semantic level. Linguistic variation emerges and is reinforced through language use in context, continuously adapting to social and cognitive constraints. Language use thus provides excellent data for studying (changing) socio-cultural practices as well as the (general) mechanisms of human communication.

In my talk I focus on two opposing but complementary effects to be observed in the dynamics of language use: innovation and conventionalization. Innovation leads to an expansion of linguistic options by new linguistic coinages, e.g. new words entering language or known words being used in new contexts. Conventionalization leads to a reduction of options by convergence in linguistic usage, i.e. the tacit agreement on "how to say things" often associated with a specific style or register. I will show that while innovation and conventionalization pull in different directions, they interact in specific ways to keep language intact for communication.

The underlying approach is corpus-based, using data-driven methods. Language models (e.g. word embeddings) are combined with selected information-theoretic measures (entropy, surprisal), providing models of language use and indices of linguistic variation (here: with special regard of innovation and conventionalization). I will focus on the domain of scientific writing (English) from a diachronic perspective with side glimpses at translation in the domain of European Parliament.

About the speaker

Elke Teich
Department of Language Science and Technology
Saarland University

Elke Teich is a full professor of English Linguistics and Translation at the Department of Language Science and Technology, Saarland University, Saarbrücken, Germany. Since 2014 she has been the head of the Collaborative Research Center "SFB 1102 Information Density and Linguistic Encoding" funded by the German Research Foundation (DFG). She is currently a principal investigator on two projects in SFB 1102, one on diachronic language change and one on human translation, as well as the Saarbrücken Cluster of Excellence Multimodal Computing and Interaction (MMCI) and the German CLARIN project (Common Language Resources and Technology Infrastructure). Elke Teich is an editorial board member of several journals and book series, including 'Languages in Contrast' (Benjamins) and 'Linguistics and the Human Sciences (Equinox)'. She is a regular reviewer for national and international funding agencies, including Deutsche Forschungsgemeinschaft (DFG), Humboldt Foundation, Schweizer Nationalfonds and the Finnish Academy.

Teich's expertise ranges from descriptive grammar of English and German over (multi-lingual) register analysis with a special focus on scientific language to translatology. She worked on machine translation, automatic text generation, corpus linguistics and the digital humanities at the following academic institutions: Gesellschaft für Mathematik und Datenverarbeitung (Fraunhofer), Information Sciences Institute (ISI)/USC Los Angeles, University of Sydney, Macquarie University and Technical University Darmstadt. Her research focus in the last 10 years has been on developing computationally based approaches to modelling language variation and change.

Organizers:

Stefania Degaetano-Ortlieb, Department of Language Science and Technology, Universität des Saarlandes
Anna Kazantseva, National Research Council of Canada
Nils Reiter, Institute for Natural Language Processing (IMS), Stuttgart University / Institute for Digital Humanities (IDH), Cologne University
Stan Szpakowicz, School of Electrical Engineering and Computer Science, University of Ottawa

Program Committee:

Beatrice Alex, University of Edinburgh, United Kingdom
Melanie Andresen, Hamburg University, Germany
JinYeong Bak, Sungkyunkwan University, South Korea
Andre Blessing, University of Stuttgart, Germany
Gosse Bouma, University of Groningen, The Netherlands
Julian Brooke, University of British Columbia, Canada
Paul Buitelaar, National University of Ireland, Galway, Ireland
Miriam Butt, University of Konstanz, Germany
Gerard de Melo, Tsinghua University, China
Thierry Declerck, Deutsche Forschungszentrum für Künstliche Intelligenz GmbH, Germany
Stefanie Dipper, Ruhr-University, Bochum, Germany
Jacob Eisenstein, Georgia Institute of Technology, United States
Anna Feldman, Montclair State University, United States
Mark Finlayson, Florida International University, United States
Antske Fokkens, Vrije Universiteit Amsterdam, The Netherlands
Udo Hahn, Friedrich-Schiller-Universität Jena, Germany
Mika Hämäläinen, University of Helsinki, Finland
Serge Heiden, École normale supérieure de Lyon, France
Graeme Hirst, University of Toronto, Canada
Fotis Jannidis, Würzburg University, Germany
Adam Jatowt, Kyoto University, Japan
Mike Kestemont, University of Antwerp, Belgium
Dimitrios Kokkinakis, University of Gothenburg, Sweden
Stasinos Konstantopoulos, National Centre of Scientific Research "Demokritos", Greece
Markus Krug, Würzburg University, Germany
Jonas Kuhn, University of Stuttgart, Germany
John Lee, City University of Hong Kong, Hong Kong
Chaya Liebeskind, Jerusalem College of Technology, Israel
Tom Lippincott, Johns Hopkins University, United States
Barbara McGillivray, The Alan Turing Institute, United Kingdom
Vivi Nastase, University of Stuttgart, Germany
Borja Navarro Colorado, University of Alicante, Spain
John Nerbonne, University of Freiburg, Germany
Pierre Nugues, Lund University, Sweden
Petya Osenova, Sofia University and IICT-BAS, Bulgaria
Andrew Piper, McGill University, Canada
Thierry Poibeau, CNRS Paris and Lattice, France

Georg Rehm, DFKI, Germany
Martin Reynaert, Tilburg University, Radboud University Nijmegen, The Netherlands
Pablo Ruiz Fabo, Université de Strasbourg, France
Marijn Schraagen, Utrecht University, The Netherlands
Eszter Simon, Petőfi Literary Museum, Hungary
Caroline Sporleder, Göttingen University, Germany
Elke Teich, Saarland University, Germany
Ulrich Tiedau, University College London, United Kingdom
Ted Underwood, University of Illinois, Urbana-Champaign, United States
Krishnapriya Vishnubhotla, University of Toronto, Canada
Rob Voigt, Northwestern University, United States
Menno van Zaanen, South African Centre for Digital Language Resources, Potchefstroom, South Africa
Kalliopi Zervanou, Utrecht University, The Netherlands
Heike Zinsmeister, University of Hamburg, Germany

Invited Speaker:

Elke Teich
Department of Language Science and Technology, Saarland University
"Linguistic variation and the dynamics of language use"

Table of Contents

Workshop program

Invited talk

Linguistic variation and the dynamics of language use
Elke Teich

Regular talks

Automatic Topological Field Identification in (Historical) German Texts
Katrin Ortmann

Exhaustive Entity Recognition for Coptic: Challenges and Solutions
Amir Zeldes, Lance Martin and Sichang Tu

Neural Machine Translation of Artwork Titles Using Iconclass Codes
Nikolay Banar, Walter Daelemans and Mike Kestemont

Measuring the Effects of Bias in Training Data for Literary Classification
Sunyam Bagga and Andrew Piper

ERRANT: Assessing and Improving Grammatical Error Type Classification
Katerina Korre and John Pavlopoulos

Life still goes on: Analysing Australian WW1 Diaries through Distant Reading
Ashley Dennis-Henderson, Matthew Roughan, Lewis Mitchell and Jonathan Tuke

Interpretation of Sentiment Analysis in Aeschylus's Greek Tragedy
Vijaya Kumari Yeruva, Mayanka ChandraShekar, Yugyung Lee, Jeff Rydberg-Cox, Virginia Blanton and Nathan A Oyler

Finding and Generating a Missing Part for Story Completion
Yusuke Mori, Hiroaki Yamane, Yusuke Mukuta and Tatsuya Harada

Posters

History to Myths: Social Network Analysis for Comparison of Stories over Time

Clément Besnier

`clem@clementbesnier.fr`

Abstract

We discuss on how related stories can be compared by their characters. We investigate character graphs, or social networks, in order to measure evolution of character importance over time. To illustrate this, we chose the Siegfried-Sigurd myth that may come from a reinterpretation of events that occurred in the fifth and sixth centuries in the Merovingian dynasty. The *Nibelungenlied*, the *Völsunga saga* and the *History of the Franks* are the three resources used. Annotations are made available for future research.

Dans ce papier, nous discutons de la manière dont des histoires apparentées peuvent être comparées. À travers des graphes de personnages, ou de réseaux sociaux, nous mesurons l'évolution de l'importance de personnages au fil du temps. Pour illustrer cela, nous traitons le mythe de Siegfried-Sigurd qui pourrait venir d'une réinterprétation d'événements qui ont eu lieu au cinquième et sixième siècles sous la dynastie mérovingienne. La *Chanson des Nibelungen*, la *saga des Völsung* et l'*Histoire des Francs* sont les trois ressources utilisées. Les annotations sont rendues publiques pour de futures recherches.

1 Introduction

The legend of Siegfried-Sigurd had a major place in the Germanic tradition. The best-known extant texts of the legend are the Norse *Völsunga saga* (**VOL**) and the continental Germanic *Nibelungenlied* (**NIB**). These two texts present similar sets of characters and events. They are often seen as reporting historical events that occurred in the 5th and the 6th centuries. This period was largely told in *Decem Libri Historiarum* (**DLH**). In this paper, we use the **DLH** as a historical source to quantify borrowings into **NIB** and **VOL**. To encourage further study in this domain, we made annotations and graphs available[1].

This paper begins with a summary of the texts 1. Next, in 3 we review recent analyses of these texts as well as methods to extract information from social networks. In 4, we present in detail the data used in subsequent analyses. The construction of character networks for our and the comparison between texts are explained in 5. Finally, results will be discussed in 6.

2 The legend of Siegfried, the dragon-slayer

2.1 *Völsunga saga*

VOL tells the destiny of a family from *Sigi*, an offspring of Odin himself, to *Svanhildr*, *Sigurðr*'s[2] daughter. *Sigurðr*, son of *Sigmundr* son of *Völsungr*, later kills a dragon named Fafnir after events involving gods becomes possessor of cursed gold. He later wakes *Brynhildr* up (a myth similar to the tale *Sleeping Beauty*) and they promise to marry each other. Yet *Sigurðr* marries Guðrún, daughter of *Gjúki* and *Grímhildr* and *Brynhildr* marries *Gunnar*, *Guðrún*'s brother, after a treason permitted by magic use. When it is unveiled, *Brynhildr* orders *Gunnar* to kill *Sigurðr*, so *Gunnar* incites *Guttormr* to kill

[1] github.com/clemsciences/LaTeCH-CLfL-2020-besnier

[2] ð is pronounced like th in 'this'.

Proceedings of LaTeCH-CLfL 2020, pages 1–9
Barcelona, Spain (Online), December 12, 2020.

Sigurðr, what he does. *Brynhildr* regrets and kills herself. Later *Guðrún* marries *Atli*, king of the Huns. The cycle of revenge leads *Atli* to kill *Gunnar*, *Guðrún* to kill *Atli*. After she tried to kill herself, *Guðrún* is married by force to *Jonakr* and her daughter *Svanhildr*, (that she got with *Sigurðr*), once grown up, is coveted by *Jörmunrekkr*, king of the Goths. Once again, jealousy and revenge lead *Svanhildr* and *Guðrún* to be killed. Finally, all *Sigi*'s lineage was killed.

2.2 *Nibelungenlied*

NIB has two main parts. The first focuses on *Siegfried*'s exploits on the marriages between *Siegfried* with *Kriemhild*, a Burgundian princess, and *Gunther*, who is *Kriemhild*'s brother, with *Brünhild*, a distant queen. A betrayal is at the origin of the second marriage and *Brünhild* allows *Hagen* to murder Siegfried. In the second part, *Kriemhild* seeks vengeance against *Hagen*. She marries *Etzel*, king of the Huns, thinking his power could help her. They invite the Burgundian court to their castle for a feast. *Kriemhild* and the Burgundian dynasty are at last killed.

2.3 Similarities in these stories

These two medieval texts present a similar set of characters, with similar names, and the plots are comparable. The question of common origins has been controversial: did they come from a long oral Germanic myth or were they built up from scholarly matter? Both proposed origins for **NIB** and **VOL** stories are manifest when we see historical characters who lived in the 5th and 6th centuries with e.g. *Brünhild* (**NIB**) and *Brynhildr* (**VOL**) corresponding to *Brunichildis*, queen of the Merovingian dynasty ; *Etzel* (**NIB**) and *Atli* (**VOL**) corresponding to *Attila*, king of the Huns, an Asian people)

We are in possession of a historical text that relate events that occurred in the Merovingian dynasty: the *Decem libri historiarum* (**DLH**), the *Ten Books of History*, more known as the *History of the Franks*).

2.4 *History of the Franks*

DLH was written by Gregory of Tours, a bishop who was a witness to the Frankish dynasty events. He first retells the history of the world from a Christian point of view, starting from God's creation of the cosmos to the death of Saint Martin of Tours, who was also a bishop of Tours. He then recounts in detail events that happened to Clovis and his offspring up to author's death.

2.5 Other sources

Other sources might have been used for this work, but will be left for further work. We mention them here because of their relevance from mythological and historical points of view.

- Poems of the *Poetic Edda* contain many heroic poems that display characters present in **VOL**. Such characters are *Helgi* in *Helgaqviða Hundingsbana in fyrri*, *Helgaqviða Hiorvardzsonar*, *Helgaqviða Hundingsbana onnor*, *Grípisspá*, *Reginn* in *Reginsmál*, *Fáfnir* in *Fáfnismál*, *Sigridrifomál*, *Brot af sigurdarqviðo*, *Guðrún* (*Sigurðr* is her first husband, *Atli*, the second, *Jónakr* the third) *Gudrúnarqviða*, *Brynhildr*, wife of *Gunnar* who always loved *Sigurðr*, in *Helreid Brynhildar*, and *Atli* in *Atlaqviða*, etc.

- *Gesta Danorum* was written in Latin by Saxo Grammaticus. He recounted the story of Denmark's kings. The first part is on legendary kings and the second part is on historical kings.

- Historical sources like *Getica* by Jordanes [3], *Lex Burgundionum* [4] that give more information concerning the Burgundian dynasty.

3 Related work

3.1 Philological investigations

Germanic mythology gives rise to many questions about its origins and its forms. Karl Lachmann believes that **NIB** is a coherent work made up of a collection of 20 songs, and he proposed such a recon-

---

[3] IORDANIS DE ORIGINE ACTIBUSQUE GETARUM (www.thelatinlibrary.com/iordanes1.html)

[4] Lex Burgundionum (www.dmgh.de/mgh_ll_nat_germ_2_1/index.htm#page/(III)/mode/1up)

struction. In contrast, Andreas Heusler states that **NIB** is a creation of a single poet, working from a deliberate choice of sources.

Similarities of narrative elements in other Scandinavian and in continental Germanic sources, e.g. reported in (Thorp, 1937; Thorp, 1938), show that **NIB** and **VOL** could not only be purely unconditioned creations of poets at one time. Kratz (1962) advances the idea of an amalgamation between different oral traditions in the Germanic area. No philologist denies that there is a link between **NIB** and **VOL** to the Merovingian and Burgundian dynasties (Fichtner, 2004; Schütte, 1921) and that **DLH** was an available source at the time of composition. Fichtner (2004) also shows correspondences between the four main characters of **NIB** (*Brünhild*, *Kriemhild*, *Siegfried* and *Gunther*) and historical characters, e.g. *Kriemhild* was inspired by *Brunichilde*, *Fredegunde* and *Chrodechilde*'s lives. The author also found new evidence that justify supernatural features like *Siegfried*'s invulnerability.

3.2   Character graph analysis

Characters are persons or person-like entities (gods, speaking animals) that are present, or just mentioned, in a plot. Over the past twenty years or so, scholars of fictional works have employed character graph analysis, or social network analysis, for story analysis (decomposition, summarisation) and classification of such works. Broadly, as analysed in (2019), these methods can be broken down into three steps:

1. identification and extraction of characters in the text,

2. identification and extraction of their interactions,

3. generation of the corresponding graph.

Such networks have already been used to support literary theories as in (Jayannavar et al., 2015). Questions about the historicity of stories have been investigated (Mac Carron and Kenna, 2013). However, this is only seen as plausibility by looking at whether social networks in stories are similar to networks constructed from historical sources. Historicity is either assumed or not mentioned.

3.3   Character network for mythological analysis

Mythological networks have common features, as summarised in (Kenna and MacCarron, 2017). They usually involve small-worlds, and are structurally balanced. This means that they have features found in graphs of real persons' interactions.

Character networks may describe stories at the level of character as well as at the level of the whole story. The best well-known Indian epic, the Mahabharata, was studied in English translation in (Das et al., 2016). The aim was to give an overall analysis in terms of sentiment and emotion, and on the roles played by its characters.

Scandinavian culture and texts have been investigated using comparable methods, such as the analysis of Icelandic settlement in (Mac Carron and Kenna, 2013). The authors gathered a large set of sagas, that contain overlapping elements, and produced analyses of the individual sagas and a single network from a merge of all sagas. They found common features and dissimilarities in the graphs, and concluded that social interactions found in the sagas are realistic.

An overall study of myths was accomplished in (Mac Carron, 2014), in which the **NIB** and **VOL**, among others, were analysed. The authors were able to extract communities structured as generations and other dynasties from **VOL**, whereas **NIB** did not reveal such structure, because it focuses on one generation of characters, and maintains the same set of characters throughout the story.

3.4   Works on historical characters

Contrary to works of fiction, historical texts present characters in a less clearly defined way. Social networks in aid of historical analysis in a language other than English was employed in (van de Camp and van den Bosch, 2011). The historical period is relatively recent, in the sense that the language (Dutch) used is close to contemporary Dutch. They studied interactions between people in a sentiment analysis perspective.

Table 1: Texts used for experiments

Name	Language	Estimated date of composition	Number of tokens/unique tokens	Main constituents
DLH	Vulgar Latin	6th	123272/25270	10 books
NIB	Middle High German	12th	81936/8008	39 chapters
VÖL	Old Norse	12th	26779/4631	41 chapters

3.5 Myth comparison and reconstruction

The research thread in computational story comparison closest to the present work is myth comparison and reconstruction, such as (Thuillard et al., 2018). Further out, but with similar methods, we have studies on meaning change or sound change analysis. All these tasks use methods largely used in bioinformatics for phylogenetic reconstruction. This helps build family trees of genes, which in return, helps analyse evolution through time and space. These methods will not be used in this paper, but they can be useful for future work on the subject.

4 Data

- **DLH** text was retrieved using the CLTK[5] (Johnson and Burns, 2014). The original manuscript is lost, but several Carolingian manuscripts remain. The author, Gregory of Tours, considered that his own Latin was poor, despite his high literary studies. It is often considered as a Late Latin text.

- **VOL** text comes from a manuscript written in the XVth century and now conserved in the Royal Danish Library[6]. This was digitised by **Heimskringla**[7], a project whose aim is to gather normalised texts of medieval Scandinavia. The author is unknown. The text is split into 41 chapters.

- **NIB** text comes from the manuscript C of the Nibelungenlied [8] this is often seen as the most representative of available manuscripts and is the oldest codex (UNESCO, 2008), however, it seems not to be the most archaic concerning the content. The text is split into 39 chapters.

5 Character network analysis

According to the generic process of character analysis sketched out in subsection 3.2, this work is on fiction for **NIB** and **VOL**, and **DLH** is historical, yet most of processes are similar.

Figures 1 and 2 summarise the workflow followed in the present work. The three main processes are described more precisely in the following subsections.

5.1 Character extraction

Characters can represent women, men, gods, and creatures. From all proper nouns in the texts, we removed place names, and for identification reasons, we did not keep devices (like swords that were given names in Germanic myths) and categories of people like the inhabitants of cities or countries, or names of peoples. Characters in texts appear as proper nouns, nouns and pronouns. However, in this work, only proper nouns were used to find occurrences of characters.

During data preparation, proper nouns were extracted by means of a semi-supervised method.

First, tokenisers for Latin, Old Norse and Middle High German from CLTK (Johnson and Burns, 2014) were applied; then, as texts are normalised, tokens with a first capital character were considered as potential proper nouns. Next, we removed proper noun candidates that were also found with a lower case as first character. Finally, translations were used in parallel with the original texts to manually check if they were proper nouns. An index of proper nouns were also used when they existed (it was the case for

---

[5] github.com/cltk/lat_text_latin_library that gathers texts from thelatinlibrary.com/gregorytours.html

[6] Ny kgl. Saml. 1824 b 4to (digitalesamlinger.hum.ku.dk/Home/Samlingerne/34897)

[7] heimskringla.no/wiki/Main_Page

[8] www.hs-augsburg.de/ harsch/germanica/Chronologie/12Jh/Nibelungen/nib_c_00.html

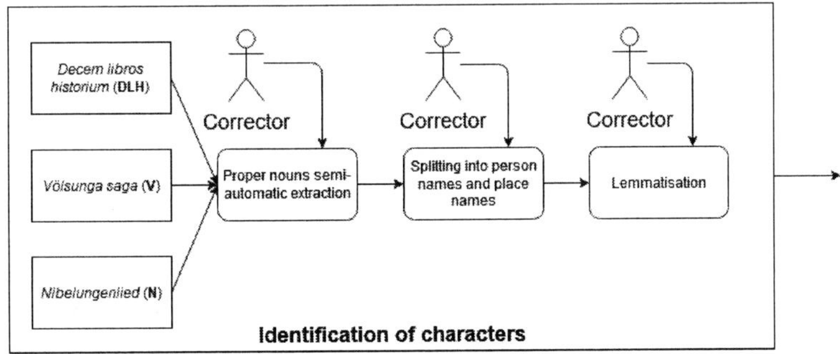

Figure 1: Character extraction

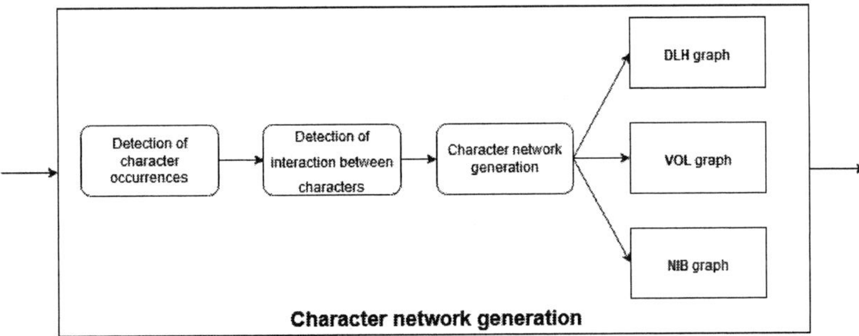

Figure 2: Interaction extraction

DLH (von Sali, 1892) and for **NIB** (Anonymous, 2011)). The issue was that they were in German and in French (for **NIB**, the lemmas of proper nouns were given in Middle High German). Finally proper nouns were split into three categories: names of persons, gods and creatures; names of places; and names of objects. Only the first category was used. The rest might be useful for future work.

5.2 Character interaction analysis

Once characters in the three texts were found, whether and how they interact to each other was determined, the very nature of interactions may be captured by analysing syntactic and semantic features of sentences where at least two characters appear. This approach was unfortunately not possible due to the lack of corpus analysis tools for Old Norse and Middle High German.

The easiest and fastest way to pick out interactions between characters is to capture their co-occurrences in a relatively narrow textual window. It was not possible to plan annotations of interactions for the whole texts in the way that Agarwal (Agarwal et al., 2012) did. The window size was chosen according to the nature of the texts. **NIB** is a poem whose basic structure is the stanza that contains four long verses. A window size of 3 stanzas was employed to capture interactions. For **VOL** and **DLH**, the smallest unit is the sentence, and the window size was set at 5 sentences.

5.3 Graph extraction

The procedures described in the two previous subsections (subsection 5.1, subsection 5.2) yielded respectively the set of characters for each text, and the set of their interactions. These were modeled as the set of nodes and the set of edges for each text. We did not keep characters that are not linked to any other characters.

Such graphs can be generated from the whole text or from a chapter. Smaller text units may lack information due to the sparse distribution of character occurrences in texts. Generating a graph from a whole text gives a static overview of character interactions. *A contrario*, generating a graph for each chapter returns a dynamic view of the relations between characters (Agarwal et al., 2012).

Table 2: Character graph features: n number of characters, N number of nodes, E number of edges, $\bar{D}$ average of degrees, D_{max} maximum of degrees.

Name	n	N	E	$\bar{D}$	D_{max}
DLH	784	332	1011	6.09	83
NIB	67	50	202	8.08	35
VÖL	115	55	163	5.93	24

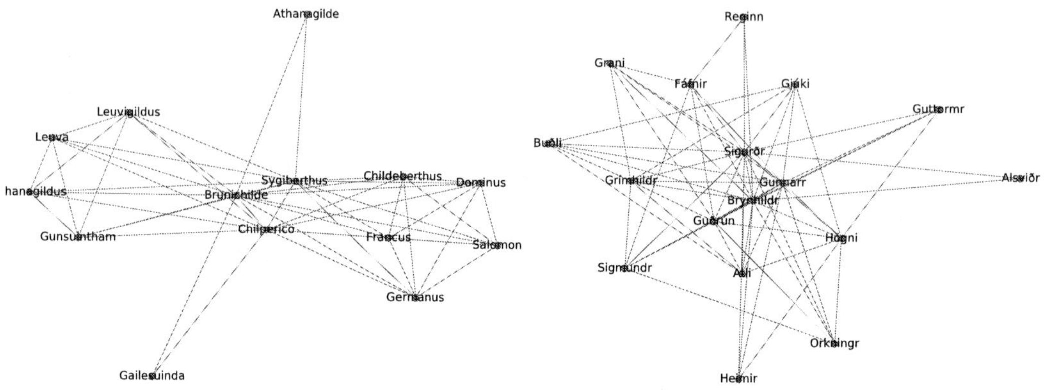

Figure 3: Brunichilde in **DLH**.

Figure 4: Brynhildr in **VOL**

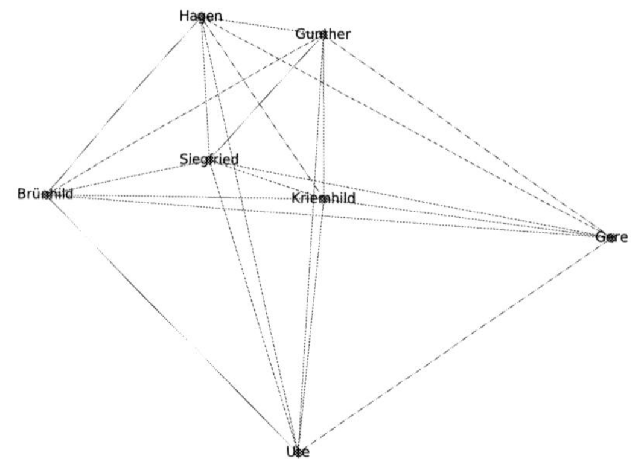

Figure 5: Brünhild in **NIB**

5.4 Comparison of graphs

Comparing graphs is still an open task, especially when they do not have the same size (Wills and Meyer, 2020).

Fortunately, we can still compare their global features, such as degrees, betweeness and closeness centrality (Mac Carron and Kenna, 2013; Kenna and MacCarron, 2017).

Our aim is to find features that are similar and different in the three stories. Similarities may show us what has been preserved in character relationships and differences may show what has evolved over time.

We chose features that show importance of characters. They are degree centrality (normalised number of characters connected to a character), eigenvector centrality (shows influence of a character with help of eigenvalues of adjacency matrix), closeness centrality (reciprocal of the average shortest path distance between a character and its reachable characters), betweeness centrality (number of shortest paths passing through a character). For more details concerning definitions of these features, see (Labatut and Bost,

Table 3: Graph features for 10 characters that occur at least in two of the three studied texts. Here d is for degree centrality, e for eigenvector centrality, c for closeness centrality, b for betweeness centrality and n for the number of neighbours (i.e. the degree), r for the rank of highest degrees.

DLH							VÖL							NIB						
Name	d	e	c	b	n	r	Name	d	e	c	b	n	r	Name	d	e	c	b	n	r
Sygiberthus	0.15	0.19	0.48	0.08	50	7	Sigurðr	0.44	0.38	0.55	0.34	24	1	Siegfried	0.44	0.26	0.60	0.04	22	5
Guntharius	0.08	0.13	0.43	0.02	28	24	Gunnarr	0.33	0.33	0.47	0.07	18	3	Gunther	0.46	0.27	0.62	0.06	23	3
Brunichilde	0.04	0.06	0.40	0.01	13	55	Brynhildr	0.30	0.31	0.50	0.11	16	6	Brünhild	0.12	0.10	0.47	0.00	6	27
Sigimundus	0.02	0.04	0.36	0.00	8	104	Sigmundr	0.31	0.26	0.46	0.14	17	5	Siegmund	0.16	0.13	0.49	0.00	8	22
Attila	0.02	0.04	0.39	0.00	7	122	Atli	0.17	0.20	0.42	0.01	9	8	Etzel	0.44	0.25	0.64	0.16	22	6
Alaricus	0.08	0.16	0.46	0.02	28	22	missing	-	-	-	-	-	-	Alberich	0.10	0.08	0.47	0.00	5	29
Theodoricus	0.13	0.17	0.48	0.08	44	8	missing	-	-	-	-	-	-	Dietrich	0.32	0.22	0.58	0.05	16	10
missing	-	-	-	-	-	-	Högni	0.31	0.25	0.46	0.17	17	4	Hagen	0.72	0.32	0.76	0.36	36	1
missing	-	-	-	-	-	-	Grímhildr	0.17	0.22	0.42	0.01	9	9	Kriemhild	0.52	0.28	0.64	0.08	26	2
Ragnacharius	0.02	0.04	0.37	0.00	6	144	Reginn	0.07	0.08	0.41	0.28	4	32	missing	-	-	-	-	-	-
Farro	0.01	0.03	0.36	0.00	4	195	Fáfnir	0.13	0.17	0.45	0.03	7	16	missing	-	-	-	-	-	-

2019). We used NetworkX[9] (Hagberg et al., 2008), a Python library for modeling graphs and computing metrics.

In this paper, we used main characters that are common to at least 2 texts and compared to each other. Common characters were found in (Schütte, 1921). A second criterium is to keep characters from 2 different texts if they are phonologically similar. It let us study 10 characters presented in table 3.

More precisely, similarities between **DLH** and **VOL** and between **DLH** and **NIB** show us what has been preserved over the six centuries that approximately separate these works. Differences, however, are more tricky to analyse because they can be due to evolution, innovations or borrowings.

As it is visible in table 2, the **DLH** has too many characters compared to the other texts. Then it is opportune to just keep books that contain our characters of interest. For comparison between stories, we only kept the second, the third and the fourth chapter of **DLH** because this is where the main similar characters found in **NIB** and in **VOL** are. With this social network, we extracted features and got results visible in table 3.

6 Interpretation

Sygiberthus remained a main character and even got a strong importance in **VOL** (high rank of degrees as well as other measures) despite the fact that he was killed at the middle of the story. *Guntharius* appears as a main character that is in the shade of other more prominent characters (high closeness and relatively low other measures). As a king or prince at the court of Burgundy, *Gunnar* and *Gunther* got a stronger role (higher measures and rank) compared to *Guntharius*. This is because the plot was more centered onto the Burgundian kingdom. *Brynhildr* and *Brünhild* has almost a similar role to *Gunnar*, *Gunther* although her role is more limited because she disappeared at the middle of **NIB** and **VOL** (see below for a deeper analysis of her ego-graphs). *Sigimundus* got a higher role in the Germanic tradition. *Attila* got a more important role in the Germanic tradition with poems with his name. His name was feared for centuries after his death. *Alaricus* plays a one-time role in **DLH** that may explain why his fate in the myth was not equal (he is not mentioned in **VOL** and in **NIB** he plays a role but was transformed into a dwarf). *A contrario*, *Theodoricus* plays a central role without being at the top. He has a small influence on events but often participates. His tradition remained in some texts only. He has his own saga *Thiðrekssaga* and is also called *Dietrich von Bern* in the continental Germanic tradition. *Hagen* and *Högni* do not play exactly the same role in **NIB** and **VOL**. His role is essential in **NIB** where both his influence and importance are very high, but his place does not make him a protagonist because of his attitude. This is a feature that is not captured by graph metrics, but could be analysed by sentiment analysis. *Ragnacharius* and *Farro* are anecdotal in **DLH** while **VOL** made them important (they are mythical beings) in regard to the hero, whereas they simply do not appear in **NIB**.

Brünhild's ego-graphs (figures 3, 4 and 5) deserve some explanations. The closest characters con-

---

[9]networkx.org

nected to her are her relatives and her husband for the three texts. **DLH** have many characters of a small interest in the story. **VOL**. Some characters did not find correspondences in table 3 because they have names without phonetic similarities with other characters of the other texts. An other fact that shows the limit of our approach is that, for example, a character like *Chilperico* does not appear directly in **VOL** and **NIB** because their features were transferred to other characters like Gunther in **NIB**. Such transfer is not always analysable with tools we used, because, for example, *Brünhild* in **NIB** and in **VOL**has features from many characters in **DLH** like *Gailswintha* (Fichtner, 2004), who is not in *Brunichilde*'s ego-graph. Distant characters in one text may have their features merged in one of the characters in an other text six centuries later.

7 Conclusion

This work provides an annotated (named-entities) corpus of a related myth. A character-based graph was used to analyse similarities and differences between the texts. Some characters got more importance while others vanished. Future research can include an analysis of phonetic evolution for such proper nouns so that it is a marker of common characters. More sources could be included in the analysis because some characters do no appear in all mythical texts of the Germanic tradition. Characters may appear in texts but not directly with same names and same features: role and name reassignments are quite common in these texts and need better models of characters in a myth to be detected and quantified.

Acknowledgements

I thank Kyle J. Johnson and John Stewart for their valuable remarks and their support. I also thank the other CLTK contributors that help improve our understanding of the ancient world.

References

Apoorv Agarwal, Augusto Corvalan, Jacob Jensen, and Owen Rambow. 2012. Social network analysis of alice in wonderland. In *Proceedings of the NAACL-HLT 2012 Workshop on computational linguistics for literature*, pages 88–96.

Anonymous. 2011. *Nibelungenlied*. Reclam.

Debarati Das, Bhaskarjyoti Das, and Kavi Mahesh. 2016. A computational analysis of mahabharata. In *Proceedings of the 13th International Conference on Natural Language Processing*, pages 219–228.

Edward G. Fichtner. 2004. Sigfrid's merovingian origins. *Monatshefte*, 96:327–342.

Aric Hagberg, Pieter Swart, and Daniel S Chult. 2008. Exploring network structure, dynamics, and function using networkx. Technical report, Los Alamos National Lab.(LANL), Los Alamos, NM (United States).

Prashant Jayannavar, Apoorv Agarwal, Melody Ju, and Owen Rambow. 2015. Validating literary theories using automatic social network extraction. In *Proceedings of the Fourth Workshop on Computational Linguistics for Literature*, pages 32–41, Denver, Colorado, USA, June. Association for Computational Linguistics.

Kyle P Johnson and Patrick Burns. 2014. Cltk: The classical language toolkit.

Ralph Kenna and Pádraig MacCarron. 2017. A networks approach to mythological epics. In *Maths Meets Myths: Quantitative Approaches to Ancient Narratives*, pages 21–43. Springer.

Henry Kratz. 1962. The proposed sources of the "nibelungenlied". *Studies in Philology*, 59(4):615–630.

Vincent Labatut and Xavier Bost. 2019. Extraction and analysis of fictional character networks: A survey. *ACM Computing Surveys (CSUR)*, 52(5):1–40.

P Mac Carron and R Kenna. 2013. Network analysis of the íslendinga sögur-the sagas of icelanders. *Eur. Phys. J. B*, 86(arXiv: 1309.6134):407.

Pádraig Mac Carron. 2014. *A network theoretic approach to comparative mythology*. Ph.D. thesis, PhD thesis, Coventry University, UK.

Gudmund Schütte. 1921. The nibelungen legend and its historical basis. *The Journal of English and Germanic Philology*, 20(3):291–327.

Mary Thorp. 1937. The unity of the nibelungenlied. *The Journal of English and Germanic Philology*, 36(4):475–480.

Mary Thorp. 1938. The archetype of the nibelungen legend. *The Journal of English and Germanic Philology*, 37:7–17.

Marc Thuillard, Jean-Loïc Le Quellec, and Julien d'Huy. 2018. Computational approaches to myths analysis: Application to the cosmic hunt.

UNESCO. 2008. Memory of the world register the song of the nibelungs, a heroic poem from mediaeval europe (germany).

Matje van de Camp and Antal van den Bosch. 2011. A link to the past: Constructing historical social networks. In *Proceedings of the 2nd Workshop on Computational Approaches to Subjectivity and Sentiment Analysis (WASSA 2.011)*, pages 61–69, Portland, Oregon, June. Association for Computational Linguistics.

Ludwig Rudolf von Sali. 1892. *Leges Burgundionum (MGH LL nat. Germ. II 1)*. Reclam.

Peter Wills and François G Meyer. 2020. Metrics for graph comparison: A practitioner's guide. *Plos one*, 15(2):e0228728.

Automatic Topological Field Identification
in (Historical) German Texts

Katrin Ortmann
Department of Linguistics
Fakultät für Philologie
Ruhr-Universität Bochum
`ortmann@linguistics.rub.de`

Abstract

For the study of certain linguistic phenomena and their development over time, large amounts of textual data must be enriched with relevant annotations. Since the manual creation of such annotations requires a lot of effort, automating the process with NLP methods would be convenient. But the required amounts of training data are usually not available for non-standard or historical language. The present study investigates whether models trained on modern newspaper text can be used to automatically identify topological fields, i.e. syntactic structures, in different modern and historical German texts. The evaluation shows that, in general, it is possible to transfer a parser model to other registers or time periods with overall F_1-scores >92%. However, an error analysis makes clear that additional rules and domain-specific training data would be beneficial if sentence structures differ significantly from the training data, e.g. in the case of Early New High German.

1   Introduction

To study the development of language over time, sufficient amounts of textual data from different time periods need to be enriched with linguistic annotations. For example, to investigate the historical development of certain syntactic phenomena like extraposition or object order in the middle field of the German sentence, annotated corpora from all relevant language stages, e.g. Middle High German, Early New High German, and modern German, would be needed. However, since the creation of annotations requires a lot of manual effort, historical corpora are rarely annotated with linguistic information beyond the morpho-syntactic level like sentence or clause structure. This limits investigations of syntactic change to qualitative studies on small data sets, often with limited statistical significance. Complementing the manual approaches with quantitative studies on large amounts of annotated texts could validate their results as well as unveil new patterns in the data. To reduce the annotation effort required for the application of quantitative methods, there is a growing interest in the use of NLP methods to automate the annotation task. But the necessary amounts of training data usually do not exist for non-standard or historical language. The present study investigates whether modern newspaper training data can be used to automatically identify topological fields, i.e. syntactic structures, in various modern and historical German texts.

The remainder of this paper is structured as follows: Section 2 covers the theoretical background of the study and gives a short introduction to the topological field model before Section 3 summarizes previous approaches to the automatic identification of topological fields. Section 4 describes the data sets used in this study and Section 5 explains the selected approach for the automatic topological field identification. In Section 6 the evaluation results are presented, including a detailed error analysis, followed by a conclusion in Section 7.

2   Topological Field Model

The topological field model (Höhle, 2019) is a widely used theory-neutral framework for the description of syntactic structures in German sentences. While German is considered to have a relatively free word order, the topological fields provide a clear structure on the clause level. In German, there are three different clause

Proceedings of LaTeCH-CLfL 2020, pages 10–18
Barcelona, Spain (Online), December 12, 2020.

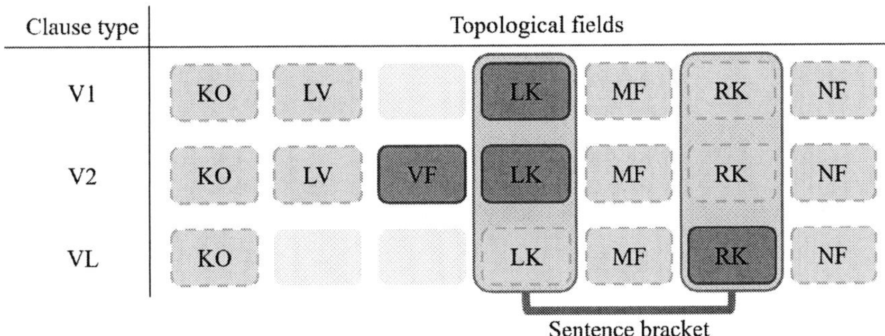

Figure 1: Simplified topological field model for verb-first (V1), verb-second (V2), and verb-last (VL) clauses with mandatory (*blue*) and optional fields (*light blue*, dashed lines). Positions that are never occupied are colored in *light gray*.

types, which are characterized by the position of the finite verb. Figure 1 illustrates the linear order of fields for verb-first (V1), verb-second (V2), and verb-last (VL) clauses. In the present study, a simplified version of the annotation scheme suggested by Telljohann et al. (2015) is used. The following fields are considered:

VF The pre-field (*Vorfeld*) of the sentence is obligatory in V2 clauses and always consists of exactly one constituent. Often this is the subject, but it can also be almost any other, possibly complex constituent, e.g. conditional clauses.

LK The left sentence bracket (*Linke Klammer*) is obligatory in V1 and V2 clauses and optional in VL clauses. In V1 and V2 clauses, it contains a single finite verb, whereas in VL clauses the position can, instead, be filled with a complementizer and, hence, is often also referred to as C. Following Telljohann et al. (2015), it can be occupied by subordinating conjunctions and relative and interrogative pronouns or phrases.

MF The middle field (*Mittelfeld*) is surrounded by the LK to the left and/or the RK to the right and can contain any number of constituents.

RK The right sentence bracket (*Rechte Klammer*) is also often referred to as verb complex VC (Telljohann et al., 2015). It contains the non-finite verbs, verb particles, and in VL clauses also the finite verb.

NF The post-field (*Nachfeld*) is located to the right of the (possibly empty) RK and can contain any number of constituents. While it is the default position for certain types of subclauses, it often also comprises other 'heavy' elements like relative clauses that are extraposed from the middle field.

KO The coordination field (*Koordinationsfeld*) subsumes the KOORD and PARORD fields from Telljohann et al. (2015) and contains all conjunctions that coordinate sentences, clauses, or fields. The conjuncts themselves are not evaluated here.

LV Left dislocations (*Linksversetzung*) contain material that is moved in front of the pre-field.

Except for the sentence brackets and the coordination field, all fields may contain embedded clauses. Figure 2 shows an example annotation with nested topological fields from the data set of this study.

3   Related Work

There has been a number of different approaches to the automatic identification of topological fields in German. The first studies (Neumann et al., 2000; Müller and Ule, 2002; Hinrichs et al., 2002) used rule-based approaches, implemented with finite-state cascades, to identify the sentence brackets and, based on this, the other topological fields. For this rule-based approach, Neumann et al. (2000) report an overall F_1-score of about 87%. Veenstra et al. (2002) show that for sentence brackets, i.e. fields that contain a very restricted

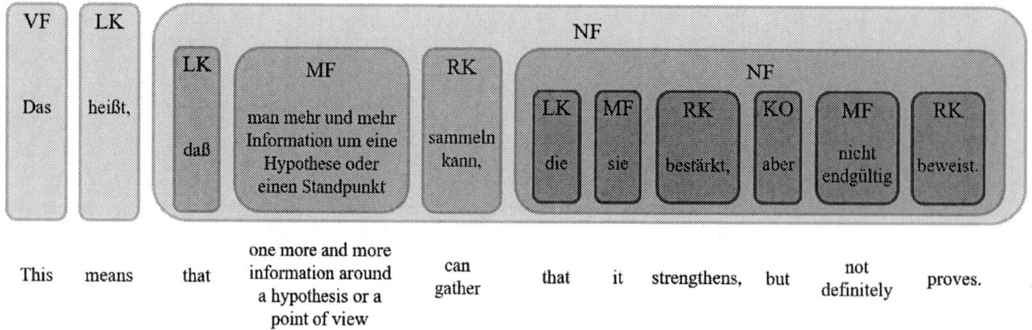

'This means that one can gather more and more information around a hypothesis or a point of view that strengthens it, but does not definitely prove it.'

Figure 2: Example sentence from the present study with nested topological fields.

set of elements, such rule-based systems can yield competitive results. For the identification of more complex topological fields and embedded clauses, though, using (probabilistic) parsers seems more promising: Becker and Frank (2002) train a non-lexicalized chart parser on a probabilistic context-free grammar and achieve labeled recall and precision values of about 93%. Klatt (2004) describes a bi-directional bottom-up parsing approach for non-recursive topological field recognition, resulting in an overall F_1-score of about 95%. de Kok and Hinrichs (2016) treat topological field annotation as a sequence labeling task. They use a bi-directional LSTM and achieve an overall accuracy of 97% for non-recursive topological field identification. For recursive topological field annotation, Cheung and Penn (2009) apply the Berkeley parser (Petrov et al., 2006) and report an F_1-score of 95% on the Tüba-D/Z corpus and 91% on the NEGRA corpus. They observe the best results for sentence brackets with F_1-scores >98%. F_1-scores of about 95% or more are also achieved for coordinations and the pre- and middle field. The post-field is recognized less reliably with about 83% and left dislocation with only 7%. All of these approaches focus on standard German (newspaper) text.

To date, there has only been one attempt to automatically identify topological fields in historical data. Using CoNLL-RDF and SPARQL, Chiarcos et al. (2018) implement a deterministic rule-based parser for topological field identification in Middle High German. It relies on grammars and expert knowledge and makes use of the manual annotations provided in the Reference Corpus of Middle High German (ReM). However, in the absence of a manual gold standard annotation, the accuracy of the parser is not evaluated and thus remains unclear.

4 Data

Although the topological field model is widely used for the description of German syntactic structures, only few corpora actually provide topological field annotations. The Tüba-D/Z corpus (Telljohann et al., 2015)[1] is the largest available data set, consisting of 3,816 German newspaper articles that are manually annotated with POS tags and topological fields. Discounting headlines and other fragments, which do not receive a topological field annotation, it contains 92,505 sentences with 606,755 fields. For this study, the corpus is split into a training (80%), development (10%), and test set (10%). Most of the studies described in Section 3 use previous versions of this corpus for training and/or evaluation.

To investigate how well the automatic identification of topological fields can be transferred to other domains, the present study includes two additional data sets for modern German. The Tüba-D/S corpus (Hinrichs et al., 2000) consists of 14 spontaneous speech dialogues from a business context, which were manually transcribed and annotated with POS tags and topological fields. Discounting fragments, the data set comprises 19,523 sentences with 107,432 fields. The data set of Ortmann et al. (2019)[2] contains a

---

[1] Release 11.0 in CoNLL-U v2 format, `http://www.sfs.uni-tuebingen.de/ascl/ressourcen/corpora/tueba-dz.html`

[2] `https://github.com/rubcompling/konvens2019`

| | **Newspaper** | | | **Modern** | | **Historical** | |
	Train	*Dev*	*Test*	*Spoken*	*Written*	*HIPKON*	*DTA*
#Docs	3,075	377	364	14	78	53	29
#Sents	73,884	9,345	9,276	19,523	462	342	414
#Toks	1,534,476	190,794	192,156	263,303	7,224	4,210	16,251
Fields							
KO	11,195	1,521	1,458	3,274	123	66	252
LV	1,080	159	138	477	41	20	64
VF	86,923	10,804	10,875	21,982	514	290	441
LK	130,321	16,322	16,345	31,013	819	398	1,081
MF	138,756	17,390	17,449	30,375	819	327	1,356
RK	88,455	10,912	11,087	14,211	493	406	1,156
NF	35,076	4,404	4,427	6,170	245	350	478
Total	491,806	61,512	61,779	107,502	3,054	1,857	4,828

Table 1: Overview of the data sets. Only sentences with a gold standard annotation are considered.

collection of five different written registers: Wikipedia articles, fiction texts, Christian sermons, TED talk subtitles, and movie subtitles. The data is provided with manually annotated POS tags and was enriched with topological fields for this study. Without fragments, it consists of 462 sentences with 3,054 fields.

Besides the modern data, the present study also includes two historical German corpora to assess whether topological fields can be identified automatically in texts from different time periods, without any historical training data available. The HIPKON corpus (Coniglio et al., 2014) contains sermons from the 12th to the 18th century and offers manual annotations for 342 sentences from the entire time span (except 15th century). Because HIPKON was created for the investigation of post-fields, only sentences with a post-field are annotated. For the present study, these sentences were manually enriched with topological fields, yielding a total amount of 1,857 fields. As HIPKON is the only corpus annotated with a custom POS tagset specifically for historical data, for this study it was mapped to the German standard tagset STTS (Schiller et al., 1999). The second historical corpus, the German Text Archive DTA (BBAW, 2019), is provided with automatically generated linguistic annotations, including sentence boundaries and POS tags. For this study, 414 sentences from 29 texts published between 1562 and 1912 were selected and annotated with a total number of 4,828 topological fields. The DTA sample includes texts from a variety of genres: five newspaper texts and three texts each from the genres funeral sermon, language science, medicine, gardening, theology, chemistry, law, and prose. For every genre, the texts were randomly selected from three (five) different centuries. Since the POS tagging and sentence segmentation accuracies in the sample were considered too low to use them as an evaluation basis, POS tags and sentence boundaries were manually corrected during topological field annotation.[3] Table 1 gives an overview of the data used in the study. The manually annotated data sets and additional resources can be found in this paper's repository at `https://github.com/rubcompling/latech2020`.

5 Topological Field Identification

The best results for recursive topological field identification are, so far, reported by Cheung and Penn (2009), who apply the unlexicalized latent variable-based Berkeley parser (Petrov et al., 2006)[4] to the identification of topological fields in German newspaper text. In the present study, their approach is transferred to different data sets, including modern non-standard and historical German texts. To train the Berkeley parser, the Tüba-D/Z training data is converted to a treebank format. Only sentences with a gold standard annotation are used for training. To ensure the applicability to different data sets, the model cannot be based on word forms, which differ significantly between modern and historical writings. Instead, the POS tags, which are consistent across data sets, are taken to form the basic text. To meet the required input format of the parser without supplying word forms, the topological field annotations must be modified. A top-level sentence node is added and artificial pre-terminal nodes are inserted where necessary so that each pre-terminal corresponds to exactly one terminal symbol as it would be the case for words and POS tags in a

---

[3]The POS error rate in the DTA texts from the sample ranges between 1.3% and 15% (avg: 6.3%). The sentence F_1-score for the sample lies between 54.1% and 100.0% (avg: 86.7%).

[4]`https://github.com/slavpetrov/berkeleyparser`

Field	Modern									Historical					
	Newspaper			Spoken			Written			HIPKON			DTA		
	Prec	Rec	F_1	Prec	Rec	F_1	Prec	Rec	F_1	Prec	Rec	F_1	Prec	Rec	F_1
KO	92.69	87.79	90.17	84.94	52.77	65.10	100.00	56.10	71.88	93.94	93.94	93.94	85.63	56.75	68.26
LV	68.57	53.73	60.25	22.15	15.95	18.54	60.00	7.50	13.33	0.00	0.00	0.00	69.57	26.23	38.10
VF	95.49	97.58	96.53	87.73	97.57	92.39	96.37	99.41	97.87	88.78	99.26	93.73	78.13	94.93	85.71
LK	98.78	99.75	99.27	97.81	99.00	98.40	97.95	99.88	98.90	96.00	97.96	96.97	89.87	91.83	90.84
MF	94.61	97.74	96.15	89.45	98.20	93.62	95.87	99.37	97.59	85.80	97.69	91.36	74.24	92.18	82.24
RK	99.05	99.52	99.29	97.40	99.60	98.49	98.99	99.59	99.29	94.74	95.94	95.33	88.36	97.04	92.50
NF	83.11	86.09	84.57	63.26	67.18	65.16	82.95	80.00	81.45	86.22	84.59	85.40	53.22	65.75	58.75
Overall	95.80	97.45	96.61	90.87	95.02	92.90	96.15	95.09	95.62	90.85	93.99	92.39	80.05	88.34	83.99

Table 2: Evaluation results for all fields and data sets. The numbers for Precision, Recall, and F_1-score are given in percent.

standard syntax tree. The parser is trained with default options[5] using the larger topological field tagset of the Tüba-D/Z corpus (Telljohann et al., 2015) during training, which is then mapped to the simple scheme as described in Section 2 for evaluation. Becker and Frank (2002) note that this strategy of training on more fine-grained categories and evaluating on a coarser tagset can improve the accuracy of topological parsing. To run the Java-based Berkeley parser, it is invoked in interactive mode via the command line and always returns the single best parse.

6 Evaluation and Results

For the evaluation of the automatic topological field identification, the parser output is compared to the gold standard annotation and labeled precision and recall are calculated. Here, true positives are fields that cover the correct span of tokens and are labeled with the correct field tag. The evaluation only considers the token span covered by a field, independently of possibly intermediate embedded fields. Punctuation at the edge of fields is removed before evaluation. If fields in the parser output have incorrect boundaries or do not exist at all in the gold standard, they are counted as false positives. If a field is present in the gold standard, but there is no corresponding field in the parser output, this is counted as a false negative. Only sentences for which there is a gold annotation are evaluated.

Table 2 gives an overview of the results for all data sets and fields. As could be expected, the parser achieves the best results on the Tüba-D/Z test data, i.e. the type of data it was trained on, with an F_1-score of 96.6%. This is comparable to the results of Cheung and Penn (2009), who report an F_1-score of 95.2% for a (much smaller) part of the same corpus. For the two other modern data sets, the parser reaches an overall F_1-score of 95.6% (written) and 92.9% (spoken). For the historical data, accuracies differ between data sets. While the results for the HIPKON corpus are comparable to the modern spoken data, the overall F_1-score for the DTA is much lower with about 84.0%. Like in previous studies, the sentence brackets are annotated with the highest accuracy in all data sets, followed by the pre- and middle fields, while the results for post-fields are worse for all data sets. Left dislocations are recognized even more rarely by the parser. The results for the coordination field vary between data sets, as well as the proportion of sentences the parser can analyze without errors (31%–79%). In general, correctly analyzed sentences are on average shorter and contain fewer fields. For some fields, it makes a difference if they are embedded in other fields or contain embedded fields themselves. For example, post-fields and left dislocations are recognized less often and less accurately if they do not contain other fields. This can be explained by the characteristics of the training data: Post-fields and left dislocations are rare in newspaper texts and mostly contain 'heavy' elements, i.e. longer clauses. Besides those general observations, every corpus poses different challenges to the parser. To better understand the differences between data sets and the causes of errors, in the following, the results for the different corpora are analyzed in more detail and a qualitative error analysis is carried out.

---

[5]Training options: `java -Xmx1024m -cp BerkeleyParser-1.7.jar edu.berkeley.nlp.PCFGLA.GrammarTrainer -treebank SINGLEFILE -out grammar.gr -path treebank.txt`

Newspaper Except for post-fields and left dislocations, all fields in the Tüba-D/Z test data are recognized with F_1-scores between 90% and 99%. The sentence brackets are identified with the highest accuracy, followed by the pre- and middle field and coordinations. For all fields (except KO and LV), at least 40% of the false positives have incorrect boundaries but overlap with the gold annotation. This value is highest for the middle field, where 82% of the false positives only have incorrect boundaries. This can, for example, be the case if the right sentence bracket is empty and the parser regards the middle and post-field as a single field, resulting in a false positive middle field and a false negative post-field. In total, four out of five sentences from this data set are analyzed without any error. On average, those sentences are ten words shorter than sentences containing errors. Errors mostly occur with elliptical constructions, fragments, and parenthetical phrases as well as sentence structures that are uncommon in standard written German and therefore rare in the training data. This observation is in alignment with Cheung and Penn (2009), who also identify parentheticals as the main error cause in their study. Further error sources are quotes and reported (direct) speech, as well as left dislocations and post-fields without internal structure. Overall, the newspaper data is annotated with high accuracy, reproducing the results of prior studies.

Spoken While the sentence brackets and pre- and middle fields are recognized with F_1-scores $>92\%$, only two thirds of the coordinations and post-fields are identified correctly in the spoken data. Left dislocations are recognized with an F_1-score of only 18.5%. Again, many false positives overlap with the gold standard annotation, especially in the case of pre- (59%) and middle fields (80%), which often erroneously stretch across left dislocations or post-fields, in turn leading to low recall values for the latter fields. Almost two thirds of all sentences in the spoken data set are analyzed without errors. On average, these sentences contain nine words less than incorrect sentences. Errors mostly result from the divergence between spoken and written language structures, for instance incomplete utterances, repeated words, or unrelated clauses and fragments in a single sentence. Still, it can be stated that, despite the differences between written training and spoken test data, the majority of the fields is recognized with fairly high accuracy and, if similar data should be processed automatically, using part of the spoken data as additional training resource could further improve the results for this text type.

Written Looking at the modern written data set, the evaluation shows that texts from different registers can be analyzed with comparable accuracy as newspaper data. The parser performs best on the Wikipedia articles (F_1: 99%) while for the other registers the F_1-score ranges between 94% and 96%. Although the data shows a slightly different distribution of fields with more left dislocations, post-fields, and co-ordinations, the parser still recognizes most fields with high F_1-scores. Also, half of the false positives overlap with the gold standard annotation: More than two thirds of the false middle fields and more than half of the false post-fields only have incorrect boundaries. 58% of the sentences are analyzed completely correctly. For many sentences, missing coordination fields are the only error. Since coordinating conjunctions are not always annotated in the training data, the parser often does not recognize them in the test data, leading to low recall for the KO field. Using simple rules to add missing coordination fields, the recall for the KO field in this data set can be raised from 56% to 97% while keeping the precision at 100%, thus improving the F_1-score of this field to 98%. Further common causes of errors are direct and reported speech, especially in sermons and fiction texts, and the higher proportion of left dislocations and post-fields in informal, spoken-like language.

HIPKON The results for the first historical corpus are comparable to those of modern spoken data. For most fields, the F_1-score is $>90\%$ and, despite the higher proportion of post-fields resulting from the corpus design, post-fields are analyzed with a higher F_1-score in this historical text sample than in the other corpora. For left dislocations, the opposite is true: Although they are more frequent in the data set, no LV field is recognized in the HIPKON sample. Either the corresponding tokens are not analyzed at all or they are analyzed as part of the pre-field, which is also reflected in the high percentage of pre-fields with incorrect boundaries. In general, more than half of all false positives overlap with the gold standard annotation. The proportion is highest for the post-field with 74% and ranges between 38% and 57% for the other fields. About two thirds of the sentences from this data set are analyzed without errors by the parser. While the recall only shows minor changes with respect to the age of the text, the precision decreases for older texts, reflecting their increasing divergence from the modern training data. Common error causes for this data set include empty middle fields like in (1), which are relatively frequent in the HIPKON corpus due to its specific focus on the post-field.

(1) *vñ [LK wólte] [RK gan] zů fínem vatt' vnd fprechē.*
   'And wanted to go to his father and speak.'

Adding historical training data or implementing simple rules, in these cases, could prevent the wrong identification of a middle field if, for example, it is preceded by a right bracket or starting with verbal elements. Additional rules could also improve the identification of post-fields, which are often not recognized by the parser. By simply labeling non-analyzed tokens following a post-field or right bracket as post-field, the recall for this field can be increased by six percentage points to over 90%. Another common cause for errors in this historical data set are left brackets like relative adverbs and particles that no longer exist in modern German, e.g. as in (2):

(2) *nach mittē tage [LK do] er hat gefclâfen*
   'after the middle of the day where he had slept'

While these tokens were annotated as relative adverbs or particles with the original custom POS tagset, the information about their relative function was lost during conversion to the modern STTS tagset, preventing the parser from identifying them. Since one missing bracket can easily change the complete analysis of a sentence, the explicit marking of these tokens as left brackets results in improvements of all fields from pre- to post-field. If older historical data should be analyzed reliably, available information about the relative function of tokens must somehow be transferred to the modern tagset, e.g. by adding a special tag and corresponding training data or by (mis-)using an existing tag for relativizers. Overall, the evaluation of the HIPKON data shows that, by using the POS tags as input, it is generally possible to transfer a model from modern to historical data although some special adjustments and/or historical training data would be beneficial to further improve the reliability of the automatic analysis.

DTA The results for the second historical corpus are substantially worse than for the other data sets. Only the sentence brackets are identified with F_1-scores $>90\%$, while the other fields range only between 38.1% and 85.7%. Like for the other corpora, the results are worst for left dislocations: Only a quarter of them is recognized, while the rest is mostly skipped by the parser, especially if they do not contain embedded fields. Coordination fields are also often not recognized, but adding the same simple rules as for the modern written data can increase the recall for the KO field from 56.8% to 90.1%, improving the F_1-score of this field by 20 percentage points.

Again, half of all false positives result from incorrect field boundaries. Two thirds of the false middle fields and more than half of the false right brackets and post-fields overlap with the corresponding gold standard annotation. But only 30% of all sentences are analyzed without errors. Those sentences are on average 26.5 words shorter and contain on average 6 fewer fields than sentences with one or more errors. This already indicates that the sentences in the DTA are very long and complex. The average sentence length in the sample is 39 words, compared to 19 words in the modern newspaper texts (spoken: 10, written: 14, HIPKON: 12), with a maximum embedding depth of 10 fields, i.e. one field containing nine other nested topological fields, compared to a maximum depth of 6 fields in the newspaper data (spoken: 5, written: 4, HIPKON: 3). Long and complex left dislocations and deeply embedded post-fields are very common in the data set, as well as embedded structures within the middle field, which are infrequent in modern German. Furthermore, the data contains many parenthetical constructions that, even for human annotators, are hard to process and understand.

The often extreme sentence length and complexity and the deep embedding of fields is a typical characteristic of the Early New High German data and not covered by the modern training data, which explains the high amount of errors. While the parser is mostly able to recognize local, clause-internal structures, e.g. left and right brackets surrounding a middle field, it often fails to identify larger structures, especially in complex constructions, e.g. with several embedded post-fields. The different historical use of punctuation further exacerbates the problems, for example with reported speech and parenthetical constructions. The same can be said about the fact that writers during this time period commonly left out right sentence brackets, which makes embedded clauses even harder to recognize and analyze correctly, for example in (3):

(3) *Ob diefes wol eine lóbliche Sache / wodurch vielmal folche Seuche abzuhalten [...]: So bezeuget doch die tágliche Erfahrung / daß [...]*

'Although this (is) a laudable thing, whereby often such an epidemic can be prevented [...], daily experience shows that [...]'

Also, similar to the HIPKON corpus, the DTA sample contains many adverbial left brackets that the parser cannot recognize, leading not only to missing left brackets but also to incorrect surrounding fields. Since these error sources become less frequent over time, there is a clear relationship between the age of the text and how well the parser performs: precision and recall both decrease with increasing age of the text, with the effect being stronger for precision. This observation holds for all genres in the sample, except funeral sermons, which are only available for earlier time periods. The highest F_1-scores are reached for the most recent newspaper and chemistry texts, the lowest for the oldest texts from the genres of language science, law, and newspaper.

It has to be kept in mind, though, that the texts in this study are already corrected for sentence boundaries and POS tags. Using the original annotations, the results would be even worse, especially for older texts where POS error rates are high. When the parser is supplied with the original POS tags (and gold sentence boundaries for evaluation purposes), the overall F_1-score decreases by almost 10 percentage points to 75.6%. For many older texts, there is an even larger reduction in F_1-score of 20 or more percentage points. Using the original sentence segmentation can be expected to further reduce the accuracy. While missing sentence boundaries do not necessarily cause problems, the low precision values (avg: 83%) would lead to many incomplete fields crossing sentence boundaries. This highlights the importance of reliable basic annotations like sentence and token boundaries or POS tags.

Overall, the evaluation of this data set shows that texts from the Early New High German period, which were written by skilled writers or scientists like it is the case for the DTA sample, can only unsatisfactorily be analyzed with models purely trained on modern German. While additional rules could certainly improve the automatic field identification to a certain extent, it is unlikely that a parser will be able to reliably analyze such complex sentences without sufficient similar training data.

7 Conclusion

The present study has investigated the automatic identification of topological fields in different modern and historical German texts using only modern newspaper text as training data. The evaluation has shown that, in general, transferring a model from modern newspaper data to other registers or time periods is possible. Using the Berkeley parser, different non-standard and spoken modern data sets as well as sermons from the 12th to the 18th century can be analyzed automatically with overall F_1-scores >92%. For the most common fields like sentence brackets or the middle field, the accuracy can be considered sufficient for qualitative and quantitative research based on the automatic field identification.

However, additional rules and especially additional training data for specific data sets could be very beneficial if sentence structures or the distribution of fields differ substantially from modern newspaper language. The evaluation has shown that texts from the Early New High German period, in particular, often exhibit such complex structures that they are hard to process even for human annotators. As a result, the parser only reaches an overall F_1-score of 84% on the DTA data set. Future work has to unveil whether time- or genre-specific training data can improve these results and enable a reliable identification of all topological fields in various text types from all time periods. Since creating such training resources is effortful and time-consuming, the presented automatic analyses could be used for pre-annotation, subsequently improving their accuracy by adding further training material.

Acknowledgments

This work was funded by the Deutsche Forschungsgemeinschaft (DFG, German Research Foundation) – Project-ID 232722074 – SFB 1102 (Project C6). I am greatful to the student annotators Anna Maria

Schroeter, Anna Ehlert, Doreen Scholz, Larissa Weber, Sara Klein, and Jennifer Wodrich for the annotations. Also, I would like to thank the anonymous reviewers for their helpful comments.

References

BBAW. 2019. Deutsches Textarchiv. Grundlage für ein Referenzkorpus der neuhochdeutschen Sprache. Berlin-Brandenburgische Akademie der Wissenschaften; http://www.deutschestextarchiv.de/.

Markus Becker and Anette Frank. 2002. A stochastic topological parser for German. In *COLING 2002: The 19th International Conference on Computational Linguistics.*

Jackie Chi Kit Cheung and Gerald Penn. 2009. Topological field parsing of German. In *Proceedings of the Joint Conference of the 47th Annual Meeting of the ACL and the 4th International Joint Conference on Natural Language Processing of the AFNLP: Volume 1 - Volume 1*, ACL '09, page 64–72, USA. Association for Computational Linguistics.

Christian Chiarcos, Benjamin Kosmehl, Christian Fäth, and Maria Sukhareva. 2018. Analyzing middle high German syntax with RDF and SPARQL. In *Proceedings of the Eleventh International Conference on Language Resources and Evaluation (LREC 2018)*, Miyazaki, Japan, May. European Language Resources Association (ELRA).

Marco Coniglio, Karin Donhauser, and Eva Schlachter. 2014. HIPKON: Historisches Predigtenkorpus zum Nachfeld (Version 1.0). Humboldt-Universität zu Berlin. SFB 632 Teilprojekt B4.

Daniël de Kok and Erhard Hinrichs. 2016. Transition-based dependency parsing with topological fields. In *Proceedings of the 54th Annual Meeting of the Association for Computational Linguistics (Volume 2: Short Papers)*, pages 1–7.

Erhard W. Hinrichs, Julia Bartels, Yasuhiro Kawata, Valia Kordoni, and Heike Telljohann. 2000. The Tübingen Treebanks for Spoken German, English, and Japanese. In Wolfgang Wahlster, editor, *Verbmobil: Foundations of Speech-to-Speech Translation*, pages 550–574. Springer, Berlin.

Erhard W Hinrichs, Sandra Kübler, Frank Henrik Müller, and Tylman Ule. 2002. A hybrid architecture for robust parsing of German. In *Proceedings of the Third International Conference on Language Resources and Evaluation (LREC 2002)*.

Tilman N. Höhle. 2019. Topologische Felder. In Stefan Müller, Marga Reis, and Frank Richter, editors, *Beiträge zur deutschen Grammatik: Gesammelte Schriften von Tilman N. Höhle*, pages 7–89. Language Science Press, Berlin.

Stefan Klatt. 2004. Segmenting real-life sentences into topological fields - for better parsing and other nlp tasks. In *KONVENS 2004. 7. Konferenz zur Verarbeitung natürlicher Sprache*. Ernst Buchberger.

Frank Henrik Müller and Tylman Ule. 2002. Annotating topological fields and chunks - and revising POS tags at the same time. In *COLING 2002: The 19th International Conference on Computational Linguistics.*

Günter Neumann, Christian Braun, and Jakub Piskorski. 2000. A divide-and-conquer strategy for shallow parsing of German free texts. In *Proceedings of the Sixth Conference on Applied Natural Language Processing*, ANLC '00, pages 239–246, USA. Association for Computational Linguistics.

Katrin Ortmann, Adam Roussel, and Stefanie Dipper. 2019. Evaluating Off-the-Shelf NLP Tools for German. In *Proceedings of the Conference on Natural Language Processing (KONVENS)*, pages 212–222.

Slav Petrov, Leon Barrett, Romain Thibaux, and Dan Klein. 2006. Learning accurate, compact, and interpretable tree annotation. In *Proceedings of the 21st International Conference on Computational Linguistics and 44th Annual Meeting of the Association for Computational Linguistics*, pages 433–440.

Anne Schiller, Simone Teufel, Christine Stöckert, and Christine Thielen. 1999. *Guidelines für das Tagging deutscher Textcorpora mit STTS (Kleines und großes Tagset)*. Retrieved from http://www.sfs.uni-tuebingen.de/resources/stts-1999.pdf.

Heike Telljohann, Erhard W. Hinrichs, Sandra Kübler, Heike Zinsmeister, and Kathrin Beck. 2015. *Stylebook for the Tübingen Treebank of Written German (TüBa-D/Z)*. Seminar für Sprachwissenschaft, Universität Tübingen, Tübingen, Germany.

Jorn Veenstra, Frank Henrik Müller, and Tylman Ule. 2002. Topological field chunking for German. In *Proceedings of the 6th conference on Natural language learning - Volume 20*, pages 1–7.

Exhaustive Entity Recognition for Coptic: Challenges and Solutions

Amir Zeldes
Georgetown University
amir.zeldes@georgetown.edu

Lance Martin
Catholic University of America
71martin@cua.edu

Sichang Tu
Georgetown University
st1018@georgetown.edu

Abstract

Entity recognition provides semantic access to ancient materials in the Digital Humanities: it exposes people and places of interest in texts that cannot be read exhaustively, facilitates linking resources and can provide a window into text contents, even for texts with no translations. In this paper we present entity recognition for Coptic, the language of Hellenistic era Egypt. We evaluate NLP approaches to the task and lay out difficulties in applying them to a low-resource, morphologically complex language. We present solutions for named and non-named nested entity recognition and semi-automatic entity linking to Wikipedia, relying on robust dependency parsing, feature-based CRF models, and hand-crafted knowledge base resources, enabling high accuracy NER with orders of magnitude less data than those used for high resource languages. The results suggest avenues for research on other languages in similar settings.

1 Introduction

Recent developments in high quality NLP have been likened to a tsunami (Manning, 2015), powered largely by Big Data for tasks such as Named Entity Recognition (NER), and continuous meaning representations in the form of word embeddings, for English and other languages (Upadhyay et al., 2016; Peters et al., 2018). Meanwhile, low resource and historical languages have not been able to take advantage of these advances for several reasons: 1. Gold datasets for most tasks are much smaller – English OntoNotes 5.0 NER (Hovy et al., 2006) has 1.7M words, more than all digitized text available in many ancient languages; 2. Work on embeddings often assumes at least $\sim$30 million words of training data (Cao et al., 2018);[1] 3. For historical and non-standardized languages, orthographic variation, regional differences, lacunae and other phenomena make learning from unlabeled data exceptionally hard.

In this paper, we report on a series of experiments, including successes and failures, in creating historical language resources for the Coptic language. The main contributions of this work are threefold:

1. We provide a new dataset annotated for entity types, named and non-named, nested entities, and entity linking, i.e. connecting spans of text to a table of specific people, places and other identifiers.

2. We evaluate recent NLP approaches to NER in a low resource setting and show that they do not perform adequately for the needs of (Digital) Humanists.

3. We present an alternative approach relying on dependency parsing, feature-based CRF models and a modest sized knowledge base, which are less labor intensive to produce than million-word training datasets, and offer a way forward for high accuracy NER in a morphologically complex, low resource historical language.

The Coptic language Coptic is the last stage of Ancient Egyptian, written in the first millenium CE in a modified Greek alphabet with additional letters derived from Egyptian Demotic script. Coptic writings

---

[1]This limitation has also been recognized in NER work targeting Latin (Erdmann et al., 2016), where models based on word embeddings did not yield competitive results.

Proceedings of LaTeCH-CLfL 2020, pages 19–28
Barcelona, Spain (Online), December 12, 2020.

are abundant, ranging from religious writings, such as hagiographies, homilies, magical texts, and ascetical treatises to social documents including letters, legal documents, and administrative records (Bagnall, 2009; Fournet, 2020). A vast amount of original compositions survive next to translated texts, especially of religious writing. Many early monastic centers wrote extensively in Coptic and many Manichaean and gnostic works survive only or primarily in Coptic. Although it was rarely the most common bureaucratic language, Coptic papyri provide crucial information about official and economic affairs in Egypt during Roman, Byzantine, and Arab rule. As such, Coptic literature is important to general history and the history of Christianity and other religions in and outside Egypt in antiquity.

Coptic grammar presents challenges to automated processing, including agglutinative morphology (fusion of multiple affixes to content words, as in (1)), incorporation (e.g. compound verbs which contain fused verbal arguments, as in (2)), and spelling variation which characterizes many ancient texts, including for widespread Greek loanwords (3).

(1) ⲛⲉ-ⲁ-ⲥ-ⲧⲣⲉ-ϥ-ⲥⲱⲧⲙ   *ne-a-s-tre-f-sōtm* 'she had made him hear'
PRET-PST-she-CAUS-he-hear

(2) ϩⲉⲧⲃ-ⲯⲧⲭⲏ   *hetb-psychē* '(to) soul-kill' = *hōtb* 'kill' + *psychē* 'soul'

(3) ⲕⲟⲗⲗⲧ6ⲉ   *kollyk^{y}e* 'group', misspelled for *kollēgion* (Gr. form of Lat. *collegium*)

In (1), the sequence corresponding to 'she had made him hear' is spelled in Coptic without spaces (or hyphens), meaning segmentation is needed before individual words, and then entities, can be recognized. In (2), a compound verb fuses to 'soul', changing the form of the verb and again requiring splitting. In (3), spelling variation makes the Greek *kollēgion* hard to recognize.

These challenges are not the focus of this paper, and our results below will be based on normalized, gold segmented text. However they mean that in practice, entity recognition will degrade when applied to automatically segmented and normalized text. Since humanists often have very high standards of accuracy, we therefore require robust solutions, as well as possibilities of incorporating semi-automatic correction steps, which we discuss below.

Entity recognition Entity annotation for DH studies can encompass three related but distinct tasks:

- Narrow NER, which identifies words referring to *named* entities, and classifies them as PERson, PLACE, ORGanization etc. Named entities are often assumed not to overlap, possibly creating awkward spans (e.g. [UK]PLACE [Prime Minister Boris Johnson]PER, in which the place span is outside of the person span, despite belonging to the same syntactic phrase).

- The more exhaustive task of Non-named/Nested Entity Recognition (NNER), including all spans referring to an entity, including overlapping entities (e.g. [[[*LA*]PLACE *police*]ORG *chief*]PER).

- Entity Linking, sometimes referred to as Wikification, in which notable entities are associated with a unique identifier, often a corresponding article about the entity in Wikipedia.

For Coptic, we are interested in all three, since texts include unnamed people and places of interest (unspecified 'monks', unnamed locations such as 'the monastery') which scholars may want to find, count and compare in texts. For named entities (esp. people/places), identities are important but difficult to find with string searches, since names repeat frequently ('Johannes' can be John the Baptist, St. John the Evangelist, Apa Johannes the Archimandrite, etc.), and marking up unique identities allows linking resources to data from other projects and languages, increasing their utility and discoverability. In the following, we present a new dataset for Coptic (N)NER and Wikification (Section 2), test out-of-the-box and custom approaches to our tasks (Section 3) and discuss some applications for humanities research using entities (Section 4). Section 5 draws the conclusion and suggests directions for further study.

2   Data

Entity annotation As an underlying dataset we chose the Coptic Treebank (Zeldes and Abrams, 2018) from the Universal Dependencies project (V2.6, `https://universaldependencies.org/`), which contains close to 50,000 genre-balanced tokens (30K train, and 10K each dev/test) annotated for gold dependency syntax, POS tags and lemmatization, covering both native and translated texts. For automatic annotation using the tools in the next section we use the larger dataset made available by Coptic Scriptorium (approx. 1M words, `http://copticscriptorium.org`) which we aim to make searchable for entity information. We annotate 10 entity types, shown in Table 1 with their proportions in the corpus. Although some of the types, such as events, plants, organizations and animals, are comparatively rare, they are nevertheless distinct and potentially very interesting; for example, events cover turning points in stories, such as a person's death, a war or conquest, famine, etc., while organizations often identify factions in theological and military conflicts (the Catholic Church, Diocletian's army, etc.). When NER is applied at scale, we expect them to be useful in conducting research on the underlying entity types.

entity type	%	examples	entity type	%	examples
ABSTRACT	28.72	'humility'	PERSON	39.92	'all angels'
ANIMAL	1.09	'200 horses'	PLACE	10.87	'Alexandria'
EVENT	2.00	'his death'	PLANT	1.00	'wheat'
OBJECT	9.79	'bottles'	SUBSTANCE	1.43	'water'
ORGANIZATION	0.86	'the army'	TIME	4.31	'ten years'

Table 1: Entity types in our data with examples and percentages.

As an annotation interface we use the version controlled online editor GitDox (Zhang and Zeldes, 2017) , shown in Figure 1, which visualizes entity spans as boxes, color-coded for entity type, and enforces strict entity nesting (entities only overlap fully contained entities), as well as no crossing of sentence boundaries (based on the Coptic Treebank's sentence splits).

Figure 1: Annotation interface.

To assess the reliability of our annotations, we carried out an inter-annotator agreement study by double annotating 1,162 tokens, containing 147 entities after adjudication. The annotators both had college level training in Sahidic Coptic and previous experience annotating Coptic corpora for other categories, such as part-of-speech tagging. Since measuring agreement on nested entities is non-trivial due to overlapping entities, we compute several metrics:

1. Cohen's Kappa, based on a single gold label per token, such that each token reflects the category of its deepest nested span (e.g. "for the army of Diocletian" becomes [O, B-org, I-org, I-org, B-per], since an organization begins at word 2, and continues until a person begins at the last word). This results in 21 possible tags (2 * entity types + 'O').

2. Micro-averaged mutual precision, recall and f-score, taking each annotator as a control for the other. Precision and recall take the perspective of annotator #1, but can equally be reversed.

3. Head accuracy: ignoring spans, what proportion of head nouns are assigned correct types.

The results are shown in Table 2, including scores for span agreement without entity types. Agreement is far above chance, with a typed and untyped kappa of .85 and .9 respectively, falling in the so-called 'perfect' bracket of 0.8–1.0 (Landis and Koch, 1977). Precision, recall and f-scores are harder to interpret, since neither annotator corresponds to a 'ground truth'; however, since we use the same metrics to evaluate systems below, these values help give a ceiling for automatic accuracy in Section 3.

	kappa	F1	precision	recall	head acc
typed	0.859	0.807	0.785	0.829	0.903
untyped	0.902	0.883	0.859	0.908	N/A

Table 2: Results of the inter-annotator agreement experiment.

Comparing typed and untyped metrics, we also see annotators agree much better on spans than on entity types. To understand why, we examine cases like (4)–(5).

(4)   mn [hah n-kah] haro-u   'it has no [soil]$_{OBJ/SUBST}$ under them'
        not much of-earth below-them

(5)   [nē] ne nt-a-u-jo-ou   ejm-p-kah   et-nanou-f '[those]$_{PER/PLANT}$ sown on the good ground'
        those are REL-PST-they-sow-them upon-the-earth REL-good-it

In (4), annotators disagreed whether 'earth' is a SUBSTANCE or concrete OBJECT, which is murky in context. In (5), as part of a parable in which Jesus likens people to plants, the PLANT in one analysis, is resolved as a PERSON in the other. It seems likely that NLP tools will err in assigning the more common category to ambiguous words across such contexts. At the same time, the head-based metrics shows that annotators mostly agree on entity types when exact spans are ignored (about 90% of the time). Most disagreements are due to entities omitted by one of the annotators, as in (6), where one annotator ignored 'sky' in 'birds of the sky' as non-referential, while another treated it as a PLACE.

(6)   n-halate n-[t-pe]   'The birds of [the sky]$_{PLACE}$'
        the-birds of-the-sky

While not perfect, the analysis suggests that human-quality scores of around 90% would provide a good basis for humanists' work using the entity annotations, with at least some of the disagreements revolving around weakly referential cases, which may be of less interest to researchers (see Section 4).

Entity Linking   For entity linking, we followed the broadly used approach of linking mentions of named entities to their corresponding Wikipedia articles (Milne and Witten, 2008; Shnayderman et al., 2019), i.e. Wikification. Using Wikipedia as a table or authorities brings a number of advantages and disadvantages, though we feel the former outweigh the latter substantially. The main advantages are obtaining an existing high quality table of authorities, and the wide range of other projects using Wikipedia identifiers, including resources linked in multiple languages (McNamee et al., 2011). Many notable Coptic person entities are not indexed in other relevant inventories, but do have Wikipedia pages. At the same time, Wikipedia identifiers are also available in the largest subset of projects, including broad projects on antiquity, such as Pleiades, and targeted ones adjacent to ours, such as Syriaca.[2]

Due to the high coverage of Wikipedia (especially for people) and the desirability of re-using common, existing identifiers, we opted to annotate our gold entity dataset with Wikipedia identifiers, which included 610 named entity types, of which 441 were found to have Wikipedia articles, amounting to 104 unique identities (i.e. distinct articles). The remainder consisted of minor entities or unknown/unidentified people mentioned in texts, such as 'Bibrus', an unidentified minor character in the Dormition of John, or Mahlon in the Book of Ruth. We evaluate the feasibility of using these seed annotations for automatic Wikification in Section 3, and give plans for wikifying more data in Section 5.

Availability   Our annotations are made freely available online under a Creative Commons Attribution (CC-BY) 4.0 license, matching the license of the Coptic Treebank. To facilitate re-use and interoperability, data is versioned on GitHub in UD's CoNLL-U format, Corpus Workbench format (Christ, 1994), PAULA stand-off XML (Dipper, 2005) and TEI XML (`https://tei-c.org/`).

---

[2]For example `http://syriaca.org/place/572.html` and `https://pleiades.stoa.org/places/727070` are both aligned with the Wikipedia entry for Alexandria, meaning their entries can easily be aligned with ours.

3 Experiments in Automatic Entity Recognition

Mention detection   Before we can evaluate entity classification and linking, we must first find entity span candidates in texts. As baselines we consider: a. using all and only nouns as entity spans (NOUN); and b. using all and only sequences of words attested as an entity in the training data (LOOKUP). The NOUN strategy will only recall single token mentions, and include incorrect non-referring expressions. LOOKUP should have few false positives, but low recall, since novel strings in the test data will be missed.

As competitive solutions we consider two families of methods: 1. In PARSE, entities are assumed to cover the spans of phrases headed by nouns, as identified by the syntax tree; 2. SEQUENCE: sequences of words in the corpus are scanned and classified as entities using a neural sequence tagger. Since we have reference syntax trees for our data, we can evaluate performance with gold and predicted trees from an automatic parser.

As a 'sequence' based system, we train a state of the art NNER system (Yu et al., 2020), which relies on a bidirectional recurrent neural network (RNN) with biaffine attention. The system scores spans based on start and end token indices, considering all possible spans, including nested mentions, and outputs a probability for each span category, or 'no-entity' (='O(outside)' in BIO encoding) for spans not predicted as mentions. The system relies on word embeddings, which we provide using Word2Vec (Mikolov et al., 2013) based on ∼1 million tokens of unannotated, automatically segmented Coptic text from Coptic Scriptorium (Zeldes and Schroeder, 2015) with a vocabulary size of ∼11,000 types and 50 dimensional representations.

method	exact span match			fuzzy head span		
	R	P	F1	R	P	F1
LOOKUP	0.386	0.555	0.455	0.591	0.849	0.697
NOUN *(gold tags)*	0.123	0.111	0.117	0.855	0.773	0.812
NOUN *(pred tags)*	0.121	0.107	0.113	0.853	0.756	0.802
PARSE *(gold parse)*	0.879	0.862	**0.870**	0.948	0.929	**0.938**
PARSE *(predicted)*	0.831	0.815	**0.823**	0.941	0.922	**0.931**
SEQUENCE *(10)*	0.463	0.651	0.541	0.611	0.859	0.714
SEQUENCE *(binary)*	0.653	0.732	0.690	0.793	0.725	0.757

Table 3:   Results for automatic entity mention span detection, exact span match on the left and fuzzy match containing entity heads on the right.

Table 3 gives scores for baselines (NOUN and LOOKUP) and the competitive approaches (PARSE and SEQUENCE). For NOUN and PARSE we provide separate scores for gold versus predicted POS and trees, using Marmot (Müller et al., 2013) as the tagger, and MaltParser (Nivre, 2009) for parsing. For SEQUENCE, we tested two scenarios: 10-way classification (typed entities) and binary classification (entity/non-entity), which should be easier to learn given the limited data. In all cases, metrics evaluate correct/incorrect boundary detection, ignoring entity types. Fuzzy span scores are more lenient, matching spans that include the entity's lexical head word, even if exact boundaries are incorrect. The results confirm the suspicion that training data and/or word embedding representations are insufficient for high quality results using the neural system. The binary RNN does better by 15%, suggesting training data sparseness may be the main issue. PARSE methods are promising, indicating that investment in a higher quality parser may help. For fuzzy span scores, the small degradation of the parse-based strategy and NOUN using automatic NLP is due to the fact that tagging nouns in Coptic is comparatively easy, especially if we ignore the common vs. proper nouns distinction (both of which usually indicate mentions equally).

Entity classification   As spans for entity classification evaluation, we use automatic parser output for all strategies, except for SEQUENCE, which uses the RNN's predicted spans. Scores are assigned for both exact match (span and entity type) and fuzzy match (minimal span containing the head receiving the correct entity type). As a baseline, we select the majority class ABSTRACT for all spans identified by the parser. As a third approach, we apply Knowledge Base (KB) lookup. To create our KB, we annotated the most frequent 2,700 nouns from Coptic Scriptorium with possible entity types regardless of context; however to keep the experimental setup fair, we use a version of the KB with only those lexical items which are attested in the training set (about 1,300 entries). We note this approach cannot handle novel words which are not included in the KB (for these we guess the majority ABSTRACT), and has no way of disambiguating ambiguous entries (for which we guess the attested majority category from training).

Finally, we test two feature-based approaches, in which a conditional random fields (CRF) model is adopted, using scikit-learn's CRF Suite.[3] The model takes selected features as input, and outputs predicted entity type for each entity's head token position only, taking into account the most probable path of labels through each sentence. Three categories of features are extracted from the input data:

- **Grammatical features:** 1. first/last 2-3 characters of each token, giving access to some morphological affixes (e.g. initial *mnt-* forms abstracts, like English '-ness'); 2. POS tags and dependency functions; 3. syntactic parent: for example subjects of verbs like 'say' are likely to be a PERSON.

- **Numerical features:** 1. descendent span length, i.e. how many words are dependent on the current token, directly or indirectly. 2. percentile position in sentence: humans are often mentioned earlier in sentences, whereas inanimate modifiers tend to occur late; 3. sentence length.

- **Context features:** previous and next tokens and their POS tags and dependency functions.

Beyond testing the CRF classifier as a standalone solution, we also combine it with the KB resources. In this setup, input items found in the KB are classified according to their entries, and the CRF classifier is only consulted in three scenarios:

1. when there are out of vocabulary (OOV) tokens for the KB (i.e. unknown words)

2. when an item has multiple KB entries, we choose the one with the higher CRF classifier score

3. when the CRF classifier is highly confident that an item is non-referential (i.e. predicting the 'O' class with probability >95%), the entity candidate is discarded

method	span match			head match		
	R	P	F1	R	P	F1
MAJORITY	0.213	0.209	0.211	0.235	0.230	0.232
SEQUENCE	0.476	0.614	0.536	0.527	0.757	0.621
KB	0.681	0.660	0.670	0.728	0.705	0.717
CRF	0.805	0.778	0.791	0.861	0.831	0.846
CRF+KB	**0.827**	**0.810**	**0.818**	**0.889**	**0.869**	**0.879**

Table 4: Scores for entity type identification. All methods except RNN use spans predicted by the best method for mention detection.

Table 4 provides the results of all models. The RNN model (SEQUENCE) is not competitive, probably due to the limited size of training data and word embeddings. KB gains approx. 14%, showing it covers many more cases. For the CRF model, F1 scores rise to 0.79 and 0.81, indicating the feature-based model is promising. The hybrid approach (CRF+KB) performs best, due to the ability of the CRF classifier to disambiguate uncertain cases and the KB's power to capture rare and unambiguous items (e.g. less frequent categories such as PLANT or EVENT, which the CRF dismisses as unlikely).

---

[3]A reviewer has asked why a CRF classifier is useful when we cannot use BIO encoding for nested span detection. In fact, in our experiments CRFs outperformed other word-wise classifiers, such as Random Forest and Gradient Boosting, since they can constrain transitions between labels which are helpful even for head word classification. Adjacent words may have plausible but incompatible tags (e.g. for the saint 'Apa Shenoute', both words can be PERSON, but only one should be labeled as the head), and certain transitions, such as inanimate object followed by an animate possessor, can be captured by CRFs.

Wikification For entity linking, our data is too small to use neural approaches with word embedding inputs. Due to the limited training data, many relevant identities will not appear in our data, meaning a large part of the target values for linking are unknown for our system. At present we therefore use a rudimentary semi-automatic strategy, offering possible links to human annotators, who can accept or reject suggestions, and enter new links for entities that appear for the first time. Our lookup strategy uses a heuristically ordered cascade applied to all minimal spans containing a proper noun:

- If the exact entity text is known in other documents in the same corpus, prefer the most frequent link associated with it (e.g. 'John who gives baptism' in the Gospel of Mark is 'John the Baptist')[4]

- Otherwise, if the entity text has appeared elsewhere in the corpus, prefer its most frequent link (exact match for 'John who gives baptism' is better, even if the corpus has other more frequent Johns)

- Else, if the entity's head noun is known in this corpus, prefer its most frequent link ('John' in the Gospel of Mark is most often 'John the Baptist')

- Else, if the entity's head is known anywhere, prefer its most frequent link ('John' might overall most frequently refer to 'John the Apostle' in all sub-corpora)

This cascaded heuristic can only work for proper nouns that appear somewhere in the training data, and is susceptible to a majority bias (i.e. it always guesses that a 'John' in a new corpus is the most frequent John in our data).

To evaluate our strategy, we compare it with two baselines: exact match majority choice (most frequent link matching the entire entity string) and head match (most frequent entity associated with a head noun). We use both the train and dev partitions to build our lookup table, while the test set remains the same, containing some 100 identifiable entity mentions belonging to 53 distinct types.

method	acc	cov	no_err
exact	0.227	0.273	0.953
head	0.433	0.500	0.933
cascade	**0.460**	**0.500**	**0.960**

Table 5: Wikification scores – accuracy (% correct links), coverage (% entities for which a response is retrieved), and % entities with no false links (correct link matched, or entity not covered).

Table 5 shows that the cascade improves on the baselines, and that, while coverage is limited (only 50%), it rarely misclassifies an example. Errors arise due to single word names shared between multiple entities, such as John (the Apostle or the Baptist) or Paul (the Apostle, or Paul of Thebes), and context differences, such as 'Israel', which is linked to 'Kingdom of Israel (united monarchy)' when referring to King David's kingdom, but to 'Israelites' when referring to Israel as a people. We currently feed such predictions to human annotators for disambiguation.

4 Applications

Distant reading Entity information can help address a variety of research questions, as well as making data more accessible and easier to discover in the larger DH ecosystem (Schroeder, 2020). As a first way of looking at entities in Coptic text, we can consider how to visualize the global picture of entity frequencies in our data as a kind of distant reading (Moretti, 2013). Two interactive visualizations we can use for this purpose are entity term networks and recursive TreeMaps (Shneiderman, 1992).

Entity term networks visualize a head word's relationships with other words in its entity spans. Figure 2a captures part of the network for ⲙⲁ *ma* 'place'. Larger nodes represent more frequently recurring terms, and broad arrows correspond to frequent transitions. The network for ⲙⲁ gives us a clearer idea of its potential semantic relationships: often preceded by ⲡⲉⲕ/ⲡⲉⲧⲛ *pek/petn* 'your', almost always followed by ⲛ *n* 'of', continuing to nouns indicating purpose ('place of dwelling', or 'lavatory' with ⲣⲙⲏ *rmē* 'urination'), events (ϣⲉⲗⲉⲉⲧ *šeleet* 'wedding'), directions (ϣⲁ *ša* 'East') and more. Similarly, the

---

[4]This is relevant e.g. because the Treebank includes only chapters 1–9 of Mark, but we want to annotate entire works.

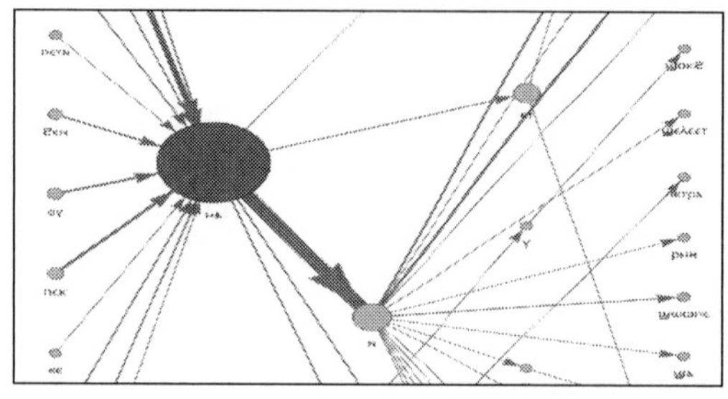

(a) Entity Network for ⲙⲁ *ma* 'place.'

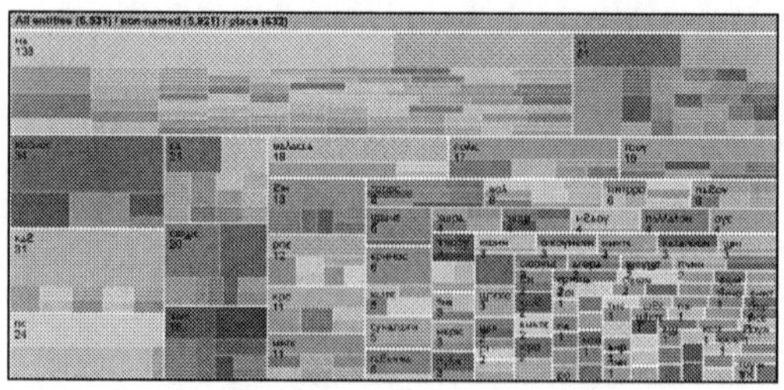

(b) TreeMap of non-named place entities

Figure 2: Distant reading visualizations.

TreeMap concisely depicts the most mentioned entities and headwords in the corpora. Following our annotation guidelines, the TreeMap initially separates named and non-named entities. These are divided into the ten entity types, and then by unique entity head words. Figure 2b shows the view of non-named place entities. The TreeMap shows that places headed by ⲙⲁ (top left, 138 cases) are most frequent, followed by ⲏⲓ *ēi* 'house' (51) and ⲕⲟⲥⲙⲟⲥ *kosmos* 'cosmos, world' (34). In lower ranks, the data evinces the importance of the desert in our corpus. Many texts center on monks who have left civilization, and their setting is often the ⲭⲁⲓⲉ *jaie* 'desert' (18). Consequently, we see our texts mention ⲭⲁⲓⲉ more than ⲡⲟⲗⲓⲥ *polis* 'city' (17), and even more so if we include Greek synonyms such as ⲉⲣⲏⲙⲟⲥ *erēmos* 'desert' (6). These visualizations allow easy interactive exploration and show patterns that may be missed when reading individual texts. Without entity annotation, such phrases cannot be trivially extracted and categorized for comparison.

Entity type proportions Another comparable quantity across texts is the proportion of named vs. non-named entities, or proportions of entity types. For the latter, we observe that sermons in the treebank (e.g. Pseudo-Athanasius, Letters of Besa) have much more abstract entities than narratives, since they concentrate on instruction, using abstractions to communicate their message and mentioning people less often. Narratives mention people more frequently, with a person/abstract ratio of 2:1 or higher, compared to ∼1:1 in sermons. Drilling down in more detail, we find exceptions such as The Life of Onnophrius and The Dormition of John: these have person/abstract ratios close to 1:1, mainly due to homiletic speeches delivered by the main characters, echoing Coptic sermons as they instruct disciples to avoid sin. This quantitative finding foregrounds an interesting commonality between seemingly unrelated texts and differences between texts from one genre.

We imagine many more findings will emerge from Coptic entity annotations, which complement detailed philological, literary, and historical inquiries. Data aggregation and visualization of different subsets of texts enable analyses based on the quantity, proportion and dispersion of entity types which we are only beginning to explore. They abstract away from individual ways of phrasing references to people and places, while linking mentions of named entities across datasets, projects, and DH tools.

5 Summary and conclusion

In this paper we presented a new annotated data set for Coptic entity classification and linking, using ten entity types, including named and non-named, potentially nested entities, and attaching named entities to corresponding Wikipedia articles, i.e. Wikification. Our annotated data represents a wide range of genres, including translated and autochthonous texts, and is freely available in a number of popular formats, including the CoNLL and TEI XML formats, under an open license, as are our tools.[5]

From a technical perspective, our results demonstrate the difficulty in applying state-of-the-art neural frameworks to nested NER in languages with modest data sizes. At the same time, the lack of availability of many millions of words for training word embeddings limits the utility of RNN architectures relying on highly informative, context sensitive information. Instead, we are able to show that a syntax-based

---

[5]Available at: `https://github.com/CopticScriptorium/corpora`, including automatically annotated silver data. Gold entity annotations have also been merged into the release of the UD Coptic Treebank, at `https://github.com/UniversalDependencies/UD_Coptic-Scriptorium`.

approach using dependency trees to identify nested noun phrases is viable and substantially more accurate for data in the several 10K-100K tokens range. Although our approach relies on the existence of such syntactically annotated data to train a parser, the size of the data set is likely to be a more realistic target for projects in similar settings to ours than the size of datasets underlying standard approaches to (N)NER in modern languages. For comparison, the Universal Dependencies treebanks for Ancient Greek and Latin include over 400,000 and 800,000 tokens respectively, meaning that the treebank used here is very modestly sized; and even with larger treebanks, those languages too lack highly expressive word embeddings based on hundreds of millions, or even billions of words, which are commonly available for modern European languages. Our methods therefore show promise for mention detection in annotating other resources for classical languages, such as freely available Ancient Greek and Latin texts available in the Perseus Digital Library (Smith et al., 2000).

For entity classification, our approach shows the robustness of feature based classifiers (Section 3), while also revealing the added value of a knowledge base (KB) architecture. A KB derived strictly from the training data is already helpful for the hybrid approach taken here (KB+CRF in Section 3), while an even broader coverage KB can be constructed with relatively low effort, which makes it possible to capture some of the rarer, but often lexically unambiguous entity types, such as names of animals or plants. For entity linking, we show modest results in terms of recall, but quite good precision which can facilitate larger manual annotation efforts by offering reliable suggestions for human review.

In Section 4 we outlined some of the applications that wide-coverage entity annotations can bring for humanists, including style and genre studies, highlighting differences between documents that are otherwise similar from the text type perspective, and bird's eye-view visualizations which allow us to examine how texts talk about entities, and how often. The data used for the example studies in this paper comes from the high quality, but small, manually annotated corpus prepared for this work. We plan to publish a much larger automatically annotated corpus of Coptic texts using the tools described here, which we expect to deliver much more comprehensive capabilities in exploring the contents of Coptic texts, many of which still have no translations that might allow exploring the content in English. Such larger scale data could also be used to link to other projects featuring entity identifiers (in Coptic or otherwise), and to lexicographic projects, such as the Coptic Dictionary Online (Feder et al., 2018), or the Database and Dictionary of Greek Loanwords in Coptic (DDGLC) (Almond et al., 2013).

6   Acknowledgments

We would like to thank Coptic Scriptorium contributors Mitchell Abrams, Elizabeth Davidson, Rebecca Krawiec, Christine Luckritz Marquis, Elizabeth Platte, Dana Robinson and Caroline T. Schroeder for their work on the annotated data, as well as the anonymous reviewers for their feedback. This work was supported by a Stage III Digital Humanities Advancement Grant from the National Endowment for the Humanities (grant HAA-261271-18).

References

Mathew Almond, Joost Hagen, Katrin John, Tonio Sebastian Richter, and Vincent Walter. 2013. Kontaktinduzierter Sprachwandel des Ägyptisch-Koptischen: Lehnwort-Lexikographie im Projekt Database and Dictionary of Greek Loanwords in Coptic (DDGLC). In Ingelore Hafemann, editor, *Perspektiven einer corpusbasierten historischen Linguistik und Philologie*, pages 283–315, Berlin. BBAW.

Roger S. Bagnall. 2009. *Early Christian Books in Egypt*. Princeton University Press, Princeton, NJ.

Yixin Cao, Lei Hou, and Juanzi Li Zhiyuan Liu. 2018. Neural collective entity linking. In *Proceedings of COLING 2018*, pages 675–686, Santa Fe, NM.

Oliver Christ. 1994. A modular and flexible architecture for an integrated corpus query system. In *Proceedings of Complex 94. 3rd Conference on Computational Lexicography and Text Research*, pages 23–32, Budapest.

Stefanie Dipper. 2005. XML-based stand-off representation and exploitation of multi-level linguistic annotation. In *Proceedings of Berliner XML Tage 2005 (BXML 2005)*, pages 39–50, Berlin, Germany.

Alexander Erdmann, Christopher Brown, Brian Joseph, Mark Janse, Petra Ajaka, Micha Elsner, and Marie-Catherine de Marneffe. 2016. Challenges and solutions for Latin named entity recognition. In *Proceedings of the Workshop on Language Technology Resources and Tools for Digital Humanities (LT4DH)*, pages 85–93, Osaka, Japan.

Frank Feder, Maxim Kupreyev, Emma Manning, Caroline T. Schroeder, and Amir Zeldes. 2018. A linked Coptic Dictionary Online. In *Proceedings of LaTeCH 2018 - The 11th SIGHUM Workshop at COLING2018*, pages 12–21, Santa Fe, NM.

Jean-Luc Fournet. 2020. *The Rise of Coptic: Egyptian Versus Greek in Late Antiquity*. Princeton, Princeton, NJ.

Eduard Hovy, Mitchell Marcus, Martha Palmer, Lance Ramshaw, and Ralph Weischedel. 2006. OntoNotes: The 90% solution. In *Proceedings of NAACL 2006, Companion Volume: Short Papers*, pages 57–60, New York.

J. Richard Landis and Gary G. Koch. 1977. The measurement of observer agreement for categorical data. *Biometrics*, 33(1):159–174.

Christopher D. Manning. 2015. Computational linguistics and deep learning. *Computational Linguistics*, 41(4):701–707.

Paul McNamee, James Mayfield, Dawn Lawrie, Douglas Oard, and David Doermann. 2011. Cross-language entity linking. In *Proceedings of IJCNLP 2011*, pages 255–263, Chiang Mai, Thailand.

Tomas Mikolov, Kai Chen, Greg Corrado, and Jeffrey Dean. 2013. Efficient estimation of word representations in vector space. In *International Conference on Learning Representations (ICLR) Workshop*, Scottsdale, AZ.

David Milne and Ian H. Witten. 2008. Learning to link with Wikipedia. In *Proceedings of the 17th ACM conference on Information and Knowledge Management*, pages 509–518, Napa Valley, CA.

Franco Moretti. 2013. *Distant Reading*. Verso, London.

Thomas Müller, Helmut Schmid, and Hinrich Schütze. 2013. Efficient higher-order CRFs for morphological tagging. In *Proceedings of EMNLP 2013*, pages 322–332, Seattle, WA.

Joakim Nivre. 2009. Non-projective dependency parsing in expected linear time. In *Proceedings of ACL 2009*, pages 351–359.

Matthew E. Peters, Mark Neumann, Mohit Iyyer, Matt Gardner, Christopher Clark, Kenton Lee, and Luke Zettlemoyer. 2018. Deep contextualized word representations. In *Proceedings of NAACL 2018*, pages 2227–2237, New Orleans, LA.

Caroline Schroeder. 2020. Coptic literature in context (4th-13th cent.): Cultural landscape, literary production, and manuscript archaeology. In *Understanding Space and Place through Digital Text Analysis*, pages 229–242. Edizioni Quasar, Rome.

Ilya Shnayderman, Liat Ein-Dor, Yosi Mass, Alon Halfon, Benjamin Sznajder, Artem Spector, Yoav Katz, Dafna Sheinwald, Ranit Aharonov, and Noam Slonim. 2019. Fast end-to-end Wikification. arXiv:1908.06785[cs.CL].

Ben Shneiderman. 1992. Tree visualization with tree-maps: 2-d space-filling approach. *ACM Transactions on Graphics*, 11:92–99.

David A. Smith, Jeffrey A. Rydberg-Cox, and Gregory Crane. 2000. The Perseus project: A digital library for the humanities. *Literary and Linguistic Computing*, 15(1):15–25.

Shyam Upadhyay, Manaal Faruqui, Chris Dyer, and Dan Roth. 2016. Cross-lingual models of word embeddings: An empirical comparison. In *Proceedings of ACL 2016*, pages 1661–1670, Berlin.

Juntao Yu, Bernd Bohnet, and Massimo Poesio. 2020. Named entity recognition as dependency parsing. In *Proceedings of ACL 2020*, Seattle, WA.

Amir Zeldes and Mitchell Abrams. 2018. The Coptic Universal Dependency Treebank. In *Proceedings of the Universal Dependencies Workshop 2018*, pages 192–201, Brussels.

Amir Zeldes and Caroline T. Schroeder. 2015. Computational methods for Coptic: Developing and using part-of-speech tagging for digital scholarship in the humanities. *Digital Scholarship in the Humanities*, 30(1):164–176.

Shuo Zhang and Amir Zeldes. 2017. GitDOX: A linked version controlled online XML editor for manuscript transcription. In *Proceedings of FLAIRS-30*, pages 619–623, Marco Island, FL.

A Survey on Approaches to Computational Humor Generation

Miriam Amin and **Manuel Burghardt**
Computational Humanities Group, Leipzig University
`miriam.amin@studserv.uni-leipzig.de,`
`burghardt@informatik.uni-leipzig.de`

Abstract

We provide a comprehensive overview of existing systems for the computational generation of verbal humor in the form of jokes and short humorous texts. Considering linguistic humor theories, we analyze the systematic strengths and drawbacks of the different approaches. In addition, we show how the systems have been evaluated so far and propose two evaluation criteria: humorousness and complexity. From our analysis of the field, we conclude new directions for the advancement of computational humor generation.

1   Introduction

Since the early 1990s, computer scientists and linguists have been trying to create jokes using algorithms. Despite this longstanding research and the current evolution of powerful approaches in deep learning and neural networks – which are very well able to simulate human behavior and creativity, e.g. with the composition of pop music (Chu et al., 2017), poetry (Ghazvininejad et al., 2017) or abstract paintings (Li et al., 2019) – no system has been able to imitate human humor and to generate jokes like a human until today. From a research perspective, the task at hand is called *humor generation*. It is part of the broader field of *computational humor* and the output of humor generation systems are typically, but not exclusively, jokes. Besides the creation of humor, the following aspects are relevant for the field of computational humor as a whole:

- **Humor recognition** is dealing with algorithms deciding whether a given sentence expresses a certain degree of humor (Mihalcea and Strapparava, 2005; Barbieri and Saggion, 2014; Cattle and Ma, 2018; Morales and Zhai, 2017). A related task is humor prediction (Chen and Lee, 2017).

- **Humor adaption systems** are systems that learn a person's humor preference and adapt their performance according to it (Weber et al., 2018; Winters et al., 2018).

- **Computational humor evaluation** research is concerned with the problem of how to evaluate a humor generating system (Valitutti, 2011; Braslavski et al., 2018).

- **Computational humor applications** are wide spread and range from systems that help mentally challenged children to learn and comprehend complex communication situations (Ritchie et al., 2007; Shah et al., 2016) to applications that can be used to make human computer interaction more pleasant on the human side (Binsted, 1995; Stock, 2006; Iwakura et al., 2018).

- **Computational humor datasets and corpora** are collected and published with the purpose of facilitating humor research methods using data analysis, statistical learning or deep learning. They range from data about humor norms of English words (Engelthaler and Hills, 2017), over data that conveys pairs of newspaper headlines with a humorous counterpart (Hossain et al., 2019) to multimodal data that includes not only linguistic, but also acoustic and facial expression features as reaction to humorous expressions in TED talks (Hasan et al., 2019).

While humor generation can be researched from both the textual and the visual perspective (Oliveira et al., 2016), this survey article is dedicated to providing an overview of only text-based systems and approaches for the computational generation of humor.

Although only a minority of the existing systems refer to humor theory explicitly, we assume that it is necessary to also consider some of the most current linguistic humor theories when discussing different computational approaches to humor generation. Among the most prominent humor theories are the following:

- Surprise disambiguation model (Ritchie, 1999; Minsky, 1984; Paulos, 1982; Shultz, 1974)
- Suls' two-stage model (Suls, 1972)
- Script-based semantic theory of humor (SSTH) (Raskin, 1984) and its extension, the General theory of verbal humor (Raskin and Attardo, 1991)

These theories agree that humor is evoked by incongruity within a text. Incongruity theories assume that a humorous text conveys two different, incompatible interpretations (also called scripts[2] or frames) that share a common part that allows us to shift from one script to another. One interpretation is usually more obvious than the other, so that the recipient begins to process only this script, until parts of the text contradict with the initial interpretation, revealing the before hidden, second interpretation. This sudden revision of understanding causes the emotions of surprise and satisfaction that is perceived as humor (Krikmann, 2006). The various theories differ in how the incongruity is created or resolved (Ritchie, 1999).

Although research on computational humor generation has been going on since the early 1990s, the field is still very heterogenous. Research is conducted by at least two different communities: humor theory/linguistics (e.g. Hempelmann, 2008; Raskin, 2012; Taylor, 2017) and natural language processing/computational linguistics (e.g. Binsted and Ritchie, 1994; Hong and Ong, 2009; Yang and Sheng, 2017). There have been attempts by the humor theory community to streamline the research activity in a series of workshops (Nijholt, 2012), however, the vast majority of existing humor systems originates from the NLP community and does not seem to pick up those more theory-driven impulses. Interestingly enough, most of the older NLP approaches also do not take into account related and previous work and for the most part seem to exist in isolation from each other (Winters et al., 2019). After all, a more recent approach aims to standardize terminology and generalize the computational template-based stream of research (Winters et al., 2019). This framework is, however, not able to capture the entirety of the existing systems and the only existing survey paper that aims at capturing activity in the field dates back to 2001 (Ritchie, 2001). With the present survey paper, we try to fill that gap by providing a comprehensive overview of the existing approaches. To be able to compare and discuss these approaches, we propose *humorousness* and *complexity* as the two main criteria for the evaluation of humor generation systems. By analyzing the strengths and weaknesses of the respective systems with regard to those criteria, we conclude directions for future research in the field.

2 Humor Generation Systems

Humor generation can be viewed as a special case of automatic text generation. Accordingly, the existing systems can be categorized as belonging to one of two major approaches to text generation: Templates and neural networks. Until Yang and Sheng's publication on an LSTM RNN for joke production in 2017, all of the previous published systems were template-based. While the early template-based systems had to be equipped with handcrafted lexicons, more recent systems have a variety of external lexical resources as source of material for generation.

It is also worth mentioning that the nature of the humorous texts produced by different systems is rather diverse. While a number of systems was focused on the generation of question-answer jokes (Raskin and Attardo, 1994; Binsted and Ritchie, 1994; Ritchie et al., 2007; Sjöbergh and Araki, 2008; Hong and Ong, 2009; Labutov and Lipson, 2012), others aimed at creating narrative jokes (Sjöbergh and Araki, 2009; Yang and Sheng, 2017; Yu et al., 2018). Furthermore, three systems generate humor

---

[2] A script, also known as frame, is 'an organized chunk of information about something' and 'contains information which is typical, such as well-established routines and common ways to do things and to go about activities' (Attardo, 1994). In a broader sense, every content word can be a script, as for example 'teacher' or 'workplace'. Scripts can also be more complex like 'packing for holidays'.

through lexical replacement, in acronyms (Stock and Strapparava, 2005), proverbs (Sjöbergh and Araki, 2008) or in SMS (Valitutti et al., 2016), and one system creates witty analogies (Petrović and Matthews, 2013).

In the following, we will give an overview of existing humor generation systems. Since neural networks have recently achieved state-of-the-art results on many tasks in natural language processing, we will start with the group of systems that apply them for the creation of jokes. This group, however, contains only two systems, whereas the vast majority (ten systems) belongs to the group of template-based approaches.

2.1 Neural systems

The most recent line of work on computational joke generation trains neural networks for language generation in a way that the output is a short humorous text. As was already mentioned, work in this branch started with Yang and Sheng's (2017) current affair jokes generator that is trained on a joke corpus and allows the user to specify the topics of the joke. They use an LSTM RNN as their network architecture and GloVe as vector representation for the training data input. As training data, the authors use a dataset of 7,699 jokes written by Conan O'Brien and news data in order to improve the model for the current affairs related language. The topic words to be selected by the user were extracted from the jokes with a POS-tagger, assuming that nouns typically represent topics. Additionally, the user can specify the words the joke starts with from a list (e.g. *'I don't know why but...'*). The authors attempt to implement a form of incongruity by not outputting the word with the highest probability, but instead picking words from the vocabulary with the probability they were assigned in the output layer. For example, for the topic words 'Kardashian' and 'President', the network generated the joke *'Yesterday to a new attractiveness that allows Bill Kardashian's wife to agree with the U .S . Presidents . In fairness , she said , "My spa".'.* It is evident from this example that the system is not capable of producing a humorous text.

Instead of training their model on a joke corpus, Yu et al. (2018) aim at creating humor through incongruity by training a neural network with a seq2seq model on the Wikipedia text corpus and using one polysemic word and two of its meanings as input for text generation. From that, the language model generates two sentences, each conveying one sense of the word. In the first of the two presented pun models (the authors call it joint model), an encoder-decoder network is trained to generate one sentence containing both senses. The second model (highlight model) is an improved version that adds more words associated with the initial senses to the decoded sentence. That is to make sure both conveyed senses are transferred to the audience explicitly enough. For example, one of the triples consisting of a polysemic word and two of its meanings as input for the joke models could be *'square: 1) a plane rectangle with four equal sides and four right angles, a four-sided regular polygon; 2) someone who doesn't understand what is going on.'* For this input, the highlight model outputs *'Little is known when he goes back to the square of the football club'* and the joint model generates *'There is a square of the family.'* Likewise Yang and Sheng's (2017) system, neither of the models' output is identifiable as joke.

In contrast to template-based humor systems that will be reviewed in the next section, neural systems pose no semantic or syntactic restrictions, which results in a fairly creative output. Despite the high level of creativity, both neural systems ultimately fail to generate actual humor.

2.2 Template-based systems

In linguistics, a template is understood to be a text with slots that can be filled with different variables. In order to compose a joke, a template needs to be associated with a schema, which is the structure stipulating the relationships between the variables of a template (Binsted and Ritchie, 1994). These relationships are typically chosen in a way to provoke incongruity and its resolution. In other words, the schema is the joking mechanism. The variable relations can be a lexical relationship like synonymy, meronymy or hyponymy, but also a phonetical relation, such as (quasi-)homonymy. All template-based systems need a source that provides information about relationships between words in order to fulfill the requirements of the schema. We propose a classification of template-based systems that focuses on the source of these information. It should be noted that template-based systems are typically less creative than neural systems, as they are in any case restricted to the constraints of the template which are pre-defined by the creator of the template.

Within the template-based strand of research we primarily distinguish between systems that use ontologies for variable selection and systems that apply quantitative measures for that end. While the first group relies on the existence of ontologies or lexicons that store relationship information that is required to fill the template explicitly, the second group calculates predefined metrics on a corpus to find the best fit for a variable arithmetically. As a third group, we have identified hybrid systems that share properties of both aforementioned groups. In the following, we present the different groups with their corresponding systems.

Ontologies for variable selection

Early generators make use of handcrafted ontologies that are tailored to the specific system. This includes the Light Bulb Joke Generator (LIBJOG, Raskin and Attardo, 1994) that produces jokes of the pattern *How many <group name> does it take to screw in a light bulb? <NumberX>. One to <activity 1> and <numberY> to <activity2>*. LIBJOG uses a lexicon of social groups and their stereotypical activities to produce jokes such as *'How many Californians does it take to change a light bulb? Twelve. One to screw it in and eleven to share in the experience.'*. Over several phases from LIBJOG-1 to LIBJOG-4, the system became incrementally more complex, allowing for more activity fields and less restricted number relations.

Binsted and Ritchie (1994) follow a similar approach by basing their punning riddle generator on a manually edited lexicon that stores lexical relationship information, such as synonymy, hyponymy and associated verbs and the phonetical feature homophony. Their system called JAPE-1 uses question-answer templates, as for example *What is <adjective> and <verb>?– <noun phrase>*. With *<noun phrase>* as user input, JAPE fills the two remaining slots based on the words' homophony, exploiting phonological ambiguity to induce humorousness. An example of such a joke is: *'What's green and bounces? A spring cabbage!'*. Figure 1 illustrates the mechanism of that joke. In total, JAPE has 15 joke templates with schemes.

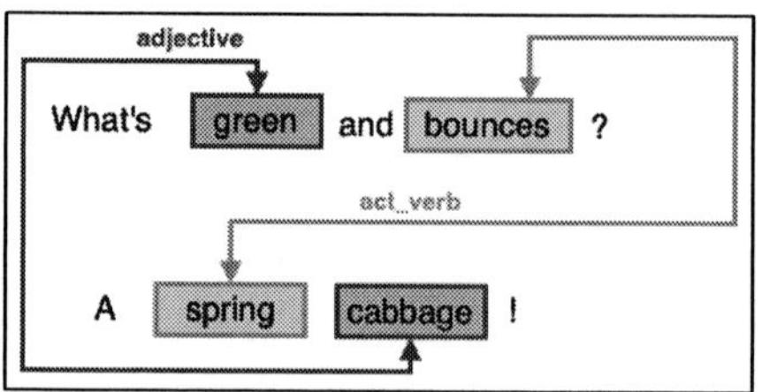

Figure 1: Illustrated example of the joke mechanism in JAPE. From: Binsted and Ritchie, 1994

Another line of systems uses freely-available ontologies and databases. Resources used by the existing systems are WordNet (Princeton University, 2010) for lexical relationships, ConceptNet (Speer et al., 2017) for semantic relationships and UniSyn (Fitt, 2002) or CMU pronouncing dictionary (Lenzo, 2007) for phonetical relationships. Furthermore, systems make use of thematic word lists for slang words or profanity. With STANDUP, Ritchie et al. (2007) present an extension of JAPE that has a user interface makes use of WordNet and UniSyn instead of the handcrafted lexicon.

HAHAcronym (Stock and Strapparava, 2005) is a system that writes out common acronyms in a humorous manner. For example, the acronym *FBI (Federal Bureau of Investigation)* becomes *Fantastic Bureau of Intimidation*. HAHAcronym makes use of WordNet, augmented with domain labels for the entries and the CMU pronunciation dictionary to take into account word rhymes and rhythms. The systems parses a given acronym to detect the syntactical form and the highest-ranking noun phrase, which remains unchanged. The other words get substituted while preserving the initial letter, the word class as well as the overall rhyme and rhythm. A substitution is chosen by exploiting semantic field opposition.

Sjöbergh and Araki's (2009) ambiguous compound generator also leverages WordNet to create jokes, this time however focusing less on inter-word relationships, but more on the provided definitions and example sentences. The system consists of two modules, creating two types of jokes, each making use of possibly ambiguous compound nouns. The first module creates jokes with the template *'I saw a <noun1> <noun2>. She (<noun1>) <WordNet example sentence>.'* For the two noun slots, the system selects compound nouns from WordNet where both parts also occur as single entries, the first as noun and the second as noun and verb. For the verb, one of the example sentences is extracted in order to complete the template to a joke such as *'I saw a fish stick. She (the fish) stuck her thumb in the crack.'* The audience initially assumes that *fish stick* is a composite, as this is the more obvious interpretation. However, this expectation is disrupted in the second sentence, when the rear part of the supposed composite turns out to be a verb. The first sentence is now reanalyzed, and the incongruity is resolved. The second type of joke Sjöbergh an Araki's system produces, follows the template *'<WordNet definition <noun1> <noun2>>.'* For this, compounds are selected when they contain at least one word that is included in WordNet itself, and by changing one letter that word must become another word present in WordNet. This compound is combined with one entry that has the original compound in its WordNet definition. From the exemplary compound *'god of war'* this would render *'Ares: (Greek mythology) Greek god of car'*. To reduce the number of jokes, the authors implement a measure of funniness and only output jokes above a certain threshold. The measure is calculated by the relation of the frequency of the selected compound between a joke corpus and a non-humorous corpus.

Hong and Ong's (2009) system uses WordNet's relation synonymy and UniSyn's pronunciation information alongside with any semantic relationship retrieved from ConceptNet. Their system creates punning riddles similar to Binsted and Ritchie's JAPE. This time, however, the algorithm is designed to first learn question-answer joke patterns from examples and then create new jokes according to the patterns. To create joke patterns, the algorithm called T-PEG marks nouns, adjectives and verbs in every joke from a POS-tagged joke corpus as candidate variables. For every tuple of candidate variables in a joke, T-PEG determines the lexical, phonetical or semantical relationship between the two variables. Those candidate variables with at least one relationship with another candidate are the final variables in the learned template. For example, from the source pun *'Which bird can lift the heaviest weights? The crane.'*, T-PEG extracts the sentence template *'Which <X1> can <X3> the heaviest <X6>? The <Y1>.'* and the word relationships *'X1 ConceptuallyRelatedTo X6'*, *'X6 ConceptuallyRelatedTo X1'*, *'Y1 IsA X1'*, *'X6 CapableOfReceivingAction X3'*, *'Y1 CapableOf X3'* and *'Y1 UsedFor X3'*. From the 39 templates the algorithm extracted, the authors found 27 (69 %) to be usable. To generate jokes, T-PEG uses the library of patterns and WordNet, Unisyn and ConceptNet to find fitting words for the slots and a keyword input from the user as a starting point.

Quantitative measures for variable selection
On the contrary to the aforementioned systems, joke generators using quantitative measures implement hypotheses about the nature of the relations, which are not expressed in explicit variable relationships but in quantitative measures, for instance n-gram co-occurrence.

Labutov and Lipson (2012a) are the first (and only) authors to explicitly implement a linguistic humor theory, based on cycles within the knowledge graph of ConceptNet. The theoretic framework they refer to is the *script-based semantic theory of humor* (SSTH) (Raskin, 1984), according to which a text is humorous (i.e. a joke) if it satisfies the following conditions: it suits partly or completely to two different scripts and these two scripts are opposite. Instead of explicitly defining the relationships between the concepts, like in STANDUP, the authors model their assumptions of how to retrieve concepts and their relations that form a joke from ConceptNet probabilistically. Based on the premise that paths in ConceptNet can be represented as scripts, the authors hypothesize that circuits, i.e. two paths that have the same root and end node, are joke candidates. Figure 2 shows an example of a circuit. From a seed concept, the algorithm performs a depth-first search and selects candidate paths, represented as a chain of relations between concepts. Modeling SSTH's script overlap, one condition for selection of a candidate path is the maximum path overlap. In order to create a meaningful and reasonable script in human language, the maximum likelihood of transition between the relations is also considered. The transition probabilities were learned before. From the found script pairs, the ones with maximum inter-script incongruity are selected. To measure incongruity, an algo-

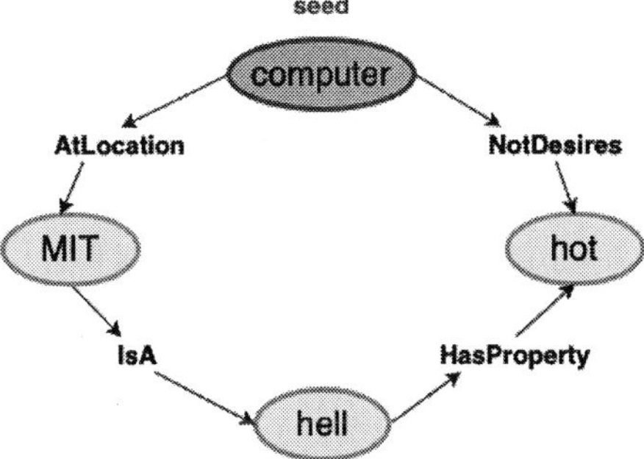

Figure 2: Example of a semantic circuit that constitutes a joke. From: Labutov and Lipson, 2012

rithm clusters all concepts in ConceptNet, so that related concepts form one cluster. The jokes are created with a small number of templates similar to the form *'Why does the A do B? Because the A is D.'* An example of a joke created by the system is *'Why is the computer hot in MIT? Because MIT is hell.'*

Petrovic and Matthews' (2013) approach strikes a similar chord by encoding the semantic relationships between the variables in a template as functions and finding the words that would minimize the result. This time, however, the candidate variables are calculated based on frequencies and co-occurrences within the Google n-gram corpus, which marks a leap towards the independence of such systems from ontologies and knowledge graphs. The joke template here is *'I like my X like I like my Y, Z.'*. The authors formulate assumptions about the variables that must be met to make the completed template funny. On the contrary to Labutov and Lipson (2012a), these assumptions, however, do not seem to originate explicitly from the theory of humor, but from a self-conceived heuristic of the authors. Besides the precondition that X and Y are nouns and Z is an adjective, the model is based on the following hypotheses: (1) The adjective should be relevant to both nouns. The model calculates the co-occurrence probability from the Google 2-gram corpus (ignoring 2-grams with less than 1,000 occurrences). (2) The less common the attribute Z, the funnier the joke. This is encoded as the reciprocal frequency of Z in the corpus. (3) The more ambiguous the attribute, the funnier the joke. The authors represent this as the reciprocal of the number of senses of Z, retrieved from WordNet. (4) The more dissimilar the nouns are, the funnier the joke. To measure the similarity, the model calculates the cosine of the angle between the two nouns, represented as vectors of all attributes used to describe them in the corpus. Dissimilarity is represented as the reciprocal similarity of X and Y. Overall, Petrovic and Matthews assume that a joke is funnier, the higher the product of all factors is, i.e. the funniness probability, given a triple (X, Y, Z), normalized over all triples. For joke calculation, the authors fix one of the nouns because of limitations in computing capacity. An example of a generated jokes is *'I like my relationship like I like my source, open.'*.

Hybrid systems

A number of systems combine ontological and quantitative approaches. Sjöbergh and Araki (2008) present a system performing Japanese stand-up comedy implementing three different joking techniques. The system starts with a proverb joke, continues with a riddle joke and ends with a joke retrieved from a human generated joke database. The succeeding joke is found on the base of the words used in the previous joke and connected by the phrase *'Speaking of <keyword>, <next joke>'*. The system generates proverb jokes by selecting a proverb from a list of common Japanese proverbs and changing two words to similar sounding dirty words. Dirty words are taken from a collection of dirty words and information about similar pronunciation from a list of the phonetic distances between Japanese graphemes. The proverb *'jack of all trades, master of none'* would for instance be modified to *'jacking off all trades, masturbate none'*. For the riddle jokes, the system checks the nouns of the previous joke for similarity with a word of the dirty words list. The jokes follow the template *'A <noun> is a <noun>, but what kind of <noun> is <hint>? – <dirty word>'*. The hint is a word that describes the noun as well as the dirty word and is generated by searching *'a <dirty word> is <hint>'* in an internet search engine. The hint found is then reviewed for its co-occurrence with noun and dirty word, again using frequencies retrieved from a search engine. An example of such a joke is *'"Speaking" is "speaking", but what is a naughty kind of speaking? – Spanking the monkey.'*.

Similar to their approach, Dybala et al. (2008) develop a pun generator that creates Japanese puns as humorous responses to a user's input as part of a conversational system. In a first step, the algorithm called PUNDA generates a candidate word for a pun. The user's input is morphologically analyzed and if any word is parsed as a noun, this word becomes the base of the pun. Pun candidates are generated from the base word using one of four possible generation patterns: homophony, initial syllable addition, internal syllable addition and final syllable addition. For example, the following candidates can be generated from the base word *katana* by 1. homophony: *katana*, 2. initial syllable addition: *akatana, ikatana, ukatana, ...* 3. final syllable addition: *katanaa, katanai, katanau, ...* and 4. internal syllable addition: *kaatana, kaitana, kautana, ...* . If any of the candidates is recognized as an actual word by a morphological analyzer, the number of hits in a Japanese search engine is determined. The word with the highest hit rate is the final candidate. In a second step, a list of all sentences that contain this word is retrieved from a sentence database. The shortest sentence with exclamation mark, or if no such sentence is found, with period is selected as the final sentence. This sentence is connected to the user's input with the pattern *'Speaking of <base word>'*. An example conversation could be the following: User: *'Natsu wa atsui desu kedo, Toukyou hodo ja nai desu'. (The summer is hot, but not as hot as in Tokyo.)* with the base word: *natsu (summer)* and the pun candidate *natsukashii (emotionally attached; loved)*. – System:

Natsu to ieba, natsukashii Nose de, kyuuyuu to waiwai! (Speaking of summer, it will be fun to meet some old friends in my beloved Nose [a town near Osaka]!)

Similar to Stock and Strapparava's (2005) HAHAcronym, Valitutti et al. (2016) generate humorous texts by word substitution. They substitute a single word in a given short text message (SMS) that serves as a template. Their 2016 study is an enhanced version of a 2013 paper by the same authors (Valitutti et al., 2013). They assume different kinds of lexical constraints that determine the funniness of a substitution: (1) Taboo: The substitution is a taboo word (dirty word e.g.) or connoted with a taboo. (2) Coherence: The substitute forms a coherent compound with its neighbors. (3) Position: The substitution takes place among the last words of the text. (4) Form: The substitute is phonetically or orthographically similar to the original word. They use WordNet, the CMU pronunciation dictionary, the Google n-gram corpus after 1990, two online dictionaries of slang words and an example list of funny autocorrection mistakes from the internet, to find suitable candidates and check them for compliance with the constraints. As input for the manipulation they use an SMS Corpus. An example of a joke that leverages the constraints form and position is *'Tmr u going to school? I meet u in pool?'* (school/pool replacement).

3 Evaluation of Humor Generation Systems

In order to compare the existing systems to each other, some basic measures for the quality of humor generation systems are needed. Although a multitude of systems has been developed so far, a standardized methodology of assessing the quality of such systems is still missing. Most previous systems chose the humorousness of the output as an evaluation criterion. The majority of approaches was evaluated by means of user studies where actual humans rated the generated jokes on a Likert scale that typically ranges from 0 (not a joke) to 5 (really funny). The first authors to introduce this method were Binsted and Ritchie (1994) and many followed their example, such as Sjöberg and Araki (2008) or Hong and Ong (2009). Yang and Sheng (2017) as well as Valitutti et al. (2016) employ a four-step Likert scale.

However, in most of the papers it remains unclear how the samples for evaluation were selected. Petrovic and Matthews (2013) for example disclose that they hand-picked the best jokes for the human assessment. Obviously, it matters a lot whether the average humor of a system is calculated on the basis of random jokes or on the basis of jokes that were pre-selected by the authors.

The main challenge in the design of humor evaluation measures is that humor is highly subjective and what makes one person laugh might not have the same effect on another person. Winters et al. (2018) show that the funniness judgements of jokes differ significantly among the test persons. Circumventing this issue, Valitutti (2011) proposes the HF (humorous frequency) as measure for the evaluation of computational humor generators. He defines HF as the fraction of funny items in a randomly generated set of jokes. Any item is either funny or not funny, i.e. in this context humorousness has a Boolean value rather than a score. To calculate the HF of a system, Boolean humorousness ratings have to be assigned to every item of a randomly selected set of jokes generated by the system. However, how a single joke is assessed remains highly subjective.

Binsted and Ritchie (1997) suggest to classify a computer-generated joke as successful when people cannot tell it apart from a human-generated joke, funniness left aside. Yu et al. (2018) conduct such an evaluation. The authors design what they call a Soft Turing Test to let test persons rate the humanness of the jokes generated by their system on a three-score Likert-scale (2–definitely human/0–definitely machine).

What all these approaches have in common, however, is that they do not consider the humor capability of the systems as a whole and rather evaluate individual jokes, or, as in the case of the HF, derive an overall evaluation of the system from the scores of the individual jokes. Consequently, the diversity of the produced material is completely disregarded in these evaluations. This overlooks the fact that a system that produces a row of almost similar jokes would not be very enjoyable for a human. Taking this factor into account, the humor capability of a system with a low complexity, i.e. a system that produces similar jokes with almost the same wording and the same production principle, should be rated lower than a system that produces a variety of jokes and joke mechanisms.

To our knowledge, none of the evaluation procedures yet has attempted to apply objective criteria to the decision of whether a given piece of text is humorous or not. However, from the insights of humor theory and research, criteria for what constitutes a joke can be concluded. Consequently, a useful measure would be not if a text is humorous or how funny a joke is, but rather whether a text is identifiable as joke or not, taking into account objective criteria.

4 Comparison of Humor Generation Systems based on their Humorousness and Complexity

The considerations in the last section give rise to two main criteria for the evaluation of humor systems: humorousness and complexity. In the following, we provide a discussion of the benefits and limitations of different systems based on these criteria. We define *humorousness* as the ability of a humor system to output text that is identifiable as a joke or a text with a humorous intent. The above introduced incongruity theories can contribute objective criteria towards this end. In this sense, a text is humorous if it conveys two different concepts, whose incompatibility is resolved in an unexpected way. We define *complexity* as the ability of a humor system to generate a variety of humorous texts, concerning syntactical and lexical features, as well as the joking mechanism. The joking mechanism describes the way in which the incongruity and its resolution is evoked.

Based on these two criteria, Table 1 provides a rating of the aforementioned systems. Due to the lack of computable metrics, we do not assign scores to the single systems. Instead, we rank the systems against each other in terms of the introduced criteria on a scale from 1 to 3 where 1 is the highest rank.

Type of joke/system name	Authors	Year	Class	H	C
Current affair joke generation	Yang and Sheng	2017	Neural	3	1
Homographic pun generation	Yu, et al.	2018	Neural	3	1
Lightbulb jokes/LIBJOG	Raskin and Attardo	1994	Template-based	1	3
Punning riddle generators/ JAPE and STANDUP	Binsted and Ritchie	1994/2007	Template-based	1	2
HAHAcronym	Stock and Strapparava	2005	Template-based	2	2
Japanese Standup	Sjöbergh and Araki	2008	Hybrid	2	2
PUNDA	Dybala et al.	2008	Hybrid	2	2
Question-Answer jokes patterns	Hong and Ong	2009	Template-based	1	2
Ambiguous compound joke generator	Sjöbergh and Araki	2009	Template-based	2	2
Humor as circuits in ConceptNet	Labutov and Lipson	2012	Template-based	1	2
Humorous analogy generation	Petrovic and Matthews	2013	Template-based	1	3
Humorous SMS generation	Valitutti et al.	2016	Hybrid	2	2

Table 1: Ranking of humor systems with regards to humorousness (H) and complexity (C)

For the assessment of humorousness, we gave rank 3 to systems that do not fulfill the criteria for jokes at all and rank 1 to systems whose output is obviously identifiable as joke. Rank 2 was given to systems that produce text that fulfills at least some joke criteria (e.g.: Valitutti's Humorous SMS generator introduces ambiguity to the texts, but it lacks unexpectedness). However, the evaluation of the jokes could only consider the jokes published by the authors, usually 3-5 examples. As mentioned before, it can be assumed that the authors manually filtered out the best jokes for the papers. Petrović and Matthews (2013) among others, admit this and Hong and Ong (2009) explicitly mention that much of the output is not funny.

With regard to complexity, we assigned rank 3 to systems without template that restricts syntactical and lexical features, rank 2 to systems that have either a variety of different templates or template with variable slots that are large enough to allow a lexical diversity and rank 1 to systems that have only one template.

This analysis reveals the strengths and weaknesses of the two approaches to humor generation. The table clearly shows that none of the systems reaches the highest rank in humorousness as well as in complexity. The template-based approaches fill the higher ranks for humorousness by implicitly including humor theory through their constraints and metrics. The neural systems on the other hands are not capable of generating humorous text at all, scoring the lowest ranks. Nonetheless, these systems reach the highest scores in complexity through their learned language model, consequently being able to generate a large variety of text. The template-based approaches fail to reach that level of complexity.

5 Conclusion: Toward Better Humor Generation Systems by Means of Linguistic Humor Theories

Our survey shows that even after more than 25 years of work on humor generation, further research needs to be conducted in order to create a system that generates text that fulfils theory-driven criteria for humor and that is able to produce a variety of texts, regarding syntactical structures and joke mechanisms. It is somewhat surprising that almost none of the present approaches refers to a linguistic humor theory explicitly. The initially introduced humor theories and their evolution, however, make very clear that textual humor is evoked by complex semantic mechanisms. A number of requirements about the involved concepts and their semantic relationships needs to be fulfilled in order to create a text that is actually humorous rather than just puzzling. These theories enable us to explain why some texts are funny and make people laugh and others do not. Hence, we believe that considering these existing humor theories will be an important step to overcome the limitations of existing joke generators.

We regard the *surprise ambiguation model* and the SSTH as the most interesting theories. The *surprise ambiguation model*, as formalized by Ritchie (1999), defines a small set of properties and entities. Based on the three entities M_1 – the obvious interpretation of the set-up, M_2 – the hidden interpretation of the set-up and M_3 – the meaning of the punchline, the model defines the following relations and properties involved in humorous texts: *Obviousness* (M_1 is more likely than M_2 to be noticed by the reader), *conflict* (M_3 does not make sense with M_1), *compatibility* (M_3 does not make sense with M_2), *comparison* (there is some contrastive relationship between M_1 and M_2) and *inappropriateness* (M_2 is inherently odd or a taboo). Winters et al. (2019 and 2018) already used these properties to identify and validate a set of metrics that are used by machine learning algorithms to extract features from existing jokes. Also, the concept of humor postulated by the SSTH has very few requirements that could be formalized pretty easily. The SSTH even implicitly gives an instruction of how a joke can be constructed from non-humorous content. In Suls' two-stages model on the other hand, whether something is humorous or not is dependent on the presence of a cognitive rule. However, a cognitive rule can be anything and is therefore not very feasible for being modeled computationally. The GVTH focuses more on a representation of the differences of jokes rather than on the humor mechanism itself.

We see great potential for the improvement of existing approaches to computational humor generation by taking into account these theoretical approaches to humor and hope that this survey will pave the way for further, more theory-driven research in this direction.

References

Salvatore Attardo. 1994. *Linguistic Theories of Humor*. Walter de Gruyter.

Francesco Barbieri and Horacio Saggion. 2014. Automatic Detection of Irony and Humour in Twitter. In *Proceedings of the Fifth International Conference on Computational Creativity, ICCC 2014*, pages 155–162, Ljubljana, Slovenia. Association for Computational Creativity.

Kim Binsted. 1995. Using Humour to Make Natural Language Interfaces More Friendly. In *Proceedings of the AI Alife and Entertainment workshop, Fourteenth International Joint Conference on Artificial Intelligence*, Montreal, Quebec, Canada. IJCAI Organization.

Kim Binsted and Graeme Ritchie. 1994. An implemented model of punning riddles. In *Proceedings of the 12th National Conference on Artificial Intelligence (AAAI '94)*, volume 1, pages 633–638, Menlo Park, CA, USA, July. Association for the Advancement of Artificial Intelligence (AAAI).

Kim Binsted and Graeme Ritchie. 1997. Computational rules for generating punning riddles. *Humor: International Journal of Humor Research*, 10(1):25–76.

Pavel Braslavski, Vladislav Blinov, Valeria Bolotova, and Katya Pertsova. 2018. How to Evaluate Humorous Response Generation, Seriously? In *Proceedings of the 2018 Conference on Human Information Interaction & Retrieval (CHIIR '18)*, pages 225–228, New York, NY, USA. Association of Computing Machinery (ACM).

Andrew Cattle and Xiaojuan Ma. 2018. Recognizing Humour using Word Associations and Humour Anchor Extraction. In *Proceedings of the 27th International Conference on Computational Linguistics (COLING '18)*, pages 1849–1858. Association for Computational Linguistics (ACL).

Lei Chen and Chong MIn Lee. 2017. Predicting Audience's Laughter Using Convolutional Neural Network. In *Proceedings of the 12th Workshop on Innovative Use of NLP for Building Educational Applications (BEA@EMNLP '17)*, Copenhagen, Denmark. Association for Computational Linguistics (ACL).

Hang Chu, Raquel Urtasun, and Sanja Fidler. 2017. Song From PI: A Musically Plausible Network for Pop Music Generation. In *Workshop Track Proceedings of the 5th International Conference on Learning Representations (ICLR '17)*, Toulon, France. International Conference on Representation Learning.

Pawel Dybala, Michal Ptaszynski, Shinsuke Higuchi, Rafal Rzepka, and Kenji Araki. 2008. Humor Prevails! - Implementing a Joke Generator into a Conversational System. In Wayne Wobcke and Mengjie Zhang, editors, *AI 2008: Advances in Artificial Intelligence*, volume 5360 of *Lecture Notes in Computer Science*, pages 214–225. Springer Berlin Heidelberg, Berlin, Heidelberg.

Tomas Engelthaler and Thomas Hills. 2017. Humor norms for 4,997 English words. *Behavior Research Methods*, 50(3):1116–1124.

Susan Fitt. 2002. Unisyn Lexicon. http://www.cstr.ed.ac.uk/projects/unisyn/

Marjan Ghazvininejad, Xing Shi, Jay Priyadarshi, and Kevin Knight. 2017. Hafez: an interactive poetry generation system. In *Proceedings of ACL 2017, System Demonstrations*, pages 43–48, Vancouver, Canada. Association for Computational Linguistics (ACL).

Md Kamrul Hasan, Wasifur Rahman, Amir Zadeh, Jianyuan Zhong, Md Iftekhar Tanveer, Louis-Philippe Morency, and Mohammed E. Hoque. 2019. UR-FUNNY: A Multimodal Language Dataset for Understanding Humor. In *Proceedings of the 2019 Conference on Empirical Methods in Natural Language Processing and the 9th International Joint Conference on Natural Language Processing (EMNLP-IJCNLP '19)*, pages 2046–2056, Hong Kong, China. Association for Computational Linguistics (ACL).

Christian Hempelmann. 2008. Computational humor: Beyond the pun? In Victor Raskin, editor, *The Primer of Humor Research*, volume 8 of *Humor Research*, pages 333–360. Mouton de Gruyter.

Bryan Anthony Hong and Ethel Ong. 2009. Automatically Extracting Word Relationships As Templates for Pun Generation. In *Proceedings of the Workshop on Computational Approaches to Linguistic Creativity (CALC '09)*, pages 24–31, Stroudsburg, PA, USA. Association for Computational Linguistics (ACL).

Nabil Hossain, John Krumm, and Michael Gamon. 2019. "President Vows to Cut <Taxes> Hair": Dataset and Analysis of Creative Text Editing for Humorous Headlines. In *Proceedings of the 2019 Conference of the North American Chapter of the Association for Computational Linguistics: Human Language Technologies (NAACL-HLT '19)*, pages 133–142, Minneapolis, MN, USA. Association for Computational Linguistics (ACL).

Ryosuke Iwakura, Tomohiro Yoshikawa, and Furuhashi Furuhashi. 2018. A Basic Study on Generating Back-Channel Humor Phrases for Chat Dialogue Systems. In *2018 Joint 10th International Conference on Soft Computing and Intelligent Systems (SCIS) and 19th International Symposium on Advanced Intelligent Systems (ISIS)*, pages 1263–1266. Publicity Committee of SCIS-ISIS.

Arvo Krikmann. 2006. Contemporary Linguistic Theories of Humour. *Folklore: Electronic Journal of Folklore*, 33:27–58.

Igor Labutov and Hod Lipson. 2012. Humor as Circuits in Semantic Networks. In *Proceedings of the 50th Annual Meeting of the Association for Computational Linguistics (Volume 2: Short Papers)*, pages 150–155, Jeju Island, Korea. Association for Computational Linguistics (ACL).

Kevin Lenzo. 2007. The CMU pronouncing dictionary. *Carnegie Melon University*.

Mao Li, Jiancheng Lv, Jian Wang, and Yongsheng Sang. 2019. An abstract painting generation method based on deep generative model. *Neural Processing Letters*, 2019:1–12.

Rada Mihalcea and Carlo Strapparava. 2005. Computational Laughing: Automatic Recognition of Humorous One-liners. In *Proceedings of the 27th Annual Conference of the Cognitive Science Society (CogSci '05)*, pages 1513–1518, Stresa, Italy. Cognitive Science Society.

Marvin Minsky. 1984. Jokes and the Logic of the Cognitive Unconscious. In Lucia Vaina and Jaakko Hintikka, editors, *Cognitive Constraints on Communication: Representations and Processes*, Synthese Language Library, pages 175–200. Springer Netherlands, Dordrecht.

Alex Morales and ChengXiang Zhai. 2017. Identifying Humor in Reviews using Background Text Sources. In pages 492–501, Copenhagen, Denmark. Association for Computational Linguistics (ACL).

Anton Nijholt, editor. 2012. *Computational Humor 2012. Proceedings 3rd International Workshop on Computational Humor*. Universiteit Twente, Enschede.

Hugo Gonçalo Oliveira, Diogo Costa, and Alexandre Pinto. 2016. One does not simply produce funny memes! – Explorations on the Automatic Generation of Internet humor. In *Proceedings of the Seventh International Conference on Computational Creativity (ICCC '16)*, pages 238–245, Paris, France. Association for Computational Creativity.

John Allen Paulos. 1982. *Mathematics and Humor: A Study Of The Logic Of Humor*. University of Chicago Press, Chicago.

Saša Petrović and David Matthews. 2013. Unsupervised joke generation from big data. In *Proceedings of the 51st Annual Meeting of the Association for Computational Linguistics (Volume 2: Short Papers)*, pages 228–232, Sofia, Bulgaria. Association for Computational Linguistics (ACL).

Princeton University. 2010. About WordNet. https://wordnet.princeton.edu/

Victor Raskin. 1984. *Semantic Mechanisms of Humor*. Springer Netherlands, Dordrecht.

Victor Raskin. 2012. A Little Metatheory: Thought on What a Theory of Computational Humor Should Look Like. In *Artificial Intelligence of Humor, Papers from the 2012 AAAI Fall Symposium*, Arlington, Virginia, USA. Association for the Advancement of Artificial Intelligence (AAAI).

Victor Raskin and Salvatore Attardo. 1991. Script theory revis(it)ed: joke similarity and joke representation model. *Humor - International Journal of Humor Research*, 4(3–4):293–348.

Victor Raskin and Salvatore Attardo. 1994. Non-literalness and non-bona-fide in language: An approach to formal and computational treatments of humor. *Pragmatics & Cognition*, 2(1):31–69.

Graeme Ritchie. 1999. Developing the Incongruity-Resolution Theory. In *Proceedings of the AISB Symposium on Creative Language: Stories and Humour*, pages 78–85, Edinburgh, Scotland. Society for the Study of Artificial Intelligence and Simulation of Behaviour.

Graeme Ritchie. 2001. Current Directions in Computational Humour. *Artificial Intelligence Review*, 16(2):119–135.

Graeme Ritchie, Ruli Manurung, Helen Pain, Annalu Waller, Rolf Black, and Dave O Mara. 2007. A practical application of computational humour. In *Proceedings of the 4th International Joint Workshop on Computational Creativity*, London, UK. Association for Computational Creativity.

Thomas R. Shultz. 1974. Development of the Appreciation of Riddles. *Child Development*, 45(1):100–105.

Jonas Sjöbergh and Kenji Araki. 2008. A Complete and Modestly Funny System for Generating and Performing Japanese Stand-Up Comedy. In *COLING 2008, 22nd International Conference on Computational Linguistics, Posters Proceedings*, pages 111–114, Manchester, UK. Coling 2008 Organizing Committee.

Jonas Sjöbergh and Kenji Araki. 2009. A Measure of Funniness, Applied to Finding Funny Things in WordNet. In *Proceedings of the Conference of the Pacific Association for Computational Linguistics 2009*, page pp 236-241. Pacific Association for Computational Linguistics.

Robyn Speer, Joshua Chin, and Catherine Havasi. 2017. ConceptNet 5.5: An open multilingual graph of general knowledge. In *Proceedings of the Thirty-First AAAI Conference on Artificial Intelligence*, pages 4444–4451, San Francisco, California, USA. AAAI Press.

Oliviero Stock. 2006. Password swordfish: Verbal humor in the interface. *Humor - International Journal of Humor Research*, 16(3):281–295.

Oliviero Stock and Carlo Strapparava. 2005. The Act of Creating Humorous Acronyms. *Applied Artificial Intelligence*, 19(2):137–151.

Jerry M. Suls. 1972. A Two-Stage Model for the Appreciation of Jokes and Cartoons: An Information-Processing Analysis. In *The Psychology of Humor*, pages 81–100. Elsevier.

Julia M. Taylor. 2017. Computational treatments of humor. In Salvatore Attardo, editor, *The Routledge Handbook of Language and Humor*, pages 456–471. Routledge.

Alessandro Valitutti. 2011. How many jokes are really funny? Toward a New Approach to the Evaluation of Computational Humor Generators. In Bernadette Sharp, Michael Zock, Michael Carl, and Arnt Lykke Jakobsen, editors, *Human-Machine Interaction in Translation: Proceedings of the 8th International NLPCS Workshop*, volume 41, pages 189–200, Frederiksberg, Denmark. Samfundslitteratur.

Alessandro Valitutti, Antoine Doucet, Jukka M. Toivanen, and Hannu Toivonen. 2016. Computational generation and dissection of lexical replacement humor*. *Natural Language Engineering*, 22(5):727–749.

Alessandro Valitutti, Antoine Doucet, Hannu Toivonen, and Jukka M. Toivanen. 2013. "Let Everything Turn Well in Your Wife": Generation of Adult Humor Using Lexical Constraints. In *Proceedings of the 51st Annual Meeting of the Association for Computational Linguistics, Volume 2: Short Papers*, Sofia, Bulgaria. Association for Computer Linguistics (ACL).

Klaus Weber, Hannes Ritschel, Ilhan Aslan, Florian Lingenfelser, and Elisabeth André. 2018. How to Shape the Humor of a Robot - Social Behavior Adaptation Based on Reinforcement Learning. In *Proceedings of the 20th ACM International Conference on Multimodal Interaction*, pages 154–162, New York, NY, USA. Association of Computing Machinery (ACM).

Thomas Winters, Vincent Nys, and Daniel De Schreye. 2018. Automatic Joke Generation: Learning Humor from Examples. In Norbert Streitz and Shin'ichi Konomi, editors, *Distributed, Ambient and Pervasive Interactions: Technologies and Contexts*, pages 360–377. Springer International Publishing.

Thomas Winters, Vincent Nys, and Danny De Schreye. 2019. Towards a General Framework for Humor Generation from Rated Examples. In *Proceedings of the 10th International Conference on Computational Creativity*, pages 274–281, Charlotte, North Carolina, USA. Association for Computational Creativity (ACC).

Er Ren Yang and Quan Sheng. 2017. Neural Joke-Generation. In *Final Project Reports of Course CS224n*. Stanford University.

Zhiwei Yu, Jiwei Tan, and Xiaojun Wan. 2018. A Neural Approach to Pun Generation. In *Proceedings of the 56th Annual Meeting of the Association for Computational Linguistics (Volume 1: Long Papers)*, pages 650–1660, Melbourne, Australia. Association for Computational Linguistics (ACL).

Neural Machine Translation of Artwork Titles Using Iconclass Codes

Nikolay Banar[1,2] **Walter Daelemans**[1] **Mike Kestemont**[1,2]

[1]CLiPS, University of Antwerp, Antwerp, Belgium

[2]ACDC, University of Antwerp, Antwerp, Belgium

{nicolae.banari, walter.daelemans, mike.kestemont}@uantwerpen.be

Abstract

We investigate the use of Iconclass in the context of neural machine translation for NL↔EN artwork titles. Iconclass is a widely used iconographic classification system used in the cultural heritage domain to describe and retrieve subjects represented in the visual arts. The resource contains keywords and definitions to encode the presence of objects, people, events and ideas depicted in artworks, such as paintings. We propose a simple concatenation approach that improves the quality of automatically generated title translations for artworks, by leveraging textual information extracted from Iconclass. Our results demonstrate that a neural machine translation system is able to exploit this metadata to boost the translation performance of artwork titles. This technology enables interesting applications of machine learning in resource-scarce domains in the cultural sector.

1 Introduction

In the age of mass-digitization, cultural heritage institutions put significant effort in making their (meta) data available to developers and researchers. Artificial intelligence, and machine learning in particular, increasingly plays an important role in this process (Fiorucci et al., 2020). Recent case studies have demonstrated successful applications of machine learning methods to cultural heritage collections. Most of this work relies on advances in computational methods and utilizes a modelling framework known as deep neural networks (LeCun et al., 2015; Schmidhuber, 2015). However, such algorithms are data-intensive and require large annotated datasets, which recently have become available in some fields (Tiedemann, 2012; Krizhevsky et al., 2012; Lin et al., 2014). These datasets contain millions of training items, which allowed researchers to achieve impressive results in many tasks. However, the construction of such materials in the domain of cultural heritage material is an even more expensive process, as it requires the intervention of highly-trained subject experts. Hence, many institutions can only offer smaller datasets, that contain just a fraction of the number of training examples that are needed to train a deep learning algorithms. Transfer learning is a common solution to overcome such a lack of training data (Ruder et al., 2019). In neural machine translation (NMT), networks are nowadays commonly pre-trained on large generic datasets of parallel sentences, before they get fine-tuned on a more specific "downstream" corpus. Such networks, however, are conventionally only exposed to the actual sentence pairs in the target domain and are ignorant of additional knowledge that might be available such as, for example, iconographic metadata about objects and their relations. In the case of artworks, computational methods that can exploit such additional knowledge are highly appealing.

This work aims to apply NMT in the context of cultural heritage metadata using Iconclass (Vellekoop et al., 1973) as a source of external knowledge. Iconclass (see Section 3.1.1) contains keywords and definitions of subjects represented in artworks. We propose a simple approach to integrate this external knowledge in an NMT architecture for artwork titles to improve the translation performance. The structure of this paper is as follows. We first present the related work in Section 2. Then, we describe the datasets and present the applied methods in more detail in Section 3. Next, we present the results of our

Proceedings of LaTeCH-CLfL 2020, pages 42–51
Barcelona, Spain (Online), December 12, 2020.

case study and discuss them in Section 4. Finally, we summarize our main contributions and findings with proposals for future work in Section 5.

2 Related Work

Modern NMT systems nowadays often work at the level of an individual sentence pair and aim to translate a source sentence into a target sentence, without making use of additional information other than the source sentence itself. The idea to concatenate a source sentence with additional information, however, is not new. This preprocessing step is appealing due to its simplicity and model-agnostic applicability. Previous approaches in this respect are generally divided into 2 categories (see examples in Table 1): (i) *extended context* (Tiedemann and Scherrer, 2017), where additional information in the source language is added to the source sentence (and sometimes to the target sentence); (ii) *data augmentation* (Bulté and Tezcan, 2019), where the source sentence is enriched with information in the target language.

Tiedemann and Scherrer (2017) investigated the benefits of the extended context approach in attention-based NMT for DE→EN subtitles (see Table 1). The source sentence was concatenated with the previous source sentence and, then, the same technique was additionally applied to the target sentence. They used a special prefix to mark tokens belonging to the extended context. Although the improvement over the baseline was moderate, the NMT models were able to utilize the additional context and to distinguish it from the main sentence. In follow-up work, Bawden et al. (2018) designed EN→FR test sets to investigate the usefulness of the previous source and target sentences in the context of NMT. They demonstrated that the concatenation strategy leads to improved performance. Agrawal et al. (2018) applied the concatenation technique with a Transformer-based architecture to EN→IT TED talks and experimentally varied the number of concatenated sentences included. There too, the extended context was demonstrated to be beneficial for Transformers. Junczys-Dowmunt (2019), finally, developed one of the best-performing systems based on the same idea in the context of the WMT19 news translation shared task for EN→DE.

Bulté and Tezcan (2019) proposed a simple and efficient data augmentation method for NMT that yielded substantial performance improvements for EN→NL and EN→HU. The source sentence was concatenated with fuzzy matches, or sentences in the target language retrieved from a translation memory, that covered the entire training set. The fuzzy matches were selected on the basis of a simple similarity measurement between each source sentence and all other source sentences from the translation memory. Then, the fuzzy source sentences with a similarity score above a given threshold were stored with their corresponding target sentences. In a subsequent study, Jitao et al. (2020) improved the previously proposed method by explicitly informing models about any relevant tokens in the fuzzy matches and incorporating distributed sentence representations (see Table 1).

Inspired by this previous work, we investigate the use of Iconclass in the context of artwork title translations. We use the definitions and keywords associated with Iconclass codes to extend and augment the artwork titles. Our main contribution is that we demonstrate that Iconclass definitions, when provided within a data augmentation strategy, improve translation performance.

extended context	source	cc_sieh cc_, cc_Bob cc_! -Wo sind sie?
	target	-Where are they?
data augmentation	source	How long does a cold last? || Combien de temps dure le vol?
	target	Combien de temps dure un rhume?

Table 1: Examples of the *extended context* approach from Tiedemann and Scherrer (2017) and the *data augmentation* approach from Jitao et al. (2020). The special prefix cc_ indicates tokens from the extended context and the special token \|\| separates the augmented sentence from the main and additional parts.

3 Methods

In this section, we describe the datasets and the methods that we utilized in our research. We justify our choice for the particular NMT model used and provide details on the experimental settings and evaluation measures.

3.1 Datasets and Preprocessing

3.1.1 Iconclass

Iconclass is an iconographic classification system used by stakeholders in the GLAM sector (Galleries, Libraries, Archives and Museums) to describe and retrieve subjects represented in the visual arts. Each subject represented in Iconclass is assigned a unique Iconclass code or identifier, that includes keywords and definitions in multiple languages (see Figure 1). In total, Iconclass contains a set of 28,000 hierarchically ordered definitions and 14,000 keywords. An Iconclass code starts with a digits ranging from 0 to 9 representing 10 main categories: (0) abstract art; (1-5) general topics; (6) history; (7) Bible; (8) literature; (9) classical mythology and ancient history. An Iconclass code can be further complemented by the options presented in Table 2. Keywords have been added to concepts to help users to retrieve relevant concepts from the database. However, the number of available keywords per language differs significantly and they do not necessary match each other across languages, as is evident from the example Iconclass codes in Figures 1b and 1c. Unfortunately, Dutch descriptions are mostly unavailable and, hence, are not utilized in this work. We extracted all information from the Iconclass codes using the Iconclass Python package[1].

N	Extension	Definition	Keywords
1	71H7	David and Bathsheba (2 Samuel 11-12)	Bathsheba, Samuel-2 11-12
	71H7**1**	David, from the roof (or balcony) of his palace, sees Bathsheba bathing	balcony, bathing, love at first sight, palace, roof, spying
2	25G41	flowers	flower
	25G41(**ROSE**)	flowers: rose	rose
3	25F23(LION)	beasts of prey, predatory animals: lion	lion
	25F23(LION)(+12)	beasts of prey, predatory animals: lion (+ heraldic animals)	Wappentier, araldica, heraldisches Symbol, heraldry, héraldique, lion

Table 2: Extension of Iconclass codes: (1) a letter or digit to increase specificity; (2) bracketed text to add the name of a specific entity; (3) bracketed text with a plus-sign to add an additional 'shade of meaning'.

3.1.2 Artwork dataset

The NL↔EN artwork dataset used below has been extracted from the database of the Netherlands Institute for Art History[2]. We deleted all duplicates from the dataset and finally obtained 21,988 sentence pairs, with the corresponding Iconclass codes for the artworks in question. We randomly selected 2,000 sentence pairs as a development set and included another 2,000 sentence pairs in the test set. The training set contains 1.35 ± 0.72 Iconclass codes per sentence/title and we randomly sample one Iconclass code per sentence/title in the development and test sets. In this work, we do not exploit the hierarchical structure of Iconclass codes and leave this worthwhile option to future work. Additional details about the datasets are provided in Table 3. We experimented with 4 different concatenation strategies. Each source sentence s_i (in English or Dutch) was concatenated using bracketed tags to the corresponding English description d_i^{en} or set of keywords in English k_i^{en} or Dutch k_i^{nl}: (1) s_i (txs) d_i^{en}

[1] https://labs.brill.com/ictestset/
[2] https://rkd.nl/en/explore/images

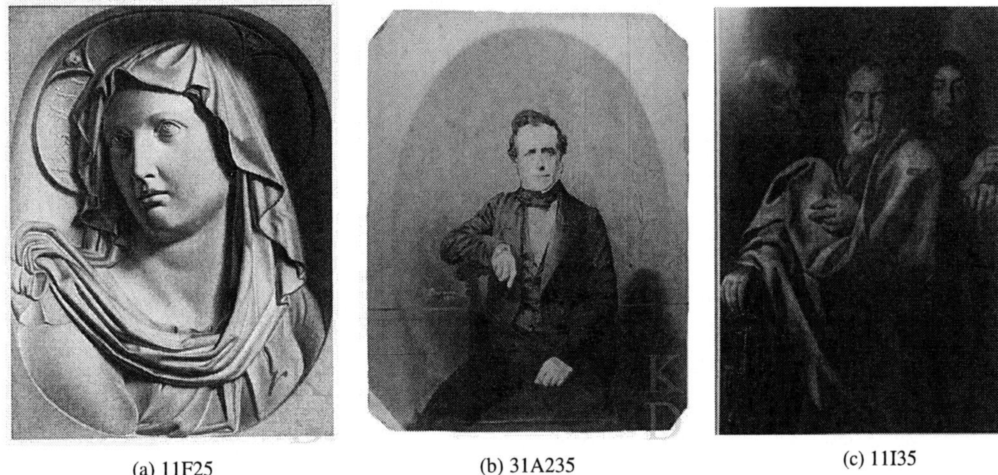

(a) 11F25   (b) 31A235   (c) 11I35

Figure 1: Examples of images assigned Iconclass codes from Posthumus (2020). The Iconclass code 11F25 provides the English definition 'Mater Dolorosa', the set of English keywords 'Mater Dolorosa, bust, full length, half-length, head , mother' and the set of the Dutch keywords 'Mater Dolorosa, buste, full length , half-length, hoofd, moeder'. The Iconclass code 31A235 is less informative with the definition 'sitting figure' and only one English keyword 'sitting'. The Iconclass code 11I35 only has an English definition: 'other groups of apostles'.

Split	EN sentence	NL sentence	EN description	EN keywords	NL keywords
Train	52.01 ± 29.64	53.75 ± 29.86	51.80 ± 34.60	26.58 ± 21.48	26.85 ± 21.78
Dev	51.90 ± 29.90	53.81 ± 30.37	52.20 ± 34.75	26.42 ± 21.65	26.84 ± 21.65
Test	51.76 ± 29.67	52.61 ± 35.05	52.61 ± 35.05	26.66 ± 21.10	26.95 ± 21.41

Table 3: Statistics of the dataset: mean and standard deviation in sentence lengths.

(txe); (2) s_i (kws) k_i^{en} (kwe); (3) s_i (kws) k_i^{nl} (kwe); (4) s_i (txs) d_i^{en} (txe) (kws) k_i^{en} (kwe). If a sentence from the training set has more than one Iconclass code, then the sentence is separately matched with each Iconclass code using one of the concatenations as shown in Table 5. We balance each concatenated sentence by adding its original version to the training and development sets in order to make the models learn both types of sentences equally well. Additionally, we use two versions of the test set in our evaluation: (1) a baseline test set, where we use original sentences without any concatenations; (2) the test set as concatenated with the corresponding additional information.

3.1.3 Pre-training

Pre-training has become a common solution to cope with small datasets across many domains in deep learning (Ruder et al., 2019). In our experiments, we used 1,777,653 sentence pairs extracted from the Europarl corpus (Tiedemann, 2012) for the NL↔EN language pair, in order to pre-train the models on a generic background corpus. We randomly selected 3,000 sentence pairs as a development set and 3,000 sentence pairs in the test set respectively.

3.2 Model Details

Banar et al. (2020) demonstrated the advantages of character-level translation over the subword-level approach for artwork titles. Hence, we exclusively resorted to character-level models in the present work. However, Banar et al. (2020) used a fusion of recurrent and convolutional models (Lee et al., 2017) that has become outdated. The recent emergence of NMT models started with recurrent neural

source	Ceres bespot door Stellio (Metamorphosen 5: 446-461)
target	Mocking of Ceres by Stellio (Metamorphoses 5: 446-461)
English definition	a little boy (Abas, Ascalabus, or Stellio) laughs at Ceres, because she drinks too avidly while she is resting at an old woman's house
English keywords	Ascalabus, boy, drinking, laughing, old woman, thirst
Dutch keywords	Ascalabus, dorst, drinken, jongen, lachend, old woman
concatenation 1	Ceres bespot door Stellio (Metamorphosen 5: 446-461) (txs) a little boy (Abas, Ascalabus, or Stellio) laughs at Ceres, because she drinks too avidly while she is resting at an old woman's house (txe)
concatenation 2	Ceres bespot door Stellio (Metamorphosen 5: 446-461) (kws) Ascalabus, boy, drinking, laughing, old woman, thirst (kwe)
concatenation 3	Ceres bespot door Stellio (Metamorphosen 5: 446-461) (kws) Ascalabus, dorst, drinken, jongen, lachend, old woman (kwe)
concatenation 4	Ceres bespot door Stellio (Metamorphosen 5: 446-461) (txs) a little boy (Abas, Ascalabus, or Stellio) laughs at Ceres, because she drinks too avidly while she is resting at an old woman's house (txe)(kws) Ascalabus, boy, drinking, laughing, old woman, thirst (kwe)

Table 4: Example concatenations of a title and the information from the Iconclass code 92M132.

source	Johannes de Doper en de H. Hieronymus
target	John the Baptist and St. Jerome
definition 1	the monk and hermit Jerome (Hieronymus); possible attributes: book, cardinal's hat, crucifix, hour-glass, lion, skull, stone
definition 2	John the Baptist; possible attributes: book, reed cross, baptismal cup, honeycomb, lamb, staff
training sentence 1	Johannes de Doper en de H. Hieronymus (txs) the monk and hermit Jerome (Hieronymus); possible attributes: book, cardinal's hat, crucifix, hour-glass, lion, skull, stone (txe)
training sentence 2	Johannes de Doper en de H. Hieronymus (txs) John the Baptist; possible attributes: book, reed cross, baptismal cup, honeycomb, lamb, staff (txe)

Table 5: Example of the concatenation of a title having multiple Iconclass codes with corresponding English definitions from 11H(JEROME) and 11H(JOHN THE BAPTIST).

networks such as GRU or LSTM memory cells (Bahdanau et al., 2014; Sutskever et al., 2014; Luong et al., 2015; Cho et al., 2014), but since then it has been established that Transformer-based architectures (Vaswani et al., 2017) persuasively outperform recurrent and convolutional models across various tasks. The Transformer model mitigates some of the limitations of recurrent and convolutional models; the Transformer, for example, includes self-attention mechanisms that can access all positions in a previous layer. Therefore, the receptive field is not as myopic as with convolutional models. Additionally, the absence of recurrent connections allows one to make the training process fully parallellizable. Therefore, such models nowadays are more appealing for our problem.

3.3 Training and Inference Details

As character-level translation works better for the translation of artwork titles (Banar et al., 2020), we applied a four-layer character-level Transformer (Vaswani et al., 2017), implemented in the OpenNMT-py framework (Klein et al., 2017). The vocabulary size was set to 300 characters and the length of sentences was limited to 450 characters. The models were trained by minimizing the negative conditional log-likelihood using the Adam optimizer (Kingma and Ba, 2014) with a batch size of 6,144 tokens and an accumulation count of 4. First, we pre-train the models on the general corpus and, then, fine-tune them on our domain-specific corpus. Each model was trained on a single GeForce GTX 1080 Ti with 11 GB RAM. In the pre-training phase, the models were initialized using the method proposed by Glorot and Bengio (2010) and trained for 100,000 updates using the Noam decay schedule (Popel and Bojar, 2018) with an initial learning rate of 2. In the fine-tuning phase, the initial learning rate was set to 0.0001. The fine-tuning was interrupted as soon as the validation loss did not decrease for 600 updates. In the decoding part of the architecture, we applied a beam search with a beam size of 25. The evaluation was conducted using three standard metrics: CHARACTER[3] (Wang et al., 2016), CHRF[4] (Popović, 2015) and BLEU-4 (Papineni et al., 2002) .

4 Results and Discussion

We present our quantitative results in Section 4.1. We divide our experimental results into two different sections. First, we assess the use of the extended context in Section 4.1.1. Second, we compare the various data augmentation strategies to the baseline in Section 4.1.2. In Section 4.2 we manually inspect a selection of outputs for the best performing model.

4.1 Quantitative Analysis

Pair	Additional Information	Type	Baseline test			Test with context		
			BLEU↑	C-TER↓	CHRF↑	BLEU↑	C-TER↓	CHRF↑
NL-EN	(a) baseline	NA	**43.25**	30.71	67.04	NA	NA	NA
	(b) keywords^{nl}	EC	42.50	30.81	66.77	42.56	30.60	66.91
	(c) keywords^{en}	DA	42.93	**30.25**	**67.21**	42.96	30.03	67.31
	(d) definition^{en}	DA	42.25	30.58	66.77	**46.02**	**29.48**	**68.32**
	(e) (d) + (c)	DA	41.96	31.23	66.47	45.88	29.79	68.17
EN-NL	(f) baseline	NA	42.99	30.82	67.75	NA	NA	NA
	(g) keywords^{nl}	DA	43.83	30.37	68.21	**43.71**	30.22	68.18
	(h) keywords^{en}	EC	43.59	30.49	68.07	43.53	30.66	67.92
	(i) definition^{en}	EC	42.93	30.94	67.73	43.20	30.80	67.77
	(j) (i) + (h)	EC	**44.00**	**30.35**	**68.23**	43.68	**29.97**	**68.37**

Table 6: Results of the experiments. The type 'EC' and 'DA' correspond to experiments with *extended context* and *data augmentation* approaches respectively. The arrows near the metrics in the column labels indicate the desired direction of improvement (i.e. whether a higher/lower score for this metric is better). The 'baseline' experiment corresponds to the models fine-tuned without any additional information. The columns 'Test with context' and 'Baseline test' correspond to translation of the sentences enriched with additional information and without it, correspondingly.

4.1.1 Extended Context

From Table 6 we can see that the models (b, h) fine-tuned with the context extended by keywords demonstrate comparable results to the baseline models (a, f) in the baseline test. Model (h) slightly outperforms the associated baseline, while model (b) is slightly worse in this testing scenario. The testing scenario with the extended context suggests that these models do not successfully manage to exploit the additional context, as there is no obvious boost in performance. For model (h), we can even observe a subtle decrease in performance. As the definitions were only available in English, the context has been extended by definitions only for EN→NL (see the models i and j). These models still show comparable performance to the baseline model (f) when translating without the extended context. The testing scenario with the extended context is also not beneficial. Therefore, we observe that the extended

---

[3] https://github.com/rwth-i6/CharacTER
[4] https://github.com/m-popovic/chrF

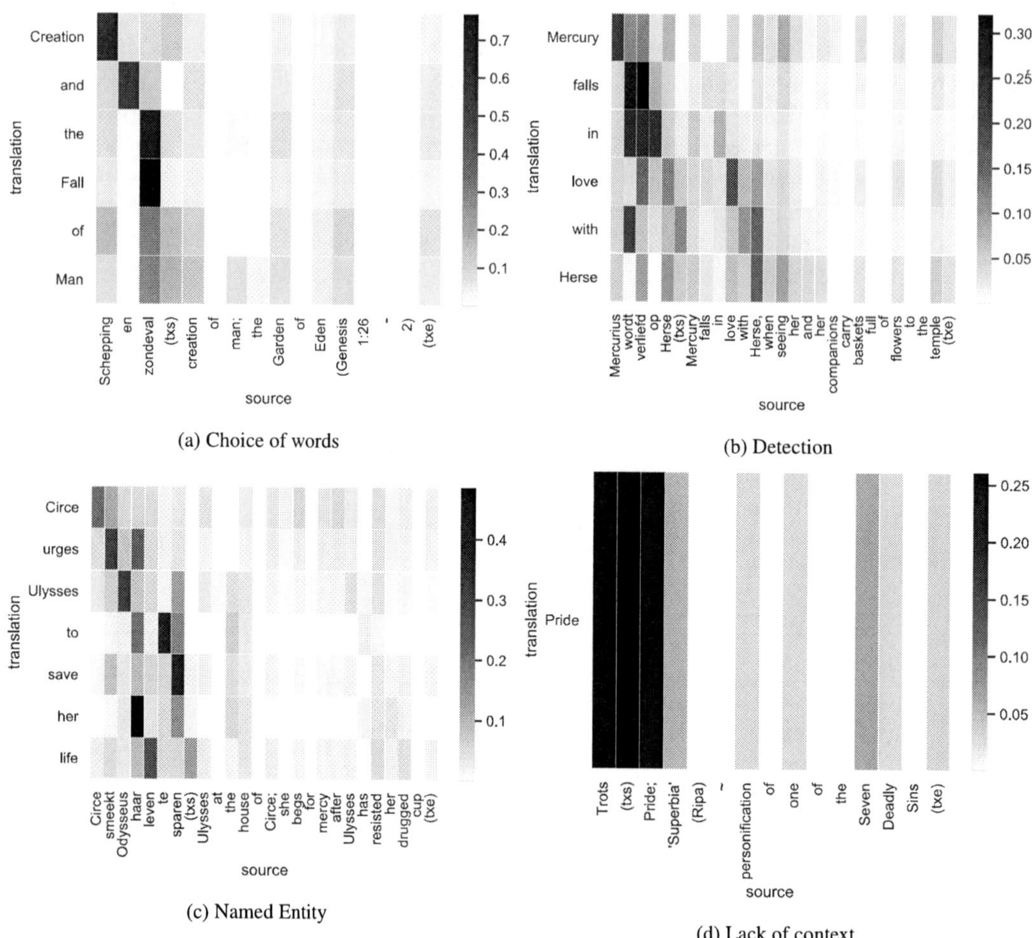

Figure 2: Example translations with attention maps for the model that uses English Iconclass definitions for data augmentation. We also provide the target sentence, translation of the model without data augmentation (**Without DA**) and translation of the baseline model (**Baseline**) fine-tuned without additional information. (a) **Target:** 'Creation and the fall of Man'. **Without DA:** 'Creation and a fall of mankind'. **Baseline:** 'Creation and a fall of mankind'. (b) **Target:** 'Mercury falls in love with Herse'. **Without DA:** 'Mercury being loved on Herse' **Baseline:** 'Mercury being loved on Herse'. (c) **Target:** 'Circe begging Ulysses to save her life'. **Without DA:** 'Circe pleading with Odysseus to save her life'. **Baseline:** 'Circe pleads with Odysseus to save her life in her life'. (d) **Target:** 'Pride'. **Without DA:** 'Christ'. **Baseline:** 'Events'.

context in the testing phase is generally not advantageous and, hence, we conclude that the use of these concatenations is not beneficial in our case.

4.1.2 Data Augmentation

As shown in Table 6, the models (c, g) fine-tuned with keywords as a source of data augmentation show comparable results to the baseline models (a, f) in the baseline testing scenario. Therefore, we conclude that the source sentences augmented by keywords are not helpful for our task. The models (d, e) utilize definitions for the data augmentation for NL→EN. These models demonstrate slightly worse performance compared to the baseline model (a) when translating without data augmentation. Translating with the source sentences augmented by definitions, however, boosts the performance of these models and we observe substantial improvement over baseline model (a) and their own non-augmented counterparts. We manually inspected the output of the model (d) and discuss some interpretive observations in the next Section 4.2.

4.2   Error Analysis

In this section, we qualitatively discuss the outputs of the best performing model (d) in the testing scenario with data augmentation from Table 6. We compare its output to that for the basic test setting, as well as to baseline model (a). We divide our findings into four main categories below.

Lexical choices. The model is able to exploit additional information in the target language in order to select words closer to target translations. From Figure 2a, we can see that the target translation is not literal and the word *Man* is absent in the Dutch counterpart. The literal translation of this sentence is *Creation and Fall*. In this case, baseline model (a) and model (d) in the basic testing scenario generate non-literal translations with the additional post-modification *of mankind*. The translation is close to the target, but it is still erroneous. Model (d) pays attention to the phrase *creation of man* from the Iconclass definition and decides to adopt the word *Man* instead of the word *mankind* as in the baseline and in the case without data augmentation.

Detection of lexical units. As mentioned in Section 3.1.1, Iconclass definitions describe subjects represented in artwork images. If a subject is widely represented in iconography, an artwork can even have the same title as an Iconclass definition or the definition can at least contain parts of the target translations. Hence, these target translations may be detected in an Iconclass definition and just copied by model. In Figure 2b, we can see that the baseline model (a) and model (d) in the basic testing scenario produce grammatically incorrect outputs. The Dutch fixed expression *wordt verliefd op* is translated almost literally as *being loved on*. However, we can see that model (d) finds a part of the right translation in the additional information and copies it.

Named entities. Artwork titles densely feature named entities in comparison to general corpora and, hence, they can be a serious issue for NMT models. Similarly to Banar et al. (2020), we observe that the models in the basic testing scenario tend to copy named entities instead of attempting a proper translation. However, we observe that if a correct named entity is provided in the additional information, the model is able to generate the correct target translation. From Figure 2c, we can see that model (d) derives the correct named entity *Ulysses*, while other scenarios are less successful.

Lack of context. The titles of artworks naturally differ from the sentences in more general corpora and can be very short. The lack of context may cause translation difficulties. In the example from Figure 2d, the title consists of only one word. The baseline model (a) and model (d) in the basic testing scenario struggle to translate the title *Pride* correctly and generate the non-sense translations *Events* and *Christ*, correspondingly. In this case, the additional information helps model (d) to generate the right answer.

5   Conclusion and Future Work

In this paper, we utilized the Iconclass framework as a source of additional information for NMT of artwork titles. We extracted English and Dutch keywords and English definitions from the Iconclass codes. This information was concatenated to the source sentences. Experiments show that augmenting the source sentences with the Iconclass definitions for the objects under scrutiny improves the overall translation quality by a considerable margin. On the basis of a manual inspection of the output, we argue that the NMT model is able to successfully capitalize on the additional information extracted from the Iconclass definitions. There are various reasons for this. Firstly, the model is able to recognize any named entities in the concatenated part (that are lacking in the actual source title) and it can correctly inject them in the translation. Secondly, the data augmentation approach improves the lexical aspects of the translation, providing useful semantic cues in the case of limited context. Thirdly, the model is able to detect correct translations in the concatenated part and integrate them appropriately in the translation. However, the augmentation of the source sentences with the keywords and any type of extended context that we applied do not show any promising results. In future work, we would like to extend the current pipeline with a model that automatically matches the source sentence with the corresponding Iconclass code. In addition, it may be beneficial to incorporate visual features extracted from artworks and, hence, to perform a multi-modal matching. Iconclass contains 28,000 hierarchically ordered definitions that makes the matching problem extremely sophisticated. We plan to investigate the feasibility of such a matching strategy.

References

Ruchit Rajeshkumar Agrawal, Marco Turchi, and Matteo Negri. 2018. Contextual handling in neural machine translation: Look behind, ahead and on both sides. In *21st Annual Conference of the European Association for Machine Translation*, pages 11–20.

Dzmitry Bahdanau, Kyunghyun Cho, and Yoshua Bengio. 2014. Neural machine translation by jointly learning to align and translate. *arXiv preprint arXiv:1409.0473*.

Nikolay Banar, Karine Lasaracina, Walter Daelemans, and Mike Kestemont. 2020. Transfer learning for digital heritage collections: Comparing neural machine translation at the subword-level and character-level. In *Proceedings of the 12th International Conference on Agents and Artificial Intelligence - Volume 1: ARTIDIGH,*, pages 522–529. INSTICC, SciTePress.

Rachel Bawden, Rico Sennrich, Alexandra Birch, and Barry Haddow. 2018. Evaluating discourse phenomena in neural machine translation. In *16th Annual Conference of the North American Chapter of the Association for Computational Linguistics: Human Language Technologies*, pages 1304–1313.

Bram Bulté and Arda Tezcan. 2019. Neural fuzzy repair: Integrating fuzzy matches into neural machine translation. In *57th Conference of the Association for Computational Linguistics (ACL)*, pages 1800–1809.

Kyunghyun Cho, Bart van Merriënboer, Dzmitry Bahdanau, and Yoshua Bengio. 2014. On the properties of neural machine translation: Encoder–decoder approaches. In *Proceedings of SSST-8, Eighth Workshop on Syntax, Semantics and Structure in Statistical Translation*, pages 103–111.

Marco Fiorucci, Marina Khoroshiltseva, Massimiliano Pontil, Arianna Traviglia, Alessio Del Bue, and Stuart James. 2020. Machine learning for cultural heritage: A survey. *Pattern Recognition Letters*, 133:102–108.

Xavier Glorot and Yoshua Bengio. 2010. Understanding the difficulty of training deep feedforward neural networks. In *Proceedings of the thirteenth international conference on artificial intelligence and statistics*, pages 249–256.

XU Jitao, Josep M Crego, and Jean Senellart. 2020. Boosting neural machine translation with similar translations. In *Proceedings of the 58th Annual Meeting of the Association for Computational Linguistics*, pages 1580–1590.

Marcin Junczys-Dowmunt. 2019. Microsoft translator at wmt 2019: Towards large-scale document-level neural machine translation. In *Proceedings of the Fourth Conference on Machine Translation (Volume 2: Shared Task Papers, Day 1)*, pages 225–233.

Diederik P Kingma and Jimmy Ba. 2014. Adam: A method for stochastic optimization. *arXiv preprint arXiv:1412.6980*.

Guillaume Klein, Yoon Kim, Yuntian Deng, Jean Senellart, and Alexander M. Rush. 2017. OpenNMT: Open-source toolkit for neural machine translation. In *Proc. ACL*.

Alex Krizhevsky, Ilya Sutskever, and Geoffrey E Hinton. 2012. Imagenet classification with deep convolutional neural networks. In *Advances in neural information processing systems*, pages 1097–1105.

Yann LeCun, Yoshua Bengio, and Geoffrey Hinton. 2015. Deep learning. *nature*, 521(7553):436–444.

Jason Lee, Kyunghyun Cho, and Thomas Hofmann. 2017. Fully character-level neural machine translation without explicit segmentation. *Transactions of the Association for Computational Linguistics*, 5:365–378.

Tsung-Yi Lin, Michael Maire, Serge Belongie, James Hays, Pietro Perona, Deva Ramanan, Piotr Dollár, and C Lawrence Zitnick. 2014. Microsoft coco: Common objects in context. In *European conference on computer vision*, pages 740–755. Springer.

Minh-Thang Luong, Hieu Pham, and Christopher D Manning. 2015. Effective approaches to attention-based neural machine translation. In *Proceedings of the 2015 Conference on Empirical Methods in Natural Language Processing*, pages 1412–1421.

Kishore Papineni, Salim Roukos, Todd Ward, and Wei-Jing Zhu. 2002. Bleu: a method for automatic evaluation of machine translation. In *Proceedings of the 40th annual meeting on association for computational linguistics*, pages 311–318. Association for Computational Linguistics.

Martin Popel and Ondřej Bojar. 2018. Training tips for the transformer model. *The Prague Bulletin of Mathematical Linguistics*, 110(1):43–70.

Maja Popović. 2015. chrf: character n-gram f-score for automatic mt evaluation. In *Proceedings of the Tenth Workshop on Statistical Machine Translation*, pages 392–395.

Etienne Posthumus. 2020. Brill iconclass ai test set. `https://labs.brill.com/ictestset/`.

Sebastian Ruder, Matthew E Peters, Swabha Swayamdipta, and Thomas Wolf. 2019. Transfer learning in natural language processing. In *Proceedings of the 2019 Conference of the North American Chapter of the Association for Computational Linguistics: Tutorials*, pages 15–18.

Jürgen Schmidhuber. 2015. Deep learning in neural networks: An overview. *Neural networks*, 61:85–117.

Ilya Sutskever, Oriol Vinyals, and Quoc V Le. 2014. Sequence to sequence learning with neural networks. In *Advances in neural information processing systems*, pages 3104–3112.

Jörg Tiedemann and Yves Scherrer. 2017. Neural machine translation with extended context. In *Proceedings of the Third Workshop on Discourse in Machine Translation*, pages 82–92.

Jörg Tiedemann. 2012. Parallel data, tools and interfaces in opus. In *Lrec*, volume 2012, pages 2214–2218.

Ashish Vaswani, Noam Shazeer, Niki Parmar, Jakob Uszkoreit, Llion Jones, Aidan N Gomez, Łukasz Kaiser, and Illia Polosukhin. 2017. Attention is all you need. In *Advances in neural information processing systems*, pages 5998–6008.

G. Vellekoop, E. Tholen, and L. D. Couprie. 1973. *Iconclass : an iconographic classification system*. North-Holland Pub. Co., Amsterdam.

Weiyue Wang, Jan-Thorsten Peter, Hendrik Rosendahl, and Hermann Ney. 2016. Character: Translation edit rate on character level. In *Proceedings of the First Conference on Machine Translation: Volume 2, Shared Task Papers*, pages 505–510.

A Two-Step Approach for Automatic OCR Post-Correction

Robin Schaefer
Staatsbibliothek zu Berlin -
Preußischer Kulturbesitz
10785 Berlin, Germany
`robin.schaefer`
`@sbb.spk-berlin.de`

Clemens Neudecker
Staatsbibliothek zu Berlin -
Preußischer Kulturbesitz
10785 Berlin, Germany
`clemens.neudecker`
`@sbb.spk-berlin.de`

Abstract

The quality of Optical Character Recognition (OCR) is a key factor in the digitisation of historical documents. OCR errors are a major obstacle for downstream tasks and have hindered advances in the usage of the digitised documents. In this paper we present a two-step approach to automatic OCR post-correction. The first component is responsible for detecting erroneous sequences in a set of OCRed texts, while the second is designed for correcting OCR errors in them. We show that applying the preceding detection model reduces both the character error rate (CER) compared to a simple one-step correction model and the amount of falsely changed correct characters.

1 Introduction

The digitisation of historical documents is a central objective for libraries, archives and museums. Using OCR, the digitised documents can be converted to electronic full text. Important advances have been achieved in OCR over recent years, mainly through the use of neural networks (Reul et al., 2018). However, in the case of historical documents there still remains a substantial amount of OCR errors that hinders the usage of the digitised documents and requires efficient methods for OCR post-correction. By defining OCR post-correction as a translation problem, current approaches are often based on neural networks (Mokhtar et al., 2018), especially sequence-to-sequence models that are inspired by successes achieved in neural machine translation (NMT) (Bahdanau et al., 2014; Luong et al., 2015). While these models perform well for data sets with a high amount of OCR errors, post-correction becomes more difficult when the CER is less severe (Amrhein and Clematide, 2018).

In this paper we present an alternative approach to OCR post-correction. Instead of solving the task in one step, i.e. by training a single translation model[1], we propose a two-step approach that avails itself of two separate models. We chose a Long Short Term Memory (LSTM) architecture (Hochreiter and Schmidhuber, 1997) for the actual sequence-to-sequence translation step (henceforth called *translator*). In addition, we inserted a model before the translator that functions as a filter by separating erroneous sequences[2] from correct ones (henceforth called *detector*). The benefits of this approach are two-fold: 1) By decreasing the proportion of correct OCRed data, the CER of the data fed into the translator is artificially increased. This is assumed to improve the translation results.[3] 2) By excluding the majority of correct sequences from the translation step, we can avoid to mistakenly insert errors in them.

This paper is structured as follows: Section 2 briefly summarizes the relevant previous work. Section 3 presents an initial OCR post-correction approach using a standard sequence-to-sequence model. It also describes the used data and the applied preprocessing steps. Afterwards, Section 4 presents our alternative two-step approach to OCR post-correction. Both components are analysed independently using different test sets. In Section 5 we show first results of the full pipeline applied to one data set. Finally, in Section 6 we discuss our results and give a short outlook.

---

[1]Although, technically speaking, a sequence-to-sequence model consists of two model components, we are calling this approach *one-step* as both components are trained simultaneously.

[2]We use the terms *sequence* and *line* interchangeably.

[3]It is crucial to note that the CER gets increased *only* by removing correct sequences with the detector model. At no point do we manually insert artificial OCR errors.

Proceedings of LaTeCH-CLfL 2020, pages 52–57
Barcelona, Spain (Online), December 12, 2020.

2   Related Work

Traditionally, the problem of OCR post-correction has been approached by the application of statistical language modelling techniques, frequently in combination with lexical resources or n-grams (Tong and Evans, 1996). String distance metrics are frequently used to generate correction candidates for erroneous tokens, aided by a probabilistic scoring mechanism or noisy channel model (Kolak and Resnik, 2002). However, these methods are less successful for historical documents that exhibit large amounts of OCR errors, historical spelling variation and where fitting language resources are scarce (Piotrowski, 2012).

Accordingly, Reffle and Ringlstetter (2013) compute a two-channel profile for historical language variation and OCR errors to improve the correction rate while minimizing the injection of new errors. This method was further improved by Fink et al. (2017) with the addition of an adaptive feedback mechanism and the treatment of non-interpretable tokens as conjectured errors. An alternative technique is Anagram Hashing (Reynaert, 2008), but more recent evaluations indicate that this approach requires fine-tuning (Reynaert, 2016). Since different OCR engines (or models) also produce different OCR error patterns, another strategy is merging multiple OCR results, supported by heuristics and lexical resources (Volk et al., 2011). OCR post-correction has also been studied as a problem of statistical (Afli et al., 2016) or neural machine translation (Mokhtar et al., 2018; Hämäläinen and Hengchen, 2019).

An overview of the recent state-of-the-art in OCR post-correction is provided by the ICDAR competition on post-OCR text correction. The competition comprises of two tasks, error detection and error correction, with evaluation sets for English and French language. The 2017 edition saw Weighted Finite-State Transducers (WFST) obtain best results in the error detection task, with an SMT/NMT system achieving the highest reduction of errors (Chiron et al., 2017). In the 2019 edition, a system based on BERT (Devlin et al., 2018) came out best for both tasks (Rigaud et al., 2019). For comparison, we refer to Amrhein and Clematide (2018) as our baseline (see Section 6).

3   The Standard Sequence-to-Sequence Approach

We first approached the OCR post-correction task by implementing a standard LSTM-based sequence-to-sequence translation model using the PyTorch framework (Paszke et al., 2019). The architecture consists of an encoder model responsible for calculating a matrix representation of the OCRed input sequence. This is used by the subsequent decoder model for creating a correct output sequence.

Data.   Using the OCR-D pipeline (Neudecker et al., 2019) [4], we processed 35 German works that were published from the 17th to the 19th century. All works are part of the corpus created by the *Deutsches Textarchiv* ("German Text Archive", DTA)[5], which contains double-keyed transcriptions, i.e. ground truth (GT). We aligned lines of GT and the OCRed documents using *dinglehopper*[6], before we calculated the CER for each individual OCR sequence. Furthermore, we removed sequence pairs with an error rate of more than 10%, which resulted in a data set of 167,848 line pairs. Given that experiments with the full data set have shown negative results, we consider this removal step necessary for training the translation model. It is important to note that the removed sequence pairs contain incorrect alignments, which we assume to be detrimental for the training process.

Following Amrhein and Clematide (2018) we applied a sliding window approach in order to 1) increase the data set size and 2) increase the importance of a token's direct context. To this end, we defined a context window of two preceding and one succeeding words around a given token (i.e. context-context-token-context). We incrementally moved this window one token at a time. Context windows never crossed page boundaries. This procedure increased our data set to 707,427 line pairs.

After this reformatting step, we removed non-German sequences using *langid* (Lui and Baldwin, 2012). The remaining line pairs were split into training (365,000 lines), validation (56,800 lines) and test sets (56,800 lines). All sets were encoded using a greedy approach inspired by the encoding mechanism used in the BERT framework (Devlin et al., 2018). Each 3-, 2- and 1-character combination occurring

---

[4]Specifically, we use the implementation from `https://github.com/qurator-spk/ocrd-galley`.
[5]`http://www.deutschestextarchiv.de/`
[6]`https://github.com/qurator-spk/dinglehopper`

in the GT received an encoding value. Referring to this character combination-encoding mapping, we encoded the OCR sequences. Whenever a 3-character encoding encountered in the OCR data did not exist in the mapping, a 2- or, if needed, 1-character encoding was chosen. Finally, the encoded sequence vectors were 0-padded to the length of 40.

Model Architecture and Results.   Both encoder and decoder models had one layer and a hidden node size of 256. The decoder further included an attention mechanism (Bahdanau et al., 2014). We trained the sequence-to-sequence model monodirectionally for 970 epochs using a learning rate of 0.0001 and a batch size of 200. In order to facilitate the task of the decoder, we made use of the teacher forcing technique (Williams and Zipser, 1989) using a ratio of 0.5. Applying the trained translator model on the test set, we achieved a CER of 1.6%. As the original CER in the test set amounts to 1.2%, this model actually increases the error rate. Referring to Amrhein and Clematide (2018), we argue that this model is not capable of efficiently correcting the low CER of this data set.

4   The Two-Step Approach

In order to improve the translator model's results, we decided on building a two-step pipeline. This pipeline consists of an initial OCR error detection model and a subsequent error translation (i.e. correction) model.[7] In this architecture, only sequences that the detector considers erroneous would be forwarded to the translator model. This procedure has the added benefit of artificially increasing the proportion of OCR errors which are fed into the translator. It also has the potential of decreasing the amount of erroneously changed correct characters.

4.1   The Detector Model

A successful detector model is characterised by a low false positive rate, i.e. by a small number of lines incorrectly classified as erroneous. Hence, we are particularly interested in increasing the detector's precision. As building a model that barely inflicts harm upon the correct data is of utmost importance, we do not prioritize a high recall, which indicates the proportion of identified incorrect sequences.

We developed a model based on a bidirectional LSTM architecture that sequentially processes an OCR sequence and outputs for every character encoding probabilities of it being erroneous or correct with respect to the GT encoding. Experiments showed that using a 3-layer structure with a hidden size of 512 yielded best results. A linear layer was set on top of the LSTM architecture, which reduced the high dimensional tensors to the output size of 3 (correct character/s, incorrect character/s, 0-padding). Logits were inputted into a softmax layer to obtain probabilities. We further used a dropout probability of 20% between LSTM layers. We trained the model for 138 epochs using a batch size of 200. Sequence-wise labels were calculated as follows: 1) Only character encodings with an error probability of $>99\%$ were treated as erroneous. 2) All sequences with at least one incorrect encoding were labelled as incorrect.

Data.   We used the data[8] described in Section 3 and applied the same preprocessing steps. However, instead of directly encoding the GT data, we used it to create class targets for the LSTM model. The OCR data was again encoded using the greedy encoding mechanism and padded with 0s.

	Predicted negative	Predicted positive
Target negative	41386	1123
Target positive	3730	10561

Table 1: Confusion Matrix (positive = incorrect sequence; negative = correct sequence)

Results.   Applying the trained detector model on the test set yielded promising results. We obtained an F1 score of 81%, a precision of 90% and a recall of 74%. In line with the objective described in this section, we obtained a high precision score and low false positive rate. This is confirmed by Table 1

---

[7]The code (two-step approach): `https://github.com/qurator-spk/sbb_ocr_postcorrection`.
[8]The data (two-step approach): `https://zenodo.org/communities/stabi/`.

(see column *Predicted positive*). Notably, we also achieved an acceptable recall, which indicates that a substantial proportion of incorrect sequences is also classified as such. Hence, the majority of incorrect sequences gets actually passed on to the translator model.

4.2 The Translator Model

The second component of our OCR post-correction pipeline is a sequence-to-sequence translation model as described in Section 3. For the sake of comparison of both approaches we refrained from making changes to the model architecture or training parameters. The model was trained for 876 epochs.

Data. We processed another 28 works using the OCR-D pipeline. After applying the same preprocessing steps as described in Section 3, the data set included 467,044 line pairs. As the translator model is to be applied on sequences classified as erroneous by the detector model, we needed to perform an additional step for the creation of training, validation and test sets. Keeping in mind that the detector model's precision is 90%, this means that we can expect 10% of the lines classified as erroneous to be actually correct. To cope with these misjudgements, we randomly added correct sequences to the erroneous lines such that each set included approximately 10% correct sequences.

However, this step severely reduced the overall size of the data set. In order to create a sufficiently large set for training, we used the vast majority of sequences to this end (196,000). As this decision resulted in small validation and test sets, we enhanced them using additional data from the respective sets used for validating and testing the detector model (final size of both sets: 22,000).

Results. Applying the translator model to the test set resulted in a reduced CER compared to the original error rate of the OCRed data. We achieved a CER of 3.6%, which is a reduction of 0.7% to the former 4.3% in the uncorrected data.

5 The Full OCR Post-Correction Pipeline

As both components have been analysed independently in Section 4, we now present results yielded by applying the full two-step pipeline on a combination of both test sets (83,600). As the detector's task is the reduction of correct sequences in the data that is to be fed into the translator, we did not remove any correct sequences manually.

Results (Detector). Applying the detector model on the test set yielded an F1 score of 79%, a precision of 87% and a recall of 72%. Although these scores are somewhat reduced compared to the results obtained by the detector if used on the first test set alone, we argue that the scores are appropriately similar to proceed with OCR post-correction using the translator model. 19,800 of the 83,600 sequences were classified as erroneous and, hence, were forwarded to the translator.

Results (Translator). Calculating the mean CER over the full test set resulted in a score of 1.1%. In order to measure the full test set's CER after the translation step has been conducted, we first applied the translator component on the sequences classified as erroneous and then combined the corrected sequences with the lines previously classified as correct. Calculating the CER on the corrected test set yielded a score of 0.9%, which is a relative improvement of 18.2%. For reasons of comparison, we fed the same test set into our one-step correction model, which achieved a CER of 2.1%. In addition, for both approaches we calculated the rates of correct characters being erroneously changed. While our two-step architecture achieved a score of 0.3%, 6% of characters were falsely changed by our one-step model.

6 Discussion and Outlook

In this paper, we presented an alternative approach to automatic OCR post-correction using a two-step architecture consisting of a detector and a translator model. While the detector model identifies erroneous sequences in an OCR data set, the translator model is used to correct these sequences. This approach has two major benefits. First, removing correct sequences from the to-be-corrected data set increases the proportion of OCR errors fed into the translator model. This is supposed to improve the translator's results. Second, a detector model with a high precision limits the amount of correct sequences processed by the translator, thereby reducing the likelihood of correct characters being erroneously changed. As a successful OCR post-correction model is supposed to leave the correct data unaltered, the importance of the second aspect should not be underestimated.

Comparisons of both approaches' results show that by inserting the detector model the translator's results can be substantially improved. Whereas the simple one-step translator model actually increases the CER from 1.1% to 2.1%, we were able to reduce the error rate to 0.9% by applying the two-step architecture. This is a relative improvement of 18.2%. While this CER improvement is smaller than the score achieved for the English monographs (pre-correction CER: 1.8%, rel. improvement: 31.3%) in Amrhein and Clematide (2018), their improvement achieved for the French monographs (pre-correction CER: 1.6%, rel. improvement: 18.3%) is similar to our result.[9] We are aware that it is difficult to directly compare our results with Amrhein and Clematide (2018) given the differences between the two studies (German vs English/French data, differences in the model hyperparameters, notable differences in pre-correction CER). However, we consider the partially similar results as a promising indicator that our two-step model can actually compete with previously proposed methods.

While the CER reduction is noteworthy in itself, a special focus should be laid on the rates of erroneously changed correct characters. The two-step approach yielded a promising rate of changed correct characters of 0.3%. However, correcting the data set with the one-step model resulted in a high rate of 6%, which indicates that the correct sub-parts of the data have been severely modified. Given that we did not use different model parameters for training both sequence-to-sequence translators, we can conclude that this reduction is associated with the insertion of the detector. In other words, our results can be interpreted as evidence for the assumption that a low CER poses a notable problem for a one-step translation model.[10]

As the detector component already strongly improves the OCR post-correction results, our future work will primarily focus on the further development of the translator component. On the one hand, we plan to improve the attention mechanism implemented in the translator's decoder model. As OCR errors are characterized by their local context, using a local attention approach (Luong et al., 2015) may have benefiting effects on OCR post-correction. Furthermore, we will investigate alternatives to the LSTM architecture. In particular, we consider the application of Generative Adversarial Networks (Goodfellow et al., 2014) as a fruitful path of future research.

Acknowledgements

This work was partially supported by the German Federal Ministry of Education and Research (Bundesministerium für Bildung und Forschung, BMBF), project grant QURATOR - Curation Technologies (Unternehmen Region, Wachstumskern, grant no. 03WKDA1A)[11]. We thank the anonymous reviewers for their helpful comments.

References

Haithem Afli, Loïc Barrault, and Holger Schwenk. 2016. Ocr error correction using statistical machine translation. *Int. J. Comput. Linguistics Appl.*, 7(1):175–191.

Chantal Amrhein and Simon Clematide. 2018. Supervised ocr error detection and correction using statistical and neural machine translation methods. *Journal for Language Technology and Computational Linguistics (JLCL)*, 33(1):49–76.

Dzmitry Bahdanau, Kyunghyun Cho, and Yoshua Bengio. 2014. Neural machine translation by jointly learning to align and translate. *arXiv preprint arXiv:1409.0473*.

Guillaume Chiron, Antoine Doucet, Mickaël Coustaty, and Jean-Philippe Moreux. 2017. Icdar2017 competition on post-ocr text correction. In *2017 14th IAPR International Conference on Document Analysis and Recognition (ICDAR)*, volume 1, pages 1423–1428. IEEE.

---

[9]Presented results of Amrhein and Clematide (2018) are referred to as *NMT context* in their paper.

[10]Importantly, our results can also be interpreted as counter-evidence against the hypothesis that the one-step translation model merely failed due to an inappropriate setting of hyperparameters.

[11]`https://qurator.ai`

Jacob Devlin, Ming-Wei Chang, Kenton Lee, and Kristina Toutanova. 2018. Bert: Pre-training of deep bidirectional transformers for language understanding. *arXiv preprint arXiv:1810.04805*.

Florian Fink, Klaus U Schulz, and Uwe Springmann. 2017. Profiling of ocr'ed historical texts revisited. In *Proceedings of the 2Nd International Conference on Digital Access to Textual Cultural Heritage*, pages 61–66.

Ian J. Goodfellow, Jean Pouget-Abadie, Mehdi Mirza, Bing Xu, David Warde-Farley, Sherjil Ozair, Aaron Courville, and Yoshua Bengio. 2014. Generative adversarial nets. In *Proceedings of the 27th International Conference on Neural Information Processing Systems - Volume 2*, NIPS'14, page 2672–2680, Cambridge, MA, USA. MIT Press.

Mika Hämäläinen and Simon Hengchen. 2019. From the paft to the fiiture: a fully automatic nmt and word embeddings method for ocr post-correction. *arXiv preprint arXiv:1910.05535*.

Sepp Hochreiter and Jürgen Schmidhuber. 1997. Long short-term memory. *Neural Comput.*, 9(8):1735–1780, November.

Okan Kolak and Philip Resnik. 2002. Ocr error correction using a noisy channel model. In *Proceedings of the second international conference on Human Language Technology Research*, pages 257–262. Morgan Kaufmann Publishers Inc.

Marco Lui and Timothy Baldwin. 2012. langid.py: An off-the-shelf language identification tool. In *Proceedings of the ACL 2012 System Demonstrations*, pages 25–30, Jeju Island, Korea, July. Association for Computational Linguistics.

Thang Luong, Hieu Pham, and Christopher D. Manning. 2015. Effective approaches to attention-based neural machine translation. In *Proceedings of the 2015 Conference on Empirical Methods in Natural Language Processing*, pages 1412–1421, Lisbon, Portugal, September. Association for Computational Linguistics.

Kareem Mokhtar, Syed Saqib Bukhari, and Andreas Dengel. 2018. Ocr error correction: State-of-the-art vs an nmt-based approach. In *2018 13th IAPR International Workshop on Document Analysis Systems (DAS)*, pages 429–434. IEEE.

Clemens Neudecker, Konstantin Baierer, Maria Federbusch, Matthias Boenig, Kay-Michael Würzner, Volker Hartmann, and Elisa Herrmann. 2019. Ocr-d: An end-to-end open source ocr framework for historical printed documents. In *Proceedings of the 3rd International Conference on Digital Access to Textual Cultural Heritage*, DATeCH2019, pages 53—-58, New York, NY, USA. Association for Computing Machinery.

Adam Paszke, Sam Gross, Francisco Massa, Adam Lerer, James Bradbury, Gregory Chanan, Trevor Killeen, Zeming Lin, Natalia Gimelshein, Luca Antiga, et al. 2019. Pytorch: An imperative style, high-performance deep learning library. In *Advances in neural information processing systems*, pages 8026–8037.

Michael Piotrowski. 2012. Natural language processing for historical texts. *Synthesis lectures on human language technologies*, 5(2):1–157.

Ulrich Reffle and Christoph Ringlstetter. 2013. Unsupervised profiling of ocred historical documents. *Pattern Recognition*, 46(5):1346–1357.

Christian Reul, Uwe Springmann, Christoph Wick, and Frank Puppe. 2018. State of the art optical character recognition of 19th century fraktur scripts using open source engines. *arXiv preprint arXiv:1810.03436*.

Martin Reynaert. 2008. Non-interactive ocr post-correction for giga-scale digitization projects. In *International Conference on Intelligent Text Processing and Computational Linguistics*, pages 617–630. Springer.

Martin Reynaert. 2016. Ocr post-correction evaluation of early dutch books online-revisited. In *Proceedings of the Tenth International Conference on Language Resources and Evaluation (LREC'16)*, pages 967–974.

Christophe Rigaud, Antoine Doucet, Mickaël Coustaty, and Jean-Philippe Moreux. 2019. Icdar 2019 competition on post-ocr text correction. In *2019 International Conference on Document Analysis and Recognition (ICDAR)*, pages 1588–1593. IEEE.

Xiang Tong and David A Evans. 1996. A statistical approach to automatic ocr error correction in context. In *Fourth Workshop on Very Large Corpora*.

Martin Volk, Lenz Furrer, and Rico Sennrich. 2011. Strategies for reducing and correcting ocr errors. In *Language technology for cultural heritage*, pages 3–22. Springer.

Ronald J. Williams and David Zipser. 1989. A learning algorithm for continually running fully recurrent neural networks. *Neural Comput.*, 1(2):270–280, June.

"Shakespeare in the Vectorian Age" – An evaluation of different word embeddings and NLP parameters for the detection of Shakespeare quotes

Bernhard Liebl & Manuel Burghardt
Computational Humanities Group
Leipzig University, Germany
{liebl, burghardt}@informatik.uni-leipzig.de

Abstract

In this paper we describe an approach for the computer-aided identification of Shakespearean intertextuality in a corpus of contemporary fiction. We present the Vectorian, which is a framework that implements different word embeddings and various NLP parameters. The Vectorian works like a search engine, i.e. a Shakespearean phrase can be entered as a query, the underlying collection of fiction books is then searched for the phrase and the passages that are likely to contain the phrase, either verbatim or as a paraphrase, are presented in a ranked results list. While the Vectorian can be used via a GUI, in which many different parameters can be set and combined manually, in this paper we present an ablation study that automatically evaluates different embedding and NLP parameter combinations against a ground truth. We investigate the behavior of different parameters during the evaluation and discuss how our results may be used for future studies on the detection of Shakespearean intertextuality.

1 Introduction

Shakespeare is everywhere. Intertextual references to the works of the eternal bard can be found across all temporal and medial boundaries, making him not only the most cited and most performed author of all time, but also the most studied author in the world (Garber, 2005; Maxwell and Rumbold, 2018). But even though countless studies on Shakespearean intertextuality have examined individual aspects of his work by means of close reading, there is still no overview, no big picture, no systematic map of intertextual Shakespeare references for larger text corpora. It is also striking that up to now hardly any computational approaches have been used to detect Shakespeare references on a larger scale. This is all the more surprising as there are many methods in the fields of computer science and natural language processing for determining the *similarity between texts* (Bär et al., 2012), which actually can be seen as a formal definition of intertextuality.

We acknowledge that the full range of intertextual phenomena cannot be covered by mere means of text similarity determination. For our understanding of intertextuality we therefore refer to the definition of Gérard Genette, who defines it as "the effective presence of one text in another text"[1] (Genette, 1993), where we understand the *effective presence* of one text in another to be a more or less objectively recognizable, explicit reference on the surface of the text. Thus, our approach will not be able to detect highly implicit and indirect references that require a lot of domain knowledge and context. The following variant of a well-known quotation from Macbeth (Shakespeare's original variant is given in square brackets) would, however, be objectively recognizable from the text and clearly classified as an intertextual reference:

> By the stinking [pricking] of my nose [thumbs], something evil [wicked] this way goes [comes]. (Terry Pratchett: "I Shall Wear Midnight").

In order to identify such objectively recognizable references in an automated way, we present an approach that investigates the potential of word embeddings (Mikolov et al., 2013) in combination with

---

[1] Original quote: "la présence effective d'un texte dans un autre".

Proceedings of LaTeCH-CLfL 2020, pages 58–68
Barcelona, Spain (Online), December 12, 2020.

other related parameters (e.g., weighting based on POS types, order of POS types, etc.). As we are aware that different word embeddings and NLP parameters will influence the results in very specific ways, we present an ablation study in which we systematically explore the effects of different parameter combinations. We hope that our evaluation will shed some more light on the role of different embeddings and NLP parameters for the detection of intertextuality in the sense of Molnar's desideratum of "interpretable machine learning" (Molnar, 2020).

2   Related work

While text reuse detection (Agirre et al., 2016; Bär et al., 2012) mainly finds application in the context of plagiarism detection and the identification of duplicate websites, there are also productive applications in the digital humanities. One example can be found in the project Digital Breadcrumbs of Brothers Grimm (Franzini et al., 2017), where computational text reuse methods are used to detect motifs of fairy tales across different languages and versions. Labbé and Labbé (2005) present a tool in the intersection of stylometry and text reuse, as they use intertextual distance to classify texts from French literature. Ganascia et al. (2014) describe an approach for the automatic detection of textual reuses in different works of Balzac and his contemporaries . Apart from these example studies, the majority of existing research on text reuse in the Digital Humanities can be located in the field of historical languages and classic studies (Bamman and Crane, 2008; Büchler et al., 2013; Coffee et al., 2012a; Coffee et al., 2012b; Forstall et al., 2015; Scheirer et al., 2014)

While clearly there has been interesting work on the problem of text reuse and intertextuality detection in various areas of the digital humanities, there are only very few studies that use computational methods to detect Shakespeare quotes (Burghardt et al., 2019; Hohl-Trillini, 2019; Molz, 2019). With this paper we contribute to computational intertextuality detection in Shakespeare studies by exploring a set of parameters that can enhance approaches to searching references based on word embeddings.

3   System design: Introducing "The Vectorian"

The Vectorian[2] is a high-performance sentence alignment search engine[3] designed around a number of explicit parameters that model different approaches to scoring sentence similarities. The search engine is also accessible via an internal batch interface for doing large hyperparameter searches, as is the case for the study presented in this paper. Throughout the rest of the section we describe the various parameters of the Vectorian step by step. An overview of the architecture is shown in Figure 1. In a preprocessing step (top half of Figure 1), we first split the search corpus into sentences and detect POS tags for each token of the sentences. Since the corpus in which we search for Shakespeare quotations consists entirely of contemporary literature, the use of *spaCy* 2.3.2 and the *en_core_web_lg-2.3.1* is unproblematic. When running a query – i.e. specific Shakespeare quotes – we run the same preprocessing on the query text but skip sentence splitting and assume a single sentence. We are aware that the selected spaCy model is not optimal for Shakespeare quotes because it does not reproduce details of Early Modern English. However, having looked at a number of samples and the assigned POS tags, we think it works good enough for this first pilot study. We plan to implement a language model that is more specific to Shakespeare as a future step. Next, the Vectorian computes similarities between tokens from the query and the search corpus based on precomputed contemporary word embeddings like *fasttext*. At this point, only word tokens are used and punctuation is ignored completely. For the Shakespearean text in the query, contemporary word embeddings pose an obvious challenge due to shifts in word meaning. We currently do not leverage historical word embeddings like *HistWords* (Hamilton et al., 2016), but plan to incorporate these in future extensions of this work. After preprocessing and storing the data in an efficient in-memory format suitable for high-performance realtime searches over a large corpus (see bottom right in Figure 1), we compute alignments based on similarity scores between the tokens (see bottom left in Figure 1). Ultimately, scores are derived from the embeddings and controlled by various parameters – the details are contained in a pipeline we refer to as *SIM_FULL* (see big box in Figure 1) and which will be described

---

[2] `https://github.com/poke1024/vectorian/tree/v4`
[3] For a similar approach see Manjavacas et al. (2019).

in more detail in the next sections (see the right half of Figure 2). Given the token similarity scores, we find optimal alignments on the sentence level using the Waterman-Smith-Beyer algorithm (Waterman et al., 1976), which we leverage through an optimized and highly customizable implementation[4].

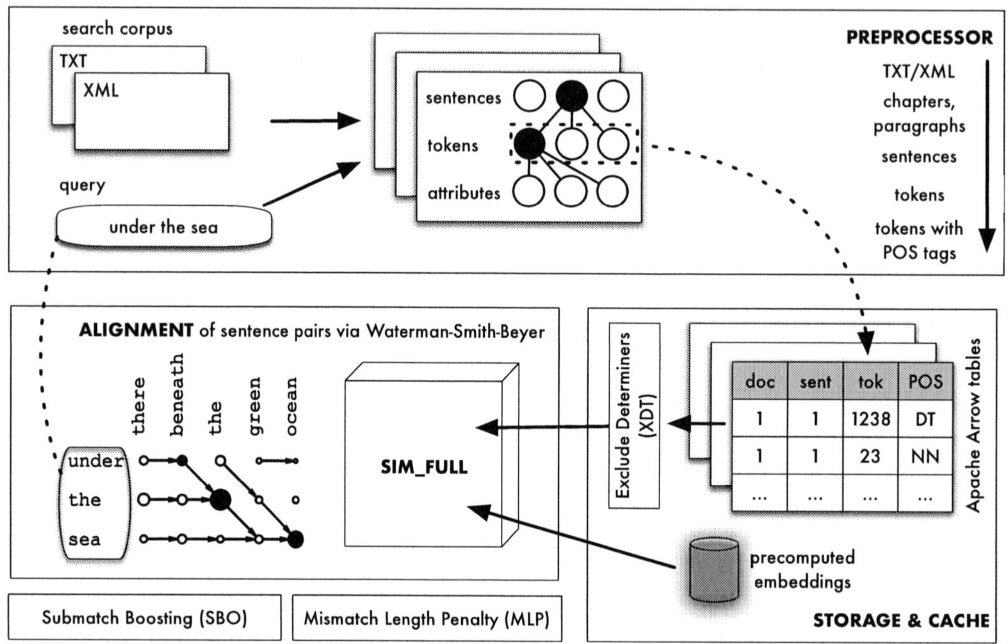

Figure 1: Simplified overview of overall architecture.

In the following we provide details on the ten parameters that are shown in Figures 1 and 2. These parameters tackle three different areas of similarity measures we found worth considering. (1) Three parameters (*XDT*, *SPW*, *PMP*) are concerned with how exactly part of speech (POS) tags contribute to the similarity computation. (2) Five parameters (*EMI*, *ESM*, *IFS*, *SIF*, *SIT*) are concerned with how to exactly compute a scalar similarity score from word embeddings. (3) Finally, two parameters (*MLP*, *SBO*) control details of how alignments are scored.

3.1 Parameters for POS Tag Influence

Exclude Determiners (XDT). A Boolean parameter. If enabled, it will perform a search as if all tokens in query and corpus that have been tagged with the universal POS tag[5] *DET* have been removed.

Semantic POS Weighting (SPW). A numeric parameter between 0 and 1. If set to 0, the similarity between two tokens is directly computed from the configured embedding metrics. If set to 1, token pair scores are weighted with the corpus token's PennTree POS tag (Taylor et al., 2003) using the weights given by Batanović and Bojić (Batanović and Bojić, 2015). As a result, and following the argumentation of Batanović and Bojić, some tokens (e.g. *VBP*) will have a greater influence on the final similarity scores than others (e.g. *NN*). If w is a token's weight according to Batanović and Bojić, we compute an overall token weight as $(1 - SPW) + (SPW \times w)$. Therefore, reducing *SPW* will gradually equalize these weights.

POS Mismatch Penalty (PMP). A numeric parameter between 0 and 1 that penalizes the similarity scores of token pairs if their universal POS tags do not match – i.e. giving tokens a lower score, even if the embedding considers them very similar. If set to 1, any POS mismatch will reduce the similarity score to 0, regardless of the embedding score. A value of 0 completely ignores POS mismatches.

---

[4] https://github.com/poke1024/simileco
[5] https://universaldependencies.org/u/pos/

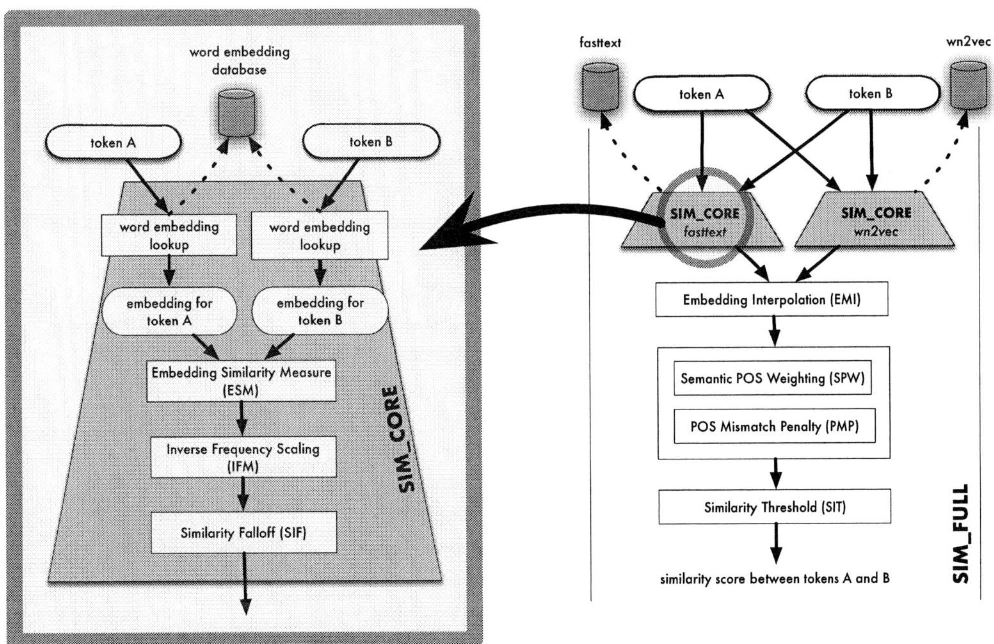

Figure 2: Steps and parameters involved in computing the similarity of two tokens. Details of the *SIM_FULL* module from Figure 1 are shown on the right side. The *SIM_CORE* sub module is shown on the left side. Solid lines show data flow, dotted lines show lookups.

3.2 Parameters for Embedding Similarity Computation

Embedding Interpolation (EMI). A numeric parameter between 0 and 1 that specifies a mixing of two embeddings. For our experiments, we use the official pretrained *fasttext* embeddings (Mikolov et al., 2018) and *wnet2vec* (Saedi et al., 2018) embeddings[6]. These two candidates were chosen as typical proponents of very different kinds of precomputed word embeddings: whereas *fasttext* is an established iteration of the *word2vec* school that are trained on unstructured corpora, *wnet2vec* is based on "ontological graphs" (Saedi et al., 2018), namely WordNet. By combining these embeddings, we hope to investigate if combining very different approaches can yield a benefit.

Our mixing computes a maximum similarity: if t is the value for *EMI*, we compute the mixed similarity s' from two original similarities s_1 and s_2 as $s' = max(2s_1(1-t), 2s_2 t)$. Therefore, a value of 0 indicates that only *fasttext* scores are used, whereas a value of 0.5 indicates that for each token pair, the maximum similarity found in either embedding is used.

Embedding Similarity Measure (ESM). Specifies how two word vectors from an embedding are turned into a scalar similarity score. The Vectorian supports three strategies: cosine similarity, the *noniterative contextual dissimilarity measure* by Jegou et al. (Jegou et al., 2010) with a neighborhood size of 100 elements and finally the rank-based similarity metric by Santus et al. (Santus et al., 2018). We refer to these strategies as *cosine*, *nicdm* and *apsynp* respectively.

Inverse Frequency Scaling (IFS). A numeric parameter between 0 and 1 that weights similarity scores with a token's inverse probability of occurence in a typical corpus. If set to to 0, no such weighting takes place, if set to 1, the similarity score for rarer words will get boosted. Specifially, if p is a token's negative log probability and s is the similarity, a new similarity score s' is computed as

---

[6]These were computed by running `https://github.com/nlx-group/WordNetEmbeddings` on 58,492 unique words from 66 novels that were part of the search corpus. As not all of these words were present in WordNet, the resulting embedding covers only 27,718 words.

$$s' = s * (-p)^{IFS} \tag{1}$$

This is a rather simplistic approach, as we currently do not model approaches such as tf-idf (Leskovec et al., 2020).

Similarity Falloff (SIF). A numeric parameter between 0 and 1 that rescales similarity scores before POS weighting. This can help to increase the distance between high and low scores. Each similarity score s is rescaled to s^{SIF}. A value of 1 obviously disables rescaling.

Similarity Threshold (SIT). A numeric threshold between 0 and 1 that is applied to similarity scores after POS weighting. Any score below this value will be set to 0 for further processing. This has the effect of reducing noise from unwanted low similarities.

3.3 Parameters for Alignment Scoring

Mismatch Length Penalty (MLP). An integer value indicating that length of a mismatch – in number of tokens – that will reduce the similarity score by 0.5 – the maximum possible score being 1. Low values will enforce no or only short mismatches, whereas higher values allow longer runs of mismatching tokens. The score penalty is modelled as an exponential function. For a mismatch of length n we compute the penalty as

$$1 - 2^{-\left(\frac{n}{MLP}\right)} \tag{2}$$

Submatch Boosting (SBO). A numeric parameter that models the score if only parts of the query get matched. Specifially, if a query contains n tokens of which m have been matched, and each individual token has a maximum score of 1 and the sum of matched token scores is s, then we compute an overall score s' using a discount factor α as follows[7]:

$$\alpha = \left(\frac{n - m}{n}\right)^{SBO} \tag{3}$$

$$s' = \frac{s}{m + \alpha(n - m)} \tag{4}$$

A value of 0 therefore indicates that no special submatch weighting takes place. Values larger than 0 decrease the impact of non-matched tokens in the overall scores, thereby making partial matches obtain higher scores.

4 Evaluation design

In this section we present an ablation study in which we automatically test different combinations of the parameters that were described in the previous section, in order to investigate how they influence the results. The ground truth required to carry out such an evaluation was derived from Molz (2019), who conducted a comprehensive study to identify references to Shakespeare in a corpus of postmodern fiction using a mixture of close and distant reading. We took a subsample of this work, which contains 73 quotes from one of Shakespeare's most popular plays: *Hamlet*. The rationale for taking only a subsample is that the ground truth cannot be considered 100% comprehensive, as was shown in related studies with the dataset (Bryan et al., 2020). We kept the sample size small in order to simplify the task of recognizing new true positives identified by the Vectorian. The 73 quotes are distributed among 31 novels that have a total size of 4,2 million tokens. Sticking to the search engine metaphor introduced in Section 2, we will treat each of the 73 Hamlet quotes as a query that is searched for in the collection of novels. In the evaluation study, each query is assigned an unranked set of expected results (as documented in the ground truth) in the corpus of novels. Each result refers to one specific sentence in a novel. Some queries have multiple expected results, e.g. for "There are more things in heaven and earth ..." our ground truth records 8 occurences in different novels. However, most queries have only 1 or 2 matches in our ground

---

[7]For simplicity, we give the unweighted case, though our implementation includes POS weighting here.

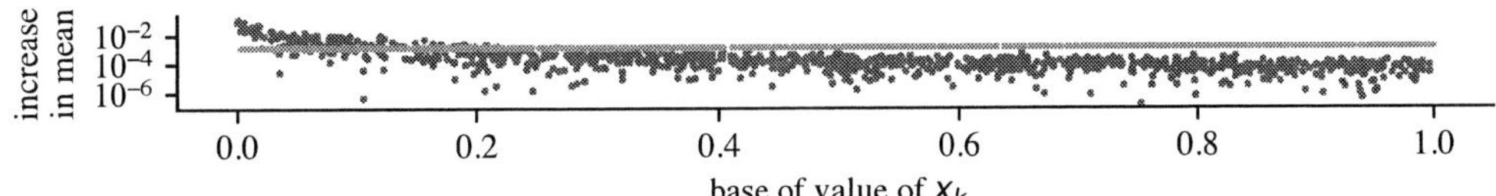

Figure 3: Scatter plot of absolute change in harmonic mean (blue) and arithmetic mean (orange) over random scores $x_1, ..., x_n$ when updating a single input score x_k by an improvement ϵ of 0.1. Y axis is logarithmic. The arithmetic mean always increases by a constant $\frac{\epsilon}{n}$ regardless of x_k's value, so in an optimizer it encourages increasing low and high scores similarly. The harmonic mean on the other hand tends to weigh the same improvement in a low input (left) considerably higher than in a high input (right) and therefore encourages increasing low inputs.

truth[8]. In total, our ground truth contains 149 result sentences for 73 unique queries. We measured the performance of each query by computing the *Discounted Cumulative Gain* (DCG) (Järvelin and Kekäläinen, 2002) against the unranked[9] ground truth for the first 50 results retrieved. DCG is a standard measure to rank the quality of a result set in information retrieval, where documents from higher ranks contribute more to the overall *gain* and documents at lower ranks contribute less, i.e. they are *discounted*.

Since a full grid search was not feasible for our parameter space, we ran an *Optuna* (Akiba et al., 2019) optimizer with the objective of maximizing a total performance score. This total performance score is computed as a mean over the DCGs of all queries. However, since some queries expect more results than others – and therefore the ideally obtainable DCGs for different queries vary – such a composite score only makes sense if all contributing DCGs have been scaled to a fixed range. Therefore we employed the commonly used formulation of Normalized DCGs (nDCGs) (Manning et al., 2008) to normalize the score for each query into the range between 0 and 1. To summarize these considerations: we used nDCG@50 for each query and then computed a mean to obtain a total performance score. We ran a first optimization with the objective of maximizing the commonly used *arithmetic* mean over all query nDCGs as the maximizing objective, and a second independent optimization with the objective of maximizing a *harmonic* mean of query nDCGs. The *harmonic* mean may seem like an unusual choice here, as its use in information retrieval is typically limited to the F-score (Manning et al., 2008). The reason we use it in this scenario, is the distribution of query difficulty in our ground truth and the specific characteristics of the *harmonic* mean. We found a very strong negative skew due to a high number of rather simplistic queries in our data. There are about 50% of queries that relate to verbatim or near-verbatim quotes of text from Shakespeare, which means that these are rather easy to detect from a text reuse perspective. About 10% of the queries on the other hand rely on implicit knowledge and are probably not easily found by the Vectorian, which relies entirely on explicit language features. The remaining 40% of the queries are neither trivial nor out of reach for the Vectorian. We therefore put them into the category *hard but feasible*. Optimizing on the *arithmetic* mean carries the risk of micro-optimizing the bulk of easy queries to an nDCG of 100%, but finding no good nDCGs for the few but more interesting queries. In order to encourage good nDCGs for *hard but feasible* queries, the *harmonic mean* seems to be a reasonable alternative. As Figure 3 illustrates, it tends to improve by higher values when low inputs get increased.

In our evaluation study, we ultimately ran optimizations for both types of means with 1,500 trials using a default configuration with *tree-structured Parzen estimators* (Akiba et al., 2019). As a caveat, it must be noted that due to the small size of our ground truth sample, our evaluation did not have a dedicated validation set. Since the parameters in our system are few and quite restricted, however, we believe the risk of overfitting is rather low. We interpret our results as a simplistic model that represents deeper characteristics of the query-result relationships given in our ground truth.

---

[8]The exact distribution is $44 : 1$ (i.e. 44 queries with one result) , $13 : 2, 5 : 3, 4 : 4, 2 : 5, 2 : 6, 2 : 8, 1 : 10$.

[9]I.e. a full score is obtained if the specified ground truth results are retrieved first, regardless of their internal order.

5 Results and Discussion

The best configuration found with *Optuna* produced nDCGs of 77.6% and 75.2% for the *arithmetic* (A) and *harmonic* (H) mean optimization objectives respectively. Since the decision what constitutes a quotation in some cases cannot be made on the language level alone and thus is highly subjective (Molz, 2019), we believe that these scores can be interpreted as a fairly good performance. The system also produced a small number of new true positive matches, which could be confirmed to be valid[10]. The specific parameter values for the best configurations are given in Table 1, together with the parameter domains that were searched. Note that *Optuna* does not use an initial starting or seeding configuration.

Parameter	Distribution	Domain	A	H
Exclude Determiners	categorical	*false, true*	*false*	*true*
Embedding Interpolation	uniform	$0 \leq x \leq 1$	1.0	0.41
Embedding Similarity Measure	categorical	*cosine, nicdm, apsynp*	*cosine*	*nicdm*
Inverse Frequency Scaling	uniform	$0 \leq x \leq 1$	0.0	0.96
Similarity Falloff	uniform	$0 \leq x \leq 1$	0.93	0.39
Semantic POS Weighting	uniform	$0 \leq x \leq 1$	0.46	0.09
POS Mismatch Penalty	uniform	$0 \leq x \leq 1$	0.77	0.43
Similarity Threshold	uniform	$0 \leq x \leq 1$	0.73	0.83
Mismatch Length Penalty	int	$0 \leq x \leq 10$	1	1
Submatch Boosting	uniform	$0 \leq x \leq 5$	0.24	0.14

Table 1: Investigated parameter domains (first three columns) and best configurations found through *Optuna* search for *arithmetic* mean and *harmonic* mean (last two columns). Numerical values are rounded to nearest multiple of 0.01.

Unfortunately, due to the skewed nature of the query problem in our ground truth, the mean value of the nDCGs tells us only little about the performance of the two variants with respect to different types of queries. Figure 4 therefore gives a detailed histogram of the query nDCGs. As argued in the evaluation design, the distribution of the *hard but feasible* queries with low scores turned out differently indeed. Most notably for *H*, we see a salient group of (orange) queries scoring between 0.4 and 0.7, while the queries scoring at nDCG 0 and 1 both have been slightly diminished. In general, this is what we hoped for. The downside however is that the beneficial *arithmetic* (blue) peak between 0.7 and 0.8 is now gone, i.e. we have lost this score for some queries.

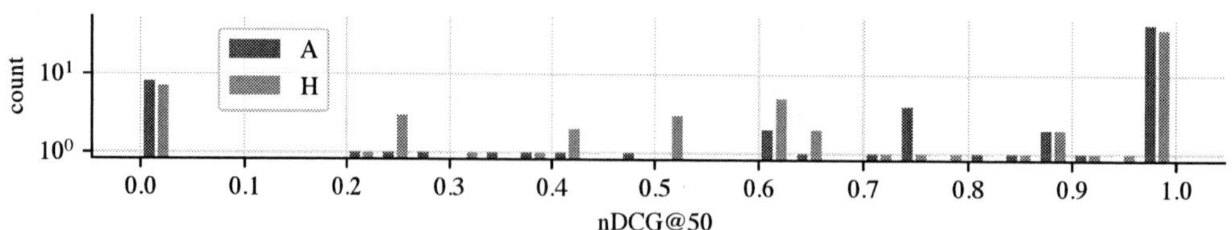

Figure 4: Histogram of nDCGs for variants *A* and *H*. Y axis is logarithmic.

Figure 5 shows the performance of both variants in terms of quantiles. Both variants operate optimally on the maximum 100% nDCG level for easy queries that are located at the quantiles above 0.5. Between the 0.15 and 0.5 quantiles however, the *arithmetic* mean variant performs better. On the other hand, the *H* variant does not show the dip below the 0.15 quantile, which seems to give it slightly better performance for some difficult queries.

---

[10]After marking these as correct, the nDCGs changed to 81.2% (for *A*)) and 78.9% (for *H*).

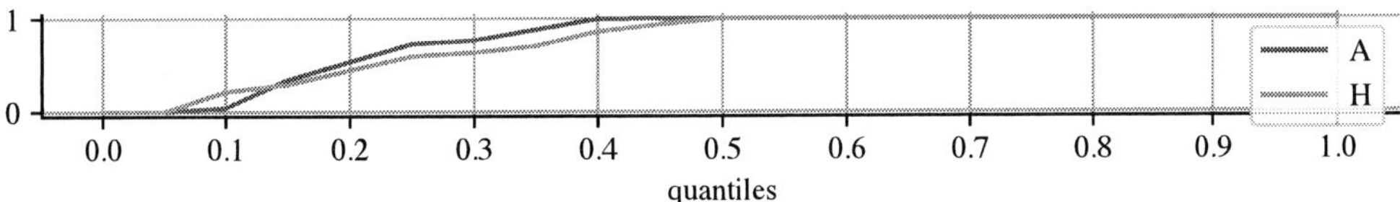

Figure 5: Quantiles of nDCGs for variants *A* and *H*.

We now discuss the parameters' importance by performing an ablation study on each of them, starting with the *harmonic* variant (see Figure 6), which shows a surprising combination[11]. *EMI* and *PMP* have no effect at all – any value produces the same optimal results – and nearly the same is true for *ESM*. In other words, the whole embedding pipeline seems to be irrelevant for the search results. Furthermore, *SPW*, *SIF*, and *IFS* are all basically *no-ops*. The only three salient choices are a *SIT* above 0.8, a *MLP* of 1 – that shows an interesting option for extending it up to 4 – and a slightly elevated *SBO* value. In summary, large parts of the Vectorian engine have been turned off in this case in order to facilitate a specific kind of search, namely looking for alignments of tokens without using any POS or embedding information.

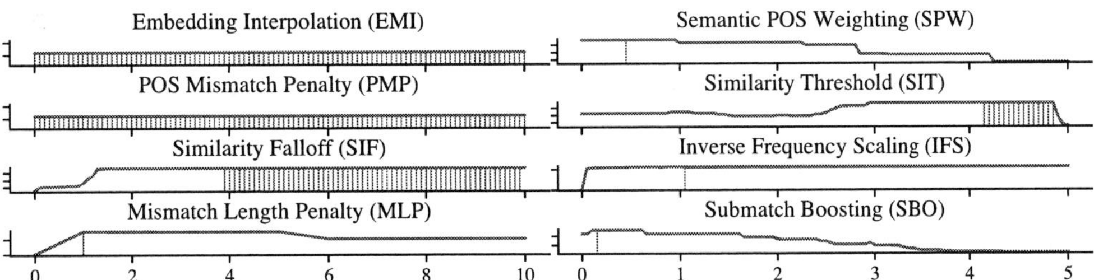

Figure 6: Ablations for various parameters of best configuration found through *harmonic* means of nDCGs. The *x* axis shows parameter values, the *y* axis shows achieved *harmonic* mean nDCG@50. Different plots expose different *y* ranges. Maximum values obtained per parameter are shaded green.

In contrast to the results for *H*, an ablation on the *A* variant shows more intertwined settings (see Figure 7). We only see one *no-op* with *SIF*, all other parameters are meaningful. *SIT*, *MLP* and *SBO* are somewhat similar to the *H* variant. The embedding and POS parameters are quite different. *SPW* has its maximum benefit between 0.4 and 0.5, meaning it should neither be turned fully on nor off[12]. The plot for *PMP* suggests that a POS mismatch should *always* override the computed similarity from an embedding and count that token pair as *not similar*. For *EMI*, we observe that the best value is not 1, as inferred in the *Optuna* search, but 0.55. This seems to confirm our assumption that mixing very different types of embedding can be beneficial. Without mixing, *wnet2vec* at 1 outperforms *fasttext* at 0. For *ESM*, *cosine* performs slightly better than *nicdm*. Both measures perform considerably better than *apsynp*.

The overall results are rather counterintuitive: If our distinction into easy and hard queries is correct, then the result would mean that the retrieval of easy queries benefits from embeddings and syntactic markers, whereas the retrieval of hard queries does not. To shed some light on what is really happening here, we looked at Recall at K (Manning et al., 2008) for both cases (see Figure 8). As expected when optimizing for nDCG, *A* excels in bringing many correct results to the very front of the result list (see $K < 3$). *H* on the other hand indeed focuses on queries with low scores – especially results that are not or hardly found at all. Starting at roughly $K = 20$ this clearly shows: *H* starts to recall more correct

---

[11]Note that the green areas indicate those parameter values that produced the best reproduction of the given ground truth.

[12]The plot suggests that applying the weights from Batanović and Bojić (2015) fully – through a parameter value of 1 – would harm the search performance considerably.

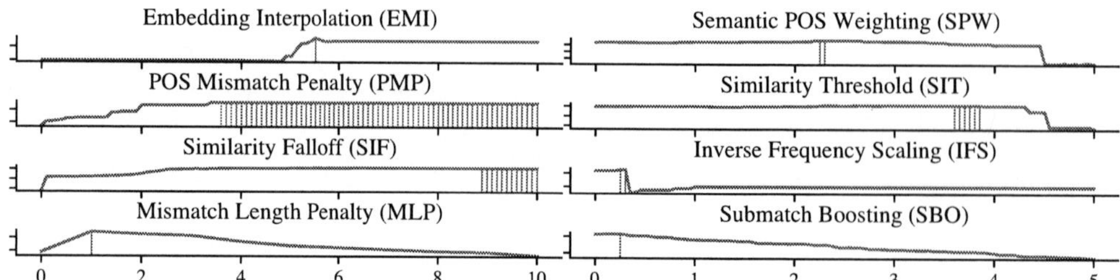

Figure 7: Ablations for various parameters of best configuration found through *arithmetic* mean of nD-CGs. The *x* axis shows parameter values, the *y* axis shows achieved *arithmetic* mean nDCG@50. Different plots expose different *y* ranges. Maximum values obtained per parameter are shaded green.

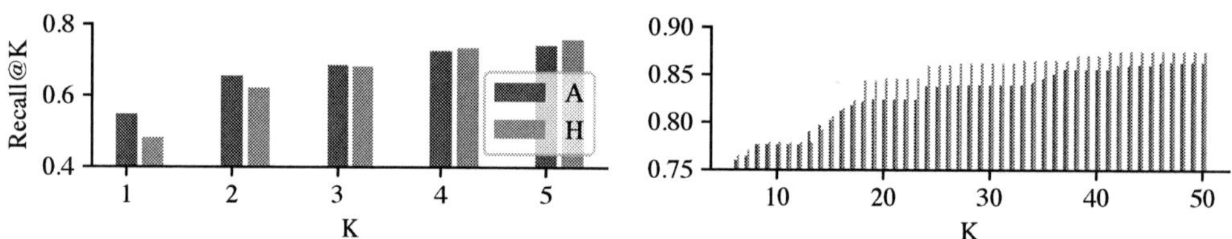

Figure 8: Recall@K for *A* and *H* variants. The *y* range differs on the left and on the right.

results than *A*. Closer inspection of the results shows that many of these *hard* queries contain only one or two tokens that exhibit any form of semantic alignment to the sentences in the ground truth. In other words, large parts of the query are ignored by the alignment engine when trying to find a match[13]. At the same time, the few tokens that do match are usually verbatim words from Shakespeare's texts. This observation explains *H*'s strategy to disable large parts of the Vectorian pipeline and basically build a verbatim single word matcher to cope with these queries.

6 Conclusion

We have investigated the optimal configuration of various explicit parameters in a text reuse detection pipeline and showed that it is able to achieve nDCGs of roughly 80% on a rather difficult test set. While for some queries focusing on the interplay of word embeddings, POS tags and alignments is optimal, other queries seem to benefit from turning off these features. We have demonstrated, how these choices are generated naturally by maximizing *arithmetic* and *harmonic* means of nDCG scores. Our analysis uncovered important ideas of what makes queries *hard* for our current architecture and indicates the need for a ground truth that is classified and balanced in terms of difficulty. As Molz (2019) described considerably more Shakespeare references in his study, we plan to enhance the ground truth accordingly and classify the quotes according to different categories (e.g. verbatim quote, semantic paraphrase, changed word order, etc.). We hypothesize that different types of quotes will result in different optimal parameter combinations. This will be investigated in more detail in a follow-up study, where we will also look into other types of embeddings and explore single parameters in more detail.

---

[13]A similar observation is true for any human expert, who, however, would have the advantage of knowing the quote's broader context from neighboring sentences.

References

Eneko Agirre, Carmen Banea, Daniel Cer, Mona Diab, Aitor Gonzalez-Agirre, Rada Mihalcea, German Rigau, and Janyce Wiebe. 2016. SemEval-2016 Task 1: Semantic Textual Similarity, Monolingual and Cross-Lingual Evaluation. In *Proceedings of the 10th International Workshop on Semantic Evaluation (SemEval-2016)*, pages 497–511, San Diego, California. Association for Computational Linguistics.

Takuya Akiba, Shotaro Sano, Toshihiko Yanase, Takeru Ohta, and Masanori Koyama. 2019. Optuna: A Next-generation Hyperparameter Optimization Framework. In *Proceedings of the 25th ACM SIGKDD International Conference on Knowledge Discovery & Data Mining*, pages 2623–2631, Anchorage AK USA, July. ACM.

David Bamman and Gregory Crane. 2008. The logic and discovery of textual allusion. In *In Proceedings of the 2008 LREC Workshop on Language Technology for Cultural Heritage Data*.

Daniel Bär, Torsten Zesch, and Iryna Gurevych. 2012. Text reuse detection using a composition of text similarity measures. In *Proceedings of COLING 2012*, pages 167–184, Mumbai, India, December. The COLING 2012 Organizing Committee.

Vuk Batanović and Dragan Bojić. 2015. Using Part-of-Speech Tags as Deep Syntax Indicators in Determining Short Text Semantic Similarity. *Computer Science and Information Systems*, 12(1):1–31, January.

Maximilian Bryan, Manuel Burghardt, and Johannes Molz. 2020. A computational expedition into the undiscovered country - evaluating neural networks for the identification of hamlet text reuse. *Proceedings of the 1st Workshop on Computational Humanities Research (CHR)*.

Marco Büchler, Annette Geßner, Monica Berti, and Thomas Eckart. 2013. Measuring the influence of a work by text re-use. *Bulletin of the Institute of Classical Studies. Supplement*, pages 63–79.

Manuel Burghardt, Selina Meyer, Stephanie Schmidtbauer, and Johannes Molz. 2019. *"The Bard meets the Doctor" – Computergestützte Identifikation intertextueller Shakespearebezüge in der Science Fiction-Serie Dr. Who*. Book of Abstracts, DHd.

Neil Coffee, Jean-Pierre Koenig, Shakthi Poornima, Christopher Forstall, Roelant Ossewaarde, and Sarah Jacobson. 2012a. The Tesserae Project: intertextual analysis of Latin poetry. *Literary and Linguistic Computing*, 28(2):221–228, 07.

Neil Coffee, Jean-Pierre Koenig, Shakthi Poornima, Roelant Ossewaarde, Christopher Forstall, and Sarah Jacobson. 2012b. Intertextuality in the digital age. *Transactions of the American Philological Association (1974-)*, pages 383–422.

Christopher Forstall, Neil Coffee, Thomas Buck, Katherine Roache, and Sarah Jacobson. 2015. Modeling the scholars: Detecting intertextuality through enhanced word-level n-gram matching. *Digital Scholarship in the Humanities*, 30(4):503–515.

Greta Franzini, Emily Franzini, Gabriela Rotari, Franziska Pannach, Mahdi Solhdoust, and Marco Büchler. 2017. The digital breadcrumb trail of brothers grimm. *Poster at the DATECH conference, Göttingen*.

Jean-Gabriel Ganascia, Peirre Glaudes, and Andrea Del Lungo. 2014. Automatic detection of reuses and citations in literary texts. *Literary and Linguistic Computing*, 29(3):412–421, 06.

Marjorie Garber. 2005. *Shakespeare After All*. Anchor Books.

Gérard Genette. 1993. *Palimpseste. Die Literatur auf zweiter Stufe*. Suhrkamp.

William L. Hamilton, Jure Leskovec, and Dan Jurafsky. 2016. Diachronic Word Embeddings Reveal Statistical Laws of Semantic Change. In *Proceedings of the 54th Annual Meeting of the Association for Computational Linguistics (Volume 1: Long Papers)*, pages 1489–1501, Berlin, Germany. Association for Computational Linguistics.

Regula Hohl-Trillini. 2019. *'Look thee, I speak play scraps': Digitally Mapping Intertextuality in Early Modern Drama*. Oxford University, Bodleian and Folger Libraries, July.

Kalervo Järvelin and Jaana Kekäläinen. 2002. Cumulated gain-based evaluation of IR techniques. *ACM Transactions on Information Systems*, 20(4):422–446, October.

Herve Jegou, Cordelia Schmid, Hedi Harzallah, and Jakob Verbeek. 2010. Accurate Image Search Using the Contextual Dissimilarity Measure. *IEEE TRANSACTIONS ON PATTERN ANALYSIS AND MACHINE INTELLIGENCE*, 32(1):10.

Cyril Labbé and Dominique Labbé. 2005. A Tool for Literary Studies: Intertextual Distance and Tree Classification. *Literary and Linguistic Computing*, 21(3):311–326, 10.

Jurij Leskovec, Anand Rajaraman, and Jeffrey D. Ullman. 2020. *Mining of Massive Datasets*. Cambridge University Press, New York, NY, third edition edition.

Enrique Manjavacas, Brian Long, and Mike Kestemont. 2019. On the Feasibility of Automated Detection of Allusive Text Reuse. *arXiv:1905.02973 [cs]*, May.

Christopher Manning, Prabhakar Raghavan, and Hinrich Schütze. 2008. *Introduction to Information Retrieval*. Cambridge University Press, USA.

Julie Maxwell and Kate Rumbold. 2018. *Shakespeare and Quotation*. Cambridge University Press.

Tomas Mikolov, Kai Chen, Greg Corrado, and Jeffrey Dean. 2013. Efficient estimation of word representations in vector space. *arXiv preprint arXiv:1301.3781*.

Tomas Mikolov, Edouard Grave, Piotr Bojanowski, Christian Puhrsch, and Armand Joulin. 2018. Advances in Pre-Training Distributed Word Representations. In *Proceedings of the International Conference on Language Resources and Evaluation (LREC 2018)*.

Christoph Molnar. 2020. *Interpretable Machine Learning. A Guide for Making Black Box Models Explainable*. https://christophm.github.io/interpretable-ml-book/.

Johannes Molz. 2019. *A close and distant reading of Shakespearean intertextuality*. Ludwig-Maximilians-Universität München, Juli.

Chakaveh Saedi, António Branco, João António Rodrigues, and João Silva. 2018. WordNet Embeddings. In *Proceedings of The Third Workshop on Representation Learning for NLP*, pages 122–131, Melbourne, Australia. Association for Computational Linguistics.

Enrico Santus, Hongmin Wang, Emmanuele Chersoni, and Yue Zhang. 2018. A Rank-Based Similarity Metric for Word Embeddings. *arXiv:1805.01923 [cs]*, May.

Walter Scheirer, Christopher Forstall, and Neil Coffee. 2014. The sense of a connection: Automatic tracing of intertextuality by meaning. *Digital Scholarship in the Humanities*, 31(1):204–217, 10.

Ann Taylor, Mitchell Marcus, and Beatrice Santorini. 2003. The Penn Treebank: An Overview. In Nancy Ide, Jean Véronis, and Anne Abeillé, editors, *Treebanks*, volume 20, pages 5–22. Springer Netherlands, Dordrecht.

M.S Waterman, T.F Smith, and W.A Beyer. 1976. Some biological sequence metrics. *Advances in Mathematics*, 20(3):367–387, June.

Vital Records: **Uncover the past from historical handwritten records**

Hervé Déjean
Naver Labs Europe
6 chemin de Maupertuis
38240 Meylan, France
herve.dejean@naverlabs.com

Jean-Luc Meunier
Naver Labs Europe
6 chemin de Maupertuis
38240 Meylan, France
jean-luc.meunier@naverlabs.com

Abstract

We present *Vital Records*, a demonstrator based on deep-learning approaches to handwritten-text recognition, table processing and information extraction, which enables data from century-old documents to be parsed and analysed, making it possible to explore death records in space and time. This demonstrator provides a user interface for browsing and visualising data extracted from 80,000 handwritten pages of tabular data.

1 Introduction

A great deal of human history is detailed in hand-written documents that have yet to be analyzed. Extracting information from such documents has, until recently, represented an extremely time-consuming and labour-intensive task. For this reason, there remains a treasure trove of untapped information that could help provide insight into, for example, the impact of industrialization on populations. Indeed, some of these records—such as those documenting epidemics—may provide useful context for our understanding of modern problems.

The recent advances in Handwritten Text Recognition (Mühlberger et al., 2019), and in Deep Learning at large, allow now us to automatically process large volumes of documents.

The *Vital Records* demonstrator, based on a collection of 80,000 pages, brings to life records that were handwritten by more than 700 different priests from 200 parishes in Germany from 1848 to 1878. The demo illustrates how state-of-the-art deep-learning methods—handwritten text recognition (HTR), table recognition (TR), and information extraction (IE)—can be used to transform these records into a digital format that can be queried and visualized in different ways to enrich our knowledge from previously unexplored sources of information.

The online demonstrator is available under this URL[1]

2 Using *Vital Records* to trace trends through history

Vital Records allows users to browse and visualize the dataset extracted from these German records using spatio-temporal criteria, in addition to the usual textual search queries (Figure 1).

Death records provide a range of useful information. As well as the name, age, date, and cause of death, the records include the profession of the deceased (Figure 3). With this information in hand, we are able to visualize trends over a given period. For example, we used these Death records to trace the evolution of professions between 1847 and 1877. The resulting graph, shown in Figure 4, shows the number of deaths recorded for which the field of profession (Stand) contains weaver (Weber), shoemaker (Schumacher), and miller (Müller). The graph may be considered a proxy for estimating the evolution of these professions during this period. It's possible, too, to spot locally relevant characteristics. For example, data extracted from these records shows a high number of glassmakers (Glasmacher) around

---

[1]https://europe.naverlabs.com/about/global-ai-rd-belt/eu-and-government-projects/vital-records

Proceedings of LaTeCH-CLfL 2020, pages 69–73
Barcelona, Spain (Online), December 12, 2020.

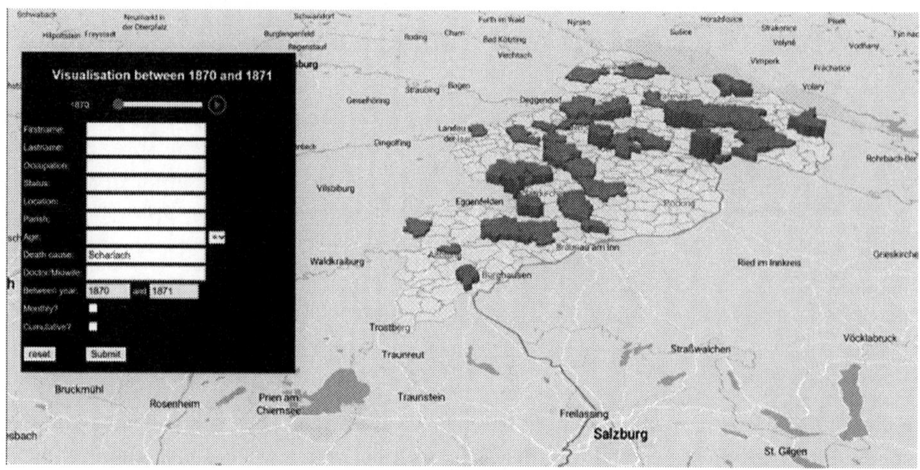

Figure 1: The user interface allows you to specify temporal and spatial criteria as well as to specify a value for each data field.

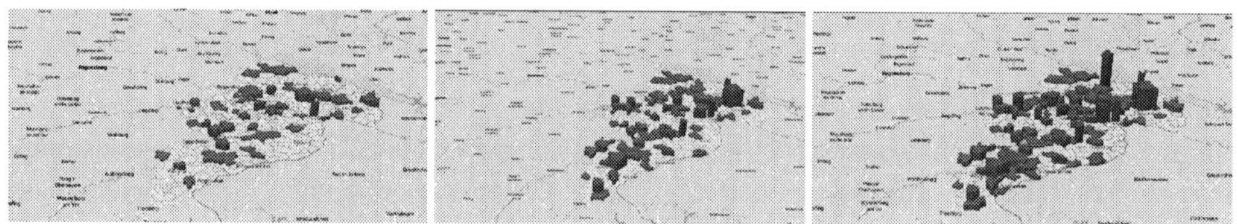

Figure 2: Example of temporal visualisation: number of deaths per parish, death cause:scarlet fever (Scharlach) in January, July and December 1871.

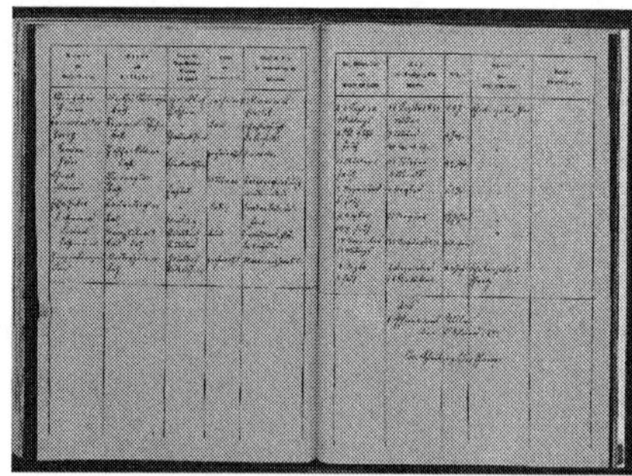

Figure 3: Example from the German records in which deaths are recorded in table format.

Zwiesel, a region that remains well-known for its production of glassware to this day. In addition to the visualization of data using graphs, *Vital Records* makes possible the development of temporal animations for which the timestep can be adjusted by year, month, or day. By combining both spatial and temporal information in this way, we are able to visualize the evolution of a given query over space and time. Our favourite query is the spread of scarlet fever in 1871.

It's also possible to track specific events, such as the opening of a hospital in a parish, or the arrival of a train line. Searching for professions containing the string *bahn* will provide you with a map of the three Bahnstrecke, or train lines: Passau-Regensburg, the Bavarian Forest Railway, and the München-Simbach.

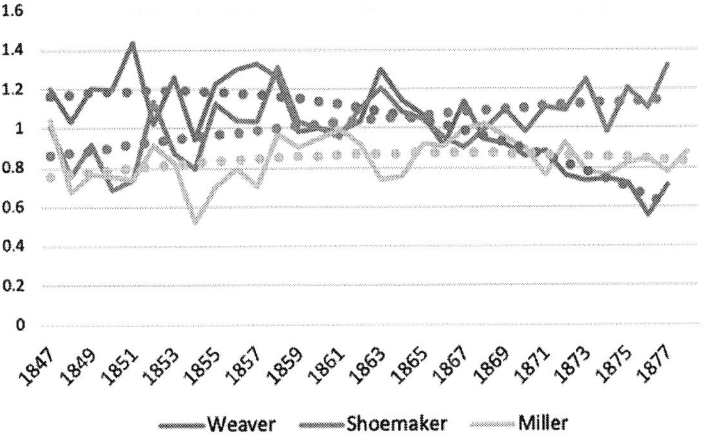

Figure 4: Visualization and data obtained from the *Vital Records* demonstrator, based on handwritten records from 200 parishes in Germany. This graph shows the evolution of the professions of weaver (blue), shoemaker (orange), and miller (yellow) between 1847 and 1877. Dotted lines represent the regression lines.

3   Deep-learning and Recognition: the Technology behind *Vital Records*

3.1   Handwritten Text Recognition

To develop this technology and create the Vital Records demo, we began by transforming handwritten tables—like the one shown in Figure 3—into a digital format. The field of handwritten document processing has improved significantly over the past few years, thanks to the neural network paradigm. First, we used the automated recognition and transcription platform Transkribus (Mühlberger et al., 2019) to transcribe 1000 pages from the German records. We then used these transcriptions to train an HTR model that could automatically digitise the information from the Death, Birth, and Wedding records of the archive. We found the character error rate (CER) to be around 10%, meaning that on average one letter out of every ten is wrongly recognised.

3.2   Table Recognition

Next, we focused on converting an image of a table into a spreadsheet (Figure 5). Understanding a page means grasping the layout, the relations between textual elements within the page, and so on. Although such 'table understanding' remains a challenge, it's one that can now be addressed with deep neural network technology (Prasad et al., 2019). We developed a neural network model that would learn how to organize a set of lines such that the information could be arranged into table rows. To achieve this, we enlisted the help of a graph convolutional network. By using the annotated collection (1000 pages containing tables that had been annotated to train the models), our system was able to recognise nine out of ten table rows. Figure 5 shows the original image and the reconstructed table using the Web interface provided by the Transkribus Plateform[2].

Building a user interface that enables experts to search the collection through space and time could provide an answer to the question 'Are the results sufficiently good to be useful to users of the archive or social historians?'

---

[2]https://transkribus.eu/r/read/projects/

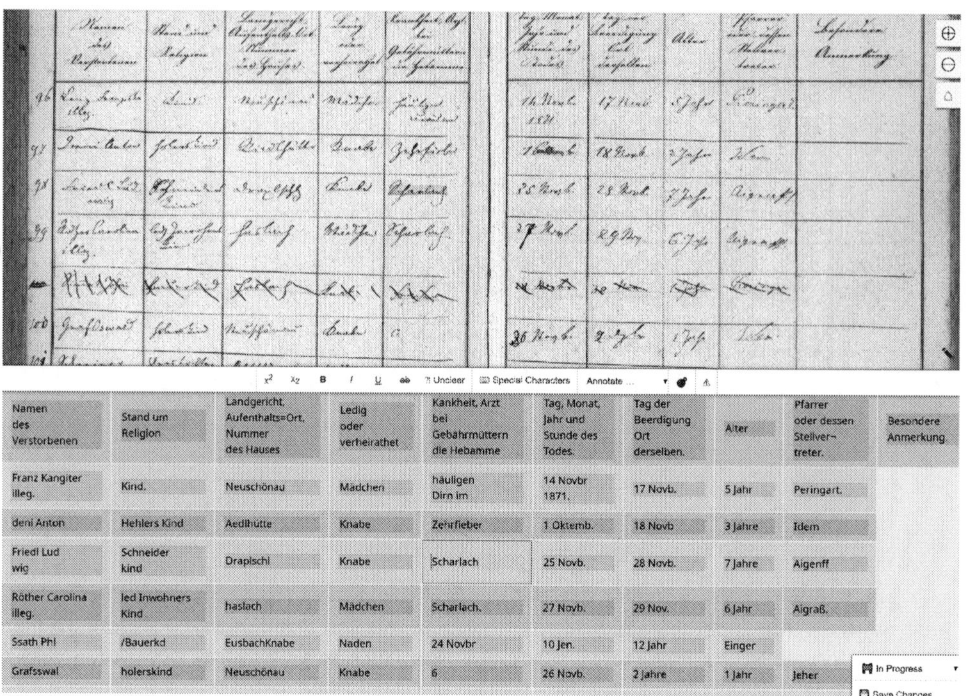

Namen des Verstorbenen	Stand um Religion	Landgericht, Aufenthalts=Ort, Nummer des Hauses	Ledig oder verheirathet	Kankheit, Arzt bei Gebährmüttern die Hebamme	Tag, Monat, Jahr und Stunde des Todes.	Tag der Beerdigung Ort derselben.	Alter	Pfarrer oder dessen Stellver~ treter.	Besondere Anmerkung.
Franz Kangiter illeg.	Kind.	Neuschönau	Mädchen	häuligen Dirn im	14 Novbr 1871.	17 Novb.	5 Jahr	Peringart,	
deni Anton	Hehlers Kind	Aedlhütte	Knabe	Zehrfieber	1 Oktemb.	18 Novb	3 Jahre	Idem	
Friedl Lud wig	Schneider kind	Draplschl	Knabe	Scharlach	25 Novb.	28 Novb.	7 Jahre	Aigenff	
Röther Carolina illeg.	led Inwohners Kind	haslach	Mädchen	Scharlach.	27 Novb.	29 Nov.	6 Jahr	Aigraß.	
Ssath Phl	/Bauerkd	EusbachKnabe	Naden	24 Novbr	10 Jen.	12 Jahr	Einger		
Grafsswal	holerskind	Neuschönau	Knabe	6	26 Novb.	2 Jahre	1 Jahr	Jeher	

Figure 5: The original image and the corresponding extracted table.

3.3 Information Extraction and Spatio-Temporal Indexing

Once the information in the table had been extracted (see Figure 5), we used a state-of-the-art named-entity recognition tool trained with synthetic data. The textual data in this kind of records are regular in terms of data type (e.g. names, dates, location, and family situation), but show some irregularities: the first column contains the person name, but sometimes her religion as well. Depending on the writer (priest) the name occurs as first name(s) - family name, or the reverse. Dates are also subject to many variations (presence of the year or not, use of Arabic or Latin numbers, abbreviation for the month). In order to cope with these variations, and also to deal with HTR errors, we wrote a text generator that allowed us to generate a large quantity of training data with these variations and errors and then train named-entity recognition tool with it to recognize each word category (first name, last name, death date,. . .).

Finally, we focused on spatio-temporal indexing. Associating each record to a geographical location and a temporal point enables navigation of the data through space and time. We achieved spatial indexing simply, through metadata at the parish level (since we know the parish associated with each book). The second indexing step, i.e. temporal indexing, requires information to be extracted from each record. Even if there is a dedicated column for this in every type of record, its extraction and normalization requires some processing. This is because the string extracted from the image by the HTR must be normalized and converted to a timestamp that a computer can handle. Furthermore, although the month and day are usually written in the record itself, the year may be 'factorized' at the page level, might only exist in the first record of the page, or could even occur a few pages before the one being processed (something a human would not have an issue inferring). Detecting this is still noisy and we're currently working on our model to improve its ability to appropriately extract this data.

4 Future work

We have almost finished processing the Birth and Wedding records, and will be adding them to the demo soon, along with the ability to search across the three types of records. We hope that one outcome of this upgrade will be the automatic generation of family trees.

Some issues in terms of Information Extraction are still pending and seem to require a specific step to solve them: for instance the idem/ditto sign occurring regularly in columns in order to avoid to repeat the same value (figure 3, last column).

Additionally, a major milestone will be to infer demographic information from these data, such as the population size, and some demographic statistics (birth and death rate, for instance). This can only be computed/estimated when the three types of records are linked, enabling identification of the same person across the three records (Sylvester and Hacker, 2020; Özgür Akgün et al., 2020).

5 Conclusion

In summary, *Vital Records* uses information extracted (via HTR and TR machine-learning technology) from archival documents to enable users to visualize trends through history, and even to track specific events. The demonstrator that we have developed, based on data obtained from German parish records between 1848 and 1878, showcases the spatio-temporal capabilities of the demonstrator.

Acknowledgements

We would like to thanks the reviewers for their interesting feedback. Many thanks to the Archive of the diocese of Passau, Germany for having provided the data and their valuable expertise. Part of this work has received funding from the European Union's Horizon 2020 research and innovation programme under grant agreement No 674943 (project READ). We would also like to thank all archives who contributed to the historical dataset.

References

Günter Mühlberger, Louise Seaward, Melissa Terras, Sofia Ares Oliveira, Vicente Bosch, Maximilian Bryan, Sebastian Colutto, Hervé Déjean, Markus Diem, Stefan Fiel, Basilis Gatos, Albert Greinoecker, Tobias Grüning, Günter Hackl, Vili Haukkovaara, Gerhard Heyer, Lauri Hirvonen, Tobias Hodel, Matti Jokinen, Philip Kahle, Mario Kallio, Frédéric Kaplan, Florian Kleber, Roger Labahn, Eva Maria Lang, Sören Laube, Gundram Leifert, Georgios Louloudis, Rory McNicholl, Jean-Luc Meunier, Johannes Michael, Elena Mühlbauer, Nathanael Philipp, Ioannis Pratikakis, Joan Puigcerver Pérez, Hannelore Putz, George Retsinas, Verónica Romero, Robert Sablatnig, Joan-Andreu Sánchez, Philip Schofield, Giorgos Sfikas, Christian Sieber, Nikolaos Stamatopoulos, Tobias Strauß, Tamara Terbul, Alejandro H. Toselli, Berthold Ulreich, Mauricio Villegas, Enrique Vidal, Johanna Walcher, Max Weidemann, Herbert Wurster, and Konstantinos Zagoris. 2019. Transforming scholarship in the archives through handwritten text recognition. *Journal of Documentation*, 75(5):954–976.

Animesh Prasad, Hervé Déjean, and Jean-Luc Meunier. 2019. Versatile layout understanding via conjugate graph. In *2019 International Conference on Document Analysis and Recognition, ICDAR 2019, Sydney, Australia, September 20-25, 2019*, pages 287-294. IEEE.

Kenneth M. Sylvester and J. David Hacker. 2020. Introduction to special issues on historical record linking. *Historical Methods: A Journal of Quantitative and Interdisciplinary History*, 53(2):77–79.

Özgür Akgün, Alan Dearle, Graham Kirby, Eilidh Garrett, Tom Dalton, Peter Christen, Chris Dibben, and Lee Williamson. 2020. Linking scottish vital event records using family groups. *Historical Methods: A Journal of Quantitative and Interdisciplinary History*, 53(2):130–146.

Measuring the Effects of Bias in Training Data for Literary Classification

Sunyam Bagga
.txtLAB
McGill University
sunyam.bagga@mcgill.ca

Andrew Piper
Department of Languages, Literatures, and Cultures
McGill University
andrew.piper@mcgill.ca

Abstract

Downstream effects of biased training data have become a major concern of the NLP community. How this may impact the automated curation and annotation of cultural heritage material is currently not well known. In this work, we create an experimental framework to measure the effects of different types of stylistic and social bias within training data for the purposes of literary classification, as one important subclass of cultural material. Because historical collections are often sparsely annotated, much like our knowledge of history is incomplete, researchers often cannot know the underlying distributions of different document types and their various sub-classes. This means that bias is likely to be an *intrinsic* feature of training data when it comes to cultural heritage material. Our aim in this study is to investigate which classification methods may help mitigate the effects of different types of bias within curated samples of training data. We find that machine learning techniques such as BERT or SVM are robust against reproducing certain kinds of social and stylistic bias within our test data, except in the most extreme cases. We hope that this work will spur further research into the potential effects of bias within training data for other cultural heritage material beyond the study of literature.

1 Introduction

One of the challenges facing researchers working with cultural heritage data is the difficulty of producing historically representative samples of data (Bode, 2020). While we have access to very large collections of digitized material (e.g. Hathi Trust, Gale), we often lack knowledge about the distributions of different types of documents and their stylistic qualities within these collections (not to mention within the broader sweep of history more generally). Researchers aiming to build collections for historical study using automated methods are thus faced with a two-part challenge: first, the collection of reliable training data given the absence of annotated data within larger collections; and second, the mitigation of potentially unknown biases within such training data when scaling to the classification of larger historical collections.

In this work, we attempt to measure the effects of such potential *unknown* biases within training data for the purpose of literary classification by testing cases of *known* bias. In essence, we want to simulate the following scenario. A researcher wishes to construct a large sample of historical documents from within a given heritage repository using automated methods. Because there is no consistently annotated data for her purposes, she constructs a small training data sample by hand based on her domain expertise, either by randomly sampling from the larger collection or building around some prior disciplinary consensus. As she moves to implement a process to automatically classify documents based on her training data, she is left with a fundamental uncertainty: Because the underlying distribution of different stylistic and social features of the data within the larger collection are unknown, and given that her sample represents a tiny fraction of all documents, how confident can the researcher be that whatever biases may be present in the training data will (not) be reproduced in the subsequent automated annotations?

Proceedings of LaTeCH-CLfL 2020, pages 74–84
Barcelona, Spain (Online), December 12, 2020.

To model this scenario, we work with a collection of data in which the underlying distributions of stylistic and social features are known and then test a variety of cases of increasing bias within the training data to measure its effects on the test data. We assess three separate forms of stylistic and social bias, which include genre, dialogue, and authorial gender, as well as a variety of classification techniques, including the use of data augmentation, to identify conditions under which the reproduction of bias is minimized. In all cases, the goal of our classification task is the detection of *fiction* from a larger collection of documents. The identification of fictional or "literary" documents within large historical collections is a pressing need for the field of literary studies and has been taken up in several cases (Underwood et al., 2020; Underwood, 2014; Bode, 2020). As yet, however, no assessment has been made of the potential effects of bias within the training data used for such annotation exercises.

As we discuss in detail in Section 5, we surprisingly find that current state-of-the-art techniques in NLP such as BERT (Devlin et al., 2019) (or even SVMs) are robust against reproducing all three kinds of bias within our test data, except in the most extreme cases. One bias in particular, authorial gender, appears to exhibit no effect at all in classification tasks, even under the most extreme circumstances.

2   Related Work

2.1   Bias in NLP

Numerous studies in recent years have analyzed different kinds of biases in NLP systems. They span a wide variety of NLP tasks such as abusive language detection (Sap et al., 2019), language modeling (Lu et al., 2018), learning word embeddings (Bolukbasi et al., 2016; Caliskan et al., 2017), and machine translation (Vanmassenhove et al., 2018), among others. For example, Sap et al. (2019) find that African American English tweets are twice as likely to be labelled offensive compared to others, demonstrating racial bias in hate speech detection systems, while Bolukbasi et al. (2016) and Caliskan et al. (2017) show that word embeddings trained on popular datasets strongly exhibit gender stereotypes. In each of these cases, research demonstrates that biases encoded in the training data used for automated detection tasks is reproduced in NLP outputs.

Recent work by Blodgett et al. (2020) has emphasized that in light of the numerous ways "bias" has been interpreted and studied in the literature that researchers explicitly state both their working understanding of bias and also the concrete social harms that can follow from bias in NLP. Our concern in focusing on text classification for cultural heritage materials is designed to address the problem of historical representation and the role that automated systems play in the construction of our understanding of the past. Biases in training data could lead to misleading representations of the past, which could in turn lead to "harms of representation" identified by Blodgett et al. (2020) with respect to different, often historically marginalized social groups. For example, training data that does not adequately reflect women's participation in the production of literature could in turn generate historical samples that severely under-represent women's role in the history of literature. Similar concerns could be raised about racial, ethnic, or regional identities. Moreover, Zadrozny (2004) show that some machine learning classifiers are affected by the problem of sample selection bias, that is, when the training data consist of randomly drawn samples from a different distribution than the test data about which the learned model is expected to make predictions.

2.2   Data Augmentation for NLP

Due to the lack of large-scale and reliably annotated data in historical collections, many researchers will necessarily have to begin with manually collected training data, which in most cases constrains the size and diversity of training data.

Data augmentation has been proposed as a strategy to help train more robust models by improving the quantity and quality of training data. It is commonly and effectively used in the domains of computer vision (Krizhevsky et al., 2017), speech (Cui et al., 2015), and is now being explored for NLP tasks (Wei and Zou, 2019). To date, no work has experimented with data augmentation for the task of literary classification. Here, we experiment with two forms of data augmentation: (1) the Easy Data Augmentation (EDA) model that has been shown to provide performance gains across five classification tasks

(Wei and Zou, 2019), and (2) a hand-engineered model consisting of augmentation techniques such as back-translation (Yu et al., 2018), crossover (FM, 2019), and substituting proper names (Section 3.3).

2.3 Literary Text Classification

Within the larger field of text classification, very few studies have experimented with optimizing classification within the literary domain. Yu (2008) implement naive bayes and support vector machines (SVMs) for two literary classification tasks. Allison et al. (2011) show that compute algorithms and digital methods can be successfully used to build predictive models (if not explanatory models) for literary genres. More recently, Underwood et al. (2020) released a large collection of volumes that were predicted to be fiction through algorithmic modeling. They implement regularized logistic regression using a feature set that consists of unigrams (words) along with a few structural features. Our work provides further understanding of the relationship between classifiers and the prediction of literary documents.

3 Methodology

The goal of our experiments is to test the effects of bias in training data on the classification of test data belonging to the domain of literature. For our purposes, following the work of Underwood et al. (2020), we attempt to predict whether a document is a work of "fiction" within a binary classification task (fiction/non-fiction) and modulate different stylistic features, which we describe in Section 4. In this section, we describe the dataset followed by the classification algorithms used along with the data augmentation techniques applied to the training data.[1]

3.1 Dataset

The data used in this paper consists of 866 digitized works of "bestselling" contemporary writing according to Amazon.com and published between 2000 and 2016 (Piper and Portelance, 2016). The breakdown of works are based on Amazon's genre tags and include: 200 works of non-fiction, comprised of a variety of sub-genres including history, biography, policy, self-help, etc.; 235 works of "Mystery" novels, 220 works of "Science Fiction," and 211 "Romance" novels. All works were selected based on their ranking within the "bestselling" sorting mechanism on Amazon and reviewed by hand for genre appropriateness.

3.2 Classification Algorithms

We experiment with a diverse set of classification algorithms using both traditional machine learning and deep learning for this supervised learning task.

Traditional Machine Learning. We implement the following learning algorithms that are commonly used for classification: Logistic Regression, Support Vector Machines (SVM), Random Forests and Gradient Boosting Classifier (GBC). A crucial aspect of the text classification pipeline is feature representation. We represent the input text as a bag of word n-grams which is one of the most simple yet effective methods for feature vectorization. We experiment with unigrams, bigrams, trigrams and all three word n-grams combined, and pick the one which yields the best performance in a 5-fold cross validation test. Simultaneously, we perform cross-validated hyperparameter tuning for each of our learning algorithms. The algorithms and features are implemented using the scikit-learn library (Pedregosa et al., 2011).

Deep Learning. Deep learning models have achieved state-of-the-art results in many text classification tasks (Minaee et al., 2020). In this work, we implement a number of deep learning models: Convolutional Neural Networks (CNN), Long Short-Term Memory Networks (LSTM), Bi-directional LSTM, and Stacked Bi-directional LSTM. For the input embedding layer to the network, we experiment with: (1) using static pre-trained GloVe embeddings (Pennington et al., 2014), (2) using the dynamic deep contextualized ELMo representations (Peters et al., 2018) which utilizes transfer learning. We use the cross entropy loss function and Adam optimizer (Kingma and Ba, 2014) for learning network weights.

Recently, many transformer-based models have been proposed in the field that have outperformed all other learning models on several NLP tasks including text classification. We implement two such models

---

[1]We make our code and metadata publicly available at https://github.com/sunyam/bias-literary-classification.

EDA	CDA
1. Synonym Replacement: Replace N random words from the sentence with one of their synonyms.	**1. Crossover**: generates new instances by swapping halves of two instances with the same label (inspired by genetic algorithm's crossover).
2. Random Insertion: Insert a random synonym of a random word in the sentence at a random position in the sentence. Do this N times.	**2. Back-translation**: generates paraphrases of the input (English) text by translating it to another language and translating it back to English. We use four languages – French, Korean, German, Spanish.
3. Random Swap: Randomly choose two words in the sentence and swap their positions. Do this N times.	**3. Proper Names**: We generate two new instances by: (1) deleting all proper names in the input text; (2) substituting all proper names with random names.
4. Random Deletion: Randomly remove each word in the sentence with probability p.	

Table 1: Data augmentation techniques implemented in this work. As recommended by Wei and Zou (2019), we generate 16 instances per training instance for both EDA and CDA ($N = 25$ and $p = 0.05$).

here: Bidirectional Encoder Representations for Transformers (BERT) (Devlin et al., 2019) and XLNet (Yang et al., 2019). More specifically, we first load these large pre-trained models and fine-tune them on our literary classification task. The deep learning models are implemented using PyTorch (Paszke et al., 2019), AllenNLP (Gardner et al., 2017) and Transformers (Wolf et al., 2019) libraries.

3.3 Data Augmentation

The shortage of labeled training data is a major concern for many supervised learning tasks since data annotation is a time-consuming and expensive process. This has led to the idea of data augmentation which refers to increasing the size and diversity of training data without actually collecting new data. In this work, we implement two sets of data augmentation techniques: Easy Data Augmentation (Wei and Zou, 2019) and a set of other techniques we group under the name Custom Data Augmentation (CDA). They are presented in Table 1. Note that we use the Google Translate API[2] for back-translation; for proper names, we use the Stanford Named Entity Recognizer (Finkel et al., 2005) to locate them in the text and NameDatabases[3] for sampling random names. Additionally, we also merge EDA and CDA where 8 augmented instances are generated using the former and 8 using the latter.

4 Experiment Design

In this section, we introduce our experimental setup to test the robustness of the classifiers when presented with different forms of bias in the training data, grouped into the following three categories: genre, dialogue, and gender. Our research question is which classification techniques (if any) mitigate different types of known biases in the training data when it comes to accurately classifying test documents?

In all cases, we hold our test set constant and then manipulate our training data according to different kinds of stylistic and social features described below, and evaluate each model's performance. We begin by establishing a baseline where the distribution of the feature of interest (e.g. genre, dialogue, gender) is the same for both the train and test sets. We then gradually distort the training data and measure observed declines in model performance using the evaluation metrics described below. The size of the training data remains constant throughout: 200 fiction and 200 non-fiction documents.[4] A "document" refers to a 500-word passage randomly sampled from a single work. When sampling passages, we condition on the middle 40% of the work in order to avoid paratext at the beginning or end of a work. Additionally, we

---

[2]https://py-googletrans.readthedocs.io/
[3]https://github.com/smashew/NameDatabases
[4]With the exception of Uniform-Genre experiment where we use 201 fiction documents, 67 from each genre.

experiment with using longer passages from these volumes (up to 10,000 words) as described in Section 5. Finally, we sample no more than 1-3 passages per work for each scenario.

4.1 Genre

An important characteristic of fictional documents is the way they consist of a variety of sub-types, one aspect of which can be captured through the notion of "genre." While the term genre can be interpreted in different ways, we use it here to mean stylistic distinctions among literary documents that have a strong "thematic" orientation. Genres such as "mystery," "science fiction," or "romance," address significantly different real-world scenarios, which may affect the nature of characterization, narrative voice, or event-types. Research has shown that such generic distinctions exhibit a strong degree of categorical difference from the perspective of machine learning (Underwood, 2016; Piper and Portelance, 2016).

We thus hypothesize that training data that is biased with respect to genre may produce biased representations when it comes to the prediction of test data. If a researcher generated (unknowingly) a training data sample based mostly or only on science fiction, for example, would this training data produce predictions that were 1) less accurate with respect to the broader *fiction* category and 2) less equally distributed among other kinds of genres *within* the category of fiction (i.e. biased towards science fiction)?

Train-Set Scenarios.   This experiment is broken down into four training data scenarios listed below.

1. Uniform: We keep the fiction train-set uniformly distributed across the three genres, where the fiction set consists of 1/3 Mystery, 1/3 Romance and 1/3 SciFi passages. This scenario corresponds to the red dot in Figure 1.

2. Genre-Dominated: For each genre, we begin with 50% of the training data being dominated by that genre and increase the genre dominance by 10% until the entire training set consists of a single genre (i.e. 100%). The other two genres are split evenly for each scenario.

Test Set.   We keep the test set static across the four scenarios: 99 non-fiction documents and 99 fiction documents equally distributed across the three genres (similar to Scenario 1).

4.2 Dialogue

While there are no systematic studies on the prevalence and distinctiveness of dialogue within fiction (whether over time or by genre), narrative theory suggests that the emphasis or avoidance of dialogue by writers indicates an important quality of fictional narrative (Genette, 1983). As a representation of oral speech, dialogue captures a distinctive stylistic quality of fictional documents that strongly departs from the linguistic norms and codes of narration and description (Bal, 2017). We thus hypothesize that imbalances with respect to the underlying distribution of dialogue within training data will pose challenges for the accurate prediction of fiction and may bias future samples from adequately capturing the underlying distribution of dialogue within a specific sub-domain of fiction.

Sampling.   To create our sample of documents, we first process all documents using BookNLP (Bamman et al., 2014) which allows us to identify words that appear in dialogue. We then divide passages into two groups: "with dialogue" and "no dialogue." To select passages with dialogue, we condition on all passages with dialogue from each work and keep the top two passages in terms of percentage of quoted words. Doing so, we observe that the average percentage of quoted words in our "with dialogue" sample is 81.2%. To select passages with no dialogue, we sample passages that have zero quoted words. We only sample from the Mystery novels to control for the effects of genre.

Train-Set Scenarios.   For our training scenarios, we begin with a train set consisting of 0 fiction passages with dialogue and gradually increase the number of passages with dialogue to 10%, 20%, 30%, ... up until 100%. As with the genre experiments, non-fiction data is kept constant.

Test Set.   The test set is kept static across all train-set scenarios. It contains 100 non-fiction passages and 100 fiction passages where 50 passages are drawn from our "with dialogue" sample and 50 from the "no dialogue" sample.

4.3 Authorial Gender

A great deal of work in the NLP community as well as literary studies has focused on problems of gender bias when it comes to the use of word embeddings (Caliskan et al., 2017; Bolukbasi et al., 2016), classification techniques (Mandell, 2019), and modeling more generally (Bode, 2020). Empirical work has demonstrated that gender represents an important form of social inequality within the literary realm (Underwood et al., 2018; Weinberg and Kapelner, 2018; Kraicer and Piper, 2019). It is thus imperative to develop methods of data curation that do not reproduce or amplify such historical inequalities. In this set of experiments, we explore the effects that biases with respect to authorial gender might have on predictive accuracy and balance when it comes to classifying works of fiction. We manually annotate our gender assignments based on identified gender via the author's public biography. While we found no non-binary authors in our study, it is important to acknowledge that the binary labels we use here are for heuristic purposes of identifying potential bias and are not designed to capture a more diverse understanding of gender. In order to control for the effects of genre, we once again only sample from the Mystery novels.

Train-Set Scenarios. As with our dialogue experiments, we begin with 0% men novelists where all passages of fiction are written by women authors and gradually increase the number of fiction passages written by men to 10%, 20%, 30%, ..., until 100%.

Test Set. Consistent with our other experiments, we use a static test set with 100 non-fiction passages and 100 fiction passages with 50% of fiction written by men and 50% by women.

4.4 Evaluation

In order to assess the effects of bias within our training data, we evaluate our classifiers across the following two dimensions. In all cases, we compare performance with respect to a baseline where the distributions in the train and test sets mirror each other.

- Accuracy: We report standard performance metrics such as F1-score, accuracy, precision, and recall to address the question: did the increase of bias result in a decline of overall predictive accuracy?

- Balance: Our second evaluation goal is to capture distortions in the positive predictions for each of our scenarios. Here we are asking whether an increase in bias in training data leads to an increase in imbalanced sub-classes within our overall class of fiction. When a classifier is trained largely on a single genre or presence of dialogue or gender, is it able to equally identify fiction that does not belong to that genre, level of dialogue or gender? This is in many ways the more important measure for our purposes because it allows us to see how biased training data impacts the underlying distribution of a feature of interest. Will biased training data produce biased samples? To measure this, we report the relative entropy of the true positives for a given classification task. An entropy of 0 would mean that there is no class imbalance produced among the different sub-types of fiction tested, while higher entropy indicates greater skew towards a single sub-type. Table 2 indicates the relationship between entropy scores and class imbalances for the genre experiment.

5 Results and Discussion

5.1 Classifier Performance

Which classifiers perform best at our task of literary classification? In order to systematically compare performance, we start by implementing all classifiers for the *Uniform* Genre experiment setting. The classification metrics and relative entropy for a diverse set of classifiers and augmentation techniques are shown in Table 2.[5] As expected, transformer-based models perform very well on this task with BERT outperforming all other classifiers by at least 2 or more F1 points. Convolutional Neural Networks that utilize transfer learning through ELMo embeddings (F1 = 0.9) perform much better than their GloVe embeddings counterpart (F1 = 0.87).

---

[5]Due to space constraints, we only present a subset of the top performing classifiers here. Specifically, Random Forest, GBC, and LSTM-based models did not perform well on this task and are not shown in Table 2.

Classifier	F1-score	Precision	Recall	Accuracy	True-Positives Distribution	Relative Entropy
BERT	**0.9394**	0.9394	0.9394	0.9394	{mys: 0.3226, sci: 0.3333, rom: 0.3441}	0.00034
BERT + EDA	0.9333	0.9479	0.9192	0.9343	{rom: 0.3516, mys: 0.3187, sci: 0.3297}	0.00083
XLNet	0.9175	0.9368	0.899	0.9192	{rom: 0.3596, mys: 0.3034, sci: 0.3371}	0.00241
CNN (ELMo) + EDA	0.91	0.8571	0.9697	0.904	{sci: 0.3438, rom: 0.3438, mys: 0.3125}	0.00099
LogReg + EDA	0.9029	0.8692	0.9394	0.899	{sci: 0.3333, mys: 0.3333, rom: 0.3333}	0.0
SVM + EDA and CDA	0.9009	0.8835	0.9192	0.899	{sci: 0.3516, mys: 0.3077, rom: 0.3407}	0.00158
CNN (ELMo)	0.9005	0.8482	0.9596	0.8939	{rom: 0.3474, sci: 0.3368, mys: 0.3158}	0.00078
SVM + EDA	0.8986	0.8611	0.9394	0.8939	{sci: 0.3333, mys: 0.3333, rom: 0.3333}	0.0
BERT + CDA	0.898	0.9072	0.8889	0.899	{rom: 0.3636, mys: 0.3182, sci: 0.3182}	0.00203
LogReg + EDA and CDA	0.8955	0.8824	0.9091	0.8939	{sci: 0.3333, mys: 0.3222, rom: 0.3444}	0.00036
SVM	0.891	0.8393	0.9495	0.8838	{rom: 0.3298, sci: 0.3404, mys: 0.3298}	0.00011
LogReg	0.89	0.8455	0.9394	0.8838	{rom: 0.3333, sci: 0.3333, mys: 0.3333}	0.0
LogReg + CDA	0.8768	0.8558	0.899	0.8737	{mys: 0.3146, rom: 0.3483, sci: 0.3371}	0.00088
SVM + CDA	0.875	0.8349	0.9192	0.8687	{mys: 0.3187, rom: 0.3516, sci: 0.3297}	0.00083
CNN (GloVe)	0.8732	0.8158	0.9394	0.8636	{rom: 0.3548, sci: 0.3226, mys: 0.3226}	0.00102

Table 2: Performance of classifiers across the two dimensions for Genre (Uniform) experiment. Note that both train and test set are uniformly distributed across genres, and Relative Entropy is calculated between the True-Positives distribution and the test-set distribution {mys: 0.333, sci: 0.333, rom: 0.333}.

The traditional learning models – SVM and Logistic Regression – achieve somewhat comparable F1-scores of 89%. Moreover, these algorithms are the only ones to achieve a perfect entropy score of 0. It is worth mentioning, however, that BERT's entropy score of 0.00034 also yields a TP-distribution that is extremely close to the ideal test-set distribution.

Does Data Augmentation Help? We observe marginal performance gains of about 1 F1-point with EDA for Logistic Regression, SVM, and CNN. However, the performance drops by 0.6% for BERT. Our Custom Data Augmentation (CDA) technique does not improve the F1-score for any of the classifiers. From these empirical observations, we conclude that the augmentation techniques implemented in this work do not provide significant performance gains for this classification task on our data.

Passage-Length. In addition to 500-word passages, we experiment with using longer passages – 1,000 to 10,000 words – from these volumes. We find that SVM's F1-score goes up from 0.891 when using 500 words to 0.955 with 10,000 words.[6] The peak is achieved at 5,000 words with an F1-score of 0.959.

Given these findings, we continue our bias analysis only implementing BERT and SVM without any data augmentation for all subsequent experiments using 500-word passages.

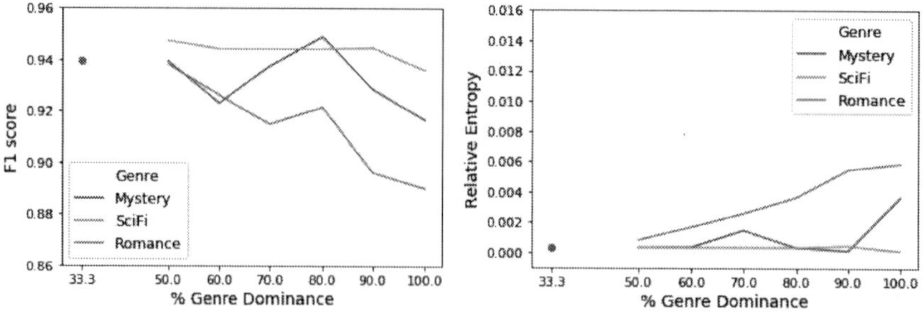

Figure 1: BERT's performance across the two evaluation-dimensions on the Genre experiments.

5.2 Bias Analysis

Genre Bias. Figure 1 shows BERT's performance according to both F1 score (left) and relative entropy (right) for the three different scenarios where a given genre dominates the training data by increasing

---

[6]Note that BERT's performance stays approximately constant at 0.94 since the pre-trained model's max length is restricted to 512 tokens. This is because the model learns positional-embeddings with sequence lengths of up to 512 tokens only.

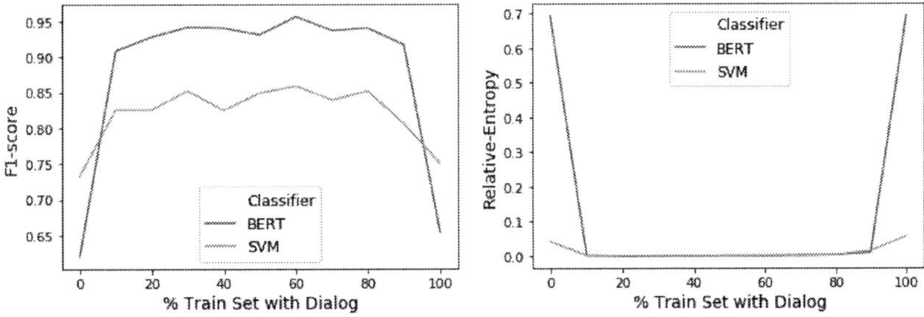

Figure 2: BERT and SVM's performances across the two dimensions on the Dialog experiments.

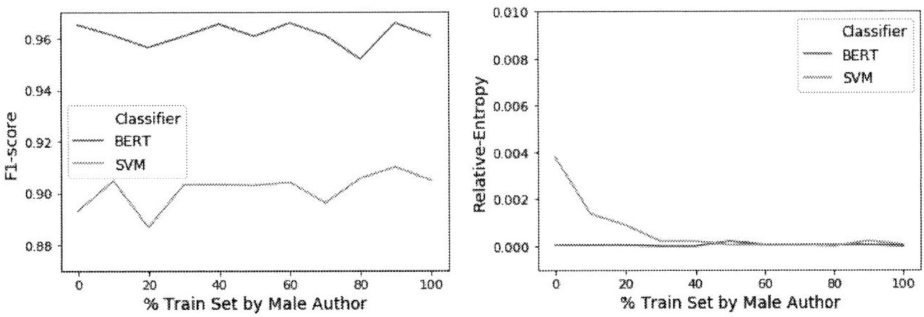

Figure 3: BERT and SVM's performances across the two dimensions on the Gender experiments.

amounts. We can see that when training data and test data mirror each other, BERT achieves an F1-score of 0.939 and an almost-perfect entropy score of 0.00034 (red dot). As we introduce more genre imbalance, we see little performance decrease until 90% imbalance has been achieved. When the train-set is 100% Romance, the F1-score goes down 5 points to 0.89 and the relative entropy goes up to 0.00585 which corresponds to a TP-distribution that is slightly biased towards romance: {sci: 0.296, rom: 0.383, mys: 0.321}. SVM also exhibits a similar trend[7] (not shown here) with its entropy going up to 0.04 where 43% of the True Positives belong to romance. In sum, BERT appears to be robust against genre biases as long as training data is not biased upwards of 90% for a single genre.

Dialogue Bias. Figure 2 shows both SVM and BERT's performance when we change the distribution of fiction passages with dialogue in the training set. Both classifiers' performance is stable across both dimensions except for the most extreme case (i.e. 100% of the train-set has dialogue or no dialogue). Somewhat surprisingly, as long as a classifier does not learn that fiction *only* consists of dialogue (or the opposite), it should not condition on types of fiction with a differential preference for dialogue.

Gender Bias. The findings of this experiment are presented in Figure 3. As can be seen, both BERT and SVM's performance is relatively stable and constant across F1-score and relative entropy. Unlike the other two experiments' findings, this holds true even for the most extreme cases of authorial gender imbalance in the train-set. While there appears to be an asymmetry with respect to gender bias - training data of all women authors will produce more imbalance than training data with all men - the relative entropy (of 0.0037) corresponds to an imbalance of 45.6% men and 54.4% women even in the most extreme case.

6 Conclusion

In this paper, we have tested different classifiers, different data augmentation techniques, and different forms of training data bias to assess their effects on the task of literary classification. Overall, we

---

[7]In fact, this trend is consistent across all different passage lengths we experimented with. Due to space constraints, the rest of the plots are provided in the GitHub repository.

have found that BERT is the best-performing classifier with SVMs comparable with text-passages above 5,000 words in length. Data augmentation as we have implemented it provides little performance gain. Finally, the stylistic and social biases tested here exhibit little effect except in the most extreme cases ($>$ 90% bias for a given category) suggesting that at least for the purposes of literary text classification, underlying biases in training data are not as impactful as researchers have initially hypothesized. Nevertheless, our work is limited in its historical scope (different historical periods may exhibit different effects), cultural specificity (our effects have only been observed on English-language documents), classification task (other types of classification may perform differently), and stylistic breadth (stylistic features important to other domains or research questions may behave differently). It is also important to emphasize that while classifiers can mitigate the propagation of bias within training data scenarios (up to a point and under certain conditions), they cannot address biases built into the underlying digital collections from which new collections are created (Bode, 2020). We hope that these experiments provide a useful framework for further refining our understanding of the effects of bias on multiple forms of cultural classification. Future work will want to test different classification scenarios, types of stylistic or social bias, multiple linguistic contexts, as well as further historical document types to better understand how unknown biases in training data may impact our representation of the past using digital collections.

References

Sarah Allison, Ryan Heuser, Matthew Jockers, Franco Moretti, and Michael Witmore. 2011. Quantitative formalism. Stanford Literary Lab.

Mieke Bal. 2017. *Narratology: Introduction to the Theory of Narrative*. University of Toronto Press.

David Bamman, Ted Underwood, and Noah A. Smith. 2014. A Bayesian mixed effects model of literary character. In *Proceedings of the 52nd Annual Meeting of the Association for Computational Linguistics (Volume 1: Long Papers)*, pages 370–379, Baltimore, Maryland, June. Association for Computational Linguistics.

Su Lin Blodgett, Solon Barocas, Hal Daumé III, and Hanna Wallach. 2020. Language (technology) is power: A critical survey of "bias" in NLP. In *Proceedings of the 58th Annual Meeting of the Association for Computational Linguistics*, pages 5454–5476, Online, July. Association for Computational Linguistics.

Katherine Bode. 2020. Why You Can't Model Away Bias. *Modern Language Quarterly*, 81(1):95–124.

Tolga Bolukbasi, Kai-Wei Chang, James Y Zou, Venkatesh Saligrama, and Adam T Kalai. 2016. Man is to computer programmer as woman is to homemaker? debiasing word embeddings. In D. D. Lee, M. Sugiyama, U. V. Luxburg, I. Guyon, and R. Garnett, editors, *Advances in Neural Information Processing Systems 29*, pages 4349–4357. Curran Associates, Inc.

Aylin Caliskan, Joanna J. Bryson, and Arvind Narayanan. 2017. Semantics derived automatically from language corpora contain human-like biases. *Science*, 356(6334):183–186.

X. Cui, V. Goel, and B. Kingsbury. 2015. Data augmentation for deep neural network acoustic modeling. *IEEE/ACM Transactions on Audio, Speech, and Language Processing*, 23(9):1469–1477.

Jacob Devlin, Ming-Wei Chang, Kenton Lee, and Kristina Toutanova. 2019. BERT: Pre-training of deep bidirectional transformers for language understanding. In *Proceedings of the 2019 Conference of the North American Chapter of the Association for Computational Linguistics: Human Language Technologies, Volume 1 (Long and Short Papers)*, pages 4171–4186, Minneapolis, Minnesota, June. Association for Computational Linguistics.

Jenny Rose Finkel, Trond Grenager, and Christopher Manning. 2005. Incorporating non-local information into information extraction systems by Gibbs sampling. In *Proceedings of the 43rd Annual Meeting of the Association for Computational Linguistics (ACL'05)*, pages 363–370, Ann Arbor, Michigan, June. Association for Computational Linguistics.

Luque FM. 2019. Atalaya at tass 2019: Data augmentation and robust embeddings for sentiment analysis. In *Proceedings of the Iberian Languages Evaluation Forum (IberLEF)*.

Matt Gardner, Joel Grus, Mark Neumann, Oyvind Tafjord, Pradeep Dasigi, Nelson F. Liu, Matthew Peters, Michael Schmitz, and Luke S. Zettlemoyer. 2017. Allennlp: A deep semantic natural language processing platform.

Gérard Genette. 1983. *Narrative Discourse: An Essay in Method*. Cornell University Press.

Diederik P. Kingma and Jimmy Ba. 2014. Adam: A method for stochastic optimization.

Eve Kraicer and Andrew Piper. 2019. Social characters: The hierarchy of gender in contemporary english-language fiction. *Journal of Cultural Analytics*, 3(1).

Alex Krizhevsky, Ilya Sutskever, and Geoffrey E. Hinton. 2017. Imagenet classification with deep convolutional neural networks. *Commun. ACM*, 60(6):84–90, May.

Kaiji Lu, Piotr Mardziel, Fangjing Wu, Preetam Amancharla, and Anupam Datta. 2018. Gender bias in neural natural language processing.

Laura Mandell. 2019. Gender and cultural analytics: Finding or making stereotypes? In *Debates in the Digital Humanities*, pages 3–26.

Shervin Minaee, Nal Kalchbrenner, Erik Cambria, Narjes Nikzad, Meysam Chenaghlu, and Jianfeng Gao. 2020. Deep Learning Based Text Classification: A Comprehensive Review. *arXiv e-prints*, page arXiv:2004.03705, April.

Adam Paszke, Sam Gross, Francisco Massa, Adam Lerer, James Bradbury, Gregory Chanan, Trevor Killeen, Zeming Lin, Natalia Gimelshein, Luca Antiga, Alban Desmaison, Andreas Kopf, Edward Yang, Zachary DeVito, Martin Raison, Alykhan Tejani, Sasank Chilamkurthy, Benoit Steiner, Lu Fang, Junjie Bai, and Soumith Chintala. 2019. Pytorch: An imperative style, high-performance deep learning library. In H. Wallach, H. Larochelle, A. Beygelzimer, F. dAlché-Buc, E. Fox, and R. Garnett, editors, *Advances in Neural Information Processing Systems 32*, pages 8024–8035. Curran Associates, Inc.

F. Pedregosa, G. Varoquaux, A. Gramfort, V. Michel, B. Thirion, O. Grisel, M. Blondel, P. Prettenhofer, R. Weiss, V. Dubourg, J. Vanderplas, A. Passos, D. Cournapeau, M. Brucher, M. Perrot, and E. Duchesnay. 2011. Scikit-learn: Machine learning in Python. *Journal of Machine Learning Research*, 12:2825–2830.

Jeffrey Pennington, Richard Socher, and Christopher D. Manning. 2014. Glove: Global vectors for word representation. In *Empirical Methods in Natural Language Processing (EMNLP)*, pages 1532–1543.

Matthew Peters, Mark Neumann, Mohit Iyyer, Matt Gardner, Christopher Clark, Kenton Lee, and Luke Zettlemoyer. 2018. Deep contextualized word representations. In *Proceedings of the 2018 Conference of the North American Chapter of the Association for Computational Linguistics: Human Language Technologies, Volume 1 (Long Papers)*, pages 2227–2237, New Orleans, Louisiana, June. Association for Computational Linguistics.

Andrew Piper and Eva Portelance. 2016. How cultural capital works: Prizewinning novels, bestsellers, and the time of reading. *Post-45*.

Maarten Sap, Dallas Card, Saadia Gabriel, Yejin Choi, and Noah A. Smith. 2019. The risk of racial bias in hate speech detection. In *Proceedings of the 57th Annual Meeting of the Association for Computational Linguistics*, pages 1668–1678, Florence, Italy, July. Association for Computational Linguistics.

William E Underwood, David Bamman, and Sabrina Lee. 2018. The transformation of gender in english-language fiction. *Journal of Cultural Analytics*, 2(2).

Ted Underwood, Patrick Kimutis, and Jessica Witte. 2020. Noveltm datasets for english-language fiction, 1700-2009. *Journal of Cultural Analytics*, 4(5).

Ted Underwood. 2014. Understanding genre in a collection of a million volumes, interim report. Technical report, University of Illinois Urbana-Champaign.

William E Underwood. 2016. The life cycles of genres. *Journal of Cultural Analytics*, 1(5).

Eva Vanmassenhove, Christian Hardmeier, and Andy Way. 2018. Getting gender right in neural machine translation. In *Proceedings of the 2018 Conference on Empirical Methods in Natural Language Processing*, pages 3003–3008, Brussels, Belgium, October-November. Association for Computational Linguistics.

Jason Wei and Kai Zou. 2019. EDA: Easy data augmentation techniques for boosting performance on text classification tasks. In *Proceedings of the 2019 Conference on Empirical Methods in Natural Language Processing and the 9th International Joint Conference on Natural Language Processing (EMNLP-IJCNLP)*, pages 6382–6388, Hong Kong, China, November. Association for Computational Linguistics.

Dana B. Weinberg and Adam Kapelner. 2018. Comparing gender discrimination and inequality in indie and traditional publishing. *PLOS ONE*, 13(4):1–20.

Thomas Wolf, Lysandre Debut, Victor Sanh, Julien Chaumond, Clement Delangue, Anthony Moi, Pierric Cistac, Tim Rault, Rémi Louf, Morgan Funtowicz, Joe Davison, Sam Shleifer, Patrick von Platen, Clara Ma, Yacine Jernite, Julien Plu, Canwen Xu, Teven Le Scao, Sylvain Gugger, Mariama Drame, Quentin Lhoest, and Alexander M. Rush. 2019. Huggingface's transformers: State-of-the-art natural language processing. *ArXiv*, abs/1910.03771.

Zhilin Yang, Zihang Dai, Yiming Yang, Jaime Carbonell, Ruslan Salakhutdinov, and Quoc V. Le. 2019. XLNet: Generalized Autoregressive Pretraining for Language Understanding. *arXiv e-prints*, page arXiv:1906.08237, June.

Adams Wei Yu, David Dohan, Quoc Le, Thang Luong, Rui Zhao, and Kai Chen. 2018. Fast and accurate reading comprehension by combining self-attention and convolution. In *International Conference on Learning Representations*.

Bei Yu. 2008. An evaluation of text classification methods for literary study. *Literary and Linguistic Computing*, 23(3):327–343, 09.

Bianca Zadrozny. 2004. Learning and evaluating classifiers under sample selection bias. In *Proceedings of the Twenty-First International Conference on Machine Learning*, ICML '04, page 114, New York, NY, USA. Association for Computing Machinery.

ERRANT: Assessing and Improving Grammatical Error Type Classification

Katerina Korre
Department of Informatics
Athens University of Economics
and Business, Greece
katkorre95@aueb.gr

John Pavlopoulos
Department of Computer
and System Sciences
Stockholm University, Sweden
ioannis@dsv.su.se

Abstract

Grammatical Error Correction (GEC) is the task of correcting different types of errors in written texts. To manage this task, large amounts of annotated data that contain erroneous sentences are required. This data, however, is usually annotated according to each annotator's standards, making it difficult to manage multiple sets of data at the same time. The recently introduced Error Annotation Toolkit (ERRANT) tackled this problem by presenting a way to automatically annotate data that contain grammatical errors, while also providing a standardisation for annotation. ERRANT extracts the errors and classifies them into error types, in the form of an edit that can be used in the creation of GEC systems, as well as for grammatical error analysis. However, we observe that certain errors are falsely or ambiguously classified. This could obstruct any qualitative or quantitative grammatical error type analysis, as the results would be inaccurate. In this work, we use a sample of the FCE coprus (Yannakoudakis et al., 2011) for secondary error type annotation and we show that up to 39% of the annotations of the most frequent type should be re-classified. Our corrections will be publicly released, so that they can serve as the starting point of a broader, collaborative, ongoing correction process.

1 Introduction

Grammatical Error Correction (GEC) is the task of correcting different types of errors in written texts, usually by taking erroneous sentences as input and transforming them into correct ones. This can be achieved with a variety or even combination of techniques, such as language modeling (Bryant and Briscoe, 2018), statistical machine translation (Katsumata and Komachi, 2019), and neural machine translation (Grundkiewicz and Junczys-Dowmunt, 2018). An important step that is usually taken in these techniques is error tagging, namely "when all errors in the corpus have been annotated with the help of a standardized system of error tags" (Granger, 2003). Error tagging (or error classification) is of utmost importance as it contributes to sentence transformations in a GEC system, when the error is mapped to the correction through special tags, such as in (Omelianchuk et al., 2020). The most popular error tagger to date is the grammatical ERRor ANnotation Toolkit (ERRANT), which automatically extracts and categorizes errors from parallel original and corrected texts (Bryant et al., 2017). By employing a rule-based classifier, ERRANT is able to expand to other languages, such as German (Boyd, 2018), Spanish (Davidson et al., 2020) and Czech (Náplava and Straka, 2019). This fact makes it particularly important for second language (L2) learning, where it can provide automatic evaluation of GEC systems in several languages (Boyd, 2018; Náplava and Straka, 2019; Davidson et al., 2020). This work suggests an ERRANT improvement, by observing a major shortcoming that currently applies and suggesting the way for it to be addressed. More specific, the contributions of this work are summarised to the following:

- We demonstrate a number of false or ambiguous classifications, using a sample of the FCE dataset (Yannakoudakis et al., 2011). Although the error classifier has been evaluated to some degree (Bryant et al., 2017), we firmly believe that more investigation is needed.

Proceedings of LaTeCH-CLfL 2020, pages 85–89
Barcelona, Spain (Online), December 12, 2020.

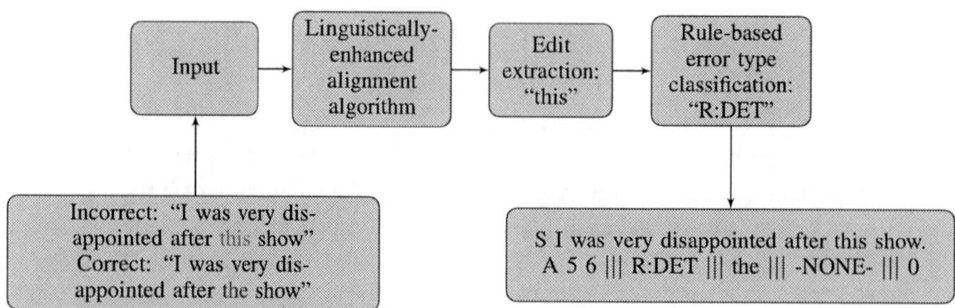

Figure 1: ERRANT system demonstration. After the input, the linguistically enhanced-algorithm aligns the two parallel sentences by making sure that items with similar linguistic properties are aligned. R:DET means that the determiner 'this' needs to be replaced with the determiner 'the'.

- We suggest re-classifications of the detected faulty items. In specific, we estimate that 39% of what has been classified as error type OTHER (the most frequent type), should have been classified to other, known error types (e.g., R:VERB).

- We publicly release our detected false classifications and our suggested re-classifications, in order to initiate a collaborative, ongoing correction process of improving the FCE dataset, which we will use for a future robust training of machine learning classifiers. In this way, we believe that any ERRANT evaluation scorers can be improved (e.g., ERRANT was employed by the most recent Grammatical Error Correction shared task: BEA-2019 (Bryant et al., 2019)).

We will first present our approach to analysing the mis-classification problem. Then we will discuss our observations on mis-classification frequencies and patterns, along with possible implications in GEC.

2 Methodology

For the purposes of this study, we are only concerned with the FCE corpus (Yannakoudakis et al., 2011). We used the FCE data file from the BEA-2019 shared task which was in M2 format and included all the extracted edits, error types and corrections. A thorough exploratory data analysis showed that the most frequent error type was R:OTHER (see Figure 2), meaning that something in the sentence needs to be replaced with something else that does not fit into a certain category. Also, there were errors of type M:OTHER and U:OTHER, i.e. something is missing and something is unnecessary, respectively. We focused our analysis only on sentences containing the most frequent error type, namely OTHER. We

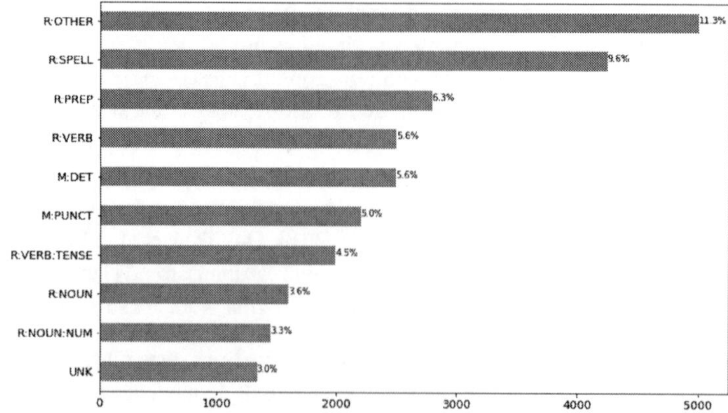

Figure 2: 21 most frequent error types in the FCE dataset, where R:OTHER type errors comprise the most frequent error type.

Code	Meaning	Description	Example
ADJ:FORM	Adjective Form	Comparative/Superlative adjective errors	more easy (easier)
ORTH	Orthography	Case and/or whitespace errors	Bestfriend (instead of best friend)
VERB:INFL	Verb inflection	Missaplication of tense morphology	getted (got), fliped (flipped)

Table 1: Three main error categories selected out of the 25 presented in (Bryant et al., 2017), serving as examples of the classification.

sampled the first 100 sentences from the FCE corpus that contain OTHER type errors (incl. M:OTHER and U:OTHER) and we manually re-labeled each of them. All of our re-classifications are publicly released as an XLSX file,[1] along with the original uncorrected sentences, the starting and ending offsets, the suggested correction, and any comments.

3 Results & Discussion

According to our re-classification, 39% of the errors could have been placed in other categories (i.e., 39 errors out of the sample of 100 sentences with one error each). Given that OTHER is the most frequent error type, a large number of sentences of the FCE corpus could potentially be re-classified to other categories. If this percentage applied to the whole FCE dataset, this would mean that 2724 out of the 6984 OTHER errors, are currently mistakenly tagged as OTHER.

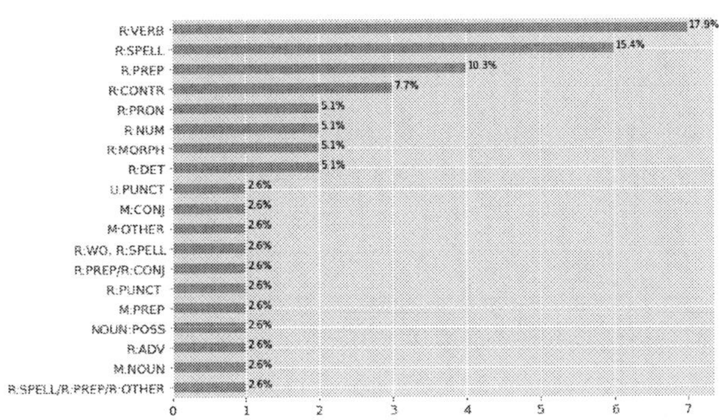

Figure 3: Error type frequencies (prev. tagged as OTHER).

The most frequent error type that was classified as OTHER was R:VERB, namely a word in the sentence has to be replaced with a verb. Spelling mistakes (R:SPELL) were also very common, accounting for about 15% of the sample. Preposition replacements (R:PREP) comprised about 10% of the sample. There were errors that were placed in other categories, as well, but as the figure shows, they account for smaller percentages.

A more qualitative demonstration is presented in Table 2. Examples 1, 3 and 4 in Table 2 contain preposition replacement errors. Example 1 and 4 are cases that possibly reflect a greater issue of ERRANT. In particular, ERRANT seems to find it easier to properly classify errors that belong to the same part of speech, or POS in short, as their correction, possibly as a result of its linguistically-enhanced alignment figure, which aligns items that are similar linguistically (Bryant et al., 2017).

In the examples, the words 'because' and 'and' are conjunctions and need to be replaced with the prepositions 'for' and 'at' respectively. Therefore, we are dealing with different POS. ERRANT ignores the option to classify the errors as R:PREP (our suggestion), and classifies them as R:OTHER instead. The specific mis-classification could be explained if we take into consideration the linguistically-enhanced alignment algorithm, which aligns linguistically similar items (see Figure 1). Because conjunctions and prepositions are different POS, ERRANT fails to assign the correct error type.

This is not the case for example 3 where the wrong preposition is replaced with a correct preposition, yet ERRANT does not provide the correct classification again. ERRANT seems to be also neglecting grammatical rules which have possibly not been implemented during the creation of ERRANT (see Figure 1 for the annotation process). For example, in sentence 2, the original sentence contains a wrong determiner 'a' in 'a person' and needs to be substituted with 'one'. In this case, the cardinal number 'one' becomes the determiner, hence the suggested error classification R:DET. Example 5 clearly con-

---

[1] https://github.com/katkorre/ERRANT-reclassification

tains a spelling mistake, but has been overlooked by ERRANT and has been put in the R:OTHER category. The error in example 6 was re-classified from R:OTHER to R:VERB. A hypothesis for the initial mis-classification could be that 'put in' is a phrasal verb, and again the linguistically-enhanced alignment algorithm prevented the correct classification. The last example could be re-classified either as R:PRON or as R:SPELL. The inability of the tool to choose between the annotation could be the reason behind the mis-classificaion.

No	FCE Sentence	Offsets	Correction	Old type	New type
1	On the other hand , the theatre restaurant was closed because unknown reasons.	10 11	for	R:OTHER	R:PREP
2	There was only a person who used to call her by this name .	3 4	one	R:OTHER	R:DET
3	I want to thak you for preparing such a good programme for us and especially for taking us to the river trip to Greenwich..	18 19	on	R:OTHER	R:PREP
4	It is in the Central Exhibition Hall and will start and ten o'clock and finish at five o'clock in the evening .	10 11	at	R:OTHER	R:PREP
5	What are you dong here, why are n't you at school ? '	3 4	doing	R:OTHER	R:SPELL
6	Also supermarket owners have put in a vast amount of money to find out the best way to place goods in order to get the most profit .	4 6	invested	R:OTHER	R:VERB
7	Your sincerely	0 1	Yours	R:OTHER	R:PRON/ R:SPELL

Table 2: Example FCE sentences that are tagged as OTHER (5th column), along with their token-based offsets (3rd column, also highlighted in red in the text) and corrections (4th column). The last column presents our suggested re-classification.

Issues like the aforementioned must not be ignored. A more robust categorization might possibly lead to a more accurate grammatical error detection and, consequently, more efficient grammatical error correction systems.

ERRANT was used in the most recent Grammatical Error Correction shared task (BEA-2019), where all system output was automatically annotated with the scorer of the toolkit (Bryant et al., 2019). Then, the automatically inferred error type was used by the participants to evaluate their performance per type. What this means, however, is that the participants are now misjudging their systems. If we assume the existence of an oracle system that always detects correctly the error type in a (FCE) sentence, then approx. 20% of the correctly detected R:VERB errors (see Fig. 3) would be considered as OTHER errors that were miss-classified, hindering the true performance of the system for the R:VERB category.

4   Conclusion

ERRANT has definitely provided an alternative, and to some degree, efficient way of annotating datasets for GEC. This is particularly important for GEC systems to be able to assess their own performance and be improved. However, we show that there is still much room for improvement regarding error type classification. Although standardizing corpora can alleviate the annotators from some of the time-consuming labour, incorrect automatic classification might deprive a GEC system from useful information. Especially, in the case of teaching, where automatic feedback is gradually gaining ground, a precise error type classification is mandatory.

In the foreground, more grammar rules should be introduced during the configuration of ERRANT. This will allow a more thorough classification, and therefore more efficient error detection and correction systems. In addition, a qualitative evaluation by linguists could ensure the quality of the classification and provide professional feedback. We release our sample of second order FCE annotations, to pose the ground for the development of a larger reference dataset. Potentially, this could be used either as a ground truth evaluation set (e.g., by rule-based systems) or as a training set by more robust machine learning classifiers.

Our next research step would be to delve into the issue of false or ambiguous error type classification further by examining and evaluating more types of errors extracted with ERRANT. We would also like to design a more systematic and thorough error classification system, by employing transfer learning and deep learning approaches.

References

Adriane Boyd. 2018. Using Wikipedia edits in low resource grammatical error correction. In *Proceedings of the 2018 EMNLP Workshop W-NUT: The 4th Workshop on Noisy User-generated Text*, pages 79–84, Brussels, Belgium, November. Association for Computational Linguistics.

Christopher Bryant and Ted Briscoe. 2018. Language model based grammatical error correction without annotated training data. In *Proceedings of the Thirteenth Workshop on Innovative Use of NLP for Building Educational Applications*, pages 247–253, New Orleans, Louisiana, June. Association for Computational Linguistics.

Christopher Bryant, Mariano Felice, and Ted Briscoe. 2017. Automatic annotation and evaluation of error types for grammatical error correction. In *Proceedings of the 55th Annual Meeting of the Association for Computational Linguistics (Volume 1: Long Papers)*, pages 793–805, Vancouver, Canada, July. Association for Computational Linguistics.

Christopher Bryant, Mariano Felice, Øistein E. Andersen, and Ted Briscoe. 2019. The BEA-2019 shared task on grammatical error correction. In *Proceedings of the Fourteenth Workshop on Innovative Use of NLP for Building Educational Applications*, pages 52–75, Florence, Italy, August. Association for Computational Linguistics.

Sam Davidson, Aaron Yamada, Paloma Fernandez Mira, Agustina Carando, Claudia H. Sanchez Gutierrez, and Kenji Sagae. 2020. Developing NLP tools with a new corpus of learner Spanish. In *Proceedings of The 12th Language Resources and Evaluation Conference*, pages 7238–7243, Marseille, France, May. European Language Resources Association.

Sylviane Granger. 2003. Error-tagged learner corpora and call: A promising synergy. *CALICO Journal*, 20:465–480, 01.

Roman Grundkiewicz and Marcin Junczys-Dowmunt. 2018. Near human-level performance in grammatical error correction with hybrid machine translation. In *Proceedings of the 2018 Conference of the North American Chapter of the Association for Computational Linguistics: Human Language Technologies, Volume 2 (Short Papers)*, pages 284–290, New Orleans, Louisiana, June. Association for Computational Linguistics.

Satoru Katsumata and Mamoru Komachi. 2019. Towards unsupervised grammatical error correction using statistical machine translation with synthetic comparable corpus.

Jakub Náplava and Milan Straka. 2019. Grammatical error correction in low-resource scenarios.

Kostiantyn Omelianchuk, Vitaliy Atrasevych, Artem Chernodub, and Oleksandr Skurzhanskyi. 2020. Gector – grammatical error correction: Tag, not rewrite.

Helen Yannakoudakis, Ted Briscoe, and Ben Medlock. 2011. A new dataset and method for automatically grading ESOL texts. In *Proceedings of the 49th Annual Meeting of the Association for Computational Linguistics: Human Language Technologies*, pages 180–189, Portland, Oregon, USA, June. Association for Computational Linguistics.

Life still goes on:
Analysing Australian WW1 Diaries through Distant Reading

Ashley Dennis-Henderson, Matthew Roughan, Lewis Mitchell, Jonathan Tuke

ARC Centre of Excellence for Mathematical and Statistical Frontiers (ACEMS)

School of Mathematical Sciences, The University of Adelaide

`{ashley.dennis-henderson,matthew.roughan,lewis.mitchell,simon.tuke}@adelaide.edu.au`

Abstract

An increasing amount of historic data is now available in digital (text) formats. This gives quantitative researchers an opportunity to use distant reading techniques, as opposed to traditional close reading, in order to analyse larger quantities of historic data. Distant reading allows researchers to view overall patterns within the data and reduce researcher bias. One such data set that has recently been transcribed is a collection of over 500 Australian World War I (WW1) diaries held by the State Library of New South Wales. Here we apply distant reading techniques to this corpus to understand what soldiers wrote about and how they felt over the course of the war. Extracting dates accurately is important as it allows us to perform our analysis over time, however, it is very challenging due to the variety of date formats and abbreviations diarists use. But with that data, topic modelling and sentiment analysis can then be applied to show trends, for instance, that despite the horrors of war, Australians in WW1 primarily wrote about their everyday routines and experiences. Our results detail some of the challenges likely to be encountered by quantitative researchers intending to analyse historical texts, and provide some approaches to these issues.

1 Introduction

World War I (WW1) was a defining event of the 20th century, and impacted millions worldwide. Researchers have studied the war, especially the experiences of those on the front lines. Primarily, this has been done through *close reading* of primary sources such as diaries and letters. However, recent advances in computational methods to analyse large text corpora offers the opportunity to analyse sources such as these through *distant reading*. Distant reading involves the application of mathematical and computational techniques from natural language processing (NLP) to perform statistical analysis of text (Jänicke et al., 2015). Distant reading has several advantages, including the ability to analyse large quantities of data and see overall patterns as well as the reduction of researcher bias. Further, distant and close reading can be combined such that interesting patterns found through distant reading can be more closely examined using close reading to determine why they occur. This work aims to use distant reading to understand what Australian soldiers went through and how they felt over the course of WW1, by analysing a unique historical data set: a large collection of transcriptions of Australian soldiers' diaries, held by the State Library of New South Wales. To our knowledge this paper represents the first NLP analysis of this data set.

This research takes advantage of the fact that diaries contain temporal information. However, extracting dates is a difficult task due to the varying manner in which dates can be written. This is further complicated by the desire to focus on the dates on which entries were written and not dates mentioned within the entries as these may refer to times and events from outside the war or at least out of the context of the current entry. In order to extract and clean dates we use a combination of regular expressions and optimisation.

Proceedings of LaTeCH-CLfL 2020, pages 90–104
Barcelona, Spain (Online), December 12, 2020.

Once dates were extracted we were able to apply topic modelling and sentiment analysis as a function of time. We are able to detect topics corresponding to particular developments of the war, and the associated sentiment for those periods. Further, we show that the diarists wrote more about everyday experiences, e.g., the time of day and meals, than they did about training and battles. This might be surprising as the war was one of the most traumatic events of the twentieth century and conventional historical narratives concentrate on the pain and suffering of the soldiers. However, in the diaries, we see the war's participants adapting their everyday lives to their circumstances, and in fact their overall sentiment across the war is surprisingly positive.

2   Corpus

We focus on Australian WW1 diaries held by the State Library of New South Wales. After the war ended, the European War Collecting Project was created by Principal Librarian William Ifould and the trustees of the Library (State Library of New South Wales, 2019). Their aim was to collect documents, including diaries, letters, war narratives, memoirs and photographs, which gave the experiences and personal feelings of those who served. In total, this collection has 966 documents, 557 of which are non-empty war diaries. A complete breakdown of the collection is given in Table 1. Since collecting these documents, the library has scanned them and used crowd sourcing to transcribe them, giving researchers access to digital (text) versions of the documents.

Type	Number	# Pages	# Words	# Authors
Diary	577	60,004	9,266,353	236
Letter	183	18,497	3,029,163	141
Letter-Diary	22	3,955	639,184	16
War Narrative	32	2,370	624,618	28
Other	152	10,418	2,159,348	111
Total	**966**	**95,244**	**15,718,666**	

Table 1: The number of each type of document in the NSW State Library Collection, along with the number of pages, words and authors. The "Other" category includes documents such as telegrams, photos, postcards, scrapbooks, and newspaper clippings. Note, there are a total of 577 diaries in this collection, however, 20 of the transcribed diaries were empty, and so we only analyse 557 diaries.

These documents can be individually downloaded from the State Library's website (State Library of New South Wales, 2020), however, we obtained the corpus directly from the Library. Before this corpus could be used it went through a variety of cleaning steps. First, the raw data was converted to a single text file per document, and a metadata table was created by using regular expressions to extract information from the document titles. Then dates had to be extracted so that we could perform analysis over time. Raw dates were extracted using regular expressions, however, several issues were found in these raw dates requiring us to clean them through optimisation. More information regarding this is given in Section 4.1. Finally, we changed all text to lowercase, removed numbers and punctuation, singularised words, converted abbreviations to the full word, and for topic modelling we removed stop words. Converting to lowercase, singularising words and converting abbreviations were all done to ensure that the various versions of a word are considered as the same word when performing our analysis. For example, "kill", "killing", and "Kills" all have the same base word: "kill". The stop words we removed were based on the `stop_words` data set in the `tidytext` package (Silge and Robinson, 2006) in R. Figure 1 shows the number of words in our diary corpus per month after this process. Unsurprisingly, the majority of entries were written between August 1914 and December 1919 — Britain, and consequently

Australia joined WW1 on August 4, 1914, and although the armistice was signed in November 1918, it took some time for the more than 100,000 Australian soldiers still in the field to be repatriated.

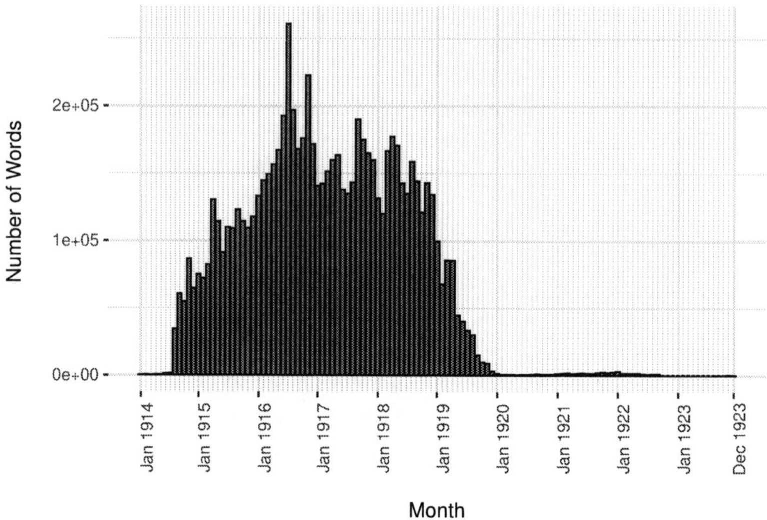

Figure 1: Number of words written in our entire diary collection per month. The majority of entries are written between August 1914 and December 1919, however there were some entries as late as 1923.

3   Related Work and Background

3.1   Analysis of Historic Documents

Our corpus has previously been studied by Caulfield (2013) and Cochrane (2015). However, their analysis was based on close reading of a small subsection of the diaries. As far as we are aware, distant reading techniques have not previously been applied to this corpus. However, distant reading techniques have been broadly applied to other historic documents. For example, Boschetti et al. (2014) used computational techniques to analyse Italian war bulletins as part of the *Memories of War* project and Ahmad et al. (2012) developed a tool to map spelling from medieval documents to modern spellings, amongst numerous other examples. Analysis of diaries presents an additional challenge as to use the important temporal data, we must extract a large number of dates.

3.2   Analysis Techniques

Topic modelling is based on the idea that documents are made up of a series of topics, which in turn are a probability distribution over words (Steyvers and Griffiths, 2007). Currently, the primary method to perform topic modelling is LDA (Latent Dirichlet Allocation) which was initially introduced by Blei et al. (2003). For a description of the mathematics behind LDA please see Blei et al. (2003). Sentiment analysis aims to determine the attitude or emotion of the author towards the content of the text. An overview of sentiment analysis can be found in Pang and Lee (2008) or Taboada (2016). An example of the use of sentiment analysis can be seen in Burghardt et al. (2019) who applied sentiment analysis to the plays of G. E. Lessing. Additional details of our use of these approaches will be provided in the following section.

4   Methods

4.1   Date Extraction

Extracting accurate dates from the diaries is important as we wish to perform our analysis over time. However, this is difficult due to the many ways in which dates are written. Raw dates were extracted using regular expressions, attempting to account for the various date formats, possible abbreviations of month and day of the week names, punctuation, and that some dates were written in French. After extracting these raw dates three main issues were discovered. First many dates were missing the month or year values, as from a human perspective it is not necessary to include this information if it was included in a previous date. In these diaries 13.91% of dates were missing the month and 53.76% were missing the year. Second, diarists sometimes wrote the wrong date, either due to not knowing the exact date or accidentally writing down the wrong day/month. The final issue is that we only want to extract the dates when the entries were written. However, regular expressions will also pick up dates of events mentioned within an entry as well as strings that look like dates such as *1st battalion*, neither of which we wish to focus on here.

We overcame these issues by creating an optimisation program which outputs dates as close as possible to the true date by (i) keeping the dates close to their raw extracted version; (ii) keeping them close to the previous date in sequence; (iii) maintaining the sequence of dates; and (iv) keeping them in the range determined by the known start and end dates of the diary. The optimisation can also exclude dates that appear out of sequence, presenting them as references. We will provide code to perform this task on request.

4.2 Topic Modelling

In this paper we focus on using LDA (Latent Dirichlet Allocation) to perform topic modelling. This model was implemented using the `topicmodels` package (Grün and Hornik, 2011) in R, using Gibbs Sampling with 10 topics and a randomly chosen seed of 1915.

The number of topics used was chosen based on four methods, by Arun et al. (2010), Cao et al. (2008), Deveaud et al. (2014), and Griffiths and Steyvers (2004), which were implemented using the `ldatuning` package (Nikita, 2020) in R. The results from each method are given in Figure 2. Based on this, we find that the optimal number of topics for Griffiths2004 is 8 or more, for CaoJuan2009 is 17 or more, for Arun2010 is 6, 7 or 10, and for Deveaud2014 is 8 - 12. We chose to use 10 topics since this falls in the range of best parameters for three of the methods.

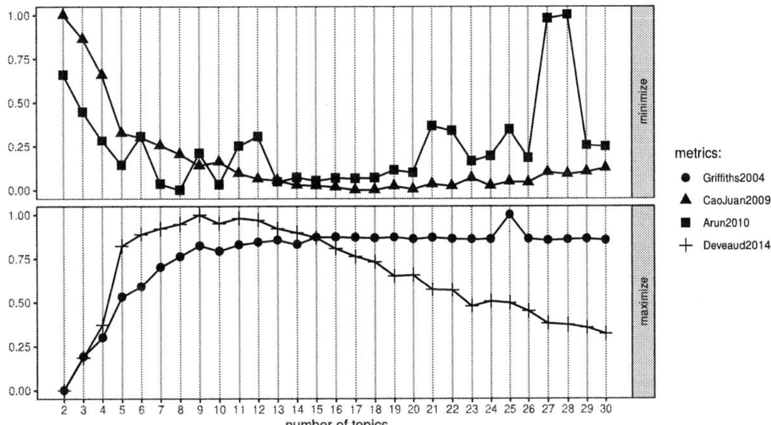

Figure 2: Results found by applying the four methods for determining the number of topics created by Arun et al. (2010), Cao et al. (2008), Deveaud et al. (2014), and Griffiths and Steyvers (2004). We chose 10 topics as it falls in the optimal range for three approaches.

4.3 Sentiment Analysis

There are three general categories of sentiment analysis: dictionary based methods (DBMs), supervised learning methods, and unsupervised learning methods (Reagan et al., 2017). We focus on DBMs as they can be applied to corpora where there is no previous known information regarding the sentiment. DBMs compare the terms within the corpus with a dictionary of terms with known sentiment values. Let $f^T(w)$

be the frequency of word w in text T, and $s_D(w)$ be the sentiment of word w in dictionary D, then the average sentiment of the text is given by (Reagan et al., 2017)

$$s_D^T = \frac{\sum_{w \in D} s_D(w) f^T(w)}{\sum_{w \in D} f^T(w)}. \tag{1}$$

For our analysis we tested the following dictionaries: AFINN, ANEW, Hului, Loughran-Mcdonald, NRC, SenticNet, SentiWordNet, and Syuzhet. These dictionaries primarily come from the `lexicon` package (Rinker, 2018) in R. The two dictionaries not available through this package are AFINN, which was accessed using the `tidytext` package (Silge and Robinson, 2006), and ANEW which was obtained from Andrew Reagan's GitHub folder: `https://github.com/andyreagan/labMT-simple/tree/master/labMTsimple/data/ANEW`. We can consider the percentage of unique words in our diaries which appear in the sentiment dictionaries, and compare this to the Brown Corpus, a standard corpus in NLP analysis. The Brown Corpus contains 1,006,770 words, including 45,215 unique words, from a collection of documents printed in the United States in 1961 (Francis and Kucera, 1971). The words contained in the Brown Corpus were obtained using the `zipfR` package (Evert and Baroni, 2007). Table 2 gives the number of words and possible sentiment values each dictionary has as well as the percentage of unique words in our diaries and the Brown Corpus which appear in the dictionaries. We note that approximately twice as many unique words from the Brown Corpus are covered by these dictionaries. This is despite the fact that our diary corpus contains more unique words (84,955 words) than the Brown corpus does. This is likely because none of these dictionaries were created for wartime text.

			Percentage (%)	
Dictionary	**Num. Words**	**Sentiment Values**	**WW1 Diaries**	**Brown Corpus**
AFINN	2,477	$(-5, 5)$	2.03	4.35
ANEW	1,034	$(1, 9)$	1.14	2.12
Hului	6,874	$\{1, 0, -1.05, -1, -2\}$	5.09	9.86
Lougran-Mcdonald	2,702	$\{-1, 1\}$	1.59	3.80
NRC	5,468	$\{-1, 1\}$	5.49	10.09
SenticNet	23,626	$(-1, 1)$	14.71	26.67
SentiWordNet	20,093	$(-1, 1)$	7.83	14.01
Syuzhet	10,738	$(-1, 1)$	8.43	16.85

Table 2: The number of words and possible sentiment values in each of the eight sentiment dictionaries, as well as the percentage of unique words in the diaries and the Brown Corpus which appear in each dictionary. We can see that SenticNet provides the broadest coverage.

In order to compare the results from different dictionaries they are required to be on the same rating scale. As five of the dictionaries are already on the scale $(-1, 1)$ we chose to convert the others to this. AFINN and ANEW were converted to this scale using the formula:

$$x_{\text{new}} = \left(\frac{\max_{\text{new}} - \min_{\text{new}}}{\max_{\text{old}} - \min_{\text{old}}} \right) (x_{\text{old}} - \min_{\text{old}}) + \min_{\text{new}}, \tag{2}$$

where x_{old} and x_{new} are the old and new value, respectively, $[\min_{\text{old}}, \max_{\text{old}}]$ is the old value range, and $[\min_{\text{new}}, \max_{\text{new}}]$ is the new value range. The Huliu lexicon was converted to the range $(-1, 1)$ by converting any word with a sentiment score of -2 to a score of -1. This could be done as a score of -2 was given to phrases that are always negative, e.g., "too much fun" (Rinker, 2019).

For both topic modelling and sentiment analysis we considered a "document" to be all of the diary entries written in a particular month.

When graphing our results we have applied a rolling mean using the `rollmean` function in the `zoo` package (Zeileis and Grothendieck, 2005) in R, with a rolling window of $k = 5$, in order to smooth out noise in the data. Due to the lack of data in 1923, as seen in Figure 1, it is not possible to calculate this rolling mean and hence, results for this year are not included.

5 Analysis

5.1 Topic Modelling

The most probable words for each of our 10 topics are shown in Appendix A. Based on the most probable words, we selected names for each of our topics, hence our topics are: *Everyday Life*, *War at Sea*, *Egypt*, *Gallipoli*, *In the Trenches (Beginning)*, *In the Trenches (Middle)*, *In the Trenches (End)*, *White Christmas*, *After the Armistice*, and *Home Again*. Note, the most probable words in all three *In the Trenches* topics are regarding battles, the Western Front and the Middle East. Hence, we differentiate these topics as *beginning*, *middle* and *end*, based on where they peak in Figure 3. The proportion of each of these topics is shown as a function of time in Figure 3.

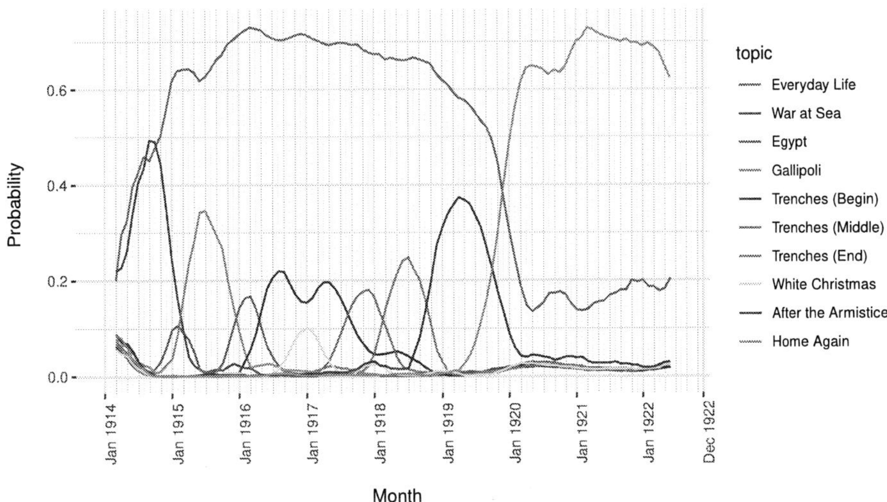

Figure 3: The proportion of each topic obtained from our LDA model, over time. Note that a rolling mean with $k = 5$ has been applied to each point.

Based on the most probable words as well as when the topics peak in Figure 3, several of these topics relate to specific developments of the war. *War at Sea* corresponds to the Australian occupation of German New Guinea and the sinking of the German raider the Emden. *Egypt* corresponds to the training of Australian troops on the outskirts of Cairo and battles around Egypt and the Suez Canal. *Gallipoli* corresponds to the Gallipoli Campaign, which for many Australian soldiers was their first experience in battle. The three *In the Trenches* topics cover the period when Australians were fighting on the Western Front and in the Middle East. The peaks in these three topics most likely correspond to specific battles such as the Battle of Romani (August 1916), the Second Battle of Arras (April-May 1917), the Battle of Jerusalem (November-December 1917), and the Battle of Hamel (July 1918). *After the Armistice* corresponds to the period after the armistice was signed in November 1918 that Australian soldiers had to wait before being sent home. For some soldiers it took up to a year to be repatriated and in this time they travelled around France and Britain as well as receiving vocational training from the AIF (Australian Imperial Force) (DVA, 2020). We also have two more general topics. *Everyday Life* is consistently the most prominent topic until December 1919. This topic includes words related to everyday things such as the time of day and meals. This shows that whilst the diarists did write about war related things, such as training and battles, they primarily focused on their ordinary day-to-day activities. After 1919 the *Home*

Again topic becomes most prominent. This is expected as this topic contains words related to being back in Australia, such as "mum", "dad" and "shopping", and corresponds to when the soldiers would have returned home.

5.2 Sentiment Analysis

Figure 4 gives the sentiment scores for our diaries over time for the eight sentiment dictionaries we considered as well as the average over these dictionaries. From this graph we first note that five of the dictionaries: AFINN, Huliu, Loughran-Mcdonald, NRC, and Syuzhet, follow the same general pattern. Further, SenticNet and SentiWordNet have a similar trend. Based on Table 2 we know that ANEW covers the least amount of words in our corpus, whilst SenticNet and SentiWordNet cover the most. This shows that our analysis is dependent on the words covered in the dictionaries. We also observe more variability in our sentiment scores in the first half of 1914 and from 1920 onwards. This would be due to only having a small amount of data for those periods as seen in Figure 1.

In the next section we compare our average sentiment curve with our topic model to understand why the sentiment peaks and dips at certain times.

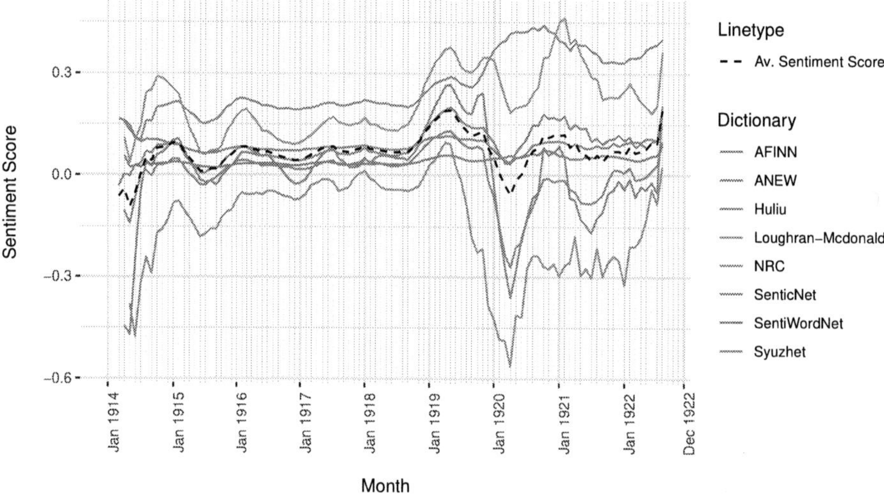

Figure 4: Sentiment scores over time for the eight dictionaries: AFINN, ANEW, Huliu, Loughran-Mcdonald, NRC, SenticNet, SentiWordNet, and Syuzhet, as well as the average of these dictionaries. Note, that before graphing we have applied a rolling mean, with $k = 5$, to each of the dictionaries.

5.3 Topic Modelling and Sentiment Analysis

The average sentiment curve shown in Figure 4 has several peaks and dips in sentiment. We investigate what these correspond to by comparing our sentiment with our topic model. Due to the variability in individual sentiment dictionaries prior to August 1914 and after December 1919 we do not consider these periods. Further, we exclude the *Everyday Life* and *Home Again* topics as they are prominent over large periods of time and hence are not likely to contribute to particular peaks and dips in sentiment. Figure 5 gives the comparison between topic probabilities and average sentiment scores.

In Figure 5 we note there are peaks in sentiment corresponding to peaks in the *Egypt* and *After the Armistice* topics, whilst there are dips in sentiment corresponding to the peaks in the *Gallipoli* and *White Christmas* topics. When arriving in Egypt for training, the soldiers would most likely have been excited about being in a new country and be keen to prove themselves in battle. This, combined with the fact that whilst in Egypt the men were able to take small trips into Cairo and around the pyramids, would lead to a more positive sentiment for that period. Contrary to this, the Gallipoli campaign would have been

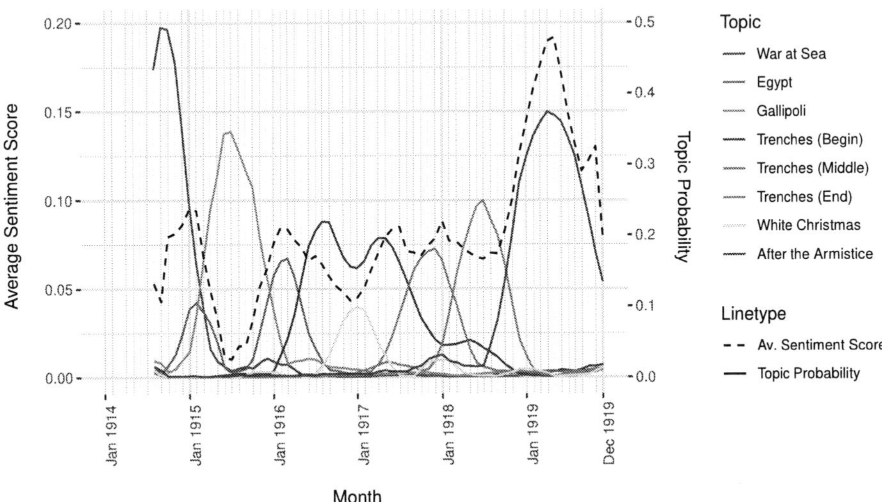

Figure 5: Average sentiment analysis scores compared to the topic probabilities (except the *Everyday Life* and *Home Again* topics).

the first battle experience for many of the soldiers leading to a more negative sentiment. Thomas Munro writes:

> "It is an awful sight to see the dead and wounded on both sides, lying out and being walked on, no possibilite [sic] to bring them in or bury them, Some of our men have been out there a month and are still there. The stench would knock you down."

One of the top 40 most probable words in the *White Christmas* topic is "miserable", suggesting that the cold weather lead to many having a more negative sentiment. Through close reading of the diaries over the months surrounding January 1917 we find several negative comments regarding the cold and wet weather. For instance, Langford Colley-Priest writes

> "Raining heavily all day which made the conditions more miserable. The mud & slush is terrible."

Further, whilst some men had a good Christmas, others didn't. The contrast between these Christmas' are seen in the following quotes:

> "Christmas dinner and tea were very merry, the rations being supplemented by a lot of luxuries ... also by plum pudding ... ", Hector McLean

> "Cold, miserable & hungry, we filed up to the cook house for our "Christmas dinner" of Bully beef Stew and buscuits [sic], as our rations were not yet to hand and our Christmas comforts were delayed somewhere.", Tom Taylor

It is not surprising that the sentiment rose after the armistice was signed. This rise in sentiment is further strengthened by the fact whilst waiting to be repatriated back to Australia soldiers spent their time travelling around France and Britain, and attending sport matches and plays (DVA, 2020).

Overall, our average sentiment during the war is always slightly positive which contradicts the typical perception of the war as horrific experience. This is most likely because the diarists predominantly wrote about everyday activities, which unlike battles, are not necessarily negative.

6 Conclusion and Future Work

This research aimed to analyse Australian WW1 diaries in order to determine what the soldiers wrote about and how they felt over the course of the war. Through the application of distant reading techniques we have seen that we can analyse large amounts of data to determine trends. Interestingly, while many people typically think of the war as a horrific experience we find that the diarists primarily wrote about their day-to-day activities. As such the diaries had an overall slightly positive sentiment, which is consistent with the positivity bias seen across human languages (Dodds et al., 2015), but is surprising for this particular corpus.

We focused on DBMs for sentiment, and found that the dictionaries used covered less of the diaries than standard texts such as the Brown Corpus. This suggests that DBMs may not be the most accurate method for determining sentiment in WW1 diaries and as such in the future we will investigate other sentiment analysis techniques such as embedding-based methods to determine if they are more applicable. Further, in the future we will write a paper detailing the difficulties with date extraction, as well as our approach and the accuracy of our method, as this is not a trivial issue.

Acknowledgements

We acknowledge the State Library of New South Wales for providing the data which made this research possible.

References

Mushtaq Ahmad, Stefan Gruner, and Muhammed Tanvir Afzal. 2012. Computational Analysis of Medieval Manuscripts: A New Tool for Analysis and Mapping of Medieval Documents to Modern Orthography. *Journal of Universal Computer Science*, 18(20):2750–2770.

R Arun, V Suresh, C.E Veni Madhavan, and M Narasimha Murty. 2010. On Finding the Natural Number of Topics with Latent Dirichlet Allocation: Some Observations. In M.J. Zaki, J.X. Yu, B Ravindran, and V Pudi, editors, *Advances in Knowledge Discovery and Data Mining, Part I*, pages 391 – 402. Springer, Berlin. Heidelberg.

David M Blei, Andrew Y Ng, and Michael I Jordan. 2003. Latent Dirichlet Allocation. *Journal of Machine Learning Research*, 3:993–1022.

Federico Boschetti, Andrea Cimino, Felice Dell'orletta, Gianluca E Lebani, Lucia Passaro, Paolo Picchi, Giulia Venturi, Simonetta Montemagni, and Alessandro Lenci. 2014. Computational Analysis of Historical Documents: An Application to Italian War Bulletins in World War I and II.

Manuel Burghardt, Christian Wolff, and Thomas Schmidt. 2019. Toward Multimodal Sentiment Analysis of Historic Plays: A Case Study with Text and Audio for Lessing's Emilia Galotti. In *4th Conference of the Association Digital Humanities in the Nordic Countries*, Copenhagen.

Juan Cao, Tian Xia, Jintao Li, Yongdong Zhang, and Sheng Tang. 2008. A density-based method for adaptive LDA model selection. *Neurocomputing*, 72(7-9):1775 – 1781.

Michael Caulfield. 2013. *The unknown Anzacs : the real stories of our national legend : told through the rediscovered diaries and letters of the Anzacs who were there.* Hachette Australia, Sydney.

Peter Cochrane. 2015. 'Diamonds of the Dustheap': Diaries from the First World War. *Humanities Australia: The Journal of the Australian Academy of the Humanities*, (6):22 – 33.

Romain Deveaud, Eric SanJuan, and Patrice Bellot. 2014. Accurate and effective Latent Concept Modeling for ad hoc information retrieval. *Document Numerique*, 17(1):61–84.

Peter Sheridan Dodds, Eric M Clark, Suma Desu, Morgan R Frank, Andrew J Reagan, Jake Ryland Williams, Lewis Mitchell, Kameron Decker Harris, Isabel M Kloumann, James P Bagrow, et al. 2015. Human language reveals a universal positivity bias. *Proceedings of the National Academy of Sciences*, 112(8):2389–2394.

DVA. 2020. Repatriation of Australians in World War I. *DVA (Department of Veterans' Affairs) Anzac Portal*.

Stefan Evert and Marco Baroni. 2007. zipfR: Word Frequency Distributions in R. In *Proceedings of the 45th Annual Meeting of the Association for Computational Linguistics, Posters and Demonstrations Sessions*, Prague.

W Francis and H Kucera. 1971. Brown Corpus Manual.

Thomas L Griffiths and Mark Steyvers. 2004. Finding scientific topics. *Proceedings of the National Academy of Sciences of the United States of America*, 101:5228–5235.

Bettina Grün and Kurt Hornik. 2011. topicmodels: An R Package for Fitting Topic Models. *Journal of Statistical Software*, 40(13):1–30.

S Jänicke, G Franzini, M F Cheema, and G Scheuermann. 2015. On Close and Distant Reading in Digital Humanities: A Survey and Future Challenges. In R Borgo, F Ganovelli, and I Viola, editors, *Eurographics Conference on Visualization (EuroVis)*.

Murzintcev Nikita. 2020. ldatuning: Tuning of the Latent Dirichlet Allocation Models Parameters.

Bo Pang and Lillian Lee. 2008. Opinion mining and sentiment analysis. *Foundations and Trends in Information Retrieval*, 2(2):1–135.

Andrew J Reagan, Christopher M Danforth, Brian Tivnan, Jake Ryland Williams, and Peter Sheridan Dodds. 2017. Sentiment analysis methods for understanding large-scale texts: a case for using continuum-scored words and word shift graphs. *EPJ Data Science*, 6(1).

Tyler Rinker. 2018. lexicon: Lexicon Data.

Tyler Rinker. 2019. Package 'lexicon'.

Julia Silge and David Robinson. 2006. tidytext: Text Mining and Analysis Using Tidy Data Principles in R. *JOSS*, 1(3).

State Library of New South Wales. 2019. Personal diaries and letters from the First World War.

State Library of New South Wales. 2020. Diarists from World War I.

Mark Steyvers and Tom Griffiths. 2007. Probabilistic Topic Models. In T Landauer, D McNamara, S Dennis, and W Kintsch, editors, *Handbook of latent semantic analysis*, pages 427–448. Lawrence Erlbaum Associates Publishers.

Maite Taboada. 2016. Sentiment Analysis: An Overview from Linguistics. *Annual Review of Linguistics*, 2(1):325–347, 1.

Achim Zeileis and Gabor Grothendieck. 2005. zoo: S3 Infrastructure for Regular and Irregular Time Series. *Journal of Statistical Software*, 14(6):1–27.

Appendix A Topics

Tables 3 - 12 give the 54 most probable words for each of the topics found using topic modelling.

rank	term	beta	rank	term	beta	rank	term	beta
1	day	0.0213	19	fine	0.0033	37	troop	0.0022
2	night	0.0132	20	till	0.0032	38	battalion	0.0022
3	morning	0.0113	21	evening	0.0032	39	horse	0.0022
4	time	0.0095	22	dinner	0.0031	40	company	0.0022
5	left	0.0070	23	received	0.0030	41	train	0.0022
6	afternoon	0.0069	24	water	0.0029	42	french	0.0021
7	pm	0.0057	25	weather	0.0028	43	boy	0.0021
8	camp	0.0050	26	brigade	0.0027	44	australian	0.0021
9	letter	0.0048	27	hospital	0.0026	45	duty	0.0021
10	arrived	0.0047	28	found	0.0025	46	heavy	0.0021
11	mile	0.0043	29	town	0.0025	47	returned	0.0021
12	home	0.0043	30	passed	0.0025	48	breakfast	0.0020
13	tea	0.0042	31	usual	0.0025	49	station	0.0020
14	hour	0.0041	32	bed	0.0024	50	tonight	0.0020
15	round	0.0039	33	cold	0.0024	51	party	0.0019
16	officer	0.0038	34	lot	0.0024	52	war	0.0019
17	line	0.0037	35	parade	0.0024	53	called	0.0019
18	leave	0.0035	36	light	0.0023	54	beautiful	0.0019

Table 3: Top 54 terms for the *Everyday Life* topic with their probabilities.

rank	term	beta	rank	term	beta	rank	term	beta
1	ship	0.0157	19	port	0.0043	37	ashore	0.0024
2	sydney	0.0092	20	deck	0.0040	38	drill	0.0024
3	german	0.0088	21	harbour	0.0040	39	crew	0.0024
4	captain	0.0074	22	emden	0.0038	40	flag	0.0023
5	officer	0.0073	23	naval	0.0035	41	herbertshohe	0.0023
6	boat	0.0073	24	administrator	0.0034	42	colombo	0.0023
7	board	0.0067	25	force	0.0034	43	commander	0.0023
8	lieutenant	0.0065	26	horse	0.0033	44	australia	0.0023
9	island	0.0064	27	melbourne	0.0031	45	holme	0.0022
10	troop	0.0058	28	major	0.0030	46	returned	0.0022
11	native	0.0056	29	government	0.0029	47	brigadier	0.0021
12	colonel	0.0050	30	cruiser	0.0027	48	sight	0.0020
13	wireless	0.0049	31	station	0.0027	49	convoy	0.0020
14	message	0.0048	32	fleet	0.0027	50	military	0.0020
15	company	0.0045	33	garrison	0.0027	51	signal	0.0020
16	rabaul	0.0045	34	steamer	0.0026	52	british	0.0020
17	received	0.0044	35	berrima	0.0025	53	war	0.0019
18	sea	0.0044	36	gun	0.0025	54	prisoner	0.0019

Table 4: Top 54 terms for the *War at Sea* topic with their probabilities.

rank	term	beta	rank	term	beta	rank	term	beta
1	cairo	0.0170	19	water	0.0040	37	serapeum	0.0022
2	canal	0.0131	20	troop	0.0039	38	oclock	0.0022
3	camp	0.0103	21	kebir	0.0039	39	trench	0.0022
4	horse	0.0098	22	regiment	0.0039	40	squadron	0.0021
5	parade	0.0097	23	train	0.0039	41	piastre	0.0021
6	ship	0.0093	24	sea	0.0038	42	maadi	0.0021
7	sand	0.0088	25	suez	0.0036	43	arab	0.0021
8	tent	0.0080	26	deck	0.0035	44	colombo	0.0021
9	desert	0.0074	27	heliopoli	0.0035	45	soldier	0.0020
10	native	0.0071	28	sydney	0.0033	46	colonel	0.0020
11	el	0.0066	29	pyramid	0.0033	47	mosque	0.0020
12	drill	0.0060	30	island	0.0030	48	infantry	0.0020
13	egypt	0.0049	31	harbour	0.0028	49	christmas	0.0020
14	boat	0.0046	32	hot	0.0027	50	wharf	0.0019
15	egyptian	0.0045	33	ashore	0.0027	51	fuller	0.0019
16	tel	0.0043	34	nile	0.0027	52	signalling	0.0019
17	camel	0.0043	35	ismailia	0.0024	53	marching	0.0019
18	alexandria	0.0040	36	port	0.0023	54	fatigue	0.0019

Table 5: Top 54 terms for the *Egypt* topic with their probabilities.

rank	term	beta	rank	term	beta	rank	term	beta
1	turk	0.0194	19	hospital	0.0048	37	island	0.0029
2	trench	0.0188	20	turkish	0.0046	38	dug	0.0029
3	gun	0.0130	21	quiet	0.0046	39	alexandria	0.0028
4	shell	0.0120	22	hill	0.0041	40	landed	0.0028
5	wounded	0.0101	23	rifle	0.0041	41	hit	0.0028
6	ship	0.0093	24	cairo	0.0041	42	aeroplane	0.0028
7	fire	0.0085	25	killed	0.0040	43	fired	0.0028
8	enemy	0.0081	26	line	0.0039	44	anzac	0.0027
9	firing	0.0076	27	shot	0.0038	45	machine	0.0027
10	beach	0.0072	28	bullet	0.0037	46	warship	0.0027
11	boat	0.0065	29	bombardment	0.0035	47	sniper	0.0026
12	position	0.0064	30	ashore	0.0034	48	pm	0.0026
13	shrapnel	0.0059	31	heavy	0.0034	49	casualty	0.0026
14	attack	0.0057	32	water	0.0032	50	damage	0.0025
15	bomb	0.0055	33	landing	0.0032	51	harbour	0.0025
16	battery	0.0053	34	gully	0.0032	52	board	0.0024
17	sea	0.0049	35	troop	0.0032	53	aboard	0.0023
18	artillery	0.0049	36	lemno	0.0030	54	dead	0.0023

Table 6: Top 99 terms for the *Gallipoli* topic with their probabilities.

rank	term	beta	rank	term	beta	rank	term	beta
1	shell	0.0153	19	bombardment	0.0052	37	fire	0.0035
2	trench	0.0153	20	marched	0.0050	38	stunt	0.0034
3	gun	0.0138	21	firing	0.0048	39	evening	0.0033
4	line	0.0131	22	battery	0.0044	40	killed	0.0033
5	fritz	0.0096	23	enemy	0.0042	41	drill	0.0032
6	german	0.0076	24	battalion	0.0042	42	london	0.0032
7	wounded	0.0069	25	horse	0.0042	43	oclock	0.0032
8	artillery	0.0069	26	machine	0.0041	44	shelling	0.0031
9	front	0.0067	27	aeroplane	0.0041	45	fatigue	0.0031
10	billet	0.0066	28	division	0.0040	46	church	0.0031
11	gas	0.0065	29	casualty	0.0040	47	hut	0.0029
12	camp	0.0065	30	attack	0.0039	48	el	0.0029
13	bomb	0.0064	31	fine	0.0039	49	wet	0.0028
14	mile	0.0059	32	parade	0.0038	50	raining	0.0028
15	plane	0.0058	33	position	0.0037	51	wood	0.0028
16	village	0.0057	34	albert	0.0037	52	dug	0.0027
17	heavy	0.0053	35	france	0.0035	53	moved	0.0027
18	road	0.0053	36	taube	0.0035	54	tommy	0.0027

Table 7: Top 54 terms for the *In the Trenches (Beginning)* topic with their probabilities.

rank	term	beta	rank	term	beta	rank	term	beta
1	road	0.0067	19	camel	0.0032	37	weather	0.0025
2	wrote	0.0057	20	raid	0.0031	38	shelling	0.0023
3	fritz	0.0055	21	barrage	0.0031	39	ridge	0.0023
4	ypre	0.0053	22	boulogne	0.0031	40	station	0.0023
5	gun	0.0048	23	wounded	0.0030	41	omer	0.0023
6	fine	0.0047	24	london	0.0030	42	lovely	0.0023
7	enemy	0.0047	25	walked	0.0029	43	deferred	0.0023
8	brigade	0.0045	26	raining	0.0028	44	rain	0.0022
9	train	0.0045	27	letter	0.0028	45	report	0.0022
10	cold	0.0043	28	pt	0.0027	46	moved	0.0021
11	dinner	0.0041	29	sister	0.0027	47	stunt	0.0021
12	bomb	0.0040	30	paris	0.0027	48	book	0.0021
13	line	0.0039	31	plane	0.0026	49	battery	0.0021
14	hut	0.0038	32	farm	0.0026	50	dump	0.0020
15	lorry	0.0037	33	de	0.0026	51	lunch	0.0019
16	bailleul	0.0037	34	miss	0.0026	52	battalion	0.0019
17	shell	0.0034	35	machine	0.0025	53	division	0.0019
18	fed	0.0033	36	messine	0.0025	54	le	0.0019

Table 8: Top 54 terms for the *In the Trenches (Middle)* topic with their probabilities.

rank	term	beta	rank	term	beta	rank	term	beta
1	fritz	0.0144	19	battery	0.0045	37	captured	0.0027
2	gun	0.0128	20	amien	0.0043	38	forward	0.0026
3	line	0.0127	21	quiet	0.0042	39	move	0.0026
4	enemy	0.0106	22	moved	0.0042	40	american	0.0025
5	shell	0.0095	23	somme	0.0040	41	wood	0.0024
6	front	0.0078	24	evening	0.0038	42	shelled	0.0024
7	plane	0.0072	25	trench	0.0038	43	hot	0.0024
8	village	0.0068	26	stunt	0.0036	44	advance	0.0024
9	road	0.0065	27	gas	0.0036	45	tank	0.0024
10	battalion	0.0064	28	shelling	0.0034	46	dug	0.0023
11	hun	0.0059	29	machine	0.0032	47	casualty	0.0023
12	prisoner	0.0059	30	viller	0.0032	48	lorry	0.0023
13	bomb	0.0053	31	dugout	0.0031	49	valley	0.0023
14	division	0.0051	32	french	0.0030	50	aussie	0.0023
15	wounded	0.0047	33	heavy	0.0030	51	river	0.0022
16	position	0.0047	34	barrage	0.0029	52	dump	0.0022
17	fine	0.0046	35	le	0.0028	53	night	0.0021
18	attack	0.0045	36	la	0.0027	54	kilo	0.0021

Table 9: Top 54 terms for the *In the Trenches (End)* topic with their probabilities.

rank	term	beta	rank	term	beta	rank	term	beta
1	cold	0.0429	19	parcel	0.0033	37	foggy	0.0022
2	snow	0.0260	20	fler	0.0032	38	albert	0.0022
3	mud	0.0150	21	camel	0.0030	39	harness	0.0022
4	christmas	0.0140	22	stable	0.0029	40	thick	0.0022
5	hut	0.0075	23	rum	0.0029	41	ribemont	0.0022
6	frost	0.0073	24	ration	0.0028	42	patient	0.0021
7	frozen	0.0071	25	freezing	0.0028	43	delville	0.0020
8	el	0.0070	26	miserable	0.0026	44	thaw	0.0020
9	snowing	0.0064	27	frosty	0.0026	45	le	0.0020
10	fritz	0.0063	28	wind	0.0026	46	amien	0.0019
11	dugout	0.0060	29	rafa	0.0025	47	blighty	0.0019
12	arish	0.0055	30	desert	0.0024	48	bazentin	0.0018
13	wood	0.0053	31	taube	0.0024	49	hun	0.0018
14	ice	0.0052	32	mametz	0.0024	50	sleet	0.0018
15	foot	0.0051	33	walked	0.0024	51	needle	0.0017
16	blanket	0.0038	34	fricourt	0.0024	52	ground	0.0017
17	bitterly	0.0037	35	snowed	0.0023	53	cleaning	0.0017
18	muddy	0.0033	36	dump	0.0022	54	headquater	0.0017

Table 10: Top 54 terms for the *White Christmas* topic with their probabilities.

rank	term	beta	rank	term	beta	rank	term	beta
1	train	0.0084	19	car	0.0035	37	noon	0.0023
2	boat	0.0069	20	met	0.0034	38	ashore	0.0023
3	ship	0.0069	21	troop	0.0034	39	city	0.0023
4	fine	0.0065	22	person	0.0032	40	cold	0.0022
5	town	0.0060	23	walked	0.0031	41	picture	0.0022
6	sea	0.0053	24	lunch	0.0031	42	le	0.0021
7	london	0.0050	25	bed	0.0030	43	passed	0.0021
8	evening	0.0049	26	house	0.0029	44	germany	0.0021
9	home	0.0047	27	board	0.0029	45	charleroi	0.0020
10	hotel	0.0047	28	dance	0.0029	46	concert	0.0020
11	deck	0.0046	29	war	0.0029	47	snow	0.0020
12	pm	0.0043	30	afternoon	0.0029	48	class	0.0020
13	de	0.0043	31	street	0.0028	49	aboard	0.0020
14	dinner	0.0041	32	girl	0.0027	50	armistice	0.0020
15	port	0.0041	33	australia	0.0025	51	hut	0.0019
16	walk	0.0038	34	visited	0.0024	52	billet	0.0019
17	leave	0.0037	35	office	0.0024	53	lorry	0.0019
18	paris	0.0035	36	aussie	0.0024	54	engine	0.0019

Table 11: Top 99 terms for the *After the Armistice* topic with their probabilities.

rank	term	beta	rank	term	beta	rank	term	beta
1	home	0.0300	19	sit	0.0044	37	train	0.0028
2	meet	0.0160	20	elli	0.0042	38	time	0.0026
3	boat	0.0126	21	tram	0.0041	39	card	0.0026
4	pm	0.0104	22	dick	0.0040	40	write	0.0025
5	tea	0.0098	23	miss	0.0040	41	arrive	0.0025
6	play	0.0092	24	tickle	0.0039	42	read	0.0022
7	ring	0.0086	25	wrote	0.0036	43	spend	0.0022
8	catch	0.0082	26	dine	0.0035	44	night	0.0021
9	bed	0.0070	27	drive	0.0035	45	chat	0.0021
10	manly	0.0063	28	roy	0.0034	46	dinner	0.0021
11	mum	0.0058	29	day	0.0033	47	visit	0.0020
12	dad	0.0054	30	piano	0.0033	48	sleep	0.0020
13	walk	0.0052	31	middle	0.0032	49	cut	0.0019
14	paddock	0.0050	32	talk	0.0031	50	lopped	0.0019
15	town	0.0049	33	otto	0.0030	51	meeting	0.0019
16	music	0.0046	34	swim	0.0029	52	dave	0.0019
17	garden	0.0045	35	rain	0.0029	53	girl	0.0018
18	george	0.0045	36	stay	0.0029	54	wharf	0.0018

Table 12: Top 54 terms for the *Home Again* topic with their probabilities.

Zero-shot cross-lingual identification of direct speech
using distant supervision

Murathan Kurfalı and Mats Wirén
Department of Linguistics
Stockholm University
Stockholm, Sweden
{murathan.kurfali, mats.wiren}@ling.su.se

Abstract

Prose fiction typically consists of passages alternating between the narrator's telling of the story and the characters' direct speech in that story. Detecting direct speech is crucial for the downstream analysis of narrative structure, and may seem easy at first thanks to quotation marks. However, typographical conventions vary across languages, and as a result, almost all approaches to this problem have been monolingual. In contrast, the aim of this paper is to provide a multilingual method for identifying direct speech. To this end, we created a training corpus by using a set of heuristics to automatically find texts where quotation marks appear sufficiently consistently. We then removed the quotation marks and developed a sequence classifier based on multilingual-BERT which classifies each token as belonging to narration or speech. Crucially, by training the classifier with the quotation marks removed, it was forced to learn the linguistic characteristics of direct speech rather than the typography of quotation marks. The results in the zero-shot setting of the proposed model are comparable to the strong supervised baselines, indicating that this is a feasible approach.

1 Introduction

All narratives imply a speaker, that is, someone who tells the story (Bal, 2017). This is the basic narrative mode. But all stories are populated by characters who typically speak to each other, as opposed to telling the story. The characters' direct speech is therefore a distinct narrative mode, though it is embedded into the narration and mediated by the narrator (Koivisto and Nykänen, 2016). Typically, prose fiction consists of passages alternating between these two modes of narrative transmission. There are also hybrid forms, such as indirect discourse and free indirect discourse (Rimmon-Kenan, 2011, Chapter 8), but for the purpose of this work we are only interested in the binary distinction between narration (the telling of the story, in which we here include any hybrid forms) and the direct speech between characters.

Recently, there has been a growing interest in the detection of direct speech, with novel approaches to problems such as distinguishing narration and speech (Jannidis et al., 2018; Ek and Wirén, 2019; Brunner et al., 2020b), keeping track of speakers (He et al., 2013; Muzny et al., 2017; Ek et al., 2018), and keeping track of addressees (Ek et al., 2018). However, the lack of annotated resources has been a hindrance for progress in this field.

It might seem that an effective strategy would be to use quotation marks (single quotes, double quotes, dashes, etc.) for distant supervision, but this is also riddled with difficulties since typographical conventions vary a lot across languages and time periods (Byszuk et al., 2020). In addition, many types of quotation marks are overloaded in the sense of being simultaneously used for other purposes, such as pauses and contractions. Presumably as a result of all this, almost all approaches to identification of direct speech have been monolingual. For example, Quintão (2014) describes identification of direct speech for Portuguese, Pareti (2015) for English, Jannidis et al. (2018) and Brunner et al. (2020b) for German, and Ek and Wirén (2019) for Swedish.

Proceedings of LaTeCH-CLfL 2020, pages 105–111
Barcelona, Spain (Online), December 12, 2020.

In contrast, the only multilingual approach that we are aware of is Byszuk et al. (2020), who collected a corpus from nine languages which they annotated manually for direct speech. Based on this, they developed a classifier for token-level identification of direct speech using BERT (Devlin et al., 2018), reaching an F-score of up to 0.9 in their leave-one-out evaluation at the language level.

Our approach has similarities to that of Byszuk et al. (2020), but, to begin with, we have adopted a low-resource scenario in which we only assume the availability of a collection of raw texts. Using a set of heuristics to automatically detect texts where quotation marks appear sufficiently consistently (similar to Jannidis et al. (2018)), we created a training corpus to be exploited for the purpose of distant supervision. In addition, we fine-tuned multilingual contextual embeddings for the corpus. Furthermore, to prevent the system from relying on the typography of quotation marks, we removed them in the version that was used for fine-tuning, thereby forcing the system to instead learn the linguistic characteristics of direct speech, notably *speech-framing expressions*. These are the cues that narrators provide to allow readers to understand and assess what the characters are saying (and in our work, also who is saying it), consisting of concatenations of a referent, verb and possibly modifiers, such as "Zoe said" or "she inserted drily" (Caballero and Paradis, 2018, pages 45, 53). To retain the relevant information, we had instead labelled each token as belonging to narration, beginning of speech or inside speech in accordance with the IOB format. We then used this corpus to develop a token-level classifier for identification of direct speech in the absence of any quotation marks, using Multilingual-BERT (M-BERT), released by Devlin et al. (2018). The experimental results show that the performance of our classifier is comparable to supervised approaches even in the zero-shot scenario. To the best of our knowledge, this is the first study of zero-shot cross-lingual identification of direct speech.

2 Method

In this section, we describe our method for training a multilingual direct-speech classifier via distant supervision, i.e. without assuming any manually labeled dataset.

2.1 Automatic Extraction of Direct Speech

Relying on quotation marks to detect direct speech leads to a number of challenges due to their typographic variations across texts and their ambiguity between different functions (e.g. dash can be used to signal a dialogue line or to indicate a sharp pause, as in *"I know you are still there – somewhere in the sky."*). However, when used consistently, quotation marks can be exploited to generate large amounts of annotations without requiring any manual work. In the first step of our pipeline, among a large collection of texts, we try to find texts which we can use to extract direct speech with high confidence. That is, contrary to Jannidis et al. (2018), we do not a priori assume the texts in the collection to use quotation marks consistently.

We firstly compile a short list of the most frequent quotation marks which consists of the following markers: «», " " , "" , – , — . Then, the texts in the collection are filtered according to the following filtering steps:

- We firstly compute the frequency of each possible quotation mark in our list and filter out the book if one of the marks does not dominantly occur, i.e. does not account for ($> 90\%$) of all the occurrences. The rationale behind this step is to eliminate the cases where several markers may be used interchangeably, hence probably not consistently, which would lead to poor quality annotations.

- We further filter the books based on the ratio of the number of speech tokens to the whole book. Specifically, we count tokens which are between the quotation mark found in the first step and only accept a book if these speech tokens constitutes more than 30% and less than 50% of the whole book, aiming to have a balanced corpus

It is worthwhile to note that we did not include the single quotation mark ' in our marker list as it is a very frequent punctuation mark used in different constructions, such as contractions. Moreover, as a quotation mark, in many languages it is only used to mark the quotations inside the direct speech (e.g.

	Training			Dev			Test		
	Speech	Narr	All	Speech	Narr	All	Speech	Narr	All
Riqua	81,614	166,684	248,298	7,662	19,389	27,051	26,125	36,691	62,816
SLäNDa	35,192	79,914	115,106	5,795	12,358	18,153	8,262	22,737	30,999
Redewiedergabe	202,499	435,465	637,964	22,990	72,775	95,765	17,084	79,423	96,507
QUAC	11,884	104,464	116,348	1,583	14,937	16,520	4,389	35,213	39,602
Silver data	271,240	403,695	674,935	75,078	85,945	161,023	-	-	-

Table 1: Statistics of how many speech and narration (narr) tokens are in the datasets, excluding the quotation marks.

Sam exclaimed "he said, 'I'll see you at the party'"). Since our annotation schema does not distinguish embedded levels of direct speech, we simply discarded single quotation mark as a direct speech signal.

As the final step, we annotate the remaining books by labeling each token within quotation marks as direct speech, and all the other tokens as narration (*O*). Following the IOB convention, we assign a special label to the first token of each direct speech chunk (*Speech-B*) whereas the remaining speech tokens are annotated with the same label (*Speech-I*). For example the sentence: *["Find any mineral?" asked Cameron, presently.]* is annotated as follows:

"	Find	any	mineral	?	"	asked	Cameron	,	presently	.
-	Speech-B	Speech-I	Speech-I	Speech-I	-	O	O	O	O	O

In line with our aim to train a general classifier which can identify direct speech without relying on any explicit typographic signal, all quotation marks are removed in the final data (thus the label – in the above example).

The collection of texts comes from Project Gutenberg. The collected books are cleaned using the *Gutenberg, dammit*[1] library which is partly based on the GutenTag project (Brooke et al., 2015). Based on the available metadata, we only considered the books which are written in English and listed as a fictional work, excluding the *plays*.

2.2 Classifier

We approach identification of direct speech as a sequence labeling problem. To this end, we use multilingual contextual embeddings, multilingual-BERT (mBERT), and apply the token classification procedure explained in the original paper by Devlin et al. (2018). The model is fine-tuned only on the automatically generated training data, as explained in the previous section.

The way data is presented to the classifier is of special significance. Direct speech and their signals (e.g., *... he, then, exclaimed ...*) tend to span over multiple sentences; hence, accurate identification of direct speech usually requires a larger context than a single sentence. Therefore, we closely follow the configuration of Brunner et al. (2020b) and the text is divided into chunks of sentences provided that there is a maximum of 100 tokens in each chunk and no sentence is cut in half. Only those sentences which are longer than 100 tokens are split into sub-sentences. The sentence boundaries are detected using NLTK's sentence tokenizer (Bird et al., 2009) for all datasets except Redewiedergabe and QUAC which were already sentence tokenized.

3 Experimental Setting

The classifiers are implemented using the Transformers library (Wolf et al., 2019). All classifiers employ mBERT and were fine-tuned for 3 epochs, with a batch size of 32 and a learning rate of 3e-5. In all experiments, the quotation marks were removed from the datasets, thus forcing the model to identify the direct speech from other linguistic cues. We evaluated our classifier on the following manually annotated datasets, each representing a different language:

---

[1]https://github.com/aparrish/gutenberg-dammit

	RiQuA			SLäNDa			Redewiedergabe			QUAC		
	P	R	F1	P	R	F1	P	R	F1	P	R	F1
Brunner et al. (2020b)	-	-	-	-	-	-	0.87	0.74	0.80	-	-	-
Supervised Baseline	0.87	0.91	0.89	0.79	0.83	0.81	0.70	0.73	0.72	0.73	0.54	0.63
Our System	0.82	0.88	0.85	0.75	0.70	0.73	0.60	0.68	0.64	0.33	0.32	0.33

Table 2: Results on the evaluated datasets in terms of (P)recision, (R)ecall and F-score. The supervised baseline was trained on the training set of each respective dataset after all quotation marks had been removed (uses mBERT). The figures for Brunner et al. (2020b) are obtained using the German BERT model, trained on the whole dataset (including the quotation marks).

- **RiQuA (English):** RiQuA is built on 11 literary 19th century texts and thoroughly annotated for direct and indirect quotation spans, cues, speakers and addressees (Papay and Padó, 2020). Since there is no official training/dev/test split for this dataset, we allocated *The Boscombe Valley Mystery* and the second passage of *Tom Sawyer* for development; *A Christmas Carol, The Lady with the Dog, The Red Headed League* and the second passage of *Emma* for test, and the remaining nine texts for training.

- **SLäNDa (Swedish):** SLäNDa is a recent annotation effort on eight Swedish novels written 1879–1940, including the annotations of speech segments, speech-framing expressions, and speakers (Stymne and Östman, 2020). We used the suggested training/test split and randomly selected four texts from the training data as the development set.

- **Redewiedergabe (German):** Redewiedergabe is the largest avaliable resource for speech, thought and writing representation (ST&WR), with annotation of four main categories: direct, indirect, free indirect and reported speech (Brunner et al., 2020a). In the experiments, we used the version of the corpus described by Brunner et al. (2020b)[2].

- **QUAC (Portuguese):** QUAC is the only corpus in the our experiments which is completely built on non-fiction text collection (Quintão, 2014). Although QUAC covers 403 news in total, only 212 of them are tagged as including direct speech. Hence, we only considered those documents in the experiments, and split the data into documents 0–150, 150–170 and 170–212 as training, development and test sets.

The detailed statistics about these datasets are provided in Table 1. As for our classifier, we prepared a training dataset with 680K words using the method described in Section 2.1, on par with the size of Redewiedergabe which is the largest corpus in our experiments. Due to lack of previous work, we compare our results against the supervised baseline which is obtained by training a separate classifier on the training set of each dataset. It must be noted that this is a very strong baseline as the classifiers are trained on the gold annotations and are monolingual in the sense that they are trained and tested on the same language.

4 Results and Discussion

The experimental results are provided in Table 2. Our model achieves performance competitive with the strong supervised baseline in all datasets except for QUAC by yielding an average F-score of 0.74 against the average F-score of 0.81 of the supervised baselines on these three datasets. Moreover, the performance is stable across different languages although relatively better for the RiQuA corpus which is also in English.

QUAC is the most challenging dataset because it is not only annotated in a zero-shot language, but also represents a non-fiction genre, namely, news. Therefore, unlike the other datasets, QUAC further tests the generalization capability of our classifier to other domains which unfortunately is not sufficient.

---

[2]https://github.com/redewiedergabe/corpus/blob/master/resources/docs/data_konvens-paper-2020.md

However, we believe that the performance is not surprising given that news tend to adopt very different linguistic cues to signal direct speech (e.g. *according to the chairman, "..."*) than that of fiction texts. Furthermore, QUAC is challenging even in the supervised setting suggested by the relatively lower performance of the supervised baseline.

A qualitative error analysis of 30 random paragraphs from each of the English and Swedish datasets indicated that the most salient characteristic of false negatives was absence of speech-framing expressions. Thus, it seems that narrators' cues to their readers were indeed useful also for the classifier. False positives were more difficult to categorize, but sometimes non-speech verbs generated false alarms, as in Example 1.[3]

(1) **It's time for me to go north,** thought Gurov as he left the platform. **High time!**

Likewise, the classifier sometimes struggled when the narration interrupting the speech extended over several sentences, as in Example 2. On the other hand, the model sometimes recognized very long narrations correctly, as in Example 3.

(2) But he made a dash, and did it: **<u>Is your master at home, my dear?</u>** said Scrooge to the girl. **Nice girl! Very.**

(3) **<u>In everything that made my love of any worth or value in your sight. If this had never been between us,</u>** said the girl, looking mildly, but with steadiness, upon him; **<u>tell me, would you seek me out and try to win me now? Ah, no!</u>**

A common problem was that the system repeatedly switched its binary decisions in the middle of clauses, resulting in spurious fragments, as in Example 4.

(4) I recognised as Peter **Jones, the official police agent, while the other was** a long, **thin, sad-faced man, with a very shiny hat and oppressively respectable frock-coat. Ha! Our party is complete,** said Holmes, buttoning up his pea-jacket and taking his heavy hunting crop from the rack.

It should be possible to handle errors of this kind by introducing a syntactic post-processing step which prevents sudden shifts between narration and speech within clauses.

Finally, as a further experiment, we evaluated our model on the indirect speech annotations of Redewiedergabe (Brunner et al., 2020a) to see if training without any quotation marks could help the model to generalize over these implicit cases, as well. However, with a recall of 0.20, it completely failed on this type of speech. Training the classifier on the same language does not help either; the classifier trained on the direct speech annotations of the same data also failed, with a recall of 0.16. Hence, this low performance is not due to the zero-shot configuration, but must be the case because direct-speech classifiers are unable to generalize to other (hybrid) forms of speech, highlighting the need for more studies on the simultaneous identification of these.

5 Conclusion

In the current study, we show that it is possible to perform zero-shot cross-lingual identification of direct speech with a performance comparable to that of supervised baselines. Since quotation marks are not in general reliable indicators of direct speech, we instead devise a set of heuristics for collecting data where they are used sufficiently consistently, and use this to elicit enough data to fine-tune contextual embeddings. As future work, we consider focusing on the cases where our model falls short, namely, generalization to (i) other domains and (ii) other speech forms. Finally, we hope that our study will also be useful in establishing a benchmark to evaluate multilingual direct-speech identification.

Acknowledgement

This work has been partly funded by an infrastructure grant from the Swedish Research Council (SWE-CLARIN, 2019–24; contract no. 2017-00626).

---

[3]In the examples, the system's predictions are displayed in boldface and the gold standards are underlined.

References

Mieke Bal. 2017. *Narratology: Introduction to the Theory of Narrative.* University of Toronto Press, Toronto, 4th edition.

Steven Bird, Ewan Klein, and Edward Loper. 2009. *Natural Language Processing with Python — Analyzing Text with the Natural Language Toolkit.* O'Reilly Media.

Julian Brooke, Adam Hammond, and Graeme Hirst. 2015. GutenTag: an NLP-driven tool for digital humanities research in the Project Gutenberg corpus. In *Proceedings of the Fourth Workshop on Computational Linguistics for Literature*, pages 42–47.

Annelen Brunner, Stefan Engelberg, Fotis Jannidis, Ngoc Duyen Tanja Tu, and Lukas Weimer. 2020a. Corpus REDEWIEDERGABE. In *Proceedings of The 12th Language Resources and Evaluation Conference*, pages 803–812.

Annelen Brunner, Ngoc Duyen Tanja Tu, Lukas Weimer, and Fotis Jannidis. 2020b. To BERT or not to BERT — Comparing contextual embeddings in a deep learning architecture for the automatic recognition of four types of speech, thought and writing representation. In *Proceedings of the 5th Swiss Text Analytics Conference (SwissText) & 16th Conference on Natural Language Processing (KONVENS).*

Joanna Byszuk, Michał Woźniak, Mike Kestemont, Albert Leśniak, Wojciech Łukasik, Artjoms Šeļa, and Maciej Eder. 2020. Detecting direct speech in multilingual collection of 19th-century novels. In *Proceedings of 1st Workshop on Language Technologies for Historical and Ancient Languages (LT4HALA)*, pages 100–104, Marseille, France. European Language Resources Association (ELRA).

Rosario Caballero and Carita Paradis. 2018. Verbs in speech framing expressions: Comparing English and Spanish. *Journal of Linguistics*, 54(1):45–84.

Jacob Devlin, Ming-Wei Chang, Kenton Lee, and Kristina Toutanova. 2018. BERT: Pre-training of Deep Bidirectional Transformers for Language Understanding. *arXiv preprint arXiv:1810.04805.*

Adam Ek and Mats Wirén. 2019. Distinguishing narration and speech in prose fiction dialogues. In *Digital Humanities in the Nordic Countries 4th Conference (DHN), Copenhagen, Denmark, March 5-8, 2019*, pages 124–132. CEUR-WS. org.

Adam Ek, Mats Wirén, Robert Östling, Kristina Nilsson Björkenstam, Gintarė Grigonytė, and Sofia Gustafson-Capková. 2018. Identifying speakers and addressees in dialogues extracted from literary fiction. In *Proceedings of the Eleventh International Conference on Language Resources and Evaluation (LREC 2018).*

Hua He, Denilson Barbosa, and Grzegorz Kondrak. 2013. Identification of speakers in novels. In *Proceedings of the 51st Annual Meeting of the Association for Computational Linguistics (Volume 1: Long Papers)*, pages 1312–1320.

Fotis Jannidis, Leonard Konle, Albin Zehe, Andreas Hotho, and Markus Krug. 2018. Analysing direct speech in German novels. *Konferenzabstracts der DHd 2018. Kritik der Digitalen Vernunft*, pages 114–118.

Aino Koivisto and Elise Nykänen. 2016. Introduction: Approaches to fictional dialogue. *International Journal of Literary Linguistics*, 5.

Grace Muzny, Michael Fang, Angel Chang, and Dan Jurafsky. 2017. A two-stage sieve approach for quote attribution. In *Proceedings of the 15th Conference of the European Chapter of the Association for Computational Linguistics: Volume 1, Long Papers*, pages 460–470.

Sean Papay and Sebastian Padó. 2020. RiQuA: A corpus of rich quotation annotation for English literary text. In *Proceedings of the 12th Language Resources and Evaluation Conference*, pages 835–841, Marseille, France. European Language Resources Association.

Silvia Pareti. 2015. Attribution: A Computational Approach. Ph.D. thesis, School of Informatics, University of Edinburgh.

Marta E. Quintão. 2014. Quotation Attribution for Portuguese News Corpora. Master's thesis, Técnico Lisboa/UTL.

Shlomith Rimmon-Kenan. 2011. *Narrative Fiction: Contemporary Poetics.* Routledge, Taylor & Francis Group, London.

Sara Stymne and Carin Östman. 2020. SLäNDa: An Annotated Corpus of Narrative and Dialogue in Swedish Literary Fiction. In *Proceedings of The 12th Language Resources and Evaluation Conference*, pages 826–834.

Thomas Wolf, Lysandre Debut, Victor Sanh, Julien Chaumond, Clement Delangue, Anthony Moi, Pierric Cistac, Tim Rault, Rémi Louf, Morgan Funtowicz, et al. 2019. Huggingface's transformers: State-of-the-art natural language processing. *ArXiv*, pages arXiv–1910.

Twenty-two Historical Encyclopedias Encoded in TEI: a New Resource for the Digital Humanities

Thora Hagen
University of Würzburg
thora.hagen@uni-wuerzburg.de

Erik Ketzan
University of Cologne
eketzan@uni-koeln.de

Fotis Jannidis
University of Würzburg
fotis.jannidis@uni-wuerzburg.de

Andreas Witt
IDS Mannheim & University of Cologne
andreas.witt@uni-koeln.de

Abstract

This paper accompanies the corpus publication of EncycNet, a novel XML/TEI annotated corpus of 22 historical German encyclopedias from the early 18th to early 20th century. We describe the creation and annotation of the corpus, including the rationale for its development, suggested methodology for TEI annotation, possible use cases and future work. While many well-developed annotation standards for lexical resources exist, none can adequately model the encyclopedias at hand, and we therefore suggest how the TEI Lex-0 standard may be modified with additional guidelines for the annotation of historical encyclopedias. As the digitization and annotation of historical encyclopedias are settling on TEI as the de facto standard, our methodology may inform similar projects.

1 Introduction

EncycNet is a TEI-annotated corpus of 22 historical German encyclopedias from the early 18th to early 20th century, over 49,300,000 word tokens, with the goal of providing a resource for NLP and to add to the growing amount of historical, lexicographical German texts in consistently annotated XML. Initial versions of the texts were provided to us by Zeno.org in a proprietary XML schema, and we then developed a TEI annotation schema that fits the diverse structures of these encyclopedias and at the same time compromises with existing encoding standards with regard to annotating lexicographic works. We then applied the annotation schema to our corpus using XSLT (Extensible Stylesheet Language Transformations, a language for transforming XML documents into other XML documents).

The TEI methodology described in detail below is intended to connect our corpus to existing annotated, lexicographic corpora (while still accurately representing the original entry structures), as well as the semantic web, and also provide similar projects working with historic encyclopedias, in a variety of languages, with a reference point.

In this paper, we first comment on the value of encyclopedia texts for humanities research, summarize related work, and provide an overview of the individual encyclopedias included in this corpus. We then present our choices for TEI annotation and other transformation objectives that intend to homogenize the data and improve shareability and incorporation into related projects. Specific encoding choices and corresponding examples from the corpus will be given when necessary. The encyclopedia corpus is openly accessible under a CC-BY license on Zenodo[1][2] while the XSLT files are available on GitHub.[3]

Following corpus publication, we will begin the creation of EncycNet as a knowledge graph, which we hope will aid research in diachronic linguistic change in the German language, enriching existing

[1]Original corpus: http://dx.doi.org/10.5281/zenodo.4159491
[2]Transformed corpus, including the ODD: http://dx.doi.org/10.5281/zenodo.4039569
[3]https://github.com/ThoraHagen/Encyc-Transformation

Proceedings of LaTeCH-CLfL 2020, pages 112–120
Barcelona, Spain (Online), December 12, 2020.

language models with explicit semantic knowledge, and humanistic examination of changes in societal attitudes over time, with centuries of aligned encyclopedia texts as evidence.

2 Related Work

2.1 Encyclopedias

Encyclopedias occupy an important role in cultural history as texts which profess to aim, naturally in manifold ways, to encapsulate the entirety of human knowledge or a specific field within a systematic form. Regardless of how one reads or responds to them, statements such as Thorndike's (1924) assertion that encyclopedias are "the most important monuments of the history of science and civilization" are profuse in the history of cultural commentary, with just one more recent example being Rosenberg's (1999) assertion that "the importance of [Diderot's *Encyclopedia*] to the Enlightenment is difficult to overstate". Encyclopedias offer scholars a wealth of text for scholars of fields too numerous to name, not only due to the many fields of knowledge covered, but also to the variety of formal and conceptual structure, including, in the German-speaking world, the *Konversationslexikon* or "conversation dictionary", intended to contain "general knowledge" for various audiences. But, as Belgum (2010) notes, "The problem with encyclopedias for the scholar [...] is the vast amount of information and commensurately large number of topics they contain", suggesting that digital humanities methods may be useful in assisting linguists, historians, and other cultural scholars in contending with the sheer length of the texts. And indeed, DH investigations of the content of encyclopedias have emerged (e.g. Seifert (2007); Hagen (2007)).

While most notable historical encyclopedias are available on the Web in some form, often as scans or plain text, many suffer from restricted access, issues of long term archiving, and sometimes unclear licensing. Some annotated encyclopedias are restricted behind paywalls, e.g. Diderot's canonical encyclopedia digitized by ARTFL project,[4] which is queryable through a web interface but requires paid subscription for full text files. Other projects have created impressive and user-friendly online interfaces for encyclopedia texts but did not share corpora openly online, e.g. the University of Trier's Krünitz Online[5] (which has deposited XML/SGML-annotated data with the University Library of Trier) and University of Heidelberg's "Hidden Grammars of Transculturality – Migrations of Encyclopaedic Knowledge and Power"[6] and "Encyclopedia Database",[7] which followed the TEI markup guidelines described by team member (Petersen, 2010). The Encyclopedia Database website no longer seems to be functional, underscoring the risk that research outputs may be rendered unusable when long-term archiving is not successful. While the Encyclopedia Database website states that data is "open-source [... and we] invite all non-commercial usage of our data, and encourage cooperation partners to exchange their materials with us", the project website also suggests that some resources still under copyright or otherwise restricted were used in the project,[8] leading us to question what rights or licenses may be attached to such data, even if it may still be obtained. EncycNet aims to improve upon this state of the art through: open access to the corpus, use of the widely-used and unrestrictive CC-BY license, long term archiving at Zenodo, and the use of a TEI standard which other projects may follow.

2.2 Choice of Annotation Standard

While TEI has become the de facto standard for annotation of lexical and related resources, there is no widespread de facto methodology for TEI encoding of encyclopedia texts, as the previous section illustrates. TEI P5 provides the module 'Dictionaries' for annotating any terminological or lexicographical texts, but its rules are designed to fit such a wide variety of these types of texts that they can be considered

---

[4] ARTFL Encyclopédie, `https://encyclopedie.uchicago.edu/`

[5] Krünitz Online, `http://www.kruenitz1.uni-trier.de/`

[6] Hidden Grammars of Transculturality – Migrations of Encyclopaedic Knowledge and Power, `https://www.asia-europe.uni-heidelberg.de/en/research/d-historicities-heritage/d11.html`

[7] Encyclopedia Database, `http://kjc-sv036.kjc.uni-heidelberg.de:8080/exist/apps/matumi/home.html`

[8] Encyclopedia Database, "Select encyclopedias and articles for digitization", `http://kjc-sv036.kjc.uni-heidelberg.de:8080/exist/apps/matumi/home-history.html`

too general (see section on TEI Lex-0 below). In this section, we briefly introduce the available choices for annotating encyclopedias and explain why TEI Lex-0 is the appropriate choice for EncycNet.

TEI has become a widespread standard for text annotation, but terminology poses a special case as already mentioned. Until P4, the TEI included a module on terminology, which was removed with P5 in 2007 as the module was deemed obsolete (due to the publication of related ISO standards). This sparked a discussion on how to best handle terminology along with the proposal of many new annotation guidelines (Van Campenhoudt, 2017). Besides simply utilizing the core elements and the module 'Dictionaries' of TEI P5 (Budin et al., 2012), there now exist a few standards for annotating lexicographic / terminographic data, most notably TBX, TEI-TBX and TEI Lex-0. Drawing specifically on previous work in annotated encyclopedias, the most extensive TEI schema was suggested by Petersen's "A Minimal Set of Tags for Marking Up Encyclopaedias" (2010), which is now mostly covered by newer standards. However, Petersen also discusses a few points, such as footnotes in entries or the importance of paragraphs, that have still not been addressed in commentary on TEI for lexicographic works (see also section 4.1).

One ISO standard leading to the removal of the terminology module is TBX (TermBase eXchange),[9] which has become a popular choice for encoding terminology. TBX is entirely separate from TEI and its dialects, even if the proposed document structure is strongly inspired by the TEI, and was adopted by ISO in 2008. TBX is flexible, can express almost any kind of terminological data, and (as with TEI) encompasses a few dialects to better fit certain needs, such as TBX-Basic or TBX-Min. TBX is generally intended to be used for onomasiological approaches, i.e. dictionaries that group all synonymous terms together based on meaning (Romary and Witt, 2014).

To compensate for the fact that TBX is not compatible with TEI, a new project called TEI-TBX (Romary, 2014) emerged to combine the two. The main idea behind the linking of TBX and TEI is to integrate this onomasiological approach back into TEI by only taking the TBX-Basics representation of an entry into account to compromise between the two standards.

A recent encoding schema supported by DARIAH is TEI Lex-0 (Romary and Tasovac, 2018), which is based on the idea of further specifying the 'Dictionary' module of TEI, especially to fit lexicographic works better. The guidelines are much more straight-forward, as more restrictions on existing tags were introduced and certain tags got removed entirely. Because these guidelines are only a customization (not a replacement) of the TEI schema, any TEI Lex-0 valid document is therefore also TEI valid. This schema, as already implied above, enforces the semasiological model (synonymous terms are grouped in alphabetical order (Romary and Witt, 2014)) as an option besides the onomasiological model, compared to TBX. As the project is community-oriented, the standard is continually updated to fit the needs of its users. Because encyclopedias follow the semasiological approach and these guidelines provide a more explicit frame than base TEI does, we chose TEI Lex-0 as our foundation for annotating EncycNet's texts.

3 Data

The original texts of the twenty-two German encyclopedias in our corpus were initially made available to us by Zeno as part of a larger, literary corpus for an earlier data transformation / preparation project. The focus of this previous project was a wide variety of literary text forms, meaning that the transformation process was designed to fit a wider variety of ambiguous XML markup (i.e. not specifically tailored for the encyclopedias which made up only part of their larger corpus). In EncycNet, we are now able to attend to the specific structures and markup of encyclopedias texts while re-evaluating previous transformation decisions, most importantly choosing a TEI P5 `<teiCorpus>` approach. For a more detailed view of the content and the size of the corpus, see Table 1.

The EncycNet corpus has also been annotated with semantic web data, namely the automatic alignment of encyclopedia headwords with DBpedia (Auer et al., 2007), which contains millions of structured and classified entities from Wikipedia, and GermaNet, a lexical-semantic net for the German language (Hamp and Feldweg, 1997; Henrich and Hinrichs, 2010), together with its aligned Wiktionary definitions (Henrich et al., 2011). DBpedia Spotlight (Daiber et al., 2013) provides a disambiguation algorithm,

---

[9]TBX, `https://www.tbxinfo.net/`

	Description	Number of Entries	Token Count
Brockhaus 1809	General lexicon targeted at the general population.	6,960	1,186,000
Brockhaus 1837	General lexicon briefly covering everyday subjects in a strictly non-scientific way, while focusing on illustrations.	7,049	2,604,000
Brockhaus 1911	General, pocketbook edition lexicon.	82,780	2,434,000
DamenConvLex. 1834	General encyclopedia explicitly targeted at middle-class women interested in education.	7,099	1,461,000
Eisler 1904	Dictionary covering philosophical terms.	3,646	845,000
Eisler 1912	Lexicon covering influential philosophers.	2,839	396,000
Goetzinger 1885	Specialist encyclopedia on the cultural history of the German people based on the existing scientific research at the time.	948	519,000
Hederich 1770	Lexicon of mythology, addressed to scholars and artists.	6,430	832,000
Heiligenlex. 1858	Biographies of saints of the catholic church.	33,481	3,095,000
Herder 1854	General lexicon with short explanations of various topics.	39,755	2,256,000
Kirchner-Michaelis 1907	Dictionary briefly covering basic philosophical terms, including their historical development.	1,817	235,000
Lemery 1721	Lexicon covering minerals, animals, and herbs. Mostly targeted at doctors, pharmacists, etc., but also at the general population.	1,769	495,000
Lueger 1904	Specialist lexicon covering technical terms.	23,465	5,246,000
Mauthner 1923	Dictionary of philosophical terms.	214	537,000
Meyers 1905	Comprehensive general lexicon targeted at the general population.	156,264	17,437,000
Pagel 1901	Biographical lexicon of important doctors of the 19th century.	2,909	528,000
Pataky 1898	Lexicon of female, German authors, covering their biographies, works and pseudonyms.	6,907	503,000
Roell 1912	Encyclopedia of the railway industry.	3,067	2,662,000
Schmidt 1902	Lexicon of the history of German booksellers and book printers.	567	380,000
Sulzer 1771	Encyclopedia of terms within the field of aesthetics.	854	816,000
Vollmer 1874	Dictionary of mythological terms and their development in different cultures.	7,078	479,000
Wander 1867	Dictionary of German proverbs.	25,762	5,242,000

Table 1: Short description as well as the number of entries and overall token count of each encyclopedia in the corpus.

while the Lesk algorithm (Lesk, 1986) was used for GermaNet.[10] In both cases, the encyclopedia glosses were used as context input for disambiguating the encyclopedia headword in semantic web classification. Table 2 shows the percentage of headwords which were able to be automatically aligned with DBpedia and GermaNet in this way, and conversely, provide estimations of the amount of knowledge in our corpus that is currently *not* part of these semantic web resources. Thus, our corpus could be used to further add entries to DBPedia and GermaNet in the future.

The original encyclopedias encode one encyclopedia entry in one <article> element, while the child element <lem> contains the headword and the child element <text> contains the gloss itself. The usage of these elements is, along with typography elements such as <i> and <u>, fairly consistent and unambiguous. However, the internal structure of a gloss can be vastly differently annotated. Most notably, <p> can indicate a paragraph, a line from a verse, or a list item. <p> elements can have an @*class* attribute assigned, but these classes do not align with their structural function, sometimes not even within the same encyclopedia. The same problem also applies to references. Apart from the issue that references are not explicitly linked, the elements <link>, <plink>, and other typographical elements can indicate a footnote, gloss reference or footnote "anchor"—and these elements are also used interchangeably. In section 4, these two main issues (basic structure and references) in the transformation

---

[10]We used DBpedia Spotlight because it is specifically tailored to DBpedia. As no such tailored tool exists for GermaNet, we opted for Lesk as the algorithm and its variants still belong to the standards of German Word Sense Disambiguation (Henrich and Hinrichs, 2012). Other tools for entity linking such as spaCys Entity Linker or DeepType (Raiman and Raiman, 2018) could have been used besides the approaches here; however at this early stage of the project our current claims do not benefit from marginal performance improvements.

	GermaNet (%)	DBpedia (%)	Internal Alignment (%)
Brockhaus 1809	32.80	51.15	71.49
Brockhaus 1837	58.04	54.38	91.84
Brockhaus 1911	24.80	37.18	73.68
DamenConvLex. 1834	47.68	43.61	70.70
Eisler 1904	46.05	25.40	57.87
Eisler 1912	10.21	5.92	21.86
Goetzinger 1885	56.54	48.31	76.26
Hederich 1770	4.45	9.38	26.26
Heiligenlex. 1858	2.34	0.35	1.10
Herder 1854	27.25	34.61	67.32
Kirchner-Michaelis 1907	58.56	29.66	75.23
Lemery 1721	7.91	18.65	41.09
Lueger 1904	28.77	24.57	46.51
Mauthner 1923	75.23	28.97	77.10
Meyers 1905	19.80	28.94	47.03
Pagel 1901	11.28	0.17	19.09
Pataky 1898	15.43	0.58	18.00
Roell 1912	24.91	27.88	35.78
Schmidt 1902	12.70	1.06	9.47
Sulzer 1771	69.67	24.71	72.01
Vollmer 1874	7.49	14.51	34.84
Wander 1867	43.75	16.06	33.27

Table 2: Percentage of encyclopedia headwords in EncycNet for which a GermaNet synset entry or DBpedia URI was automatically assigned. The last column additionally shows the amount of headwords appearing at least once in the remaining 21 encyclopedias.

will be discussed in more detail.

A markup conversion was therefore necessary to make working with these encyclopedia texts on a quantitative scale possible. For the XSL transformation process, we focused on preserving all data as a general rule. To ensure that no text instances were lost, we implemented a quantitative evaluation, i.e. compared the glosses of all original encyclopedias with their counterpart from their respective transformed encyclopedia with Python. We also carried out a qualitative evaluation by transforming the results into simple HTML and randomly manually comparing parts with their facsimile equivalent.

4 Modifying the TEI Lex-0 Guidelines and Transformation Objectives

4.1 Basic Structure

TEI Lex-0 is an actively maintained annotation schema for lexical resources and fits most needs of our corpus, including in TEI Lex-0's semasiological approach (term: definition), which relates to the canonical structure of encyclopedias, including our German ones.

The glosses of the encyclopedias do not exhibit a typically lexicographical structure such as *headword, grammatical features (and possibly many other kinds of features), short definition, usage example*. We nonetheless chose to adopt the predominant encoding style that exists for lexicographic data (<entry> structure) instead of opting for a more general approach (e.g. a <teiCorpus> structure), so that researchers working with lexicographic data might be able to integrate these encyclopedias into their workflow more easily.

An example of a minimal gloss in our encyclopedia corpus:

```xml
<?xml version="1.0" encoding="UTF-8"?>
<entry xml:id="d3e45097Brockhaus-1809" xml:lang="de">
   <form type="lemma">
      <term>Die Literatur</term>
   </form>
   <sense xml:id="d3e45097">
      <def>
         <term type="headword"><hi rend="bold">Die Literatur</hi>
         </term>, a. d. Lat. 1) im Allgemeinen die Gelehrsamkeit; 2) insbesondre
            pflegen Einige dieses Wort auf die <hi rend="italic">schoenen
            Wissenschaften</hi> einzuschraenken.
      </def>
   </sense>
</entry>
```

Besides typography-focused elements such as <hi>, there are also structure-focused elements that can be frequently found within the glosses, namely tables, verse, and lists. Within TEI Lex-0 valid documents, these structures are not allowed. We therefore slightly modified the guidelines, so that glosses may contain these elements, as well.

We also decided on another TEI modification decision concerning the content of <def> elements. In the original encyclopedia files, glosses are composed of multiple paragraphs, realized with <p> elements. The paragraphs cannot be directly transformed into <def> elements, because one paragraph usually does not align with one definition. As we did not want to lose the paragraph structure by compiling all adjacent paragraphs into one <def> element, we chose to allow <p> elements within <def> elements instead, which is not compliant with TEI P5. We argue, however, that only allowing phrase-like elements within a definition is too restrictive for encyclopedias in general, as it is possible for a definition to consist of multiple paragraphs. For our encyclopedia structure this means that <sense> elements are always composed of just one <def> element containing either two or more <p> elements or the definition directly.

Footnotes are an essential aspect of this corpus, but so far, while <note> is generally allowed, no explicit guidelines for handling footnotes in encyclopedias exist in a standardized form yet. Petersen (2010) suggests replacing all footnote references with the corresponding footnote text, however footnotes with no references still need to be addressed then and footnotes with many references pointing to them might unnecessarily inflate the text. We instead chose to include any footnotes at the end of one <def> element as a <note> element, so that in case of two or more definitions, their corresponding footnotes will be grouped with them. Single footnotes are again annotated with a <note> with an attribute @*type* as 'footnote'. In these encyclopedias, there exist cases where footnotes are not placed at the end of entries. In the *Heiligenlexikon*, for example, all footnotes are grouped at the end of one letter range. In Wander's *Sprichwörter-Lexikon*, some entries contain notes in the middle of definitions. In both cases, we moved all footnotes to the end of their respective entries if necessary, thus altering the original structure to preserve a uniform annotation. We thus suggest that: all footnotes, like entries, should carry a unique @*xml:id* identifier, should only be allowed at the end of the related definition, and should carry the aforementioned @*type* attribute to distinguish them from other notes.

4.2 Encoding References and Footnotes

Another challenge in annotating the encyclopedias was to create explicitly tagged links between references, for instance when an encyclopedia gloss contains the text *see also X* or *see external source Y*. We thus assigned reference targets with a unique identifier as a first step and five different types of references are present in the encyclopedia corpus: references to glosses, footnotes, figures, external sources, and appendices.

We first want to focus on gloss references. Previously, some references were already tagged with fairly unambiguous elements such as <link>; others are simply highlighted with elements such as <i>.

We tried to identify highlighted references next to ordinarily annotated references with distinct regular expressions as a second step, so that phrases such as *as seen in article* `<i>rhythm</i>` (translated from entry *Der Takt* in Brockhaus' *Conversations-Lexikon*) can be resolved. Following the identification procedure, every such reference is then annotated with `<ref>` and an attribute *@type* with the value 'entry'. Connecting all recognized entry references to their actual entry identifiers constitutes the last step. As an indication to what entry a reference should be linked to is firstly any attribute values from elements like `<link>` and secondly the text content of the element. Usually, either one or the other string matches exactly one entry headword. We also implemented additional rules like substring matching or switching of first and last names for persons to resolve as many references as possible.[11] However when both strings are either too ambiguous (e.g. when just the first name is given for a reference to a person), the transformation will result in no target for that entry. This can also happen when the text content irregularly contains superfluous information or is spelled differently then the targeted entry headword (and no attribute is available), such as *biography see Anna v. Gottberg née baroness v. Rottenberg* in Patakys *Deutsches Lexikon deutscher Frauen der Feder*. Sometimes entries of references could not be located even by manual search. To give an example from Brockhaus 1837: 5,644 entry references could be found from which 4,907 match a unique entry identifier. Previously, no entry references were explicitly tagged in the original XML document. References to appendices are marked as such via *@type*, but are identified and resolved in the same way, with the exception of taking 'appendix markers' (e.g. quotation marks in Meyers *Großes Konversations-Lexikon*) into account. External references in this corpus can only be identified with regular expressions and are thus far left without a target.

Two encyclopedias contain figure references: Rölls *Enzyklopädie des Eisenbahnwesens* and Lügers *Lexikon der gesamten Technik*. These references are realized with `<anchor>` elements, as the references point to different parts of the figure, and consequently require different anchors and identifiers for the same figure. We chose to collapse all identifiers pointing to the same figure onto the same figure identifier and remove the anchors, as the redundant pointing does not make sense from a digital perspective. The connection between the figure part and the reference remains intact on a human-readable basis via the references' text content.

Lastly, there exist footnote references. In the original files, footnotes were only unique within the context of one entry, but after the transformation, footnotes were assigned a distinctive identifier by concatenating the headword with the footnote number, as homonymous headwords are also numbered. For each footnote reference, the footnote with the identical number within the same entry is assigned as a target.

5   Conclusion and Future Work

With the publication of EncycNet's newly annotated encyclopedia corpus, we hope to provide a novel, digital, historical resource and advance the methodology of TEI for encyclopedia texts. We argue that encyclopedias such as these should be treated just like any other lexical resource and thus should be annotated as such, even when the gloss structure they exhibit does not follow typical standards like any other lexical resource. Our proposed methodology, a compromise between TEI and TEI Lex-0, can be summarized as follows: allow a paragraph-like structure in definitions, allow less common structures such as lists and tables in definitions, and create explicit rules for footnotes within entries. We strive to include these findings within a future, revised version of the TEI and TEI Lex-0.

While our next step in this project is the transformation of the EncycNet corpus into a knowledge graph structure, the corpus at this earlier stage may still be improved. Currently, many headword features such as synonyms, hyper- or hyponyms are marked with highlight-elements, for example. With TEI Lex-0, these features could theoretically be annotated as such. Automatically distinguishing tagged synonyms from other words marked with the same highlight tag is possible, but not realistic within the scope of an XSL transformation, which is why these features remain "unidentified" for now. A future version

---

[11] A peer reviewer stated that a confidence score for reference and footnote matches based on e.g. the preciseness of the rule (full string vs. substring) that applied for all individual matches could be of interest. As it is possible to include certitude values as an attribute from TEI's viewpoint, we would like to add this feature in a future version of the corpus.

of the corpus, where features have been explicitly tagged with the help of appropriate NLP methods and another programming language, is still conceivable. Another unresolved issue is the grouping of multiple senses in one <sense> element, which can sometimes be the case for homonyms, but also entries listing multiple persons from the same family for example. Ideally, these senses should be split into two <sense> tags within the same <entry>, as TEI Lex-0 proposes. Identifying and splitting such glosses is, similarly to identifying headword features within the definition, difficult to realize with XSLT alone but feasible with other tools.

We hope that EncycNet, in both its TEI-annotated corpus and planned RDF conforming knowledge graph form, may aid a wide variety of future research. EncycNet adds a large new resource for historical German, and diachronic language change as well as language models may use EncycNet as a source of additional historical and semantic knowledge. Given the unique role of encyclopedias in cultural history, EncycNet also offers a wealth of evidence for humanistic research. As shown in the alignment of headwords in Table 2 above, the encyclopedia texts have a broad range of overlap in subject matter, and much work could be done on, e.g., what topics different encyclopedias include and exclude, the length of entries for topics, etc., as evidence of societal attitudes of the times. As just one example, the entries in the 1834 "women's" encyclopedia could be compared to general knowledge encyclopedias of the same time period to better understand the editors' and, arguably, the contemporary society's social prejudices and biases against women. Finally, we expect that openly published, TEI-encoded encyclopedia projects will continue to emerge in a variety of languages; one recent example is the ongoing "Nineteenth-Century Knowledge Project" (Logan, 2018; Grabus et al., 2019) which digitizes historic editions of the *Encyclopedia Britannica*. We suggest that our TEI methodology could be one way that such projects may benefit from one another and enrich our understanding of encyclopedia texts.

References

Sören Auer, Christian Bizer, Georgi Kobilarov, Jens Lehmann, Richard Cyganiak, and Zachary Ives. 2007. DBpedia: A Nucleus for a Web of Open Data. In Karl Aberer, Key-Sun Choi, Natasha Noy, Dean Allemang, Kyung-Il Lee, Lyndon Nixon, Jennifer Golbeck, Peter Mika, Diana Maynard, Riichiro Mizoguchi, Guus Schreiber, and Philippe Cudré-Mauroux, editors, *The Semantic Web*, pages 722–735, Berlin, Heidelberg. Springer Berlin Heidelberg.

Kirsten Belgum. 2010. Documenting the Zeitgeist How the Brockhaus Recorded and Fashioned the World for Germans. *Publishing Culture and the 'Reading Nation'. German Book History in the Long Nineteenth Century*, pages 89–117.

Gerhard Budin, Stefan Majewski, and Karlheinz Mörth. 2012. Creating Lexical Resources in TEI P5. A Schema for Multi-purpose Digital Dictionaries. *Journal of the Text Encoding Initiative*, (3).

Joachim Daiber, Max Jakob, Chris Hokamp, and Pablo N. Mendes. 2013. Improving Efficiency and Accuracy in Multilingual Entity Extraction. In *Proceedings of the 9th International Conference on Semantic Systems (I-Semantics)*.

Sam Grabus, Jane Greenberg, Peter Logan, and Jane Boone. 2019. Representing Aboutness: Automatically Indexing 19th-Century Encyclopedia Britannica Entries. *NASKO*, 7(1):138–148.

Nadine Hagen. 2007. *A mind-map of a nation: the Australian encyclopaedia or why sharks are more important than tigers*. Shaker Verlag.

Birgit Hamp and Helmut Feldweg. 1997. Germanet-a lexical-semantic net for german. In *Automatic information extraction and building of lexical semantic resources for NLP applications*.

Verena Henrich and Erhard Hinrichs. 2010. GernEdiT-the GermaNet editing tool. In *Proceedings of the ACL 2010 System Demonstrations*, pages 19–24.

Verena Henrich and Erhard Hinrichs. 2012. A Comparative Evaluation of Word Sense Disambiguation Algorithms for German. In *LREC*, pages 576–583.

Verena Henrich, Erhard Hinrichs, and Tatiana Vodolazova. 2011. Aligning GermaNet senses with Wiktionary sense definitions. In *Language and Technology Conference*, pages 329–342. Springer.

Michael Lesk. 1986. Automatic sense disambiguation using machine readable dictionaries: how to tell a pine cone from an ice cream cone. In *Proceedings of the 5th annual international conference on Systems documentation*, pages 24–26.

Peter Melville Logan. 2018. Nineteenth-Century Knowledge Project. *JADH 2018*, page 226.

Jens Østergaard Petersen. 2010. A Minimal Set of Tags for Marking Up Encyclopaedias.

Jonathan Raiman and Olivier Raiman. 2018. Deeptype: multilingual entity linking by neural type system evolution. *arXiv preprint arXiv:1802.01021*.

Laurent Romary and Toma Tasovac. 2018. TEI Lex-0: A Target Format for TEI-Encoded Dictionaries and Lexical Resources. In *TEI Conference and Members' Meeting*, Tokyo, Japan, September.

Laurent Romary and Andreas Witt. 2014. Méthodes pour la représentation informatisée de données lexicales / Methoden der Speicherung lexikalischer Daten. *Lexicographica*, 30(1):152–186.

Laurent Romary. 2014. TBX goes TEI–Implementing a TBX basic extension for the Text Encoding Initiative guidelines. *arXiv preprint arXiv:1403.0052*.

Daniel Rosenberg. 1999. An Eighteenth-Century Time Machine: The" Encyclopedia" of Denis Diderot. *Historical Reflections/Réflexions Historiques*, pages 227–250.

Hans-Ulrich Seifert. 2007. Dewey meets Krünitz. Semi-Automized Classification in Historical Encyclopaedias. pages 95–104.

Lynn Thorndike. 1924. L'Encyclopedie and the History of Science. *Isis*, 6(3):361–386.

Marc Van Campenhoudt. 2017. Standardised Modelling and Interchange of Lexical Data in Specialised Language. *Revue française de linguistique appliquée*, 22(1):41–60.

Results of a Single Blind Literary Taste Test
with Short Anonymized Novel Fragments

Andreas van Cranenburgh
CLCG, University of Groningen
`a.w.van.cranenburgh@rug.nl`

Corina Koolen
Independent Scholar
`corinakoolen@gmail.com`

Abstract

It is an open question to what extent perceptions of literary quality are derived from text-intrinsic versus social factors. While supervised models can predict literary quality ratings from textual factors quite successfully, as shown in the Riddle of Literary Quality project (Koolen et al., 2020), this does not prove that social factors are not important, nor can we assume that readers make judgments on literary quality in the same way and based on the same information as machine learning models. We report the results of a pilot study to gauge the effect of textual features on literary ratings of Dutch-language novels by participants in a controlled experiment with 48 participants. In an exploratory analysis, we compare the ratings to those from the large reader survey of the Riddle in which social factors were not excluded, and to machine learning predictions of those literary ratings. We find moderate to strong correlations of questionnaire ratings with the survey ratings, but the predictions are closer to the survey ratings. Code and data: `https://github.com/andreasvc/litquest`

1 Introduction

It remains an open question why some novels are considered literary, while other novels such as thrillers are considered less prestigious. One position in this debate is that formal features of the text play an important role, i.e., formalism. The notion that foregrounding language is involved with the aesthetic appreciation of literary texts is supported by experimental studies (e.g., Hakemulder, 2004). Recent work investigates the role of the text in literary quality empirically on a larger scale by collecting literary ratings of novels in a large reader survey (henceforth the Riddle survey, Koolen et al., 2020). This survey provides a way to investigate the association of literary judgments and textual features directly. Can human judgments of literary quality be predicted by machine learning models from purely textual features? The answer turns out to be yes, to a substantial extent. The model by van Cranenburgh and Bod (2017) showed that textual features can explain 61% of the variation in the literary ratings.

However, machine learning may pick up on various subtle frequency differences that humans do not notice; compare the case of authorship attribution, which is arguably more difficult to do by humans by hand, than it is for a computer with a simple table of function word frequencies and cosine distances. In order to place the success of the machine learning model that can predict literariness in context, we would have to ask humans to assign ratings purely based on a text fragment, without being influenced by the prestige associated with an author's name or the title of the novel. The setup of such a 'challenge' was proposed in van Cranenburgh and Koolen (2019); however, no results were presented. Wine experts perform at chance level in blind taste tests (Hodgson, 2008); will readers be able to recognize literature?

In this paper we report on the results of a pilot version of such an experiment and analyze the results. This allows us to see the extent to which our participants agree with ratings in the Riddle survey who rate based on author and title, as well as how they compare to the machine learning models that perform a similar task. This also allows us to estimate the importance of textual features for human readers when making judgments. By looking into the motivations that the participants have given for their ratings, we

Proceedings of LaTeCH-CLfL 2020, pages 121–126
Barcelona, Spain (Online), December 12, 2020.

Rank	Novel	Genre	Author gender	Rating M	SD	Riddle rank
1	Mortier, Godenslaap	literary	male	5.8	1.2	2
2	Durlacher, De Held	literary	female	4.9	1.4	56
3	Dijkzeul, Gouden Bergen	suspense	female	4.7	1.3	156
4	Den Tex, Wachtwoord	suspense	male	4.6	1.4	147
5	Smit, Vloed	literary	female	4.3	1.6	103
6	Van der Heijden, Tonio	literary	male	4.3	1.3	7
7	Dorrestein, De stiefmoeder	literary	female	4.0	1.7	64
8	Appel, Van twee kanten	suspense	male	3.4	1.5	184

Table 1: Results of the questionnaire with a comparison to the ranking in the Riddle survey (401 novels).

also hope to identify interesting linguistic features of literary quality, which can be investigated further in future computational and literary studies work.

2 Questionnaire setup

We selected 8 originally Dutch novels for the pilot; 4 of which were rated as highly literary (5.5–7.0) in the Riddle survey, and 4 rated as neither non-literary or very literary (3-5–5.0) in that survey. We deliberately did not select non-literary novels with low ratings of less than 3.5, because previous research showed that the genre of such novels is very easy to recognize (van Cranenburgh and Bod, 2017), and we are interested in the more subtle differences between literary novels and 'not quite literary' novels. In addition, author gender is balanced, both for the literary and the not quite literary novels.

From these novels we selected fragments of 250 words, from the beginning of a chapter, though not the first chapter. We rule out the influence of author prestige by not showing any metadata of the fragments that are presented to the participants. In addition to not presenting metadata, we also anonymize the fragments; i.e., names of the main characters in the text are abbreviated to initials. Fragments are presented in an arbitrary order (although we did not shuffle the fragments across participants).

We use the same 7-point Likert scale as in the Riddle survey, which ranges from not at all literary to very literary. As in that survey, we did not give a definition of what 'literary' is, because we did not want to influence the participants. For a given fragment, participants were asked the following questions:

1. "How literary do you think this fragment is?" (7-point Likert scale)
2. "Briefly explain why you chose this rating" (text field)
3. "If a specific phrase contributed to this judgment, cite it" (text field)

We recruited participants from our social network. They range from casual to enthusiastic readers, of various genres, with ages ranging from 30–60. We collected responses from 48 participants. Compared to the 14k participants of the Riddle survey, this is a small pilot. However, for the Riddle survey, we look only at the ratings of books the participants had rated, which means that the number of ratings varies per book. It was shown that 50–100 ratings are sufficient to compute a reliable mean (van Cranenburgh and Bod, 2017). In contrast, all fragments were rated by all 48 participants in our questionnaire.

3 Literary ratings

In this first analysis, we consider the mean literary rating for each novel fragment in the questionnaire. We compare these means to the ratings in the Riddle survey and to predicted ratings from supervised models.

3.1 Comparison with the large reader survey

Table 1 presents the results as a ranking, ordered by the rating in the questionnaire. We note 4 differences in ranking. Compared to the Riddle survey, the thrillers at rank 3 and 4 are rated as more literary, while the literary novels at rank 6 and 7 are rated substantially less literary by the participants. The gap between male and female authors is less pronounced than in the Riddle survey, where literary female authors were rated 0.5 points lower than male authors, on average (Koolen, 2018). Similarly, the genre effect of suspense novels being rated lower than literary novels disappears for the novels by Dijkzeul and Den Tex. That their writing stands out is not surprising; Dijkzeul has been nominated several times for the *Gouden Strop*, the most well-known award for Dutch suspense novels, while Den Tex has won the award thrice.

It is possible that these differences are due to author prestige not playing a role in the questionnaire, but it may also be due to the difference in rating a small fragment on stylistic aspects versus a complete novel where plot may also play a role. Rating a small fragment in isolation is very different from rating a a novel one has read from memory, based only on the author and title.

When a reader rates a novel from memory, social factors will most likely come into play. If an author is known to have been acknowledged by literary institutions, for example through literary prizes and literary studies, this will add to their prestige (Verboord, 2003). And in turn, this prestige could influence a reader to award a higher rating on a scale of literary quality. Alternatively, a lack of prestige might result in a lower judgment, as is the case with suspense novels. Respondents in the National Reader Survey would explain a low rating for a suspense novel with comments such as "It's a suspense novel," signifying a tendency to associate lower literary quality with a specific genre. On the other hand, novels by female authors are seen as less literary overall, according to our larger reader survey; even when the novel judged won a literary prize (Koolen et al., 2020). In sum, prestige—of an author and/or novel—constitutes a complex web of factors, which likely plays a part in literariness judgments, as the results of the questionnaire show. Female authors and suspense authors are no longer separated from resp. the male and literary authors in literary judgment.

There are problems with this assumption, however. For example, the literary novel by female author Durlacher has a suspenseful plot which might have resulted in lower literary ratings in the Riddle survey. At the same time the writing style was praised as layered and literary, which may explain the high rating in the questionnaire—since the latter mainly invites judgments based on writing style. Dijkzeul's suspense novel is another example. One reviewer calls the plot of this novel predictable;[1] this could explain why it is rated lower in the Riddle survey than in our questionnaire, where plot plays no role. Further research is necessary to confirm these explanations.

However, it could also be that the scales are not comparable. Overall it seems that the participants in our questionnaire are more conservative, because only one novel got a rating above 5. This may be due to difficulty of rating such short fragments, which might be compared to judging a wine by tasting a drop of it; in the absence of sufficient information, we observe a regression to the mean.

3.2 Comparison with machine learning models

The plot on the left of Figure 1 shows a comparison of the ratings in our questionnaire, the Riddle survey, and two predictive models from previous work. The predictive models take the mean ratings from the Riddle survey as ground truth by training and evaluatinng on them using crossvalidation.

The first model, "BoW + tree fragments," uses a large number of textual features including word bigrams and syntactic tree fragments and is based on long novel fragments of 1000 sentences (van Cranenburgh and Bod, 2017); this model reached an R^2 of 61.1. This score was obtained using crossvalidation of a regularized linear SVM regression model. An R^2 score is a measure of the variation explained and ranges from 0 to 100, with 0 being baseline performance and 100 being a perfect score. Tree fragments where extracted based on their frequency and correlation with literary ratings in the training fold.

The second model, "LDA + paragraph vectors," addresses the harder task of predicting literary ratings from short fragments of 1000 words and only uses LDA topic weights (Blei et al., 2003) and DBOW paragraph vectors (Le and Mikolov, 2014) based on the 401 novels as document representations (van Cranenburgh et al., 2019); this model reached an R^2 of 52.2. This score was also obtained using crossvalidation, with a regularized linear model (Ridge regression). The topic weights are obtained using Mallet, while the paragraph vectors were obtained with Gensim.

For the latter model, we have identified the matching 1000 word fragment containing the 250 word fragment presented in the questionnaire, and show the corresponding prediction in Figure 1. While the

---

[1] https://www.hebban.nl/recensie/a-vd-heide-over-gouden-bergen

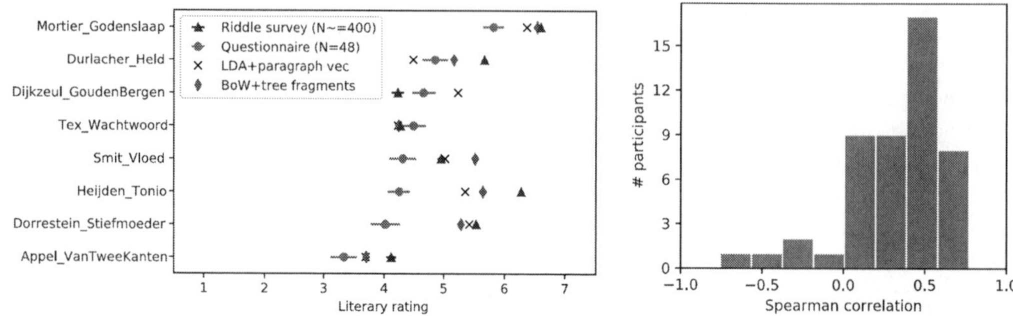

Figure 1: Left: Comparison of ratings from the questionnaire, Riddle survey and predictions from machine learning models. For the Riddle survey the average number of ratings is indicated. Error bars on ratings show standard error (note that the error bars of the Riddle survey are so small they are barely visible). Right: A histogram of Spearman correlations, showing how strongly the responses of the participants in the questionnaire are correlated with the Riddle survey.

comparison would be even more faithful if we evaluated the prediction on the exact same 250 word fragments, we opt for using the existing tuned and benchmarked model. If we take the Riddle survey as ground truth, the predictions of the models are closer than the ratings in our questionnaire, with two exceptions, Durlacher and Dijkzeul. This suggests that the predictive models may pick up on cues in the text that are not apparent to an untrained observer. However, it could also be that the participants in the questionnaire are more accurate because they were not influenced by social factors.

We can also compare our questionnaire and the Riddle survey in terms of the participants. How similar are their ratings? Because we are not interested in the precise differences in ratings, we want to focus on their rankings. We therefore compute a Spearman correlation coefficient of the ratings of each participant in the questionnaire with the mean ratings in the Riddle survey for the 8 novels. However, due this limited number of 8 data points per participant, these correlations are only presented as an exploratory analysis to give an indication of effect sizes, and we do not perform a formal hypothesis test with p-values. The plot on the right of Figure 1 shows a histogram of these correlations, showing that most participants of the questionnaire displayed a moderate to large agreement ($\rho > 0.4$) with the Riddle survey. These correlations support the construct validity of literariness as a measurable variable, since the human ratings from very different experiments agree to a large extent. If the participants would have 'failed the challenge,' we would expect the the distribution of correlations to be centered around 0, but the majority shows a positive correlation. In the Riddle survey, participants had read the complete novel they rated, but may also have been influenced by author prestige. In our questionnaire, participants were only presented with a short fragment, but were not influenced by other factors (except in the case that the participant recognized an author or novel from the fragment, which is not highly likely considering the briefness of the fragments and the anonymization of the names of the main characters).

4 Analysis of motivations

Overall, the common thread in the motivations is that elaborate and sophisticated language is seen as more literary. Most motivations refer to specific stylistic aspects. Participants also remarked that the task was hard due to the short text fragments. The following sentence was cited by multiple participants who agreed on its high literariness (our translation): "She brings out the world's blissful mongoloid smile, the grinning, wet shining zen of dumb objects, from which she blows the names off like chaff."

However, the choice of fragment likely plays a large role. The fragments were selected arbitrarily, and are not necessarily representative of the whole novel. Especially for Dorrestein, this likely played a role. In the fragment, a woman observes a group of children, followed by the following free indirect discourse (our translation): "She notices that she moves her jaws. I am Mrs Pacman. Bite, swallow, gone. Bite swallow gone." This phrase struck many participants, but it is striking that they disagreed on whether it made the fragment *more* or *less* literary. One participant cited this phrase as motivation for a 6 out of 7 ('no fixed pattern, surprising, would like to read more'), while another cited it to give a rating of 1 out of 7 due to the sudden shift in style ('a hodgepodge of old fashioned words and modern imagery'). Incidentally, such examples may be an issue for the notion of foregrounding as an explanation of literariness: while we find phrases that stand out for many of the participants, they do not agree on their effect on the literary status of the fragment. This requires further study; for example, would the participants' judgment change if more context is given?

While the fragment by Den Tex scored high in the questionnaire, several of the participants cited the mention of a soccer player, or the fact that soccer was discussed in the fragment, as a reason for judging the fragment as non-literary. This suggests that there is a perception that references to low brow, popular culture are associated with lower prestige, while literature should be about more timeless and serious matters. We can hypothesize that this is part of a heuristic: by default, references to low-brow popular culture trigger a low rating; on the other hand, such references can also appear in high literature, but in this case more context (i.e., a longer fragment) may be needed to see how such references fit in the story.

5   Discussion and Conclusion

We found a reasonable consensus for the strongest style differences in the fragments. The correlations of the Riddle survey ratings with our questionnaire ratings range from moderate to strong, which supports the construct validity of literariness as a variable. The difference between the ranking of the most and least literary fragment was preserved, and some of the changes in ranking could be explained as genre and gender effects that disappear when rating an anonymized fragment.

Participants found the task of rating short fragments hard, and the predictions by the machine learning models are closer to the survey ratings. However, the machine learning models are trained, while the participants are not. The ability of predictive models to reproduce the quality ratings should be interpreted carefully since the models may pick up on more than just literariness from the textual features, such as the aforementioned genre and gender effects. The participants agree on criteria (e.g., word usage), agree on salience of phrases, but sometimes disagree on how literary they are. This suggests that foregrounded language is not necessarily seen as literary language, and raises the question of how to identify potential linguistic markers of literary language for further study.

Our work is related to work on experimental aesthetics. In one branch of experimental aesthetics based on the ideas of Fechner (1876), the subjects' ideas on aesthetics are researched. Respondents are asked to recall as many adjectives related to aesthetic judgment as possible, for instance of literary novels. In Knoop et al. (2016), this approach leads to the conclusion that 'beautiful' and 'suspenseful' are central to descriptions of aesthetic judgment of fictional literature. This type of research is related to the influence of the text, but Knoop et al. (2016) did not ask readers to reflect on specific works. Other work on experimental aesthetics considers foregrounding effects and does present participants with novel fragments (e.g., Hakemulder, 2004) or lines of poetry (e.g., Blohm et al., 2018). However, more generally, there is more to literary quality than aesthetics. Even though there has been a focus on the aesthetic experience of literary language (cf. Van Peer, 2008), ethical, moral, affective and other motivations can play a role in literary judgments as well.

In future work, we want to determine the influence of author prestige by conducting a controlled experiment in which one group sees fragments with author names, while the other only sees the fragments. After this, a larger experiment should be conducted, with more novels, more fragments per novel, and more participants. It would be interesting to contrast general readers with readers with particular backgrounds (e.g., literature professors). Once promising linguistic markers are identified, we want to manipulate these markers in the fragments, to confirm their effect on literariness, similar to the work of Hakemulder (2004) on novel fragments and Blohm et al. (2018) on poetry.

Acknowledgments

We are grateful to Ana Guerberof, Antonio Toral, and the anonymous reviewers for helpful comments.

References

David M. Blei, Andrew Y. Ng, and Michael I. Jordan. 2003. Latent Dirichlet allocation. *Journal of machine Learning research*, 3:993–1022.

Stefan Blohm, Valentin Wagner, Matthias Schlesewsky, and Winfried Menninghaus. 2018. Sentence judgments and the grammar of poetry: Linking linguistic structure and poetic effect. *Poetics*, 69:41–56.

Andreas van Cranenburgh and Rens Bod. 2017. A data-oriented model of literary language. In *Proceedings of EACL*, pages 1228–1238.

Andreas van Cranenburgh, Karina van Dalen-Oskam, and Joris van Zundert. 2019. Vector space explorations of literary language. *Language Resources and Evaluation*, 53(4):625–650.

Andreas van Cranenburgh and Corina Koolen. 2019. The literary Pepsi challenge: intrinsic and extrinsic factors in judging literary quality. In *Digital Humanities 2019: Conference Abstracts*, Utrecht, The Netherlands.

Gustav Theodor Fechner. 1876. *Vorschule der Ästhetik*. Breitkopf & Härtel, Leipzig.

Jemeljan F. Hakemulder. 2004. Foregrounding and its effect on readers' perception. *Discourse Processes*, 38(2):193–218.

Robert T. Hodgson. 2008. An examination of judge reliability at a major U.S. wine competition. *Journal of Wine Economics*, 3(2):105–113.

Christine A. Knoop, Valentin Wagner, Thomas Jacobsen, and Winfried Menninghaus. 2016. Mapping the aesthetic space of literature "from below". *Poetics*, 56:35 – 49.

Corina Koolen. 2018. *Reading Beyond the Female: the relationship between perception of author gender and literary quality*. Ph.D. thesis, University of Amsterdam.

Corina Koolen, Karina van Dalen-Oskam, Andreas van Cranenburgh, and Erica Nagelhout. 2020. Literary quality in the eye of the Dutch reader: The national reader survey. *Poetics*.

Quoc V. Le and Tomas Mikolov. 2014. Distributed representations of sentences and documents. In *Proceedings of ICML*, pages 1188–1196.

Willie Van Peer, editor. 2008. *The quality of literature: Linguistic studies in literary evaluation*. John Benjamins Publishing.

Marc Verboord. 2003. Classification of authors by literary prestige. *Poetics*, 31(3):259 – 281.

Geometric Deep Learning Models for Linking Character Names in Novels

Marek Kubis
Adam Mickiewicz University in Poznań
Faculty of Mathematics and Computer Science
ul. Uniwersytetu Poznańskiego 4, Poznań 61-614, Poland
mkubis@amu.edu.pl

Abstract

The paper investigates the impact of using geometric deep learning models on the performance of a character name linking system. The neural models that contain graph convolutional layers are confronted with the models that include conventional fully connected layers. The evaluation is performed with respect to the perfect name boundaries obtained from the test set and in a more demanding end-to-end setting where the character name linking system is preceded by a named entity recognizer.

1 Introduction

Characters are mentioned in novels in various ways. They are referred by their first names, surnames, job titles, nick names, diminutives, honorifics and other forms that are ambiguous to some extent. This paper investigates the impact of using geometric deep learning for the purpose of linking names that refer to the same character. Geometric deep learning is a set of deep learning methods developed for non-Euclidean domains (Bronstein et al., 2017). In this preliminary study we analyze the impact of using graph convolutional networks (Kipf and Welling, 2017) and an edge based training objective on the performance of the character name linking system built upon a non-Euclidean domain of a character mentions graph.

The problem of linking all names that refer to the same character is a subject of multiple publications. Elson and McKeown (2010) perform name linking with a rule-based method as a preliminary step for attributing passages of quoted speech in narrative. The same method of linking is used by Bamman et al. (2014) for their work on modeling character types. Coll Ardanuy and Sporleder (2014) present another deterministic algorithm for character name resolution which is an integral part of their method of constructing social networks from literary artworks. Vala et al. (2015) propose a multistage pipeline for character detection that transforms the graph of character mentions by adding and removing edges between nodes that should refer to the same character. A more general problem of character identification which encompasses both name and pronoun resolution is discussed in the context of TV Shows by Chen and Choi (2016) and Choi and Chen (2018). A similar problem of character reference detection is addressed by Krug (2020) for German historic novels. A closely related task of coreference resolution was successfully approached with various deep learning models in recent years (Clark and Manning, 2016; Wiseman et al., 2016; Lee et al., 2017).

2 Dataset

For this study we use *Lalka* (English: *The Doll*) a Polish novel by B. Prus for the purpose of training and evaluation. All names that indicate the same character are annotated with a common *character identifier* which is unique within the scope of the book. The dataset is divided into training and test set that are roughly equal in size and consist of two consecutive sets of chapters. Although limited to one novel our corpus with its 150000 tokens and 192 unique characters is comparable in size to the dataset used by Choi and Chen (2018).

Proceedings of LaTeCH-CLfL 2020, pages 127–132
Barcelona, Spain (Online), December 12, 2020.

For the purpose of constructing geometric models the dataset is transformed into an adequate graphical representation of the problem. The conversion procedure has access to the entire text of the corpus and to the character identifiers of mentions that appear in the training set. We use all names that are mentioned in the text as a set of nodes. Two mentions l and r are connected by an edge, if one of the following cases holds:

1. l and r share the same lemmata // e.g. *Stanisława Wokulskiego – Stanisławem Wokulskim*

2. l is a prefix or a suffix of r // *Stanisław – Stanisław Wokulski*

3. l is a diminutive of r // *Stasiek – Stanisław*

4. l is an abbreviated form of r // *S. Wokulski – Stanisław Wokulski*

5. l and r share the same character identifier in the training set. // *Wokulski – Stanisław*

3 Models

We consider two training objectives with respect to the mentions graph that we refer to as *node* and *edge* in the rest of the paper. The first one is to predict directly the correct character identifier for every node in the graph. This objective does not require any post-processing steps, however its main disadvantage is the inability to predict identifiers for characters that are not present in the training set. The second objective is to predict the equivalence relation that holds if and only if two nodes in the mentions graph refer to the same character. This objective can be used to predict identifiers for characters that do not appear in the training set, but it requires two additional steps in order to obtain character identifiers for the nodes. First, one has to extract connected components from the graph induced by the predicted relation. Second, the character identifiers have to be determined on the basis of the mentions that belong to the same component.[1]

Figure 1 presents neural network architectures that are set up for the purpose of character name linking. All of them accept at the input vector representations of nodes that belong to the mentions graph. A single node is represented by a vector that encodes the words that belong to a mention (*word_vec*) and a vector that encodes its surrounding context (*ctx_vec*). Architectures (a) and (b) are designed for the *node* objective. They consist of a set of consecutive layers that transform node representations. The number of neurons in the last layer is equal to the number of characters in the novel. The cross-entropy loss is used for the purpose of training. Architecture (a) transforms node representations using conventional fully connected layers of neurons (*Linear* in Figure 1). It depends solely on the vector representations of nodes without taking into consideration the topology of the mentions graph. We confront this architecture with (b) where fully connected layers are replaced with dedicated graph convolutional network layers (Kipf and Welling, 2017) that utilise the edge index. This allows us to verify if there is any advantage in using structural information for the task. For the *edge* objective we develop architectures that transform node representations of (a) and (b) into representations of edges. For this purpose the *AdjacentSum* layer is introduced which returns for every edge in the mentions graph the concatenation of the corresponding node representations and their dot product, i.e.

$$e_{ij} = Concat(r_i, r_j, r_i \cdot r_j)$$

where $(i, j) \in edge\_index$ and r_i is the vector representation of node i. Furthermore, (c) and (d) are supplied with additional edge related features denoted by *edge_attr* in Figure 1. We use this vector to store textual distance between edges and to encode link types.[2] As in the case of (a) and (b) the only difference between (c) and (d) is the introduction of graph convolutional layers. However, one should notice that even though (c) does not utilise convolutions it still takes into account network topology

---

[1]For this task we select the most frequent character identifier in the connected component if any is present and fallback to the most frequent lemma otherwise.

[2]There are five one-hot encoded link types that correspond to the respective rules of connecting mentions defined in Section 2.

due to the formulation of the *edge* objective and the definition of *AdjacentSum*. Both *edge* objective architectures are trained with binary cross entropy loss to detect edges that connect mentions of the same character.

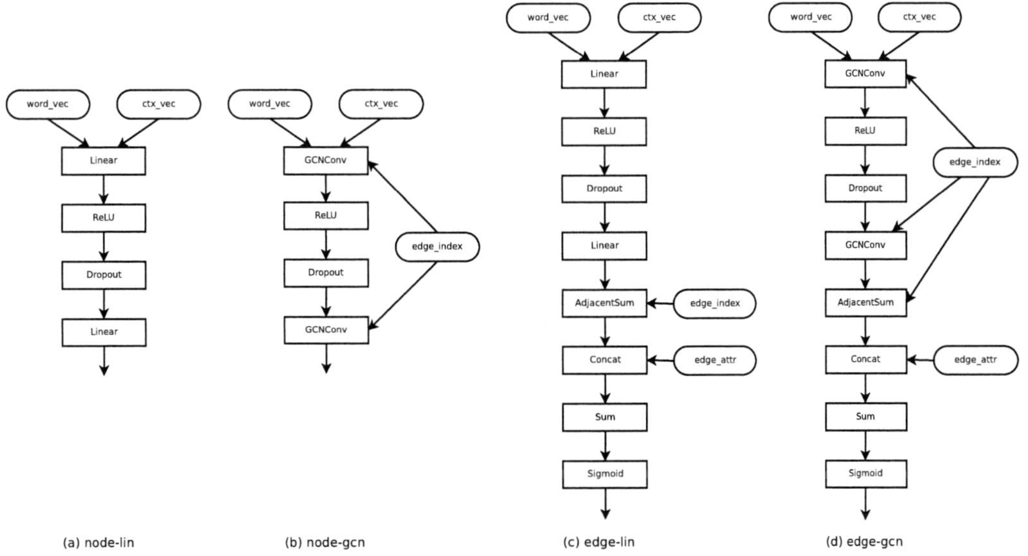

Figure 1: Neural network architectures

4   Experiments

For the purpose of evaluation we confront the neural architectures discussed in Section 3 with two baseline systems:

- *base* – a deterministic algorithm that memorizes all surface forms of character names that appear in the training set together with the corresponding character identifiers and annotates the spans of text that match the memorized surface forms with the stored character identifiers during the testing phase.[3]

- *seq* – a sequence to sequence model that learns a direct mapping from character names to their identifiers using the state-of-the-art technique of contextual string embeddings for sequence labeling (Akbik et al., 2018).

Since the graph induction procedure depends on a proper demarcation of mention boundaries we decided to conduct two types of experiments for every model. First, we use name boundaries detected by the named entity recognizer learned from the mentions that appear in the training set.[4] This is a realistic setup that we use to measure the end-to-end performance of the complete name linking system trained solely from the provided dataset without access to any additional resources. Second, we repeat the same experiment with name boundaries obtained from the test set. In this scenario the performance of the name linking model can be measured independently from the named entity recognition technique used to identify mention boundaries in the complete system. Results are reported separately for the entire set of

---

[3] Any ambiguities are resolving by selecting the most frequent character identifier.

[4] For named entity recognition we use a procedure that closely resembles the *base* algorithm. First, the surface forms of character names that appear in the training set are memorized. Then, the spans of text that match the memorized forms are annotated in accordance with the standard IOB scheme during the testing phase.

characters that appear in the test set and for the characters that where already *observed* in the training set. Micro F-score is the main metric used for the purpose of evaluation. Macro F-score which is a metric that penalizes the system for bad performance with respect to the rare characters is also reported.

Let us start the analysis of the results collected in Table 1 with the more demanding scenario of the character name linker preceded by the named entity recognizer. In this case the *node-lin* model presents similar performance to *seq* which is not unexpected taking into account that *node-lin* does not utilise topology of the mentions graph in any manner. However, if we restrict our attention to the characters that where observed in the training part of the corpus the differences between *seq* and *node-lin* become more apparent with the former being more performant with respect to the micro f-score and the latter with respect to the macro f-score. Both *node-lin* and *seq* do not surpass the second baseline which is a far simpler solution to the problem. The *node-gcn* model outperforms both baselines which proves that there is a clear benefit in incorporating structural information into the model. Furthermore, the *edge-lin* and *edge-gcn* models which incorporate the structure of the graph in the training objective perform better than *node-gcn*, especially with respect to the macro f-score. One should also notice than there is no observable advantage of using graph convolutional layers instead of linear layers in case of models designed for the *edge* objective. In fact, the connected components extracted from the relations predicted by *edge-lin* and *edge-gcn* are so similar that the overall scores do not change. Although the *edge* models manifest better performance over the entire set of characters, if we focus on the characters that are present in both parts of the corpus the *node-gcn* model is a clear winner. These observations remain valid for the second evaluation scenario which utilises the mention boundaries obtained from the test set instead of the boundaries detected by the named entity recognizer.

Model	Boundaries	Characters	Micro			Macro		
			Prec.	Recall	F-score	Prec.	Recall	F-score
base	ner	all	0.9384	0.7628	0.8415	0.2293	0.2174	0.2168
seq	ner	all	0.8064	0.7644	0.7848	0.1498	0.1790	0.1520
node-lin	ner	all	0.9246	0.6790	0.7830	0.1952	0.1463	0.1572
node-gcn	ner	all	0.9298	0.7849	0.8512	0.2446	0.2506	0.2454
edge-lin	ner	all	0.8751	0.8714	**0.8732**	0.3914	0.3680	**0.3729**
edge-gcn	ner	all	0.8751	0.8714	**0.8732**	0.3914	0.3680	**0.3729**
base	ner	observed	0.9388	0.9416	0.9402	0.6531	0.6191	0.6175
seq	ner	observed	0.8072	0.9377	0.8676	0.3074	0.3796	0.3160
node-lin	ner	observed	0.8521	0.8193	0.8354	0.5609	0.4188	0.4481
node-gcn	ner	observed	0.9392	0.9680	**0.9534**	0.7208	0.7341	**0.7213**
edge-lin	ner	observed	0.7766	0.9542	0.8563	0.1522	0.1516	0.1494
edge-gcn	ner	observed	0.7766	0.9542	0.8563	0.1522	0.1516	0.1494
base	test set	all	0.9768	0.7533	0.8506	0.2415	0.2193	0.2253
seq	test set	all	0.8064	0.7644	0.7848	0.1498	0.1790	0.1520
node-lin	test set	all	0.7011	0.7011	0.7011	0.1882	0.1602	0.1565
node-gcn	test set	all	0.7961	0.7961	0.7961	0.2446	0.2679	0.2437
edge-lin	test set	all	0.9226	0.9226	**0.9226**	0.6256	0.6297	**0.6195**
edge-gcn	test set	all	0.9226	0.9226	**0.9226**	0.6256	0.6297	**0.6195**
base	test set	observed	0.9981	0.9300	0.9628	0.7886	0.6849	0.7189
seq	test set	observed	0.8072	0.9377	0.8676	0.3074	0.3796	0.3160
node-lin	test set	observed	0.8634	0.8634	0.8634	0.6162	0.4930	0.5201
node-gcn	test set	observed	0.9823	0.9823	**0.9823**	0.8770	0.8921	**0.8638**
edge-lin	test set	observed	0.9758	0.9758	0.9758	0.6498	0.6272	0.6263
edge-gcn	test set	observed	0.9758	0.9758	0.9758	0.6498	0.6272	0.6263

Table 1: Character name linking performance broken down by the source of mention boundaries and the set of characters.

5 Conclusion

In this study we investigated the impact of using graph convolutional networks and the edge based training objective on the performance of the character name linking system built upon a character mentions graph. The conducted experiments show that the structural information encoded in the mentions graph improves the performance of the character name linking system significantly. Furthermore, there are several interesting observations that can be drawn from the achieved results. First, the usage of graph convolutional layers is essential in case of the *node* models in order to be able to outperform the baseline models. Second, taking into consideration that *node-gcn* is the best performing model with respect to the observed characters, it should be used in all situations where a training set that references all the characters that are important for the given study is provided. Third, there is no observable performance drop when graph convolutional layers are replaced by linear layers in the models developed for the *edge* objective. However, taking into account that the model which utilizes graph convolutional layers contains fewer parameters, it should be preferred.

Although the results presented in this preliminary study are promising, there are several issues that require further investigation. The choice of graph convolutional networks among many geometric deep learning models was an arbitrary one. Thus, the impact of other graphical neural network architectures on the performance of the name linking system should be measured in the future. The dataset used for the study, although comparable in size to the dataset used by Choi and Chen (2018), consists of only one novel. Hence, the question of how well the obtained results generalize to novels that come from different authors and periods is left open. Finally, taking into consideration the top performance of the *node-gcn* model with respect to the observed characters, a method of indicating unobserved characters for the *node* objective should be developed.

References

Alan Akbik, Duncan Blythe, and Roland Vollgraf. 2018. Contextual String Embeddings for Sequence Labeling. In *COLING 2018, 27th International Conference on Computational Linguistics*, pages 1638–1649.

David Bamman, Ted Underwood, and Noah A. Smith. 2014. A Bayesian Mixed Effects Model of Literary Character. In *Proceedings of the 52nd Annual Meeting of the Association for Computational Linguistics (Volume 1: Long Papers)*, pages 370–379, Baltimore, Maryland, June. Association for Computational Linguistics.

M. M. Bronstein, J. Bruna, Y. LeCun, A. Szlam, and P. Vandergheynst. 2017. Geometric Deep Learning: Going beyond Euclidean data. *IEEE Signal Processing Magazine*, 34(4):18–42.

Yu-Hsin Chen and Jinho D. Choi. 2016. Character Identification on Multiparty Conversation: Identifying Mentions of Characters in TV Shows. In *Proceedings of the 17th Annual Meeting of the Special Interest Group on Discourse and Dialogue*, pages 90–100, Los Angeles, September. Association for Computational Linguistics.

Jinho D. Choi and Henry Y. Chen. 2018. SemEval 2018 Task 4: Character Identification on Multiparty Dialogues. In *Proceedings of The 12th International Workshop on Semantic Evaluation*, pages 57–64, New Orleans, Louisiana, June. Association for Computational Linguistics.

Kevin Clark and Christopher D. Manning. 2016. Deep Reinforcement Learning for Mention-Ranking Coreference Models. In *Proceedings of the 2016 Conference on Empirical Methods in Natural Language Processing*, pages 2256–2262, Austin, Texas, November. Association for Computational Linguistics.

Mariona Coll Ardanuy and Caroline Sporleder. 2014. Structure-based Clustering of Novels. In *Proceedings of the 3rd Workshop on Computational Linguistics for Literature (CLFL)*, pages 31–39, Gothenburg, Sweden, April. Association for Computational Linguistics.

David K. Elson and Kathleen R. McKeown. 2010. Automatic Attribution of Quoted Speech in Literary Narrative. In Maria Fox and David Poole, editors, *Proceedings of the Twenty-Fourth AAAI Conference on Artificial Intelligence, AAAI 2010, Atlanta, Georgia, USA, July 11-15, 2010*. AAAI Press.

Thomas N. Kipf and Max Welling. 2017. Semi-Supervised Classification with Graph Convolutional Networks. In *5th International Conference on Learning Representations, ICLR 2017, Toulon, France, April 24-26, 2017, Conference Track Proceedings*.

Markus Krug. 2020. *Techniques for the Automatic Extraction of Character Networks in German Historic Novels.* Ph.D. thesis, Universität Würzburg.

Kenton Lee, Luheng He, Mike Lewis, and Luke Zettlemoyer. 2017. End-to-end Neural Coreference Resolution. In *Proceedings of the 2017 Conference on Empirical Methods in Natural Language Processing*, pages 188–197, Copenhagen, Denmark, September. Association for Computational Linguistics.

Hardik Vala, David Jurgens, Andrew Piper, and Derek Ruths. 2015. Mr. Bennet, his coachman, and the Archbishop walk into a bar but only one of them gets recognized: On The Difficulty of Detecting Characters in Literary Texts. In *Proceedings of the 2015 Conference on Empirical Methods in Natural Language Processing*, pages 769–774, Lisbon, Portugal, September. Association for Computational Linguistics.

Sam Wiseman, Alexander M. Rush, and Stuart M. Shieber. 2016. Learning Global Features for Coreference Resolution. In *Proceedings of the 2016 Conference of the North American Chapter of the Association for Computational Linguistics: Human Language Technologies*, pages 994–1004, San Diego, California, June. Association for Computational Linguistics.

Sonnet Combinatorics with OuPoCo

Thierry Poibeau, Mylène Maignant, Frédérique Mélanie-Becquet, Clément Plancq
LATTICE (CNRS & ENS/PSL & Univ. Sorbonne nouvelle)
1, rue Maurice Arnoux, 92120 Montrouge, France
{firstname.lastname}@ens.psl.eu

Matthieu Raffard, Mathilde Roussel
Atelier Raffard-Roussel
189 rue Ordener, Bâtiment B4, atelier 68, 75018 Paris, France
raffard.roussel@gmail.com

Abstract

In this paper, we describe OuPoCo (*l'Ouvroir de Poésie Combinatoire*), a system producing new sonnets by recombining verses from existing sonnets, following an idea that Queneau described in his book *Cent Mille Milliards de poèmes, Gallimard, 1961*. We propose to demonstrate different outputs of our implementation (a Web site, a Twitter bot and a specifically developed device, called *La Boîte à poésie*) based on a corpus of 19th century French poetry. Our goal is to make people interested in poetry again, by giving access to automatically produced sonnets through original and entertaining channels and devices.

1 Introduction

The starting point of the OuPoCo project is the book by Raymond Queneau *Cent Mille Milliards de poèmes* (*A Hundred Thousand Billion Poems*, in English) (Queneau, 1961). The book is composed of ten sonnets printed on separate strips, allowing thus a hundred thousand billion of different readings. The combinatory poetics characteristic of this book encourages the reader to play with the meanings of the poems, the various language registers present in the book or simply with its movable form. It is this stimulating relationship between poetry and constraints, which constituted the central mainspring of this project.

Queneau's book seems an ideal candidate to be transposed on a computer since a machine can perfectly combine verses and produce a comprehensive list of all the possible poems. But Queneau's work is still under copyright, which prevent us from working directly on the sonnets contained in his book. This is the reason why, instead of working on Queneau's poems, we decided to focus on a collection of 19th century French poetry instead. Beyond the availability of massive databases in this field, which facilitated the creation of our corpus, 19th century poetry also appeared as a fertile ground to reflect upon the sonnet and to work and play with various constraints. This means that original poems have to be analyzed so as to determine the rhyme, as well as other features (length of a verse, topics addressed, etc.).

This paper is thus about OuPoCo, *l'Ouvroir de Poésie Combinatoire*, a system able to generate sonnets by recombining verses taken from a corpus of French 19th century poetry. We describe the project, the different project outputs and the interest of this experience to reconnect people with poetry and literature in an entertaining way.

2 The Corpus

The first part of this research consisted in gathering a corpus of French sonnets from the 19th century. We first used available resources freely available on the Web, especially the Gutenberg project, Wikisource and Gallica, a rich collection of digitized resources provided by the Bibliothèque nationale de France

Proceedings of LaTeCH-CLfL 2020, pages 133–137
Barcelona, Spain (Online), December 12, 2020.

(the French national libray). The BnF later gave us access to an even larger corpus of French poems[1], so that the implementation currently integrates a corpus of more than 4,000 French sonnets.

All major French authors from the 19th century are included in the database, but also some less known ones. Each sonnet is encoded in a XML format along with related metadata; a TEI version of the database is publicly available (see `https://github.com/clement-plancq/oupoco-api`) and is regularly expanding.

3 Corpus and Rhyme Analysis

The OuPoCo project has nothing to do with the recent neural approach to poetry generation (Ghazvininejad et al., 2017; Van de Cruys, 2020), but it requires to get access to a formal representation of rhymes (as proposed by (Beaudouin, 2002)). In order to do this, the first step is to get a phonetic transcription of the last word of each verse, but this is not enough: for example, "*aimé*" and "*aimée*" have the same phonetic transcription, but do not rhyme, according to French rhyming rules (feminine and masculine words, for example words that end with *-é*, as opposed to *-ée*, do not rhyme); there are also cases where the phonetic transcription is slightly different but words actually rhyme (for example with sounds like $[e]$ and $[\varepsilon]$). All these cases are not marginal and must be handled appropriately.

Phonetisation (the process of transforming a word into a phonetic transcription) is done with eSpeak, a free software available on the Web (`http://espeak.sourceforge.net`), that provided satisfactory results on our data. We analyse the whole verse and not only the last word of each verse, so that a full rythmic analysis is possible. However, as we have just seen, the phonetic transcription provided by eSpeak is not enough.

A series of rules written in Python had thus to be defined to get a proper analysis of rhyme derived form the phonetic transcription of the last word of each verse. These rules are manually defined and maintained, as there is no way they could be learnt directly from the data. A part of these rules can be easily derived from a treaty of French versification, but another part is directly linked to the output of eSpeak as we have to overwrite some phonetic distinctions produced by this software that are not relevant to analyse poetry.

The sonnet generator uses this analysis to produce sonnets, with different possible structures, respecting the rules of French versification (the code and the resources used, especially the sonnet database, are open source and freely available for research, see: `https://github.com/clement-plancq/oupoco-api`).

4 Constrainsts

In the footsteps of the OuLiPo and following the comments of Queneau who did not like the idea of pure random poetry generation, we chose to implement constraints to enable the reader to interact with the database, control the generation process in different ways, and discover 19th century French literature from a different and more playful angle.

The first constraint correspond to the different existing forms of sonnets proposed in the course of history. Giacomo da Lentini, Petrach, Marot, Peletier, Shakespeare and Spencer all proposed and initiated a slightly different rhyming scheme (for example, Marot proposed the following structure: ABBA ABBA CCD EED, while Petrarch proposed several slightly different structures: ABBA ABBA CDE CDE / ABBA ABBA CDC DCD / ABBA ABBA CDE DCE, etc.). All these forms of sonnets are available and the user can choose any structure s/he prefers for generation.

The second constraint enables the reader to generate random sonnets from texts within a chosen time framework. In other words, the reader selects a period of twenty or thirty years for example that s/he wants to explore on the timeline, and sonnets are generated according to this time frame. This option makes it possible to have a quick overview of the productions of French sonnets over a period. Thanks to this option, it is for example possible to note that very few French sonnets were written at the beginning of the 19th century while their production tends to increase 20 years or so later.

---

[1]This corpus is available for research on the Bibliothèque nationale de France website: `api.bnf.fr/sonnets-de-gallica`

The third constraint deals with the authors themselves. The reader can select one or multiple poets as the source corpus to generate new sonnets. It is thus possible to explore the poems written by Baudelaire for instance, or to combine them with the ones written by Rimbaud or Verlaine.

The fourth constraint is based on a semantic analysis of the original sonnets. Six main themes were identified (beauty, love, death, nature, spirituality), later on reduced to five, as melancholy and death were hard to distinguished. A sample of sonnets were annotated using these categories (50 sonnets per category) and a classifier trained on the manually annotated corpus. It is thus possible to generate sonnets based on the part of the corpus that have been classified as pertaining to a specific theme. Note that the annotation operates at the sonnet level, whereas generation operates at the verse level. However, we assume that the theme gives a general flavor to the text, not every verse has to be relevant from a thematic point of view.

The approach is quite simple from a computational point of view. However, it is difficult to control on the fly the number of sonnets that can be generated, depending on the number of contraints chosen by the end user. It is however important to keep track of this, otherwise the end user may frequently arrive at a dead end, with a number of contraints that prevents the possibility to generate new sonnets (a basic rule being that one verse cannot rhyme with itself, and even cannot be selected twice).

5 Overview of the Demonstration

The main interest of the OuPoCo project is to present French poetry through a new and original setting. With our system, poetry is not any more just a literary genre (Derrida and Ronell, 1980), but a dynamic object that can be manipulated and experienced. For lots of people, poetry is seen at best as something related to school years, at worse as something boring and uninteresting from the past. Our new setting, in itself, makes it possible to show that playing with poetry can be fun. Our setting puts in perspective the notion of text coherence (Reinhart, 1980) since the result of the generator can be more or less satisfactory from a semantic point of view.

It is possible to interact with OuPoCo through a web site (https://oupoco.org/fr, see figure 1).

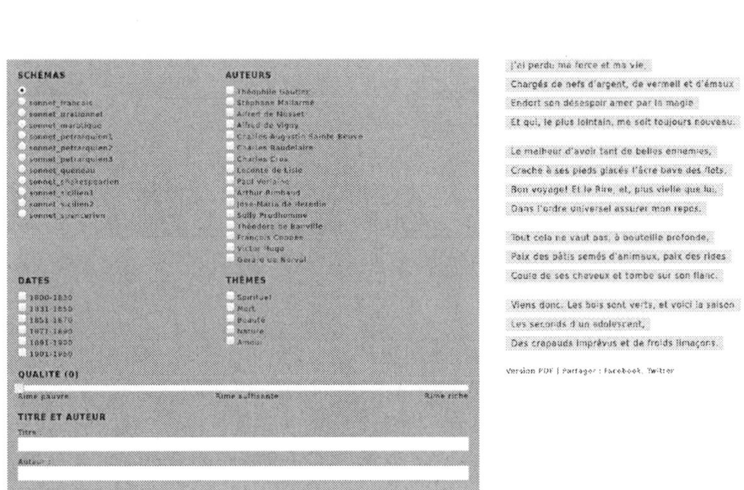

Figure 1: An overview of the system on the Web. On the left, the set of possible constraints; on the right, an example of generated sonnet

It is also possible to regularly have a look at the bot posting a quatrain every 6 hours on Twitter (see figure 2). Finally, we also had a collaboration with a duo of artists who produced a "poetry box" (*La boîte à poésie*, see figure 3), a portable version of the original idea that can be demonstrated in public events (based on Raspberry Pi components). Through these devices our goal is to reach a wider audience and engage people to reconnect with poetry.

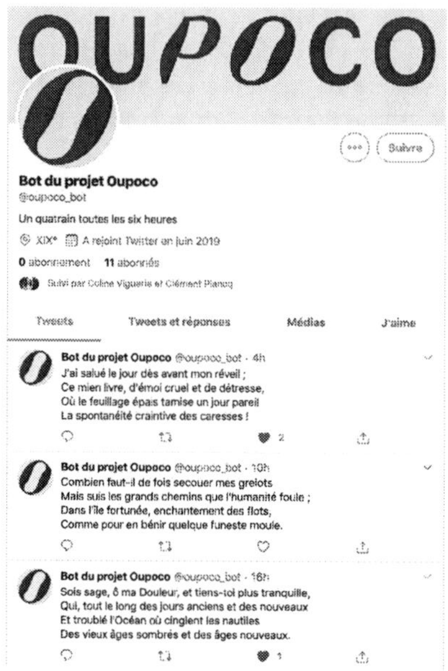

Figure 2: The Oupoco bot on Twitter

6   Evaluation and Interest of the System Output

At the crossroad between surrealism and absurdism, generated sonnets are generally quite funny and convey a dreamlike atmosphere. The themes specific to the Romantic period – such as love, whether it is magnified or lost, death or the fleetingness of time to name but a few – contribute to creating bizarre but intriguing poems. If most of them lack coherence in terms of punctuation or pronouns, these syntactic confusions can actually reinforce their poetic overtones.

The OuPoCo system is intended to be presented in front of an audience, to elicit reactions. We did not perform a formal evaluation, as we would be unable to provide meaningful evaluation criteria (Gervás, 2013) and moreover, as this is not the goal. The interest is to create reactions, to use our piece of software as a mean to make people rediscover poetry and literature.

One should also note that, because the machine produces structurally impeccable sonnets, the experiencer is unconsciously encouraged to find coherence in them, simply because we are used to coherence in our everyday life and because incoherence is bewildering (Reinhart, 1980). The second consequence is a frequent need for the experiencer to go back to the original poem, to see where from a given verse originates (tooltips always allows the experiencer to go back to the original sonnet). The project is thus not just a sacrilege game over venerated texts, but a way to make people experience and rediscover poetry.

7   Conclusion

We have described OuPoCo, a system inspired by Queneau and implemented through different devices. It aims at reconciling people with literature, especially poetry, a genre that is not very popular outside the educational system. The project was also the opportunity of a collaboration with a couple of artists who produced *La Boîte à poésie*, an interesting spin-off of the project mixing art and technology. In the future, we plan to study the potential impact of our system in different (real world) contexts, especially in educational settings.

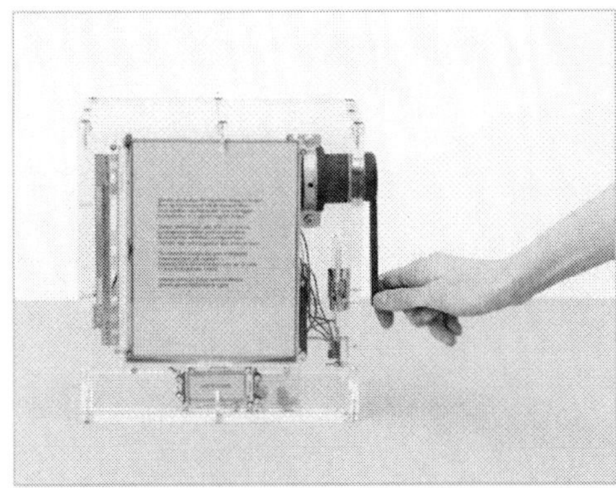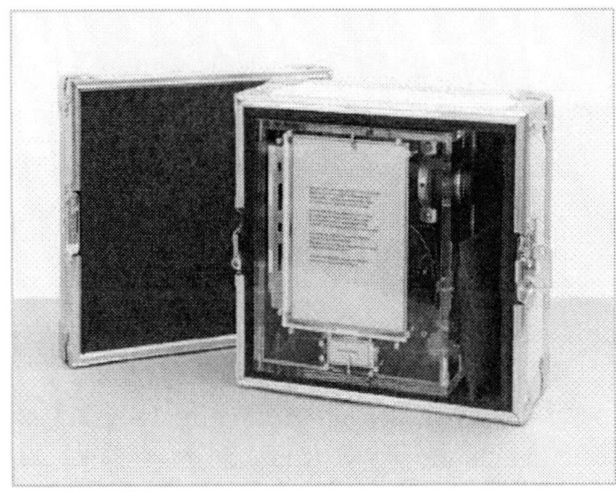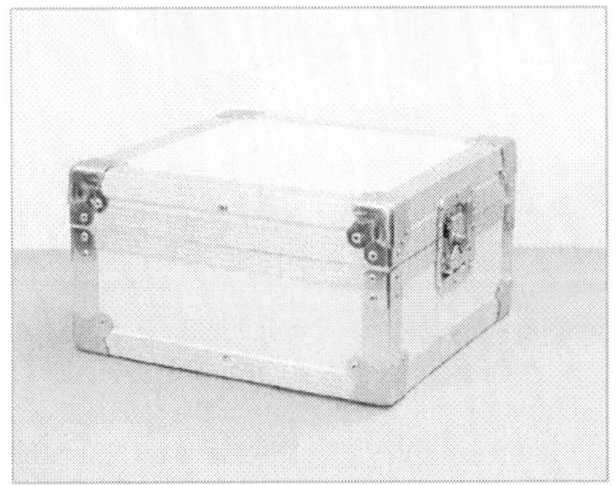

Figure 3: La Boîte à poésie, integrating the OuPoCo sonnet generator. This device has been developed by Atelier Raffard-Roussel, a couple of artists based in Paris. See `http://www.raffard-roussel.com/fr/projets-boite-a-poesie/` for details.

Acknowledgements

This work has received support of Translitteræ (Ecole universitaire de recherche, program "Investissements d'avenir" ANR-10-IDEX-0001-02 PSL* and ANR-17-EURE-0025). This work was also supported in part by the French government under management of Agence Nationale de la Recherche as part of the "Investissements d'avenir" program, reference ANR19-P3IA-0001 (PRAIRIE 3IA Institute).

References

Valérie Beaudouin. 2002. *Mètre et rythmes du vers classique. Corneille et Racine*. Honoré Champion (Lettres numériques), Paris.

Jacques Derrida and Avital Ronell. 1980. On narrative: The law of genre. *Critical Inquiry*, 7(1):55–81.

Pablo Gervás. 2013. Computational modelling of poetry generation. In *Artificial Intelligence and Poetry Symposium, AISB Convention*, University of Exeter.

Marjan Ghazvininejad, Xing Shi, Jay Priyadarshi, and Kevin Knight. 2017. Hafez: an interactive poetry generation system. In *Proceedings of ACL 2017, System Demonstrations*, pages 43–48, Vancouver, Canada.

Raymond Queneau. 1961. *Cent mille milliards de poèmes*. Gallimard, Paris.

Tanya Reinhart. 1980. Conditions for text coherence. *Poetics Today (Narratology II: The Fictional Text and the Reader)*, 1(4):161–180.

Tim Van de Cruys. 2020. Automatic poetry generation from prosaic text. In *Proceedings of the 58th Annual Meeting of the Association for Computational Linguistics*, Held online.

Interpretation of Sentiment Analysis in Aeschylus's Greek Tragedy

Vijaya Kumari Yeruva
Dept. of CSEE
Univ. of Missouri-KC
vyq4b@mail.umkc.edu

Mayanka Chandrashekar
Dept. of CSEE
Univ. of Missouri-KC
mckw9@mail.umkc.edu

Yugyung Lee
Dept. of CSEE
Univ. of Missouri-KC
leeyu@umkc.edu

Jeff Rydberg-Cox
Dept. of English
Univ. of Missouri-KC
rydbergcoxj@umkc.edu

Virginia Blanton
Dept. of English
Univ. of Missouri-KC
blantonv@umkc.edu

Nathan A Oyler
Dept. of Chemistry
Univ. of Missouri-KC
oylern@umkc.edu

Abstract

Recent advancements in NLP and machine learning have created unique challenges and opportunities for digital humanities research. In particular, there are ample opportunities for NLP and machine learning researchers to analyze data from literary texts and to broaden our understanding of human sentiment in classical Greek tragedy. In this paper, we will explore the challenges and benefits from the human and machine collaboration for sentiment analysis in Greek tragedy and address some open questions related to the collaborative annotation for the sentiments in literary texts. We focus primarily on (i) an analysis of the challenges in sentiment analysis tasks for humans and machines, and (ii) whether consistent annotation results are generated from the multiple human annotators and multiple machine annotators. For human annotators, we have used a survey-based approach with about 60 college students. We have selected three popular sentiment analysis tools for machine annotators, including VADER, CoreNLP's sentiment annotator, and TextBlob. We have conducted a qualitative and quantitative evaluation and confirmed our observations on sentiments in Greek tragedy.

1 Introduction

Recent advancements in NLP and machine learning have created unique opportunities for digital humanities research. In particular, sentiment analysis toolkits provide a way to explore the representation of emotions in literary texts such as ancient Greek Tragedy. Aristotle defined *tragedy* as a medium for bringing out emotions, especially pity and fear. Greek tragedies express a plethora of emotions via the characters and their narratives. Recent advancements in the NLP and machine learning make it possible to conduct a systematic analysis of these sentiments and emotions using computational tools.

Recent work has explored the differences between sentiments and emotions in Greek Tragedy and contemporary society. There have been two contrasting views on a universal emotion across time and space. On the one hand, Kalimtzis used David Cairn's school of thought that "cultures exhibit points of overlap that make them mutual intelligible," in other words, having "naive assumption of shared humanity" (Kalimtzis, 2014). In contrast, Konstan endorses the opposing view that emotions observed in Greeks of the classical period are different from the modern ones (Konstan, 2015; Muellner and others, 1996). In recent years, there has been scholarly work focused on comparing the contemporary population's emotional impact based on Greek Tragedy and horrific contemporary events (Munteanu, 2017), or even focusing on the role of emotions in ancient Greek diplomatic practice (Gazzano, 2019).

Sentiment analysis could be used as a training step for machines to perform more complex tasks like emotion detection. However, sentiment analysis is not an easy task for a machine because of the multiple and often unpredictable variables applied to interpret a given sentence. Typically, sentiment in context is

Proceedings of LaTeCH-CLfL 2020, pages 138–146
Barcelona, Spain (Online), December 12, 2020.

an incredibly complex task for machines. A study (Min and Park, 2019) presented a highly complex and dynamic system for reflecting the rich structure of human interaction and communication and identifying associated sentiments and topics by characterizing relationships explicitly. It demonstrated how these methods could be used to explore Victor Hugo's Les Misérables.

In our study, sentiment analysis on Greek Tragedy was conducted using both social media trained sentiment analysis tools and human annotators. This work is an initial step in exploring promising research on the modern understanding of ancient emotion. Furthermore, to conduct advanced sentiment analysis in machine learning, we need well-annotated data that can be used to teach machines about emotion in Greek Tragedy. The human-in-the-loop (Wu et al., 2019; Tsakalidis et al., 2018) has received attention for the potential of human and machine collaboration. More reliable data can be collectively annotated for in-depth study in machine learning from this kind of collaboration.

In this paper, we explore the challenges and benefits from the human and machine collaboration for sentiment annotation about sentiments in Greek Tragedy and address some open questions related to the collaborative annotation. We are particularly interested in analyzing why similar or different behaviors or opinions may be observed from the machine and human annotators–and what a comparison of human annotators and machine annotators can teach us about how humans and machines read emotion. We mainly focus on (i) an analysis of the challenges in sentiment analysis tasks for humans as well as machines and (ii) whether consistent annotation results are generated from multiple human annotators and multiple machine annotators.

2 Study Domain: Greek Tragedy

For this study, Aeschylus's essays were obtained in TEI conformant XML texts from the Perseus Digital Library (Smith et al., 2000; Rydberg-Cox, 2011). We extracted sentences based on stratified sampling, as shown in Table 1. We used the sentiment annotations ranging from 'extremely positive' to 'extremely negative' (also known as diversity sampling (Munro, 2019)).

Table 1: Greek Tragedy Survey Dataset

Essay Name	Sentences	Total# of Sentence
Eumenides	8	115
Prometheus Bound	11	138
Seven Against	7	82
Agamemnon	12	188
Suppliant Women	4	107
Persians	8	122
Total	50	752

2.1 Research Questions

There are two main goals of this paper:

RQ1: *What is the level of agreement between multiple human and machine annotators when evaluating sentiments? If the agreement is low, what are the reasons behind it? From the human annotators' evaluation, what is the impact of context towards their sentiment rankings?* To appropriately characterize or measure the mutual (dis)agreement between human annotators, we performed the statistical analysis and studied: (i) the correlation between sentiment annotation and the change in sentiment annotation when read in context, (ii) the correlation between sentiment annotation and survey sentence length, and (iii) the correlation between sentiment annotation and the number of words expressed emotions or sentiments.

RQ2: *What are the primary properties of annotators (humans or machines) that can "coexist" with sentiment annotations and (dis)agreement of sentiments in different segments and episodes?* We will assess the annotation by comparing human and machine agreement and disagreement and conduct both qualitative and quantitative evaluation regarding agreement and disagreement between human annotators. For the qualitative assessment, we will identify the most controversial question that shows the highest standard deviation among the human sentiment annotations. The survey questions will be explored further to explain the challenges of sentence-level annotation, contextual-level annotation, machine-level annotation, sentimental terms, and the survey sentence length. We will calculate Cohen's Kappa scores to describe the quality of human annotators' annotations for the quantitative evaluation.

Table 2: Survey Questions

ID	Questions	Answers
Q1	Sentiment for a given sentence (dialogue or partial of dialogue)	*Extremely Positive, Moderately Positive, Neutral, Moderately Negative, Extremely Negative*
Q2	Words that lead to sentiment discussion	*Word list from a given sentence*
Q3	Sentiment for a given sentence with the context defined	*Extremely Positive, Moderately Positive, Neutral, Moderately Negative, Extremely Negative*

2.2 Survey Design for Human Annotation

For the human annotation study, we have used a survey-based approach to access the human ability to analyze sentiment in Greek tragedy. For our study, 61 college students in the humanities were asked to rate the sentiments expressed in sentences extracted from the texts.

2.2.1 Design of Survey Questions

We asked students to focus on: (1) "sentiment" in a sentence (referred to as the target sentence), (2) the words in the target sentence that contributed to the annotated "sentiment." and (3) the "sentiment" of the target sentence within a given context (referred to as the sentence-in-context).

- Question 1 (Q1) aims to capture the sentiment expressed by a sentence, with no knowledge about the speaker or the play. This question is designed to capture the sentiment perceived by the annotator by reading a sentence in isolation.
- Question 2 (Q2) aims to understand why that annotator thinks a sentence exhibits a particular sentiment. The second question is designed to realize the interpretability component of the sentiment selected in Q1.
- Question 3 (Q3) aims to capture the sentence's sentiment within a broader context and if the human understanding of sentiment in a given sentence changes when that sentence is read in context. We represent the context by providing sentences before and after the given sentence from Question 1.

Table 2 shows the three questions that were posed for each sentence that the students were asked to annotate. The sentiment was categorized into the following categories: [*Extremely Positive, Moderately Positive, Neutral, Moderately Negative, Extremely Negative*].

2.2.2 Hypothesis and Observations

We had several assumptions about human annotators completing this task. First, the human annotators would not be broadly familiar with the Greek tragedies from which the sentences were drawn and would not be able to infer the broader context from a single sentence. Determining sentiment accurately in a single sentence without context is not an easy task. The sentiment annotation might change when it is understood within a broader context. Second, the sentiment expressed in many sentences is ambiguous and there may be subtle differences between the ways that different annotators perceive sentiment in a given sentence (e.g., extremely negative and negative). This ambiguity is also correlated with the number of words that express sentiment in any given sentence. Thus, it is even tricky for multiple human annotators to offer a consistent assessment of each sentence.

In our study, 50 sentences were randomly selected from the corpus of Greek tragedy for human annotation. On average, each sentence was annotated by fifteen human annotators (13-17 annotators per question). Of the human annotators, three types of sentiment questions were posed. (Q1) "sentiment" in a sentence (referred to as the target sentence), (Q2) the words in the target sentence that contributed to annotated "sentiment," and (Q3) the "sentiment" of the target sentence within a given context (referred to as the sentence-in-context).

2.3 Model Design for Machine Annotation

For machine annotation, we selected three popular sentiment analysis tools, VADER (Hutto and Gilbert, 2014), CoreNLP's sentiment annotator (Socher et al., 2013), and TextBlob (Loria, 2017). VADER (Hutto and Gilbert, 2014) is a rule-based model for sentiment analysis that was empirically constructed by a gold standard list of linguistic features and sentiment in microblog-like contexts. Developers demonstrated its effectiveness compared to the state-of-practice benchmarks and shallow machine learning algorithms.

VADER's sentiment intensity valence is ranged from -1 (most extreme negative) to +1 (most extreme positive). Stanford CoreNLP's sentiment annotator (Socher et al., 2013), which was designed with Recursive Neural Tensor Networks and the Stanford Sentiment Treebank, achieved 80.7% accuracy on fine-grained sentiment prediction. It has five sentiment classes, very negative to very positive (from 0 to 4) at a sentence level. TextBlob (Loria, 2017) determines sentiment in two measures, namely polarity and subjectivity. The polarity score describes the sentiment intensity in a range from -1.0 to 1.0. The subjectivity score ranges from 0.0 to 1.0, where 0.0 is very objective, and 1.0 is very subjective.

3 Experimental Results and Evaluation

These models for sentiment analysis are based on the lexical, grammatical, and syntactical conventions of model sentiment. Expressing sentiment intensity is determined by rules that might differ from sentiments as they are expressed in the literary texts. Our initial hypothesis is that human annotations of sentiments in Greek tragedy will be similar to the machine annotations and validate the applicability of these toolkits for literary texts. This is determined as follows: First, machine annotators face similar challenges to those of human annotators. Since machine annotators rely on a dictionary of word meanings, they can be consistently applied for sentiment analysis. However, some terms from Greek tragedy may not be adequately de-

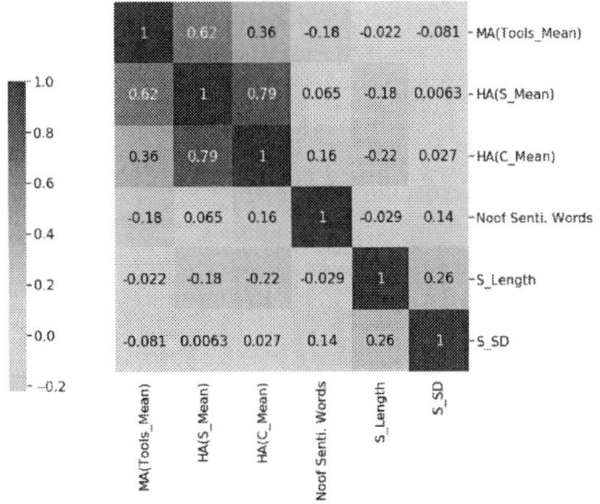

Figure 1: Correlation Testing

termined by machine annotators. Contemporary meanings in social media, for which the sentiment analysis tools were developed, may not align. Second, machine annotators have their own discrete sentiment annotations. For example, the annotation ratings for VADER, CoreNLP, and TextBlob vary. For simplicity, we have normalized them into five annotations, consistent with the human annotations ranging from extremely positive (1) to extremely negative (5). Finally, since machine annotators cannot determine a sentiment annotation when the input is given with the surrounding context, it is difficult for multiple machine annotators to get a consistent annotation result.

We used correlation tests to determine whether the values of quantitative variables change in conjunction with each approach. First, we computed the pairwise correlation coefficients for quantitative variables using the Pearson coefficient (r) and represented them in a heatmap. Second, we checked whether the variation between the sets of variables is monotonic (increasing or decreasing) or whether the data's underlying distribution is normal. Correlation coefficients ranged from -1.00 to +1.00. A positive value indicates a positive correlation – one variable is increasing, and so does the other – while a negative value indicates a negative correlation – one variable is increasing and the other decreasing.

Table 3 shows six hypothetical variables and Figure 1 illustrates the correlations of these variables: positive correlations are displayed in red and negative correlations in light blue. Color intensity is proportional to the correlation coefficients. We have also extended the Pearson coefficient correlation (r) with additional coefficients such as Spearman (ρ) and Kendall's tau (τ), and the overall graphs shown in Figure 2 are shown with consistent correlations for five variables and three coefficient values.

Table 3: Hypothetical Variables

Variable	Description
MA	*Machine Annotation (Mean)*
HS	*Human Annotation in Sentence (Mean)*
HC	*Human Annotation in Context (Mean)*
SW	*#Sentiment Words*
SL	*Sentence Length*
SD	*HA Standard Deviation*

As seen from Figure 1 and Figure 2, there are four positive correlations (HS-HC, HS-MA, HC-MA, SL-SD) and two negative correlations (HS-SL, HC-SL). The human-to-human annotation (HS-HC),

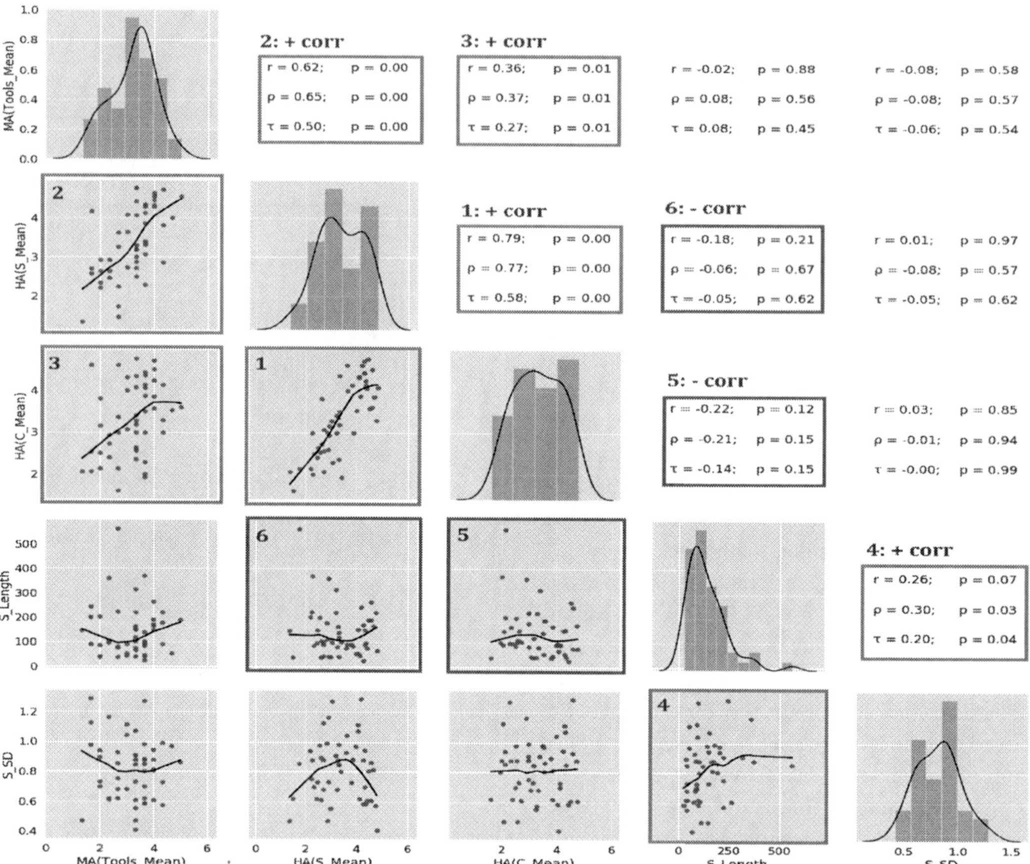

Figure 2: Correlation Testing between Machine Annotations (MA), Human Annotations (HA), Survey Sentence Length (S_Length), and Standard Deviation of Human Annotations (S_SD). Where r: Pearson, ρ: Spearman, and τ: Kendall's tau correlation's value. The green boxes (Cases 1, 2, 3, 4) indicate a positive correlation while the red boxes (Cases 5,6) indicate a negative correlation.

which is even in two different settings such as sentence and context, and the human-to-machine annotation (HS-MA) show the two highest correlations with coefficient values of 0.79 and 0.62, respectively. The human annotations for a sentence and the sentence length (HS-SL) and human annotations for a sentence in context and the sentence length (HC-SL) show the two lowest correlations with coefficient values of -0.22 and -0.18. Figure 1 shows no significant correlation between the human annotations for a sentence and the number of sentiment words (HS-SW).

3.1 Human and Machine Collaboration in Sentiment Annotation

Human-machine co-annotation is the first step towards interactive machine learning. Most of the current work in interactive machine learning ultimately uses human annotations as interpretability for the existing system (Wu et al., 2019; Smith-Renner et al., 2020; Lertvittayakumjorn and Toni, 2019). In this collaborative annotation system, humans and machines are given the same task to facilitate a compare and contrast analysis. We assess the questionnaire's ability to detect agreement or disagreement of human and machine annotators and then determine if there were significant correlations between variables for human and machine collaboration for sentiment annotation in Greek tragedy.

3.1.1 Agreement Among Human Annotators

We have evaluated the degree of the agreement among multiple annotators (13 to 17 annotators) using two approaches. First, we analyzed the standard deviation for the human annotators (13 to 17 annotators per question) for 50 questions. We have categorized the 50 questions into six categories: (1) SD $\leq$ 0.55,

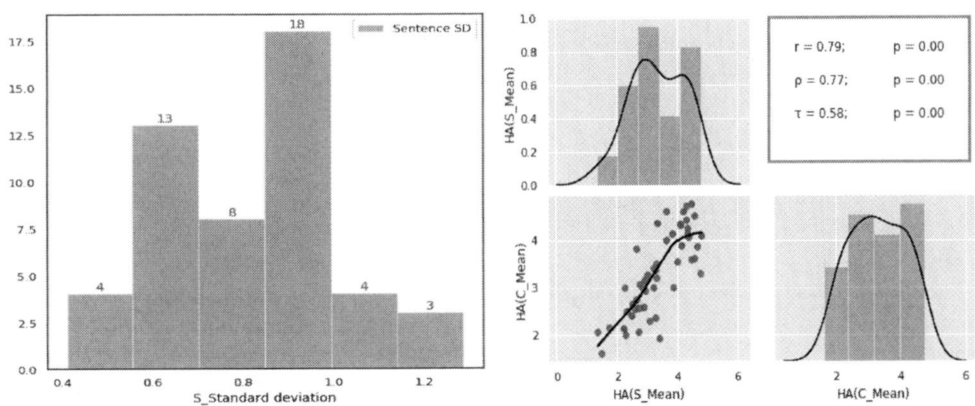

Figure 3: (a) Standard Deviation Distribution of HS (b) Correlation between HS and HC

(2) $0.56 \leq SD < 0.70$, (3) $0.70 \leq SD < 0.84$, (4) $0.85 \leq SD < 1.00$, (5) $1.00 \leq SD \leq 1.15$, and (6) $1.16 \leq SD < 1.30$ as shown in Figure 3(a). The mean of human annotations for both sentence and context are positively correlated with a Pearson correlation value of 0.79, as shown in Figure 3(b). One of the three most controversial survey questions ($1.16 \leq SD < 1.30$) is shown in Table 4. This survey question from the play *Agamemnon* was rated 3.07 (Neutral) in the sentence in isolation to 2.28 (Moderately Positive) in context by 13 annotators.

Second, we considered the correlation analysis using three coefficient measures, such as the Pearson coefficient correlation (r), Spearman (ρ), and Kendall's tau (τ). Figure 4 shows that the human annotations for both sentence (HA) and context (HC) are positively correlated to the machine annotations (MA) with the Pearson correlation values of 0.62 and 0.36, respectively. Similarly, Spearman (ρ) and Kendall's tau (τ) values show the positive correlations for HA and MA, HC, and MA.

Table 4: Sentiment Annotation with High Standard Deviation (SD=1.27)

	Essay Name	*Agamemnon*
Sentence	**Survey Question**	**Survey Question in Context**
High SD	(Mean: 3.07) *Exile though I was, I laid my hand upon my enemy, compassing every device of cunning to his ruin.*	(Mean: 2.28) *But grown to manhood, justice has brought me back again. Exile though I was, I laid my hand upon my enemy, compassing every device of cunning to his ruin. So even death would be sweet to me now that I behold him in justice's net.*

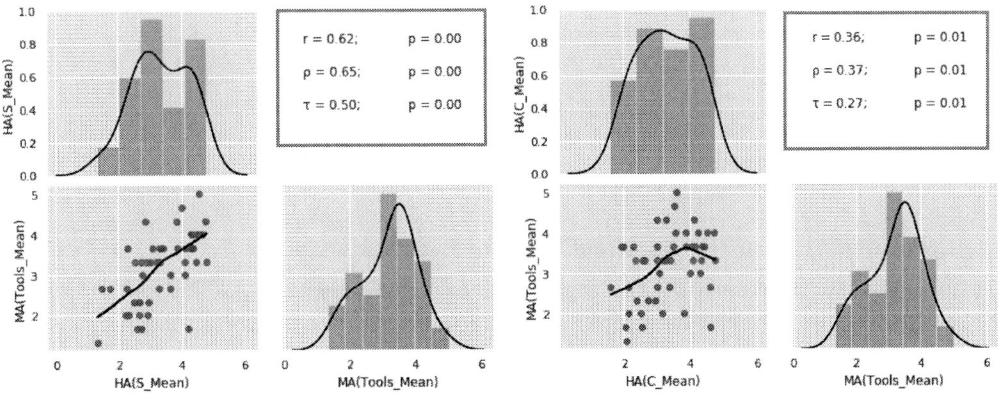

Figure 4: (a) Correlation between HS and MA (b) Correlation between HC and MA

3.1.2 Agreement between Human Annotators and Machine Annotators

For human and machine annotation, we computed Cohen's Kappa Correlation (Cohen, 1960), one of the most commonly used statistics to test inter-rater reliability (Tsakalidis et al., 2018). Kappa value of $<$ 0 indicates Poor agreement, $0.01 - 0.20$: Slight agreement, $0.21 - 0.40$: Fair agreement, $0.41 - 0.60$: Moderate agreement, $0.61 - 0.80$: Substantial agreement, and $0.81 - 1.00$: Almost perfect agreement.

The inter-rater reliability for HS and MA was evaluated, and the kappa value of 0.11 was computed for the HS-MA. Then, we conducted it for three individual machine annotators (VADER, CoreNLP, and TextBlob). The kappa values of 0.23, 0.13, -0.05 were reported for HS-VADER, HS-CoreNLP, and HS-TextBlob. Among machine annotators, the agreement between VADER and human annotators (HS) shows the best kappa value, 0.23, compared to others, which is a *fair agreement*, according to Kappa Correlation.

3.2 Sentiment Change With Context

We have evaluated the impact of context on the survey question regarding the annotators' sentiment annotations. The introduction of context is an attempt to determine, using the theory of Michel Foucault, if sentiment in the context of Greek tragedy is a 'discursive object', a product of 'discourse' (Kalimtzis, 2014; Foucault, 1970). Figure 5 depicts the distribution of sentiment annotations of sentences from Greek tragedy without context and with context. The figure shows the sentiment annotation distributions of the survey questions without context in blue and with the context in yellow. Table 5 shows the most change in sentiment annotations. First, the mean of annotation by 14 annotators changes negatively from 3 (Neutral) to 3.8 (leaning towards Moderately Negative) by adding the context to the survey question. Second, the

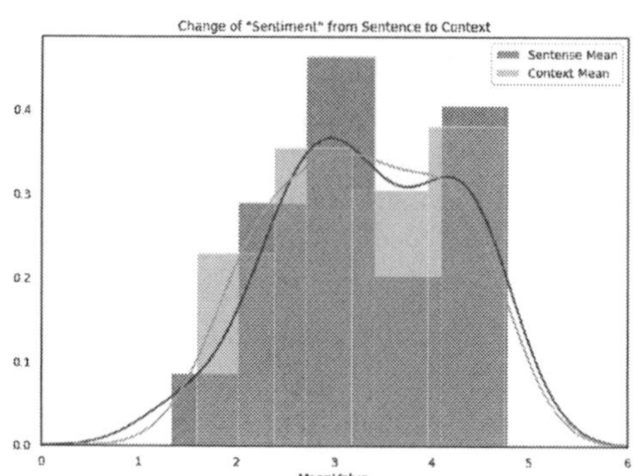

Figure 5: Sentiment Change With Context

mean of annotation by 15 annotators changes negatively from 3.4 (Neutral) to 1.9 (leaning towards Moderately Positive) by adding the context to the survey question. This shows the impacts of the sentiment change due to the existence of context.

Table 5: Sentiment Change in Context

	Essay Name	*Eumenides*
Change	**Survey Question**	**Survey Question in Context**
Negative $3 \Rightarrow 3.8$	(Mean: 3.0) *I will give you strong proof of this.*	(Mean: 3.8) *I am not a suppliant in need of purification, nor did I sit at your image with pollution on my hands. I will give you strong proof of this. It is the law for one who is defiled by shedding blood to be barred from speech until he is sprinkled with the blood of a new-born victim by a man who can purify from murder.*
Positive $3.4 \Rightarrow 1.9$	(Mean: 3.4) *Lord Apollo, you know how to do no wrong; and, since you know this, learn not to be neglectful also.*	(Mean: 1.9) *Lord Apollo, you know how to do no wrong; and, since you know this, learn not to be neglectful also. For your power to do good is assured.*

3.3 Correlation between Sentence Length and Sentiment Annotation

Human sentiment annotation tends to be negative for short sentences while positive for long sentences. Our results show that the higher the standard of deviation, the more the disagreement among annotators. Figure 6 shows that the sentence length (SL) is negatively correlated to human sentiment annotations (HA) and VADER's, while SL is positively related to standard deviations of human annotation (SD). Sentence length and standard deviation of human annotations for the sentence are positively correlated with a Pearson correlation value of 0.26, as shown in Figure 6(d). This indicates that longer sentences in the questionnaires tend to show more disagreement among annotators.

Regarding the relationship between the sentence length and sentiment annotation, Table 6 shows a short sentence is rated as *Extremely Negative* (mean: 4.28) by 14 human annotators and *Extremely Negative* by VADER. At the same time, a long sentence is rated as *Moderately Positive* (mean: 1.73) by 15 human annotators and *Extremely Positive* by VADER. Similar patterns are shown in the sentiment annotations for the question in context.

Table 6: Sentence Length and Sentiment Annotation

	Essay Name	Eumenides
Sentence	**Survey Question**	**Survey Question in Context**
Short	(Mean: 4.28) *Oh, oh, the shame of it!*	(Mean: 4.42) *I am breathing fury and utter rage. Oh, oh, the shame of it!* **What anguish steals into my breast!**
Long	(Mean: 1.73) *For us, the remnant of the Argive host, the gain has the advantage, and the loss does not bear down the scale; so that, as we speed over land and sea, it is fitting that we on this bright day make this boast: The Argive army, having taken Troy, at last, has nailed up these spoils to be a glory for the gods throughout Hellas in their shrines from days of old. Whoever hears the story of these deeds must extol the city and the leaders of her host, and the grace of Zeus that brought them to accomplishment shall receive its due measure of gratitude.*	(Mean: 2.14) **Our misfortunes should, in my opinion, bid us a long farewell.** *For us, the remnant of the Argive host, the gain has the advantage, and the loss does not bear down the scale; so that, as we speed over land and sea, it is fitting that we on this bright day make this boast: The Argive army, having taken Troy, at last, has nailed up these spoils to be a glory for the gods throughout Hellas in their shrines from days of old. Whoever hears the story of these deeds must extol the city and the leaders of her host, and the grace of Zeus that brought them to accomplishment shall receive its due measure of gratitude.*

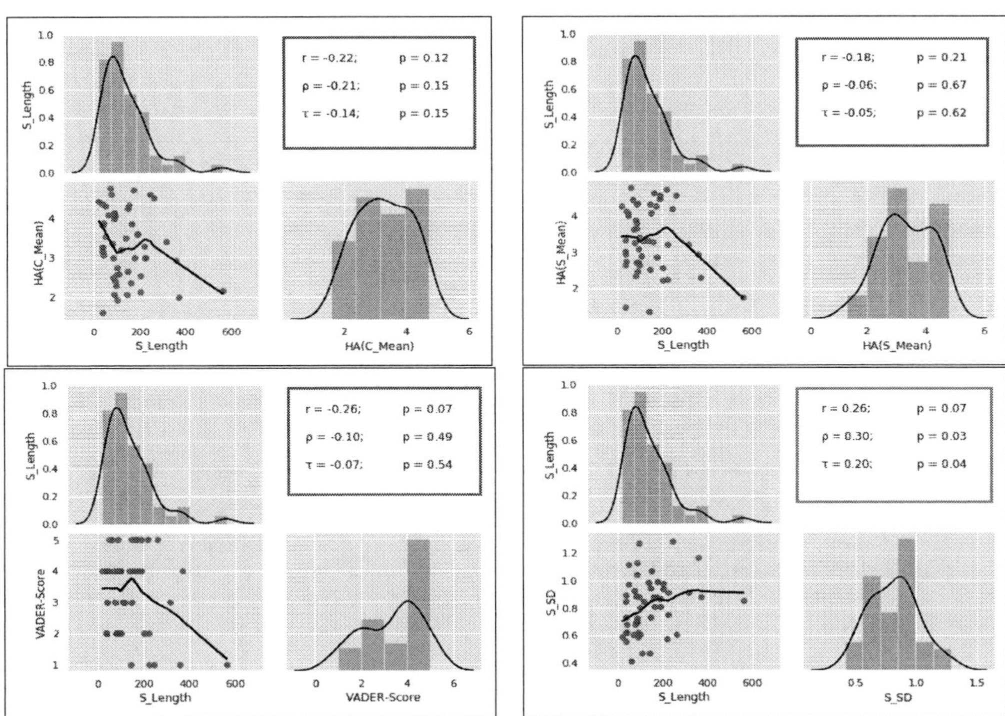

Figure 6: Correlations: (a) SL and HC (b) SL and HS (c) SL and VADER (d) SL and SD

4 Conclusions

This study explored the following questions: *What is the level of agreement between multiple human and machine annotators when evaluating sentiments in Greek tragedy? If the agreement is low, what are the reasons behind it?* First, we have conducted a coefficient correlation analysis with six variables using Pearson, Spearman, and Kendall and found that there are positive correlations for human-to-human annotation as well as human-to-machine annotation and negative correlations for human annotation and sentence length. Second, we have conducted the inter-rater reliability between human and machine annotators, and the results are either fair or slight agreement. The inter-rater reliability between human and machine annotators confirms the high performance of computational sentiment analysis (especially VADER) and their applicability to literary texts such as Greek tragedies.

References

J Cohen. 1960. A coefficient of agreement for nominal scales educ psychol meas. *SAGE Publications Inc*, 20:37–46.

Michel Foucault. 1970. The archaeology of knowledge. *Information (International Social Science Council)*, 9(1):175–185.

Francesca Gazzano. 2019. Greek ambassadors and the rhetoric of supplication. some notes. *KTÈMA Civilisations de l'Orient, de la Grèce et de Rome antiques*, 44:53–69.

Clayton J Hutto and Eric Gilbert. 2014. Vader: A parsimonious rule-based model for sentiment analysis of social media text. In *Eighth international AAAI conference on weblogs and social media*.

Kostas Kalimtzis. 2014. *Taming Anger: The Hellenic Approach to the Limitations of Reason.* A&C Black.

David Konstan. 2015. Affect and emotion in Greek literature. *Oxford Handbooks Online*.

Piyawat Lertvittayakumjorn and Francesca Toni. 2019. Human-grounded evaluations of explanation methods for text classification. In *Proceedings of the 2019 Conference on Empirical Methods in Natural Language Processing and the 9th International Joint Conference on Natural Language Processing (EMNLP-IJCNLP)*, pages 5198–5208.

Steven Loria. 2017. Textblob: Simplified text processing [a python (2 and 3) library for processing textual data].

Semi Min and Juyong Park. 2019. Modeling narrative structure and dynamics with networks, sentiment analysis, and topic modeling. *PloS one*, 14(12):e0226025.

Leonard Charles Muellner et al. 1996. *The anger of Achilles: Mēnis in Greek epic.* Cornell University Press.

Robert Munro. 2019. Human-in-the-loop machine learning.

Dana LaCourse Munteanu. 2017. The paradox of literary emotion: An ancient Greek perspective and some modern implications. *Nuntius Antiquus*, 13(2):263–283.

Jeff Rydberg-Cox. 2011. Social networks and the language of Greek tragedy. *Journal of the Chicago Colloquium on Digital Humanities and Computer Science*, 1(3).

David A Smith, Jeffrey A Rydberg-Cox, and Gregory R Crane. 2000. The perseus project: A digital library for the humanities. *Literary and Linguistic Computing*, 15(1):15–25.

Alison Smith-Renner, Ron Fan, Melissa Birchfield, Tongshuang Wu, Jordan Boyd-Graber, Daniel S Weld, and Leah Findlater. 2020. No explainability without accountability: An empirical study of explanations and feedback in interactive ml. In *Proceedings of the 2020 CHI Conference on Human Factors in Computing Systems*, pages 1–13.

Richard Socher, Alex Perelygin, Jean Wu, Jason Chuang, Christopher D Manning, Andrew Y Ng, and Christopher Potts. 2013. Recursive deep models for semantic compositionality over a sentiment treebank. In *Proceedings of the 2013 conference on empirical methods in natural language processing*, pages 1631–1642.

Adam Tsakalidis, Symeon Papadopoulos, Rania Voskaki, Kyriaki Ioannidou, Christina Boididou, Alexandra I Cristea, Maria Liakata, and Yiannis Kompatsiaris. 2018. Building and evaluating resources for sentiment analysis in the Greek language. *Language resources and evaluation*, 52(4):1021–1044.

Tongshuang Wu, Daniel S Weld, and Jeffrey Heer. 2019. Local decision pitfalls in interactive machine learning: An investigation into feature selection in sentiment analysis. *ACM Transactions on Computer-Human Interaction (TOCHI)*, 26(4):1–27.

Towards Olfactory Information Extraction from Text:
A Case Study on Detecting Smell Experiences in Novels

Ryan Brate and **Paul Groth**
University of Amsterdam
Amsterdam, the Netherlands
`r.brate@gmail.com`
`p.t.groth@uva.nl`

Marieke van Erp
KNAW Humanities Cluster
Digital Humanities Lab
Amsterdam, the Netherlands
`marieke.van.erp@dh.huc.knaw.nl`

Abstract

Environmental factors determine the smells we perceive, but societal factors factors shape the importance, sentiment and biases we give to them. Descriptions of smells in text, or as we call them 'smell experiences', offer a window into these factors, but they must first be identified. To the best of our knowledge, no tool exists to extract references to smell experiences from text. In this paper, we present two variations on a semi-supervised approach to identify smell experiences in English literature. The combined set of patterns from both implementations offer significantly better performance than a keyword-based baseline.

1 Introduction

We rely on our senses: touch, taste, hearing, sight and smell; to complement one another in shaping our interpretation of our environment. There is shifting historical relevance placed on smell - its worthiness for attention, its association with social standing, lifestyle, emotion, science and superstitions, and other topical associations shifting with time (Vroon et al., 1997). English language vocabulary specific to the description of smell experiences is not expansive, and, to the best of our knowledge, language technology to identify references to smell in text even less so. A topic search in the Cambridge Dictionary online of words categorised as relating to smells and smelling[1] returns fewer than 30 words, that are predominantly concerned with *intensity* or *sentiment* such as *fetid* and *reek*. Other characteristics of smell are instead often described in terms of reference smell sources as similes such as *There is a strange unwholesome smell upon the room, **like mildewed corduroys***.

In this paper, we present a dataset of annotated references to smell, which we call 'smell experiences' in literature, as well as a first approach and experiments to automatically recognise references to smells in texts.

The remainder of this paper is organised as follows. In Section 2, we discuss related work. In Section 3, we describe our corpus and its creation process. In Section 4, we present our extraction approach and experiments. In Section 5, we discuss the results. We conclude with Section 6 in which we present our conclusions and directions for future work. Our data is available at `http://doi.org/10.5281/zenodo.4199996` and the code to the experiments is available at `https://github.com/DHLab-nl/Detecting-Smell-Experiences-in-Novels`. This work is a preliminary result of the Odeuropa project which will commence formally in January 2021: `https://odeuropa.eu/`.

2 Related Work

The cultural significance of smells is a niche topic in the humanities domain, but one that has recently gained more interest with a translation of Muchembled's 2017 *La Civilisation des odeurs (XVIe siècle-début XIXe siècle)* to English (Muchembled, 2020) and Barwich's *Smellosophy: what the nose tells the*

---

[1]`https://dictionary.cambridge.org/topics/senses-and-sounds/smells-and-smelling/` Accessed: 5 August 2020

mind(Barwich, 2020) being reviewed in mainstream media.[2] While historians interested in olfaction such as (Tullett, 2019) analyse textual accounts of experienced smells, (computational) linguistic analysis of smell experiences (at least for English) has received little attention.

This lack of attention may be due to the fact that Western languages such as English and Dutch do not contain rich vocabularies for describing odorants as opposed to some other languages. In (Majid and Burenhult, 2014) Jahai and English speakers and in (Majid et al., 2018) Jahai and Dutch speakers were contrasted in describing a range of odorants. The Jahai, a group of nomadic hunter-gatherers in Malaysia, have over a dozen terms to describe odours. In the experiment, the Jahai speakers were both more consistent and greatly more controlled in the terms they used than the English and Dutch speakers relying on reference smell sources.

There is evidence that consistency in the use of smell sources in English can be conditioned. Croijmans and Majid (2016) examined the accuracy and consistency of wine experts, coffee experts and people with no expertise in identifying smells. No group was better at naming smells outside of the domain of their expertise. However, it was apparent the domain experts had developed a toolkit of common smell sources they frequently drew upon. An experiment on predicting properties of wines from experts' wine reviews confirms this (Hendrickx et al., 2016).

Sensorial lexicons have been developed that include terms related to smell (cf. Tekiroğlu et al. (2014)). However, as the initial seed words to bootstrap the lexicon for smell are limited, the olfactory clusters in such lexicons are by extension also limited. A different approach is taken in (Kiela et al., 2015), where terms related to smells are connected to their chemical compounds. While this is useful for translating olfactory information from the chemistry domain to language, it does not aid us in recognising the wide variety of expressions used in texts to describe smell experiences.

3   Literary Smell Dataset

To begin to tackle the problem of recognising smell experiences, we created a unique dataset focused on such expressions in literary texts. Specifically, by selecting texts from Project Gutenberg[3] that had the highest rate of occurrence of keywords derived from Table 1, we assembled a set 139 English literary texts. Each sentence in this collection was tokenised using NLTK[4], and POS-tagged and syntactically parsed using spaCy (Montani et al., 2020).[5] We split the set into three datasets: a harvesting dataset of 99 texts; a validation dataset of 20 texts; and an evaluation dataset of 20 texts.

From the evaluation dataset, a gold standard of manually labelled sentences was assembled consisting of seven documents, each of 100 randomly assigned sentences from multiple literary texts and annotated by a single annotator. To evaluate the inter-annotator agreement between the three annotators, one additional document consisting of 100 randomly selected sentences was annotated independently by the annotators.

Despite having chosen the harvesting, validation and extract sets for their high frequency of Table 1 derived keywords, on average only approximately 1 in 100 sentences contain a keyword. Thus, assuming that smell experiences typically contain a keyword, the evaluation set contains smell experiences in very low proportion. A gold standard set of extracts was sampled from the evaluation dataset to ensure a substantial number of smell extracts. The evaluation set was scanned for the high smell association keywords derived from Table 1. 80% of the sentences in the gold standard documents contain a Table 1 related word, the remaining 20% were randomly sampled. There is no overlap between documents, or redundancy within a document.

Annotators were asked to highlight and annotated spans according to the following criteria:[6]

---

[2]cf. `https://www.spectator.co.uk/article/where-are-the-scents-of-yesterday-entire-countries-have-lost-their-distinctive-smell` ; `https://slate.com/culture/2020/07/smells-history-book-review-france-plague-farts.html` ; `https://www.wsj.com/articles/smells-and-smellosophy-review-what-the-nose-knows-11594391739`

[3]`https://www.gutenberg.org/`

[4]`https://nltk.org`

[5]`https://spacy.io/`

[6]The full annotation guidelines can be found on our Github page

smell-only (in all contexts)	smell-only (in sensory contexts)	smell and taste only
odour(N), odorous(A)	*fragrance(N)*	pungent(A)
malodorous(A)	**musk(N)**	pungency(N)
fetid(A), foetid(A)	***fusty(A),frowsty(A)***	pungently(ADV)
whiffy(A)	*ripe(A), ripeness(N)*	*savour(N,V)*
smell(N,V), *scent(N)*	reek(N,V), stink(N,V)	**acrid(A)**
smelly(A)	*stench(N), niff(N)*	
scented(A)	sniff(V), **piney(A)**	
perfume(N)	waft(N,V), *stinky(A)*	
aroma(N), aromatic(N)	whiff(N),	
fragranced(A)		
petrichor(N)		
musty(A), musky(A)		

Note 1: A,N,V denotes adjectives, nouns and verbs, respectively
Note 2: <u>underlined</u>: words with smell strength connotations
Note 3: *italicised*: words with sentiment associations
Note 4: **bold face**: describes characteristics beyond strength or sentiment

Table 1: Results from Cambridge Dictionary 'smells and smelling' SMART Thesaurus search

Annotation tag	Number of corresponding text spans
'd'	533
'o'	129
'v'	186
's'	34
'a'	37
'n'	75

Table 2: Number of text spans by annotation tag

- 'd'. A smell description; e.g., 'An odd fragrance, a smell of damp plaster, wafted from the new house to his senses'.
  The inherent subjectivity of when precisely a smell experience becomes a description is left to the perception of the annotator.

- 'o'. A smell alluded to without expansion of its characteristics; e.g., 'A fragrance wafted from the new house to his senses'.

- 'v'. Any verb in the sentence which is associated with smell generally or with a specific smell experience within the extract; e.g., 'An odd fragrance wafted from the new house to his senses';

- 's'. Sense of smell alluded to directly; e.g., 'An odd fragrance, wafted from the new house to his senses'.

Additionally, two documents (of the aforementioned group of 7) were annotated with an additional set of tags:

- 'a'. An adjective being applied to the smell alluded to; e.g., 'An odd fragrance, a smell of damp plaster, wafted from the new house to his senses'.

- 'n'. The noun group referred to as a smell source; E.g., 'An odd fragrance, a smell of damp plaster, wafted from the new house to his senses'.

The inter-annotator agreement is measured using Cohen's Kappa (Cohen, 1960) per single gold standard document in a pairwise fashion. Specifically:

- The level of agreement with respect to those sentences which were tagged as *a smell experience*, by one or more annotators, i.e., those sentences with a text span annotated with either 'd' or 'o'.

- The level of agreement with respect to those sentences which were tagged as *a smell description*, by one or more annotators, i.e., those sentences with a text span annotated with 'd'.

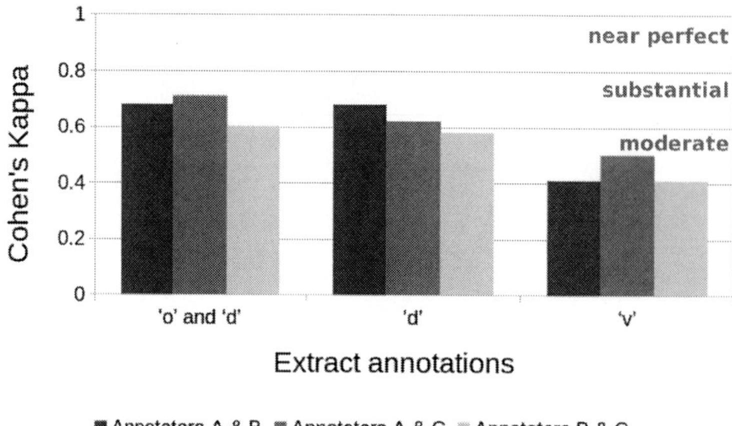

Figure 1: Cohen's Kappa scores of pairwise annotator agreement

- The level of agreement of those verbs within sentences what were tagged with 'v', i.e., verbs the annotator perceives as being related to smell generally, or in the context of the sentence.

Cohen's Kappa is a metric used to measure pairwise inter-annotator agreement. A Cohen's Kappa of 0, denotes an even probability of agreement. Landis and Koch (1977) denote a Cohen's Kappa score of 0.41 to 0.60, and .61 - 0.80 as representing *moderate* and *substantial* strength of agreement, respectively. A score of 0.81 to 1.0 can be considered as near perfect agreement.

Figure 1 shows the pairwise annotator agreement with regards the single gold standard document of 100 extracts, annotated by multiple annotators. All annotators are in *substantial* agreement in identifying all and any extracts that allude to smell, i.e., all spans labelled 'o' or 'd'. Annotators are generally in substantial agreement in identifying extracts which *describe* smell experiences, i.e., extracts with a spans labelled 'd'. Although, one pair of annotators are at the very upper end of *moderate* agreement only. Finally, in identifying verbs either highly associated with smell, or associated with smell in the context, there was only *moderate* annotator agreement.

It is reasonable to assume that human error, i.e., misreading, miscomprehending or simply skipping an extract, played some role in the observed imperfect inter-annotator agreement scores. Instances of likely human error are apparent on inspection of the gold standard, in those instances where there is arguably little room for personal subjectivity, for example, one of the three annotators did not attribute either a 'd' or 'o' tag to the span: *There was a smell of decaying leaves and of dog.*

However, a number of extracts clearly demonstrate the potential for subjectivity in smell experience interpretation, as a source for annotator disagreement, for instance, in the following extract, each of the three annotators attributed 'd', 'o' and no tag to it, respectively: *Seated beside her aromatic rest, In silence musing on her loveliness, Her knight and troubadour.*

In the following extract, one of three annotators tagged it as 'o', the other two presumably thought it sufficiently descriptive to be tagged 'd': *Between each pair of columns an elegant table of cedar bore on its platform a bronze cup filled with scented oil, from which the cotton wicks drew an odoriferous light.*

4 Extraction Approaches

As there is no known corpus annotated with smell expressions available to train a supervised smell language recogniser, we investigate pattern-based approaches to recognising such expressions. We base our approach on the concepts put forward in approaches such as the detection of hypernym-hyponym pairs (Hearst, 2000), e.g., *car is a type of vehicle*, and iterative bootstrapping (Brin, 1998) to detect author-book title pairs.

We start with seed features that are matched against the harvesting dataset. The resulting matches are then manually evaluated to identify new linguistic pattens, which are in-turn used to identify new features for the next bootstrapping round. The process can be seeded by introducing known features into the lexicon, or known patterns into the pattern set. In both (Hearst, 2000) and (Brin, 1998), this process was used to assemble a lexicon, the pattern set being effectively a by-product of the process. However, for our purposes, it is the set of patterns that is of interest, and their potential use to identify smell experiences.

The textual features targeted in prior work represented distinct real world concepts linked through a conceptual relationships. The expression of smell (in English) does not conform to a natural set of paired entities reflecting a relationship in the same way as authors and book titles do. However, surrounding adjectives, and verb and noun groups help characterise the smell experience and can therefore be targeted as complements.

A difficulty of identifying smell references over hypernym-hyponym or author-book title pairs is that there is no inherent relationship defining the number of coincident complements necessary. Instead it is a question of how restrictive we wish to make the criteria for matching sentences in the harvesting dataset. The greater the number of complements, the fewer extracts we can expect to retrieve. Thus, a too restrictive choice may result in stalling bootstrapping process. Conversely, if the choice is not restrictive enough and too many extracts unrelated to smell are returned, the process becomes uninformative. In evaluating smell related vocabulary, (Iatropoulos et al., 2018) concluded that the most commonplace words used in smell descriptions are those that could apply to a wide range of sensory contexts. This makes intuitive sense given the heavy reliance on reference smell sources to define smell characteristics. Hence, single complements are not targeted, as being too relevant outside of smell contexts. In this pilot project, we therefore focused on at least two complements in a pattern.

A basic assumption in our approaches is that found complements are indicative of the presence of a smell expression. We therefore aim to detect the following types of smell expression complements:

1. **Adjectives** modifying the smell experience perception, and the coincident **noun group** acting as the reference smell (one or more nouns modified by adjectives); E.g., *'An **odd** fragrance, a smell of **damp plaster**, wafted from the new house to his senses'*,where 'odd' and 'damp plaster' are the adjective and noun group, respectively. Thus, it is assumed that 'odd' and 'damp plaster', being coincident in defining this smell experience, are indicative of a smell experience when both present in other extracts.

2. A **noun group** acting as the reference smell, and the coincident **verb group** (adverbs, verbs, associated prepositions) describing how the smell moves; E.g., 'An odd fragrance, a smell of **damp plaster**, **wafted from** the new house to his senses', where 'damp plaster' and 'wafted from' are the noun group and verb group, respectively. Thus, it is assumed that 'damp plaster' and 'wafted from', being coincident in defining this smell experience, are indicative of a smell experience when both present in other extracts.

4.1 Approach 1: Targeting Adjective and Noun Groups

To capture and enable pattern matching with parts of speech, synonyms and flexible groupings of these in text, we start with words derived from Table 1 assembled in synonym groups. For example, <*smell_noun*> is defined to match against 'aroma', 'odour', 'scent', 'perfume' etc. The patterns further contain part of speech chunks that can match various tokens. These chunks were defined, and updated in

process, based on observed language patterns from harvesting set extracts. Listing 1 is an example of a
high-level pattern representation.

```
[<adj>] <smell_noun> _,_* _of_ <pronoun>* [<noun> {_of_ <noun>}*]
```
Listing 1: Example identified pattern

It will match the boldfaced adjective and noun groups in for example *the **warm** aroma of **multitudinous
exotics*** and *the **ammoniacal** smell of **the horses***

4.2 Approach 2: Targeting Verb and Noun Groups

As in the Adjectives & Nouns approach, we start with the same high-smell association seed lexicon
entry, *_aroma_NOUN*, as it results in a very manageable number of bootstrapped extracts. Based on the
resulting extracts, new patterns are hypothesised: e.g., from the extract *'the aroma of the **newly-sawn
timber and saw dust mingled** in the air'*, we may hypothesise the pattern *<smell_noun> _of|like_ __DET*
<pronoun>* [<noun> {_of_ <noun>}*] [<verb> prep__*]*.

This approach also includes a validation loop. As patterns with low precision risk introducing a large
volume of vocabulary into the lexicon which is unrelated to smell. The validation loop is an attempt
to limit this, by estimating pattern precision and setting a minimum acceptance threshold by taking 10
extracts per pattern and manually tagging them as *true positive, false positive*, or *unknown*. Patterns that
pass a validation threshold of 0.7 estimated precision are accepted. If no example of a pattern is present
in the validation set, it is removed.

Two variations of the patterns are retained, *identification patterns* and *extraction patterns*.
Extraction patterns target the previously discussed feature pairs, such to introduce new vocabulary into
the lexicon. Thus, extraction patterns are used to drive each iterative cycle. For example, based on
the preceding hypothesised pattern, e.g., *<smell_noun> _of|like_ __DET* <pronoun>* [<noun> {_of_
<noun>}*] [<verb> prep__*]*. Identification patterns are a superset of the extraction pattern set, and
are concerned with matching any and all smell experiences, not just matching feature pairs. Several identification patterns my be derived from a single hypothesised extraction pattern, expressing the potential
variation in matching smell experiences. The identification pattern set is our desired output from the
iterative bootstrapping process. In the final step of the approach, the extraction patterns are applied to
the harvesting set, and targeted complements are collected and added to the lexicon.

5 Evaluation and Discussion

Four complete cycles of the Adjectives & Nouns approach and three complete cycles of the Verbs &
Nouns approach were performed.

The Adjectives & Nouns approach identified 48 new identification patterns as seen in Table 3. The
majority of these patterns involve Table 1 derived words such as *<adj>* compound__ <smell_noun>*
matching *a delightful forest **aroma***, and *<adj> _with_ __DET* <pronoun>* <smell_noun> _of_
<pronoun>* <verb> <noun> {_of_ <noun>}*'* matching *heavy with the **smell** of freshly turned soil*.

Additionally, a small number of patterns identified do not involve the Table 1 vocabulary, such as
<adj> _breath|breaths_ _of_ <pronoun>* <noun> {_of_ <noun>}** matching *'...and inhale the sweet
breath of autumn, which was borne upon gentle gales'* and *'_air_* _,_ _sweet_ _with_ <pronoun>*
<noun> {_of_ <noun>}*'* matching *'the mild air, sweet with fading leaves and bracken'*.

The Verbs & Nouns approach identified 31 new identification patterns as show in Table 4. Again a
majority involve Table 1 derived words, for example *'<smell_noun> _of—like_ __DET* <pronoun>*
<noun> {_of_ <noun>}* <verb> prep_'* matching phrases such as *the aroma of **new-sawn tim-
ber and sawdust mingled** with...'*. The single example of lexico-syntactic pattern not involving Table 1 derived words, introduced the *'incense'* as synonymous with smell: *'_fumes_ _of_ _incense_ {_of_
<noun>}* __DET* <verb> prep__*'* matching for example *'the heavy fumes of incense rose up'*

Figure 2 shows the relative precision-recall performance of the group predictions, in respect of the
gold standard, with regards the pattern sets of: approach 1; approach 2; and both combined.

Cycle	Lexicon entries	New (unseen) extracts	Hypothesised (new) patterns	New id. patterns/ New ex. patterns
0	1**	91	15	15 / 13
1	519	1,509	28	26 / 22
2***	874	4,216	14	13 / 8
3	463	464	4 ****	4 / 4

**Seed word: _aroma_NOUN

*** sifted with Table 1 word search due to high volume

**** not subject to validation as cycles stopped

Note 1: Each lexicon (pair) entry is unique, and each extract is unique

Table 3: Record of iterative cycles outcomes for Approach 1: targeting coincident adjectives modifying the smell, and noun group reference smells

Cycle	Lexicon entries	New (unseen) extracts	Hypothesised (new) patterns	New id. patterns/ New ex. patterns
0	1**	91	11	10 / 9
1***	530	2,968	12	10 / 9
2	565	1,030	11 ****	11 / 8

**Seed word: _aroma_NOUN

*** sifted with Table 1 word search due to high volume

**** not subject to validation as cycles stopped

Note: Each lexicon (pair) entry is unique, and each extract is unique

Table 4: Record of iterative cycles outcomes for Approach 2: targeting coincident verb groups associated with the smell experience and noun group reference smells

It is apparent that the Adjectives & Nouns approach (red) consistently outperformed the pattern set of Verbs & Nouns approach (black); and that they target complementary smell expressions (combined approach, green). The relative performance of the combined approach with that of the Verbs & Nouns approach. The combined approach is significantly better with a 5% significance level where patterns have a precision greater than 0.75. The combined pattern set *significantly* has superior recall performance at corresponding precision cut-offs. Thus, we can conclude that targeting different feature pairs did result in patterns that target different smell extracts in the gold standard set.

6   Conclusions and Future Work

In this paper, we set out to identify smell experiences in English literary texts. We created a gold standard dataset and our experiments demonstrated that iterative bootstrapping techniques can be used to identify smell experiences in text.

Whilst the overwhelming majority of identified patterns involved keywords and phrases with a high smell association, the implementations revealed a number of new phrases used in smell contexts. Furthermore, we showed that at the very highest levels of precision, pattern group identification of smell experiences offers significantly better recall rates than a keyword search.

The focus of application of iterative bootstrapping implementations was centred on single sentence extracts for English literary texts. It would be interesting to explore the applicability of this semi-supervised method to other textual contexts, and longer-distance relationships spanning multiple sentences. Additionally, it would be informative to explore the influence of tweaking the implementation's parameters and approaches, including the pre-processing steps such as instead of using a shallow parser and experimenting with dependency grammars or semantic role labelling. With regards the precision-recall performance of the resulting pattern sets, such as exploring the influence of different seed words on the process outcomes, investigate the impact of a higher validation precision threshold for the number, and quality, of extracts returned each cycle and the corresponding identified patterns.

Our experiments demonstrated the potential use of patterns for identifying textual smell experiences in text. However, the number of extracts, and the quality of extracts in terms of smell experience density was identified as source of inefficiency which would benefit from being addressed further. The statistics presented in Table 3, for example, show the explosion in the number extracts for manual examination, in

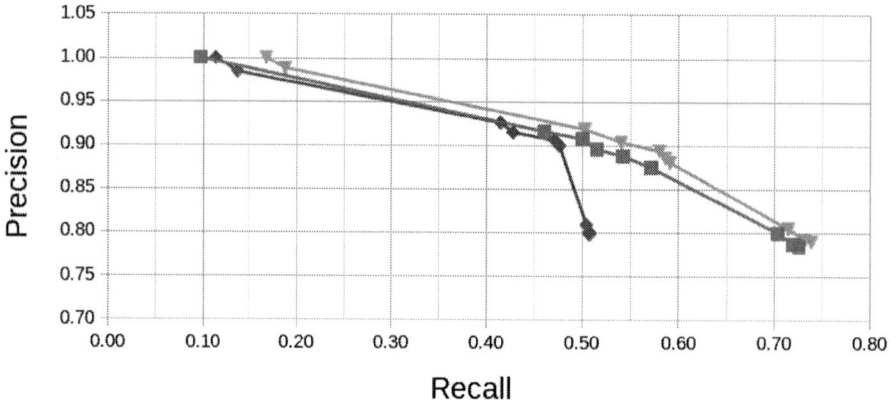

Figure 2: Group prediction precision-recall performance of the pattern sets of: approach 1; approach 2; and approach 1 and 2 combined.

certain cycles, which correspond to only comparatively few new patterns being identified.

The observed high volume of low smell experience extracts may be an inherent challenge of smell experiences relying on vocabulary which is equally, or more so, applicable in other sensory contexts. I.e., the targeting and adding to the lexicon of words with a low smell association, resulting in poorer quality extracts. However, there are a number of clear, possible avenues to explore such as increasing the validation set size, ensuring more accurate precision estimates thus improving the level of smell association of lexicon entries on average and exploring the effects of using more coincident features simultaneously, i.e., pairs were selected on the basis that if one feature alone was weakly associated with smell, two together may improve the association. More coincident features may further improve the likelihood of an extract relating to smell.

Finally, consideration as to degree of agreement between people in their interpretation, suggested a less than perfect agreement not only of the subtly nuanced aspects of smell experiences, but even at recognition of smell experiences as a broad classification. On inspection of annotations, however, it is unclear how many of these were genuine discrepancies in terms of subjective perceptions. More annotators, supported by a more comprehensive approach to tagging, e.g., requiring the annotators to explicitly note their reasoning and deliberations would help. This would offer a window into the mind of the annotators, reinforcing any conclusions that may be drawn.

Whilst there is extensive scope for further study, the experiments in this paper have shown that smell experiences can be identified, and smell experience features can be extracted from text providing a useful foundation for understanding smell usage within literature.

Acknowledgements

The authors would like to thank the annotators for taking the time to think about smelly language and tag multiple sets of sentences for us.

References

Ann-Sophie Barwich. 2020. *Smellosophy: What the Nose tells the Mind.* Harvard University Press.

Sergey Brin. 1998. Extracting patterns and relations from the world wide web. In *The World Wide Web and Databases (WebDB 1998)*, 06.

Jacob Cohen. 1960. Kappa: Coefficient of concordance. *Educational and Psychological Measurement*, 20(37).

Ilja Croijmans and Asifa Majid. 2016. Not all flavor expertise is equal: The language of wine and coffee experts. *PLoS ONE*, 11(6):e0155845.

Marti Hearst. 2000. Automatic acquisition of hyponyms from large text corpora. *Proceedings of the 14th Conference on Computational Linguistics (CoLing)*, 05.

Iris Hendrickx, Els Lefever, Ilja Croijmans, Asifa Majid, and Antal van den Bosch. 2016. Very quaffable and great fun: Applying NLP to wine reviews. In *Proceedings of the 54th Annual Meeting of the Association for Computational Linguistics (Volume 2: Short Papers)*, pages 306–312, Berlin, Germany, August. Association for Computational Linguistics.

Georgios Iatropoulos, Pawel Herman, Anders Lansner, Jussi Karlgren, Maria Larsson, and Jonas K. Olofsson. 2018. The language of smell: Connecting linguistic and psychophysical properties of odor descriptors. *Cognition*, 178:37 – 49.

Douwe Kiela, Luana Bulat, and Stephen Clark. 2015. Grounding semantics in olfactory perception. In *Proceedings of the 53rd Annual Meeting of the Association for Computational Linguistics and the 7th International Joint Conference on Natural Language Processing (Volume 2: Short Papers)*, pages 231–236, Beijing, China, July. Association for Computational Linguistics.

J. Richard Landis and Gary G. Koch. 1977. The measurement of observer agreement for categorical data. *Biometrics*, 33(1):159–174.

Asifa Majid and Niclas Burenhult. 2014. Odors are expressible in language, as long as you speak the right language. *Cognition*, 130(2):266–270.

Asifa Majid, Niclas Burenhult, Marcus Stensmyr, Josje De Valk, and Bill S Hansson. 2018. Olfactory language and abstraction across cultures. *Philosophical Transactions of the Royal Society B: Biological Sciences*, 373(1752):20170139.

Ines Montani, Matthew Honnibal, Matthew Honnibal, Sofie Van Landeghem, Henning Peters, Adriane Boyd, Maxim Samsonov, Jim Geovedi, Jim Regan, György Orosz, Paul O'Leary McCann, Søren Lind Kristiansen, Duygu Altinok, Roman, Leander Fiedler, Grégory Howard, Explosion Bot, Sam Bozek, Wannaphong Phatthiyaphaibun, Mark Amery, Björn Böing, Pradeep Kumar Tippa, Yohei Tamura, Leif Uwe Vogelsang, Ramanan Balakrishnan, Vadim Mazaev, GregDubbin, jeannefukumaru, Jens Dahl Møllerhøj, and Avadh Patel. 2020. explosion/spaCy: v2.3.2: Improved Korean tokenizer speed, experimental character-based pretraining and bug fixes, July.

Robert Muchembled. 2020. *Smells: A Cultural History of Odours in Early Modern Times.* Polity.

Serra Sinem Tekiroğlu, Gözde Özbal, and Carlo Strapparava. 2014. A computational approach to generate a sensorial lexicon. In *Proceedings of the 4th Workshop on Cognitive Aspects of the Lexicon (CogALex)*, pages 114–125, Dublin, Ireland, August. Association for Computational Linguistics and Dublin City University.

William Tullett. 2019. *Smell in Eighteenth-century England: A Social Sense.* Oxford University Press.

Piet Vroon, Anton Amerongen, Hans, and Vries. 1997. *Smell: The secret seducer.* Farrar, Straus and Giroux.

Finding and Generating a Missing Part for Story Completion

Yusuke Mori[1]   Hiroaki Yamane[2,1]   Yusuke Mukuta[1,2]   Tatsuya Harada[1,2]
[1]The University of Tokyo, [2]RIKEN
{mori, mukuta, harada}@mi.t.u-tokyo.ac.jp
hiroaki.yamane@riken.jp

Abstract

Creating a story is difficult. Professional writers often experience a writer's block. Thus, providing automatic support to writers is crucial but also challenging. Recently, in the field of generating and understanding stories, story completion (SC) has been proposed as a method for generating missing parts of an incomplete story. Despite this method's usefulness in providing creative support, its applicability is currently limited because it requires the user to have prior knowledge of the missing part of a story. Writers do not always know which part of their writing is flawed. To overcome this problem, we propose a novel approach called "missing position prediction (MPP)." Given an incomplete story, we aim to predict the position of the missing part. We also propose a novel method for MPP and SC. We first conduct an experiment focusing on MPP, and our analysis shows that highly accurate predictions can be obtained when the missing part of a story is the beginning or the end. This suggests that if a story has a specific beginning or end, they play significant roles. We conduct an experiment on SC using MPP, and our proposed method demonstrates promising results.

1   Introduction

Currently, because of the Internet, anybody can freely publish their original stories. However, it is challenging to write something that people would like and want to read. Sometimes, even professional writers fall into slumps during the writing process.

Numerous studies on understanding the secret of creating good stories have been conducted (Campbell, 1949; Propp, 1968). Rules for creating stories have been studied extensively, and "three-act structure" (Field, 2006) and "Save the cat" (Snyder, 2005) are popular examples. These works can help guide people who want to write good stories to demonstrate their creativity.

With the development of machine learning (ML) and natural language processing (NLP) technology in recent years, the creation of an automated system that supports the creative endeavors of people is now feasible (Roemmele, 2016; Peng et al., 2018; Yao et al., 2019; Goldfarb-Tarrant et al., 2019). To assist people in creating stories, it is essential to train computers to understand and create stories.

To measure the reading comprehension abilities of systems regarding stories, Mostafazadeh et al. (2016) proposed the "Story Cloze Test" (SCT). In the SCT, four sentences are presented, and the last sentence is excluded from an original five-sentence story. The objective of this task is to select an appropriate sentence from two options that complement the missing last sentence. Based on this approach, Wang and Wan (2019) proposed the "Story Completion (SC)" task in the field of generating and understanding stories. Given any four sentences of a five-sentence story, the objective of this task is to generate the sentence that is not given (known as the missing plot) to complete the story.

The ability to solve the SC is essential in the context of creative support. If writers cannot complete a story or a plot, a suitable model can provide them with the appropriate support. However, such applications are currently restricted because they require the user to know which part of a story is missing in advance. When considering an actual application, writers do not always know where their writing is

---

Proceedings of LaTeCH-CLfL 2020, pages 156–166
Barcelona, Spain (Online), December 12, 2020.

flawed, as evidenced by the vital role of editors who work with them. Of course, the editors do not just point out the missing points; they play various roles. For example, they also point out unnecessary parts. Keeping this in mind, let us understand one of the roles of the editor.

To overcome this limitation, we propose a new story comprehension method named "Missing Position Prediction (MPP)," as shown in Figure 1. An incomplete story with one sentence missing is given as input. Unlike in the SC, no information regarding the position of the missing content is given. This task aims to predict the position of the missing part. The ability to solve this task indicates that computers can identify flaws in a story's plot. In practical applications, by combining our novel task with an appropriate SC method, writers can benefit from computerized completion even if they do not know where a flaw is.

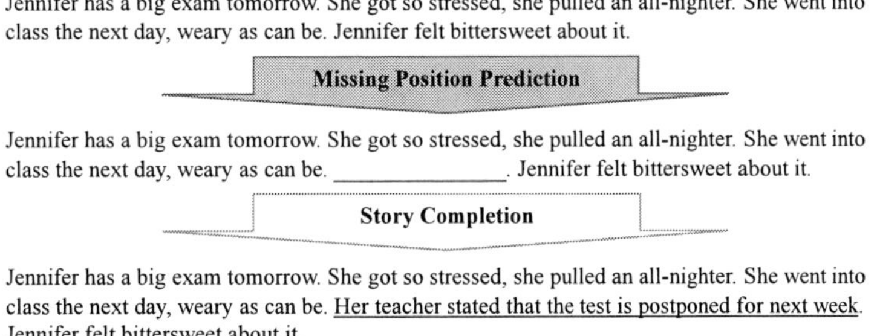

Figure 1: Example of an incomplete story and flow of MPP and SC.

Additionally, we propose a novel method for MPP and SC. Given an incomplete story, it estimates the missing part and generates a sentence to complete the story. We make our code available to support further progress on our proposed task and SC.[1]

Our main contributions are as follows:

- We propose "Missing Position Prediction (MPP)" as a story comprehension method. This method predicts the position of a missing part of an incomplete story and has significance in the contexts of story understanding, story generation, and story-writing assistance.

- We propose a novel method for MPP and SC. We first perform an experiment focusing on the MPP, and our proposed method demonstrates promising results. An analysis of the results shows that highly accurate predictions can be obtained when the missing part of a story is its beginning or end.

- Based on the results of the MPP experiment, we conduct another experiment on SC using MPP. The results of the experiment show that given an incomplete story, it is possible to restore it such that it is comparable with the original human-written one.

2 Related Work

2.1 Reading Comprehension on Stories

In some studies, to better comprehend stories, the stories were considered to be collections of events. The "Narrative Cloze Test" (Chambers and Jurafsky, 2008) is a typical example. Mostafazadeh et al. (2016) proposed the SCT as a more difficult task. The SCT presents four sentences, and the last sentence is excluded from a story composed of five sentences. The system must select an appropriate sentence from two choices that complement the missing last sentence. In addition to the task, the authors released a large-scale story corpus named "ROCStories," which is a collection of non-fictional daily-life stories written by hundreds of workers belonging to Amazon Mechanical Turk (Amazon MTurk).

In our proposed task, it is essential to understand the remaining information to infer what is missing. Regarding the example in Figure 1, the third sentence states that Jennifer is weary, and the fourth sentence mentions that she felt bittersweet. It is estimated that something mentioned as "it" is missing, and "it" is

---

[1] https://github.com/mil-tokyo/missing-position-prediction

the reason for her change of feeling. In this manner, it is necessary to identify unnaturalness – that is, the parts where the narrative arc is broken – in a story. This is a more challenging task than SCT. We believe this task is deeply related to a fundamental question in story understanding: whether or not the model understands the flow of a story.

2.2 Partial Generation of Stories

Inspired by the SCT, Zhao et al. (2018) designed "Story Ending Generation (SEG)" as a subtask of story generation. Given an incomplete story, where the last sentence is excluded from the original five-sentence story, the objective of this task is to generate the last sentence, not to select. Furthermore, based on SEG, Wang and Wan (2019) proposed the SC and investigated the problem of generating a missing story plot at any position in an incomplete story.

Additionally, in recent years, research regarding text infilling has been actively conducted (Ippolito et al., 2019; Donahue et al., 2020; Huang et al., 2020). Regarding stories, Ippolito et al. (2019) worked on complementing the missing span between left and right contexts, which they called "story infilling." In the appendix, they reported that they tried human evaluation using Amazon MTurk but their task was too hard for the average worker. Although there is no mention of why the task was too hard for the average worker, we suspect that the length of the text in their task may have been one of the reasons.

These studies require a writer to have prior knowledge of the missing parts and do not consider the case where the writer is unaware of the flaws in his/her work. The MPP aims to fill this gap.

We should note that even when there is a missing part in the story, it may be caused by writer's intention that "I want the readers to read between lines". However, the missing part can also be an unintentional mistake. To analyze if the model can understand whether the missing part is an "writer's intentional missing" is out of the scope of this study. At this stage, MPP is especially effective in the latter case, unintentional mistake. However, when a model's understanding of writer's intentional missing is achieved, it is expected that writers can also be benefited in the former case – using a method of MPP, they can know whether their intention is well understandable by readers.

As the first step, we used short stories for this task. Instead of asking average workers, we did a qualification test and only qualified workers could participate in the evaluation.

2.3 Seq2seq for Text Generation

In SEG, a simple type of the sequence-to-sequence model (Seq2seq) (Sutskever et al., 2014) and an extension using the attention mechanism are typically used as baselines (Zhao et al., 2018; Li et al., 2018; Guan et al., 2019; Mori et al., 2019).

The use of unsupervised pre-trained large neural models, such as BERT (Devlin et al., 2019) and GPT-2 (Radford et al., 2019), has become mainstream in NLP. BERT is originally trained as a masked language model and considered unsuitable for text generation compared with models using a left-to-right architecture, such as GPT-2, XLNet (Yang et al., 2019), and BART (Lewis et al., 2020). However, experiments conducted by Rothe et al. (2020) using BERT and GPT-2 for Seq2seq demonstrated interesting results. Although they did not claim that BERT is optimal as a decoder, they demonstrated that BERT2BERT outperforms BERT2GPT in some generation tasks.

In this study, we extend the Seq2seq-based method for SEG to solve MPP and SC. To achieve a more natural sentence completion, we use BERT as a Seq2seq decoder and BERT-derived Sentence-BERT (SBERT) (Reimers and Gurevych, 2019) as a part of an encoder.

3 Task Description

We begin by formulating SEG and the SC, after which we formulate our proposed task.

3.1 Story Ending Generation and Story Completion

We define $S = \{s_1, s_2, ..., s_n\}$ as a story comprising n sentences. In SEG, $S' = \{s_1, s_2, ..., s_{n-1}\}$ is given as an input. The objective of the task is to generate an appropriate ending. For SC, an incomplete story consisting of $n - 1$ sentences $S' = \{s_1, ..., s_{k-1}, s_{k+1}, ..., s_n\}$, where k represents the position of

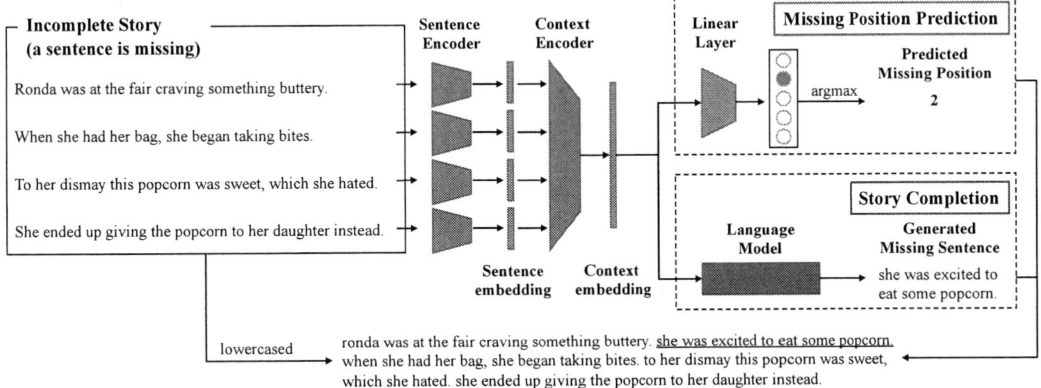

Figure 2: An overview of the proposed method.

the missing sentence in the story, is given. Next, we focus on the objective of the task that involves generating an appropriate sentence which is coherent with the given sentences. During each task, the model is trained to maximize probability $p(y|S')$, where y represents the ground truth sentence. Specifically, $y = s_n$ in SEG and $y = s_k$ in SC.

3.2 Missing Position Prediction

To overcome the issue whereby the SC model requires information regarding k, i.e., the position of the missing sentence, we propose the MPP to predict k from a given $n - 1$ sentences, as shown in Figure 1. Similar to the SC, an incomplete story comprising $n - 1$ sentences $S' = \{s_1, ..., s_{k-1}, s_{k+1}, ..., s_n\}$ is given as an input. However, any information regarding k is not given. The order of the sentences is known, but the missing position is unknown. Specifically, s_{k-1} and s_{k+1} are treated as continuous sentences. Our objective is to predict k from the input. In other words, the model is trained to maximize probability $p(missing = k|S')$.

4 Proposed Method

Hierarchical approaches have demonstrated effectiveness in story generation (Fan et al., 2018; Ravi et al., 2018). We propose a novel method with a hierarchical architecture for the MPP and SC. We devise a method inspired by the two-step encoder of Hierarchical-Seq2seq, which is a simple method for SEG that we proposed in our previous study (Mori et al., 2019). The first encoder receives $S' = \{s_1, ..., s_{k-1}, s_{k+1}, ..., s_n\}$ and outputs the sentence embeddings $\{v_1, ..., v_{k-1}, v_{k+1}, ..., v_n\}$. Next, the second encoder receives the sentence embeddings and generates a distributed representation of the entire context $v_{context}$. We call the first encoder "sentence encoder," and the second encoder "context encoder." For MPP, we input $v_{context}$ into a linear layer and obtain a five-unit output. For SC, we input $v_{context}$ into a language model and obtain a sentence to complete the story. Figure 2 shows an overview of the proposed method. Although the output of the MPP can be used here, we prefer to have our model learn these two tasks simultaneously. We intend to take it up as future work to use predicted MPP for SC and vice versa.

In proposing a new task, we believe it is useful to test how well a simple method can solve the task. Analyzing the performance and characteristics of a simple method will help in the application of complex methods in future studies. Thus, we propose a new task along with a simple method.

4.1 Sentence Encoder

First, we obtain sentence embeddings v_j for each input sentence s_j in a given context. We apply SBERT in each sentence. This encoder is not fine-tuned during our training.

4.2 Context Encoder

Using the sentence embeddings obtained, we apply another encoding layer to handle context embedding $v_{context}$. Although there is a discontinuity in the input and the missing position k is not given, the order is preserved. Hence, it is considered to be appropriate to treat the input as a sequence. We propose to use gated recurrent unit (GRU) (Cho et al., 2014) as the main part of the encoder. GRU is a type of RNN and is useful in handling sequences. Ravi et al. (2018) used an RNN with GRU cells for story encoding, demonstrating that a GRU is sufficient to capture the sequence in a short story. Li et al. (2019) also used GRU and its variant in their Context Encoder. The output of the GRU is input into a linear layer and a batch normalization layer (Ioffe and Szegedy, 2015).

4.3 Language Model

We use BERT as a language model for generating sentences to fill in the missing parts. Here, BERT is used as a decoder, and the output of the context encoder is used to initialize the encoder hidden states in cross-attention. Starting from the start token, we repeat the next token prediction for sentence generation.

5 Experiment 1: Missing Position Prediction

First, we worked on learning the MPP only. In this experiment, we investigated the part of the proposed method that excludes the language model.

5.1 Dataset

set	#stories	missing position
train	78,528	Given randomly during training
dev	9,816	Given when creating dataset
test	9,817	Given when creating dataset
total	98,161	

Table 1: Overview of the dataset used.

ROCStories is a well-organized corpus and is widely used in story-generation tasks; it is typically used in SEG (Zhao et al., 2018; Li et al., 2018; Guan et al., 2019). Similarly, Wang and Wan (2019) used it for their story-completion task. Furthermore, the dataset was used by Peng et al. (2018) for controllable story generation. Qin et al. (2019) tackled "Counterfactual Story Rewriting," which is a story revising task, using their proposed TIMETRAVEL dataset built using ROCStories. Although, initially, we did consider using other datasets, such as WritingPrompts, we ultimately did not use them. Stories in WritingPrompts vary in terms of length, and therefore, the importance of a single sentence varies from one story to the other. Thus, considering the requirements of our analysis, the aforementioned dataset seemed inappropriate.

Thus, as a starting point for proposing the task, we used ROCStories. As shown in Table 1, the dataset was randomly split in the ratio of 8:1:1 to obtain the training, development, and test sets, respectively. We removed one sentence from a five-sentence story. The missing position k was randomly decided based on a discrete uniform distribution. For the development and test sets, this removal procedure was performed when creating the dataset to improve reproducibility. For the training set, we retained the original five-sentence story in the dataset and removed a sentence randomly when reading the data during training. As a result, a different sentence could be removed from the same story, with a different k value, thus acting as data augmentation.

5.2 Comparison Method

Max-pool Context. To examine the usefulness of treating context as a sequence in the proposed task, we trained another model. In this setting, a max pooling layer was used as a context encoder.

5.3 Training Details

We trained a model for 30 epochs. The validation loss for every epoch was calculated, and the state with the smallest validation loss was used for further tests. Among the trained SBERTs, we used "bert-base-nli-mean-tokens." The output dimension was 768. For the GRU context, the number of hidden units of the GRU was 256. The linear layer had 256 dimensions for both the input and output, and weights were initialized from a normal distribution with $mean = 0$, $std = 0.01$. For the max-pool context, we applied max pooling to sentence embeddings and obtained a vector with the same dimension as the sentence embedding. We then input this vector into a linear layer and obtained a 256-dimensional vector as the context vector. The linear layer for receiving the output of the context encoder and for identifying the five labels had a 256-dimensional input and a five-dimensional output. We used the Adam optimizer with a learning rate of 0.001, $\beta_1 = 0.9$, $\beta_2 = 0.999$, and a weight decay of 0. A gradient clipping with a value of 5 was used. We set the batch size to 256.

5.4 Results

For each method, we performed five trials while changing the random seed at the time of training and calculated the mean and standard deviations of the accuracy. As shown in Table 2, the GRU context achieved an accuracy of $52.2 \pm 0.220\%$, which was higher than the accuracy of the max-pool context. The results indicated the usefulness of treating context as a sequence in the proposed task.

Methods	Accuracy (%)
Max-pool Context	35.0±0.334
GRU Context	**52.2±0.220**

Table 2: Prediction accuracy, shown as $mean \pm std$. It is a five-class classification task, so the chance rate is 20%.

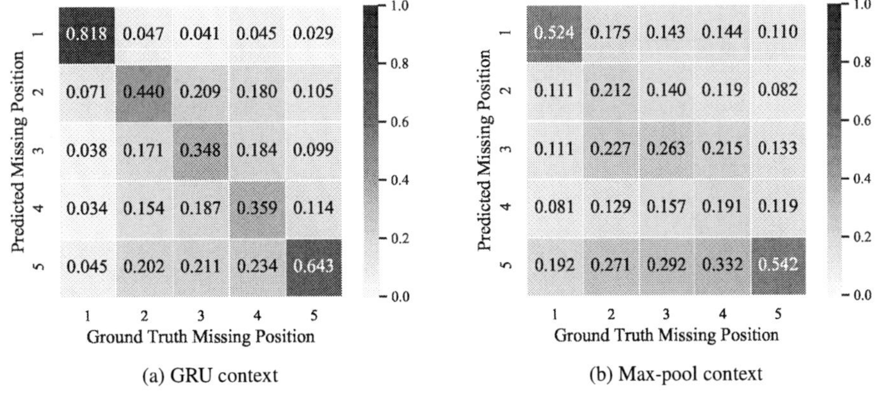

(a) GRU context

(b) Max-pool context

Figure 3: Heat maps showing the results of the (a) GRU context and (b) Max-pool context. The ground truth (GT) label is shown on the x-axis and the predicted label is on the y-axis. The squares on the diagonal line denote correct cases. The ratios of the predicted label to the GT label are shown numerically.

Hereinafter, for a more detailed discussion, we use one of the five trials as an example. The heat map in Figure 3 (a) shows which positions can be accurately identified using the GRU context method. When the sentence 1 was missing, the accuracy exceeded 80%. The results of sentences 2 to 4 exhibited lower accuracy, whereas sentence 5 had a higher accuracy.

Figure 3 (b) shows the max-pool context result for each missing position. Even though this method does not consider the sequence of the context, the prediction results for the sentences 2 to 4 are lower than those for sentences 1 and 5. Thus, it can be inferred that treating a context as a sequence does not adversely affect the prediction of missing middle sentences.

6 Experiment 2: Missing Position Prediction + Story Completion

Based on the results of Experiment 1, we conducted another experiment in which we tackled both MPP and SC. As a context encoder, we used the GRU context. We used the same dataset as in Section 5.1.

6.1 Training Details

We trained a model for 50 epochs. The validation loss for every epoch was calculated, and the state with the smallest validation loss was used for human evaluation. For the GRU context, the number of hidden units was 768. The linear layer had 768 dimensions for both the input and output. We used HuggingFace's implementation of BERT and its pre-trained model "bert-base-uncased" (Wolf et al., 2019). We calculated the total loss as follows: $L_{total} = 0.5 * L_{MPP} + 0.5 * L_{SC}$, where L_{MPP} represents the softmax cross entropy loss for MPP, and L_{SC} represents the softmax cross entropy loss for SC. We optimized the value of L_{total} using the AdamW optimizer with a learning rate of $1e - 4$, $\beta_1 = 0.9$, $\beta_2 = 0.999$, $\epsilon = 1e - 8$, and a weight decay of 0. We used a linear learning rate warmup with 4 epochs. We used a gradient clipping with a value of 1 and set the batch size to 128.

6.2 Human Evaluation

We conducted human evaluation with the help of Amazon MTurk workers. We conducted two types of tasks: a qualification test and a pair-wise evaluation task.

To choose workers with a high degree of ability to evaluate stories for participation in the evaluation task, we first conducted a qualification test. Ten randomly selected questions from the validation set of the SCT were solved by the workers, and only those workers who answered all ten questions correctly were allowed to participate in the next evaluation task.

For the pair-wise evaluation task, the qualified workers were given two similar short stories, and they were asked to choose which story gave the impression of being a complete story. The workers were given four choices as follows: Option A is more appropriate, Option B is more appropriate, both options are equally appropriate, and neither option is suitable. In this evaluation task, workers were also required to write the reason for their answer. We used 200 story pairs for comparison. The original human-written story (GT) is from the test set shown in Table 1, and our proposed model generated the other candidates based on an incomplete story. Five workers evaluated each story pair. Among the five answers obtained for each story, the most frequently chosen answers were considered as an agreement among the workers. Notably, that the workers did not do the same number of tasks. Therefore, instead of calculating the inter-annotator agreement, we decided to consider the most frequent answer.

6.3 Results

The results of the human evaluation are shown in Table 3.

Proposed	GT	both	neither
8	148	44	0

Table 3: Human evaluation results of pair-wise experiment. We used 200 stories, and each story was evaluated by five workers. The most frequently chosen answers were considered as their agreement.

Regarding the 200 stories that were autocompleted, eight were judged to be better than the original story, and 44 were judged to be equivalent to the original story. In other words, our proposed method can generate a story that is either as good as or better than a GT story with 26% probability.

7 Discussion

The results of Experiment 1 support the following two findings from Wang and Wan (2019): 1) The plot becomes more complicated as it progresses, thereby making the estimation of latter sentences more difficult and 2) for $k = 5$, four sentences in the context are continuous. Therefore, a good expression can be easily obtained, even by using an encoder that does not consider discontinuity. It is interesting to note that the beginning or the end of a story can be predicted with the highest accuracy. This appears to be related to the fact that the collection of ROCStories was performed with the following in mind: "the story should read like a coherent story, with a specific beginning and ending." In other words, the story under consideration has a specific beginning and ending. Thus, if the beginning or the ending is missing, it can be interpreted as that the methods treat the story as particularly unnatural and predict the missing position with high accuracy.

For qualitative analysis on Experiment 2, we show three examples of story pairs and human evaluations in Table 4. In the first example, the autocompleted story was evaluated to be better than the GT. MPP was a success, and a contextualized completion sentence was generated. In the second example, the autocomplete story was rated as equivalent to the GT. MPP estimated a missing location that differed from the original story but increased information differently from the GT, which was appreciated by the workers. In the third example, autocompletion did not work. It succeeded in MPP, but it failed in generating a contextualized completion sentence. The failure to generate an essential word ("contest") is pointed out. Note that the second answer appears to have been mischaracterized.

8 Conclusion

To overcome the issue of conventional SC tasks that require information regarding the position of the missing part in a story, we proposed a MPP to predict the position based on the given incomplete story. Our proposed method demonstrated that treating the context as a sequence is useful for solving this new task. We examined the prediction accuracy for each missing position and found that a prediction is easier if the beginning or the end of a story is missing. Furthermore, we tackled the combined task of MPP and SC. We conducted a pair-wise human evaluation against a human-written story, for which our proposed method demonstrated promising results.

Because we limit the study to five-sentence stories, it is unlikely that humans make mistakes in the plot. However, humans may overlook plot imperfections when considering longer, more complex stories. Thus, checking such mistakes is part of the editors' job. We proposed the task in the context of creative support, but it also can be positioned in the context of narrative understanding. Planning a story requires a form of reasoning that can move backward as well as forward. That is why SC tasks have significant meaning in story understanding and generation, and our proposed task would be a better test of a model's abilities to understand the flow of a story.

For the sake of simplicity, we proposed a simple machine-learning-based method. However, using simple bag-of-words methods or part-of-speech analysis may be effective for our proposed task. Therefore, exploring the efficacy of using methods other than those based on machine learning is left as future work.

However, our proposed task poses specific limitations. In our task, it is known that there is a missing position in the input story, and that there is only one such instance. In reality, an input story may be complete, that is, k is null. Furthermore, there may be a case in which there are multiple missing positions, that is, a case in which k has multiple values. Although dealing with these constraints is left for future studies, it is conceivable to introduce a certainty factor for the missing prediction. For example, predicting that k is null when the certainty factor is low. Although we considered a constrained case of study, we believe that our proposed task is an important step toward assisting writers in the creation of stories.

Acknowledgements

We would like to thank Yusuke Kurose, Naoyuki Gunji, and Ryohei Shimizu for helpful discussions. This work was supported by JST AIP Acceleration Research Grant Number JPMJCR20U3 and JSPS KAKENHI Grant Number JP20H05556, Japan.

Context	since the questions were complicated, i was extremely nervous. despite believing that i've failed, i turned the exam in. the teacher handed the exams back to us the next day. i ended up receiving a b.
GT	i took my class final in math today. since the questions were complicated, i was extremely nervous. despite believing that i've failed, i turned the exam in. the teacher handed the exams back to us the next day. i ended up receiving a b.
Ours	my teacher gave us a test. since the questions were complicated, i was extremely nervous. despite believing that i've failed, i turned the exam in. the teacher handed the exams back to us the next day. i ended up receiving a b.

Answers with Reasons (A: GT, B: Ours)

both	Whether it is a class final or a given test, both stories are the same and therefore both complete.
neither	both doesn't make sense
Ours	A is jumbled and does not make sense. B is logically arranged as a story.
Ours	In "A," it wouldn't make sense that a final exam was handed back in class the next day.
Ours	B was more appropriate since it is having a continuous flow than A

Context	tom was at a local park. there was an egg hunt for the kids. tom decided to pick some eggs up. he enjoyed the treats in them.
GT	tom was at a local park. it was easter. there was an egg hunt for the kids. tom decided to pick some eggs up. he enjoyed the treats in them.
Ours	tom was at a local park. there was an egg hunt for the kids. tom decided to pick some eggs up. tom was able to get many eggs. he enjoyed the treats in them.

Answers with Reasons (A: GT, B: Ours)

both	both are complete sentences
Ours	Option B is complete as it says that tom was able to get some eggs in the hunt.
both	Both of them can be considered complete. Story A tells us it is Easter (and story B doesn't) while Story B tells us Tom picked many eggs (and story A doesn't). Both of those details could be removed and the stories would still be the same.
Ours	The fact that he was able to gather some eggs was more complete than just deciding to pick up some eggs. Story A Easter gave a better time context but did not really add as much to the story since traditionally an egg hunt is held on Easter so the omission of that in Story B was made up for Tom being able to gather some eggs.
both	Both stories have a starting, content and ending.

Context	timothy loved to dance. timothy didn't have much confidence in himself. it took everything he had to dance with all of his self doubt. everyone loved his dancing and he won the contest.
GT	timothy loved to dance. there was a dance contest that was coming up soon. timothy didn't have much confidence in himself. it took everything he had to dance with all of his self doubt. everyone loved his dancing and he won the contest.
Ours	timothy loved to dance. he decided to take dance lessons. timothy didn't have much confidence in himself. it took everything he had to dance with all of his self doubt. everyone loved his dancing and he won the contest.

Answers with Reasons (A: Ours, B: GT)

GT	Only B makes sense and a complete story.
GT	A is more correct and arranged
GT	Story A doesn't mention the contest which Timothy ends up winning, therefore misses an important piece of the story.
GT	Story B mentions that there was a dance contest at the start and that he won it at the end. Story A only mentions a contest abruptly at the end making it seem out of place.
GT	B is more good

Table 4: Examples of original and autocompleted stories, followed by answers and reasoning by MTurk workers. The GT was not originally lowercased, but it was lowercased in our pair-wise evaluation task to compare with autocomplete stories. Additionally, the context given to the model is not lowercased, but it is lowercased here to make it easier to compare with the GT and our proposed method.

References

Joseph Campbell. 1949. *The Hero with a Thousand Faces*. Pantheon Books.

Nathanael Chambers and Dan Jurafsky. 2008. Unsupervised learning of narrative event chains. In *Proceedings of the 46th Annual Meeting of the Association for Computational Linguistics: Human Language Technologies*, pages 789–797, Columbus, Ohio, June. Association for Computational Linguistics.

Kyunghyun Cho, Bart van Merriënboer, Çağlar Gülçehre, Dzmitry Bahdanau, Fethi Bougares, Holger Schwenk, and Yoshua Bengio. 2014. Learning phrase representations using rnn encoder–decoder for statistical machine translation. In *Proceedings of the 2014 Conference on Empirical Methods in Natural Language Processing*, pages 1724–1734, Doha, Qatar, October. Association for Computational Linguistics.

Jacob Devlin, Ming-Wei Chang, Kenton Lee, and Kristina Toutanova. 2019. BERT: Pre-training of deep bidirectional transformers for language understanding. In *Proceedings of the 2019 Conference of the North American Chapter of the Association for Computational Linguistics: Human Language Technologies, Volume 1 (Long and Short Papers)*, pages 4171–4186, Minneapolis, Minnesota, June. Association for Computational Linguistics.

Chris Donahue, Mina Lee, and Percy Liang. 2020. Enabling language models to fill in the blanks. In *Proceedings of the 58th Annual Meeting of the Association for Computational Linguistics*, pages 2492–2501, Online, July. Association for Computational Linguistics.

Angela Fan, Mike Lewis, and Yann Dauphin. 2018. Hierarchical neural story generation. In *Proceedings of the 56th Annual Meeting of the Association for Computational Linguistics (Volume 1: Long Papers)*, pages 889–898, Melbourne, Australia, July. Association for Computational Linguistics.

Syd Field. 2006. *The Screenwriter's Workbook, Revised Edition*. Delta Trade Paperbacks.

Seraphina Goldfarb-Tarrant, Haining Feng, and Nanyun Peng. 2019. Plan, Write, and Revise: an interactive system for open-domain story generation. In *Proceedings of the 2019 Conference of the North American Chapter of the Association for Computational Linguistics (Demonstrations)*, pages 89–97, Minneapolis, Minnesota, June. Association for Computational Linguistics.

Jian Guan, Yansen Wang, and Minlie Huang. 2019. Story ending generation with incremental encoding and commonsense knowledge. In *Proceedings of the Thirty-Third AAAI Conference on Artificial Intelligence*, pages 6473–6480, Honolulu, Hawaii, January–February. AAAI Press.

Yichen Huang, Yizhe Zhang, Oussama Elachqar, and Yu Cheng. 2020. INSET: Sentence infilling with INter-SEntential transformer. In *Proceedings of the 58th Annual Meeting of the Association for Computational Linguistics*, pages 2502–2515, Online, July. Association for Computational Linguistics.

Sergey Ioffe and Christian Szegedy. 2015. Batch normalization: Accelerating deep network training by reducing internal covariate shift. In Francis Bach and David Blei, editors, *Proceedings of the 32nd International Conference on Machine Learning*, volume 37 of *Proceedings of Machine Learning Research*, pages 448–456, Lille, France, July. PMLR.

Daphne Ippolito, David Grangier, Chris Callison-Burch, and Douglas Eck. 2019. Unsupervised hierarchical story infilling. In *Proceedings of the First Workshop on Narrative Understanding*, pages 37–43, Minneapolis, Minnesota, June. Association for Computational Linguistics.

Mike Lewis, Yinhan Liu, Naman Goyal, Marjan Ghazvininejad, Abdelrahman Mohamed, Omer Levy, Veselin Stoyanov, and Luke Zettlemoyer. 2020. BART: Denoising sequence-to-sequence pre-training for natural language generation, translation, and comprehension. In *Proceedings of the 58th Annual Meeting of the Association for Computational Linguistics*, pages 7871–7880, Online, July. Association for Computational Linguistics.

Zhongyang Li, Xiao Ding, and Ting Liu. 2018. Generating reasonable and diversified story ending using sequence to sequence model with adversarial training. In *Proceedings of the 27th International Conference on Computational Linguistics*, pages 1033–1043, Santa Fe, New Mexico, USA, August. Association for Computational Linguistics.

Yitong Li, Zhe Gan, Yelong Shen, Jingjing Liu, Yu Cheng, Yuexin Wu, Lawrence Carin, David Carlson, and Jianfeng Gao. 2019. Storygan: A sequential conditional gan for story visualization. In *Proceedings of the IEEE/CVF Conference on Computer Vision and Pattern Recognition*, June.

Yusuke Mori, Hiroaki Yamane, Yusuke Mukuta, and Tatsuya Harada. 2019. Toward a better story end: Collecting human evaluation with reasons. In *Proceedings of the 12th International Conference on Natural Language Generation*, pages 383–390, Tokyo, Japan, October–November. Association for Computational Linguistics.

Nasrin Mostafazadeh, Nathanael Chambers, Xiaodong He, Devi Parikh, Dhruv Batra, Lucy Vanderwende, Push-meet Kohli, and James Allen. 2016. A corpus and cloze evaluation for deeper understanding of commonsense stories. In *Proceedings of the 2016 Conference of the North American Chapter of the Association for Computational Linguistics: Human Language Technologies*, pages 839–849, San Diego, California, June. Association for Computational Linguistics.

Nanyun Peng, Marjan Ghazvininejad, Jonathan May, and Kevin Knight. 2018. Towards controllable story generation. In *Proceedings of the First Workshop on Storytelling*, pages 43–49, New Orleans, Louisiana, June. Association for Computational Linguistics.

Vladimir IAkovlevich Propp. 1968. *Morphology of the Folktale (Translated by L. Scott)*. University of Texas Press.

Lianhui Qin, Antoine Bosselut, Ari Holtzman, Chandra Bhagavatula, Elizabeth Clark, and Yejin Choi. 2019. Counterfactual story reasoning and generation. In *Proceedings of the 2019 Conference on Empirical Methods in Natural Language Processing and the 9th International Joint Conference on Natural Language Processing*, pages 5043–5053, Hong Kong, China, November. Association for Computational Linguistics.

Alec Radford, Jeff Wu, Rewon Child, David Luan, Dario Amodei, and Ilya Sutskever. 2019. Language models are unsupervised multitask learners.

Hareesh Ravi, Lezi Wang, Carlos Muniz, Leonid Sigal, Dimitris Metaxas, and Mubbasir Kapadia. 2018. Show me a story: Towards coherent neural story illustration. In *Proceedings of the IEEE Conference on Computer Vision and Pattern Recognition*, June.

Nils Reimers and Iryna Gurevych. 2019. Sentence-BERT: Sentence embeddings using Siamese BERT-networks. In *Proceedings of the 2019 Conference on Empirical Methods in Natural Language Processing and the 9th International Joint Conference on Natural Language Processing*, pages 3980–3990, Hong Kong, China, November. Association for Computational Linguistics.

Melissa Roemmele. 2016. Writing Stories with Help from Recurrent Neural Networks. In *AAAI Conference on Artificial Intelligence; Thirtieth AAAI Conference on Artificial Intelligence*, pages 4311 – 4312, Phoenix, AZ, February. AAAI Press.

Sascha Rothe, Shashi Narayan, and Aliaksei Severyn. 2020. Leveraging pre-trained checkpoints for sequence generation tasks. *Transactions of the Association for Computational Linguistics*, 8:264–280.

Blake Snyder. 2005. *SAVE THE CAT! The Last Book on Screenwriting You'll Ever Need*. Michael Wiese Productions.

Ilya Sutskever, Oriol Vinyals, and Quoc V. Le. 2014. Sequence to sequence learning with neural networks. In *Proceedings of the 27th International Conference on Neural Information Processing Systems - Volume 2*, NIPS'14, pages 3104–3112, Cambridge, MA, USA. MIT Press.

Tianming Wang and Xiaojun Wan. 2019. T-CVAE: Transformer-based conditioned variational autoencoder for story completion. In *Proceedings of the Twenty-Eighth International Joint Conference on Artificial Intelligence*, pages 5233–5239. International Joint Conferences on Artificial Intelligence Organization, July.

Thomas Wolf, Lysandre Debut, Victor Sanh, Julien Chaumond, Clement Delangue, Anthony Moi, Pierric Cistac, Tim Rault, R'emi Louf, Morgan Funtowicz, and Jamie Brew. 2019. HuggingFace's Transformers: State-of-the-art natural language processing. *ArXiv*, abs/1910.03771.

Zhilin Yang, Zihang Dai, Yiming Yang, Jaime Carbonell, Russ R Salakhutdinov, and Quoc V Le. 2019. XLNet: Generalized autoregressive pretraining for language understanding. In H. Wallach, H. Larochelle, A. Beygelzimer, F. d'Alché-Buc, E. Fox, and R. Garnett, editors, *Advances in Neural Information Processing Systems 32*, pages 5753–5763. Curran Associates, Inc.

Lili Yao, Nanyun Peng, Weischedel Ralph, Kevin Knight, Dongyan Zhao, and Rui Yan. 2019. Plan-and-Write: Towards better automatic storytelling. In *Proceedings of the Thirty-Third AAAI Conference on Artificial Intelligence*, pages 7378–7385, Honolulu, Hawaii, January–February. AAAI Press.

Yan Zhao, Lu Liu, Chunhua Liu, Ruoyao Yang, and Dong Yu. 2018. From plots to endings: A reinforced pointer generator for story ending generation. In *Proceedings of Natural Language Processing and Chinese Computing*, volume abs/1901.03459.

TL-Explorer: A Digital Humanities Tool for Mapping and Analyzing Translated Literature

Alex Zhai*
EA 4073-GERiiCO
Univ. Lille, F-59000
Lille, France
alexhezhai@gmail.com

Zheng Zhang*
Schlumberger
Clamart, France
zzhang54@slb.com

Amel Fraisse
EA 4073-GERiiCO
Univ. Lille, F-59000
Lille, France
amel.fraisse@univ-lille.fr

Ronald Jenn
EA 4074-CECILLE
Univ. Lille, F-59000
Lille, France
ronald.jenn@univ-lille.fr

Shelley Fisher Fishkin
Stanford University
Stanford, CA
sfishkin@stanford.edu

Pierre Zweigenbaum
LIMSI-CNRS
Université Paris-Saclay
Orsay, France
pz@limsi.fr

Abstract

TL-Explorer is a digital humanities tool for mapping and analyzing translated literature, encompassing the World Map and the Translation Dashboard. The World Map displays collected literature of different languages, locations, and cultures and establishes the foundation for a variety of further analysis. It is comprised of three global maps for spatial and temporal interpretation. A further investigation into an individual node on the World Map — representing one edition or translation — leads to the Translation Dashboard. Collected translations are processed in order to build multilingual parallel corpora for a large number of under-resourced languages as well as to highlight the transnational circulation of knowledge.

Our first rendition of TL-Explorer was conducted on the well-traveled American novel, *Adventures of Huckleberry Finn*, by Mark Twain. The maps currently chronicle nearly 400 translations of this novel and the dashboard supports over 30 collected translations. However, the TL-Explore is easily extended to other works of literature and is not limited to type of texts, such as academic manuscripts or constitutional documents to name a few.

1 Introduction and Motivation

From a global perspective, human knowledge of culture and heritage has been shared, explored, and preserved for nearly centuries through translation. The art of translating texts is largely to thank for our ability to learn about and from other cultures, and vice versa. It is crucial to recognize that every person is shaped by their culture and identity. Hence, every body of knowledge, regardless of type of classification, is similarly impacted by specific historical, geopolitical, and sociocultural factors. TL-Explorer is created not only with this diversity in mind, but also as a tool to explore these nuances as they are reflected in translated literature.

TL-Explorer is designed to provide users with a feeling of continuity as they explore translated texts. The tool begins at a broad starting point — a global view of the entire collection of texts — and allows the user to smoothly zoom into a particular geographic region, individual editions or translations in that region, and specific chapters and paragraphs within the selected literature. The TL-Explorer uses a Geographic Information System (GIS) to create the World Map and NLP techniques to generate the Translation Dashboard.

2 Prior Work

2.1 Digital Humanities Mapping Tools

Hypercities (Presner et al., 2014) introduced a digital humanities mapping tool for exploring and interacting with the layered histories of city and global spaces. Spatialization tools or geographic information

---

*equal contribution

Proceedings of LaTeCH-CLfL 2020, pages 167–171
Barcelona, Spain (Online), December 12, 2020.

systems (GIS) such as Carto[1], Open Street Map (OpenStreetMap contributors, 2017), QGIS (QGIS Development Team, 2009), Harvard Worldmap (Guan et al., 2012), Spatial Data Explorer (Kollen, 2016) and Unfolding (Nagel et al., 2013) are also useful tools for digital humanities mapping.

2.2 Parallel Corpora Construction and Analysis Tools and Resources

There exist many construction and analysis tools for parallel corpora such as Uplug (Tiedemann, 2003), PENCIL (Kakoyianni-Doa et al., 2013) and The Sketch Engine (Kilgarriff et al., 2014), but there remain very little designed specifically for translated literature.

While the interpretive nature of literary translations has caused a lag in their adoption as a source for NLP development, multiple recent projects have developed parallel corpora based on well-known texts including the *Harry Potter* series and *Le Petit Prince*.

2.3 Alignment Visualization Tools

While there already exist alignment visualization tools such as ANNIS (Druskat et al., 2016), SWIFT Aligner (Gilmanov et al., 2014), Cario (Smith and Jahr, 2000), VisualTCA (Gomes et al., 2007) and MkAlign (Fleury and Zimina, 2007), most of them focus on word alignment. Further, even though some of these tools provide sentence alignment visualization, they are meant to be an intermediate step before the lexicon level. There are currently no other tools that allow users to explore data in a chapter-paragraph-sentence/word, coarse-to-fine fashion. Moreover, these tools are not oriented towards literary texts, which is more challenging for alignment approaches. Though alignment should be as confident as possible (Xu et al., 2015), this is complicated by the fact that a literary translation may include deliberate changes to the text inserted by the translator, and may not be a literal translation.

3 TL-Explorer

3.1 World Map Viewer

The World Map is the base tool in the TL-Explorer and provides a geographic display of collected translation information. It is separated into three maps: the Home Map, Heat Map, and Time Map, which display the same information in different views.

3.1.1 Home Map

The Home Map (see Figure 1) is the first map. It provides a global view of all the gathered texts, and each node represents one edition or translation. Nodes are placed at the location of publication, not based on the language of translation. Texts that are geographically close to each other are grouped into a cluster, represented by the light-yellow circles, with a number that reflects the number of texts in that cluster. A search function in the top left corner of the interface allows the user to search the map by title of the text. In the bottom left corner, a label identifies the number of texts being represented. The key informs the user of the types of languages represented on the map: English original, well-resourced language, medium-resourced language, and under-resourced language.

The World Map allows the user to zoom in from a global view to country view and even as close as specific streets. By clicking on a node, a pop-up displays the following information of the selected text: title, language, series/collection, edition, contributors (translators, editors, cover artists, and illustrators), date of publication, publisher, publisher city, and page count. If there is a digital version of the translation, the pop-up will include a link to it.

3.1.2 Time Map

The Time Map documents in chronological order developments of the literature of interest. The year is controlled by a scroll-bar below the map. As the years progress, nodes appear and accumulate. For example, Figure 1 displays the translation of *Adventures of Huckleberry Finn* up to the year 1940.

---

[1]https://carto.com/

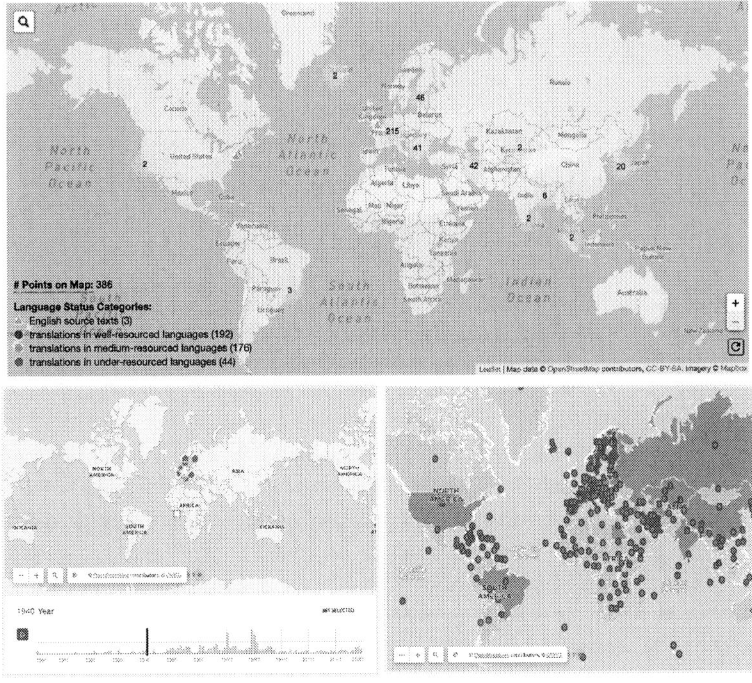

Figure 1: **Home Map** The width and height ratios of the maps have been changed to conserve space.

3.1.3   Heat Map

The third map is the Heat Map, which displays translation count for each country and provides insight on which areas are more frequently represented (see Figure 1). It is aggregated using the data at a certain time, and changes as more data is added, such as a new translation or language.

3.1.4   Crowdsourcing for Data Curation

There are currently 386 points or translations on the maps. However, the TL-Explorer is immensely scalable. The TL-Explorer has a form where the user can submit all the information they have pertaining to an individual translation. After data-vetting, the point will be added as a new node to the maps.

3.2   Translation Dashboard

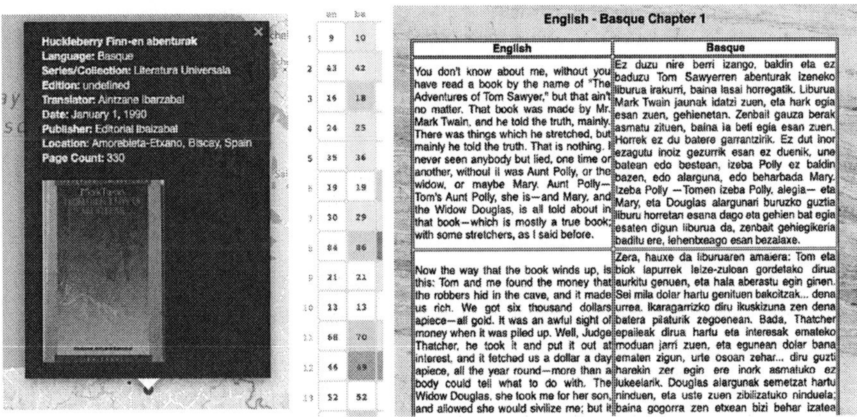

Figure 2: Translation Dashboard, example with a Basque translation

The field translation studies bridges comparative literature and corpus linguistics. While corpus linguists are likely to have at least basic programming skills and a broad familiarity with computational methods, the equivalent "digital humanities" training is less common in comparative literature. As a result, corpus linguists are more likely to focus on comparatively large-scale computational text analysis, and comparative literature scholars tend to conduct close examinations of a small number of texts.

The Translation Dashboard is designed as an adjunctive tool for researchers in translation studies grounded in the comparative literature tradition. It provides a reading environment that could display the visualizations and text in parallel in order to allow scholars to easily see patterns of structural divergence between the source text and translations at different levels of granularity.

Text is aligned at the paragraph, sentence, and world level using Natural Language Processing algorithms, including the IBM Models 1 and 2 for Statistical Machine Translation(Collins, 2011) and the Gale-Church Algorithm(Gale and Church, 1993).

3.2.1 Paragraph Count Analysis

After selecting a specific node on the World Map, the default view of the Translation Dashboard displays a per-chapter paragraph count, based on newlines and white space in that source text. The deviation in paragraph count between a source text and its translation is reflected in the color variation in the Heat Map within the table (see Figure 2, center image). An exceedingly high divergence from the source paragraph count alerts the scholar that there may be data cleaning issues (e.g. one instance where each line in a poem embedded in a narrative was treated as a new paragraph), but a moderate divergence can reflect the translator's deliberate stylistic choices about how the flow of the narrative should be rendered. A translation studies scholar in the literary tradition may use this information to select chapters for a close-reading analysis.

3.2.2 Paragraph Alignment

When the user selects an individual chapter in the text, they can view a display that presents both the original English chapter and the chapter in the translation. The tool displays the two parallel to each other to allow for easy comparison.

We divided chapters into 3 major categories based on the differences in their paragraph counts compared to the original English version: *exact-match*, *large-difference*, and *small-difference*. Different paragraph aligners may apply to different categories.

For *exact-match* chapters, our hypothesis is that their paragraphs were translated one to one. No further paragraph alignment methods are needed. This hypothesis has been confirmed for most of the *exact-match* cases by the human validation experiment.

Large-difference cases are normally caused by different ways of splitting quotations, so we provide a text pre-processing option before paragraph alignment when long quotations have been found under *large-difference* cases. This pre-processing option splits quotations into paragraphs according to the same standard in all translations. Experiments have shown that this action can significantly reduce differences in paragraph counts and sometimes move a chapter from the *large-difference* category to the *small-difference* category.

For the majority *small-difference* cases, we applied the Gale-Church algorithm(Gale and Church, 1993). Here we treat paragraphs as sentences so as to feed them into this sentence alignment algorithm. The tool is easy to use, and thus easy for a native speaker to provide feedback on the accuracy of the alignments.

4 Conclusion

Encompassing both of the World Map and the Translation Dashboard, the TL-Explorer allows for analysis of translated literature at an exceptional range of specificity. The World Map provides a global view that can be shrunken into exact coordinates and streets and the Translation Dashboard allows for intense analysis of two texts from entire works to specific sentences. The TL-Explorer similarly serves a purpose of preservation and globalization, representing a large number of under-resourced languages and a transnational circulation of knowledge.

References

Michael Collins. 2011. Statistical machine translation: Ibm models 1 and 2. *Columbia Columbia Univ.*

Stephan Druskat, Volker Gast, Thomas Krause, and Florian Zipser. 2016. corpus-tools. org: An interoperable generic software tool set for multi-layer linguistic corpora. In *LREC*.

Serge Fleury and Maria Zimina. 2007. Exploring translation corpora with mkalign. *Translation Journal*, 11(1).

William A Gale and Kenneth Church. 1993. A program for aligning sentences in bilingual corpora. *Computational linguistics*, 19(1):75–102.

Timur Gilmanov, Olga Scrivner, and Sandra Kübler. 2014. Swift aligner, a multifunctional tool for parallel corpora: Visualization, word alignment, and (morpho)-syntactic cross-language transfer. In *LREC*, pages 2913–2919.

Felipe Tassario Gomes, Thiago Alexandre Salgueiro Pardo, and Helena de Medeiros Caseli. 2007. Visualtca: Uma ferramenta visual on-line para alinhamento sentencial de textos paralelos. In *Anais do XXVII Congresso da Sociedade Brasileira de Computação-V Workshop em Tecnologia da Informação e da Linguagem Humana (TIL)*, pages 1729–1732.

Weihe Wendy Guan, Peter K Bol, Benjamin G Lewis, Matthew Bertrand, Merrick Lex Berman, and Jeffrey C Blossom. 2012. Worldmap–a geospatial framework for collaborative research. *Annals of GIS*, 18(2):121–134.

Fryni Kakoyianni-Doa, Stefanos Antaris, and Eleni Tziafa. 2013. A free online parallel corpus construction tool for language teachers and learners. *Procedia-Social and Behavioral Sciences*, 95:535–541.

Adam Kilgarriff, Vít Baisa, Jan Bušta, Miloš Jakubíček, Vojtěch Kovář, Jan Michelfeit, Pavel Rychlý, and Vít Suchomel. 2014. The sketch engine: ten years on. *Lexicography*, pages 7–36.

Christine Kollen. 2016. Spatial data explorer: Providing discovery and access to geospatial data at the university of arizona.

Till Nagel, Joris Klerkx, Andrew Vande Moere, and Erik Duval. 2013. Unfolding–a library for interactive maps. In *International Conference on Human Factors in Computing and Informatics*, pages 497–513. Springer.

OpenStreetMap contributors. 2017. Planet dump retrieved from https://planet.osm.org . `https://www.openstreetmap.org`.

Todd Presner, David Shepard, and Yoh Kawano. 2014. *Hypercities thick mapping in the digital humanities.*

QGIS Development Team, 2009. *QGIS Geographic Information System.* Open Source Geospatial Foundation.

Noah A Smith and Michael E Jahr. 2000. Cairo: An alignment visualization tool. In *LREC*.

Jörg Tiedemann. 2003. *Recycling Translations – Extraction of Lexical Data from Parallel Corpora and their Application in Natural Language Processing.* Ph.D. thesis, Uppsala University, Uppsala, Sweden. Anna Sågvall Hein, Åke Viberg (eds): Studia Linguistica Upsaliensia.

Yong Xu, Aurélien Max, and François Yvon. 2015. Sentence alignment for literary texts. *LiLT (Linguistic Issues in Language Technology)*, 12.

Association for Computational Linguistics
209 N. Eighth Street
Stroudsburg, Pennsylvania 18360